COUNTRY SCHOOLWOMEN

Nadine Wrought and her fourth-grade class, Ivanhoe School, 1931.

COUNTRY SCHOOLWOMEN

Teaching in Rural California,
1850–1950

KATHLEEN WEILER

STANFORD UNIVERSITY PRESS

STANFORD, CALIFORNIA

Stanford University Press
Stanford, California
© 1998 by the Board of Trustees of the
Leland Stanford Junior University
Printed in the United States of America

CIP data appear at the end of the book

For my mother

ACKNOWLEDGMENTS

I began research on this project in 1987–88 with the support of a Spencer Fellowship from the National Academy of Education. That year I spent several months in California as an affiliated scholar at the Stanford Institute for Research on Gender, exploring local archives and interviewing retired teachers. This was the first of numerous trips to California between 1987 and 1993. I began by interviewing retired teachers who had known my mother. These teachers suggested others. A notice in the Tulare County Retired Teachers Association newsletter and an opportunity to describe my research at a meeting of the Kings County Retired Teachers Association led me to a number of other retired teachers who kindly agreed to be interviewed. Alice Royal of Visalia, a retired teacher, took me on a guided tour of the State Historical Park at the black town of Allensworth, including the beautifully restored two-room schoolhouse. Betty Rivers of the California Department of Parks and Recreation shared her own research on Allensworth. I was given lunch by the members of the Kings County Historical Society, was greeted courteously by residents of the Tule River Indian Reservation, and visited small schoolhouses in the foothills of the Sierra Nevada and elaborate mission-style town schools built in the 1920s. Annie Mitchell, the unofficial historian of Tulare County, graciously shared her notes on early teachers with me.

I explored large and small archives throughout California, helped by university archivists and county librarians. I worked extensively in the local history collection of the Kings County Public Library and the Annie Mitchell History Room of the Tulare County Public Library. I also used the collections of the Bancroft Library, the California State Library and Archives in Sacramento, the Federal Archives at San Bruno, the Regional

Oral History Archive at the University of California at Berkeley, the Holt Atherton Center for Western Studies at the University of the Pacific, and special collections at UCLA, Stanford University, the University of California at Riverside, the Harvard Graduate School of Education, San Francisco State University, San Jose State University, Fresno State University, and Bakersfield State University. I want to acknowledge the invaluable support I was given by these librarians and archivists, who took time from their many other duties to help me. Research trips and time to write were supported by a Spencer Foundation postdoctoral fellowship, a Faculty Development Grant from Tufts University, a National Endowment for the Humanities fellowship, and a year at the Mary Ingraham Bunting Institute at Radcliffe.

The help I received from colleagues and friends made this work possible. Many colleagues and friends followed the development of this project and gave invaluable constructive criticism. I want to thank in particular Joyce Antler, Sari Biklen, Deborah Britzman, Ron Butchart, Michele Clark, Sam Clark, Geraldine Clifford, Anna Davin, Sara Freedman, Maxine Greene, Ronna Johnson, Sandra Joshel, Polly Kaufman, Linda Perkins, Dan Perlstein, Sally Schwager, Maxine Seller, Roger Simon, David Tyack, Courtney Vaughn, and Sandy Zagarel. My year as a fellow at the Bunting Institute at Radcliffe in 1992–93 gave me an ideal environment for writing. The community of women scholars, activists, poets, novelists, and artists at the Bunting provided the kind of working conditions any writer would desire; I want especially to thank Malena DeMontis, Marguerite Feitlowitz, and Marcie Hershman for their thoughtful and caring support. The political and personal community of the editorial collective of *Radical Teacher* continues to provide comradeship so rare in these harsh times. A Fulbright fellowship to Australia gave me the opportunity to share this work with Australian colleagues. I want to thank Jane Kenway, Jill Blackmore, Alison McKinnon, Donna Dwyer, Jill Sanguinetti, The Melbourne Feminist History Group, and in particular Lyn Yates and Marjorie Theobald, for their hospitality and critical insights. My family has supported me through difficulties in ways they may not even know. Peter Weiler was my most careful and helpful reader. He, Emma Weiler, Corey Steinman, and Sarah Weiler have inspired me with their confidence and love, and Anna Weiler Steinman and Justin Steinman Weiler have given us all joy and hope for the future. During my many research trips to California I was given hospitality and friendship from family and friends. I want to thank Graciela Perez-Travisan, Lisa Rofel, Mary Babcock Stull, Jane Such, Richard Such, M'K Veloz, Dan Weiler, and Louise Weiler for their good food, conversation, and care for me.

Norris Pope and Pamela MacFarland Holway of Stanford University Press have been gracious and supportive of this project, and Anne Canright did an extraordinary job of copyediting an unwieldy manuscript. Most of all I want to thank the retired teachers who allowed me into their homes and shared their memories and thoughts. Although I have used pseudonyms in the text when giving direct quotations in order to protect their privacy, I want to list their names here in appreciation for their kind generosity: Eva Ammons, Hazel Anderson, Ethel Rivers Bachman, Jean Bergemann, Ray Bessey, Veva Blunt, Elizabeth Booth, Madeleine Cochrane, Marjorie Cummins, Verna Cunningham, Thelma Dawes, Hoot Gibson, Edith Rivers Gist, Nancy Hanada, Mercedes Hinkle, Gerald Jacobus, Mary Beth Jadwin, Joanne Ledbetter, Rosalie Lewellyn, Mary McDowell, Rosa McGuire, Mamie Moon, Prudence Oleson, Katherine Rafenstein, Irene Rivers Rawley, and Jewell Wall.

The woodcuts at the beginning of each chapter are taken from 1935 and 1936 issues of "California Schools," a monthly pamphlet made available to California teachers by the state department of education.

CONTENTS

Photographs follow p. 156.

TABLES

COUNTRY SCHOOLWOMEN

INTRODUCTION

I thought that there wasn't anybody alive in
the world but me who would know this, who
would make the connection. And I would be
the last person to do so. But perhaps this isn't
so. People are curious. A few people are. They
will be driven to find things out, even trivial
things. They will put things together, knowing
all along that they may be mistaken. You see
them going around with notebooks, scraping
the dirt off gravestones, reading microfilm,
just in the hope of seeing this trickle in time,
making a connection, rescuing one thing from
the rubbish. —Alice Munro, "Meneseteaug"

$\mathbf{A}$ny historian organizes and presents a story about
the past driven, as Alice Munro says, "to find things out," to make connections. But the motives and theoretical and political assumptions that
guide historical narratives are not always made clear. Shulamit Reinharz has pointed out that feminist researchers frequently start with an
issue that concerns them personally, something that is both "an intellectual question and a personal trouble."[1] Carolyn Steedman suggests
that historians should "observe where we are," in the sense of understanding and articulating the underlying concerns that shape our presentation of the past.[2] This book reflects my own personal and intellectual concerns.

I grew up in a small country town in the San Joaquin Valley in California, the daughter and niece of women schoolteachers, whose fathers
and brothers were small farmers. For my mother and for my aunts, teaching seemed the only way to support themselves and to contribute to the
support of their families. My mother and her sister both attended state
teachers college and began teaching when they were nineteen. In the depression, my mother supported her parents after they lost their small
family farm. When she married, she stopped teaching, as was typical—
whether because she or my father expected it or because of the married
women teachers' bar I don't know—but in the teacher shortage after the

Second World War the school principal drove out to our house and offered her a job. She said she agreed because we needed the money and because the town needed teachers so badly, but I think teaching gave her an identity; it allowed her to do valuable work that was respected and validated, at least in the eyes of children. In my childhood, my mother always taught; she never held any administrative position. She taught third and fourth grade in the town school, or combined classes in rural two- and three-room schools. It wasn't uncommon for grown young men to come to our house to see my mother and say, "Don't you remember me? In third grade?" When my mother retired, the principal, a man much younger than she, said, "She is the most loved teacher we have ever had at our school." When I look back on my mother's life I see the limitations that shaped it, choices made within the narrow parameters of what was acceptable for women. But at the same time I see much of value and much that has not been adequately recognized as being of value. In my memory, it was my mother and her friends who provided me with the example of how to live in the world with humor and compassion. They were not seen as powerful by the men who controlled the public world, but they quietly maintained the bonds of family and community.

In December 1985, my mother died of heart failure at the age of seventy-eight. When my mother died, I had just completed my doctoral thesis, a study of urban women teachers.[3] My personal trouble, my grief, my sense of loss all led me to this new project. I realized that although my mother's life as a teacher was central to her own self-identity, in fact I knew very little about that earlier life. I began a history of women teachers in order to understand and remain connected to my mother's world.

The underlying logic of this book, then, rests in a sense of loss. And as I have explored this past, I have confronted not only my own personal loss, but the loss of a wider world that has been forgotten. I also write from a belief in the truths that lie hidden in the fabric of life, truths we can't see because we can't name the pattern of which they are a part. I think, for example, of the emotional work of women, their care of children, their daily maintenance of what Dorothy Smith calls the everyday world. I remember afternoons in our kitchen when I was a child, my mother drinking coffee with her friends, who were also teachers, their bemusement as they talked about the young men who were their principals; how her friends would leave to return home to prepare meals for husbands and children, to clean, to keep things going. In the schools, they did both intellectual and emotional work to support the lives of children. Their own lives were complex and valuable, but that value was not recognized in the public world. There was no name for the pattern of what they did.

It was the value I saw in these lives and their absence in the history I had been taught that led me to undertake this history of teachers in rural California. In this book I excavate a past world I know through my own memories and the memories of others, shaped by my own feminist concerns in the present. In the course of my research I was invited into the homes of retired teachers who shared their memories with me. They lived in the foothills, in the valley, and in towns; in mobile homes, in comfortable suburban houses, and in ranch houses surrounded by carefully kept fences and sturdy cattle. When I would get out of my car on a hot summer day with my notes and tape recorder and walk through a yard with fig trees, palms, and oleander, I caught an almost physical sense of my childhood, of the past. I drove to ranches, seeing again the hard-packed dirt of farmyards; in a plain kitchen, behind the framed photographs of grandchildren and the television set, I glimpsed the china, water glasses, and pitchers of my childhood. A world was there; but was it as I imagined it?

As I explored this history more deeply, interviewing retired teachers and reading local school records and state documents, my memories were challenged as well as confirmed. The autonomy and pride in their work that teachers expressed in their narratives coexisted uneasily with evidence of increasing state control over curriculum and credentials. And the social and cultural world that my mother and other teachers helped maintain was not based on equality and community for all, but also on racist beliefs and practices. As I explored my own memories and those of retired teachers, it was impossible to ignore the white Protestant hegemony that was reproduced in the schools and community. Incidents I had forgotten came back to me: my mother's story of her uncle who one night drove with other men to the Armenian colony at the town of Yettem and fired shotguns into their homes to drive them out; her memories of the people she called "Diggers," the Indians who would come down from the hills in ragged groups to work in the fields; the Mexican children I had known from first grade who somehow vanished from my math and science classes by the time we got to high school. My sense of the lost world of women teachers was framed by myths, what Micaela Di Leonardo has called "rhetorical nostalgia."[4] Throughout my research and in this book, therefore, a tension exists between my deep belief in the value of these women's lives and evidence of the harshness and racism of the culture they helped maintain.

When I began this study, I held two other somewhat unformed and unexamined assumptions. One was that men had always controlled the work of women in schools—that education was a patriarchal space in which women cared for children in classrooms while men held positions of authority, defined issues, and set policy. The second was that "the state" was the site of a disciplinary power that shaped and controlled people's lives through surveillance and technologies of dominance. Both of these assumptions, of course, emerged from the debates among feminists and theorists associated with the left in the last two decades in North America, Australasia, and Europe. In the course of this project, I have come to question them both. First, in wider reading and in interviews, I discovered what historians of women's education have argued for some time: that historically, teaching has been a source of power for women, offering them respect, autonomy, and money. This has not always been true, has always been contested by men, and has always had to be struggled for; but for some women in some circumstances, teaching has afforded material rewards and intellectual satisfaction. Second, the state (at least in California) has itself been the site of intense conflict. Although the twentieth century saw greater knowledge and control of both teachers and children thanks to increased state supervision, required credentials for teachers, and testing of students, one of the surprises of my research was to uncover a world of articulate women educators who held positions of power at the state level, who supported one another, and who defined an alternative and positive meaning for the woman teacher. The most influential of these women was Helen Heffernan, head of elementary and rural education at the California Department of Education for forty years (1926–65). She and the women supervisors she led showed classroom teaching to be valuable and intellectually challenging, in sharp contrast to the vision of both university experts and local communities. I came in the course of this research, therefore, to see a shifting world, one in which the lives and representations of women teachers were contradictory and contested.

I have approached this study, then, not only as a "personal trouble," but also as an intellectual question. It emerges from the particular moment in which I write, a time when assumptions about theory and history are being heatedly debated. As an intellectual of my time, I am suspicious of claims to final truths; I am conscious of power, concerned about language and representations. In writing this history I have tried to remain true to these concerns and to avoid a teleological and closed story, a "heroic narrative" in which a theoretical construct is set forth as though it were true and then empirical evidence is found to reveal this truth. I have tried to remain conscious both of my own process of constructing this narrative and of the underlying logic that has informed it, of what Foucault has called a "regime of truth."

My framing of this history reflects broader trends and debates within both women's history and feminism. In the 1960s, historians writing from an explicitly political, feminist perspective began a project to re-cover women's lives from the oblivion to which they had been relegated. These histories tended to emphasize the oppression of patriarchal prac-tices and sexist ideology. Subsequent women's historians turned to the question of resistance and the ways in which women created meaning in the past. This entailed both a reconstruction of women's lives and a cel-ebration of their achievements and worth. These two concerns—to re-veal the oppressive nature of patriarchal ideology and practices, on the one hand, and to document the lives of those who have been "hidden from history," on the other—were the characteristic marks of the new women's history and continue to define the work of feminist historians. But as the outline of a history of women has begun to emerge and as feminist historians have developed an increasingly complex and nuanced body of work, conflicts over interpretation and approach have inevitably arisen.[5] These conflicts parallel debates within historical studies more broadly and reflect the impact of poststructuralism and deconstruction. Judith Newton, for example, has pointed out that from the beginning, women's historians held that "'history' is best told as a story of power re-lations and struggle, a story that is contradictory, heterogeneous, frag-mented."[6] In the United States, the influence of poststructuralism and cultural studies has led to a self-conscious examination of the underly-ing assumptions of women's history from the perspective of literary and critical theory.[7] Not only is history a creative process reflecting selection and resting on certain rhetorical effects, feminist scholars argue, but it has been deeply gendered as well. The new feminist critique emphasizes the way histories have worked, as Ann-Louise Shapiro notes, to "preserve particular developments while suppressing others" based on assumptions about gender.[8]

A recognition of the importance of gender seems essential to redress-ing the silences and distortions of patriarchal discourse. But in empha-sizing the validity and importance of excluded knowledges—what Fou-cault has called "dangerous memories"—we run the risk of accepting un-problematically memory and experience as sources of a "true past." As poststructural feminist historians such as Catherine Hall, Joan Scott, and Denise Riley have argued, the category of "experience" itself is one that needs to be carefully examined. Scott argues:

When experience is taken as the origin of knowledge, the vision of the individual subject (the person who had the experience or the historian who recounts it) be-comes the bedrock of evidence upon which explanation is built. Questions about the constructed nature of experience, about how subjects are constituted as dif-ferent in the first place, about how one's vision is structured—about language (or discourse) and history—are left aside.[9]

The argument about remembered experience is in many ways an argument about evidence and truth. The more extreme "linguistic" argument would be that what we can know is *only* language, a series of texts constructed through discursive systems that produce meaning as an effect. From this perspective, the focus of analysis should be exclusively on the process of producing meaning, for nothing else can be known. I have followed a less extreme approach here, viewing narratives as evidence of the ways in which human beings make sense of and evaluate material practices and conditions through the discourses available to them. Linda Gordon, who takes a similar position, argues that while the analysis of representations can lead to a nuanced understanding of the ways in which language can work to justify the privilege and power of dominant groups, it does not mean that the material conditions and oppressions of the past did not exist and should not be problematized.[10] Narratives can also provide evidence about material practices, about structures of feeling and events that are doubtless discursively produced in the sense of being remembered and presented in oral or written testimony, but that nonetheless occurred. A focus on the constructed quality of texts as historical evidence is similar to Gramsci's conception of consciousness as "strangely composite" or Bakhtin's competing authoritative and resisting discourses.[11] These formulations appeal to a metaphor of competing meaning systems that circulate throughout society. Individuals cannot conceptualize or make sense of what happens in their lives except through language, but language itself is not transparent; it is, in Bakhtin's famous phrase, "overpopulated with the intentions of others."[12]

In my analysis of these rural women teachers, I have been concerned both with the ways they are constructed as women in dominant discourse and with the ways they construct the meanings of their own experiences through the shifting categories available to them. Alison Prentice and Marjorie Theobald comment that "both the idea and the reality of the 'woman teacher' in history is proving evocative in ways far more complex than most of us first imagined could be the case."[13] In trying to capture this complexity, I have focused on representations, the ways in which people construct meaning from the images and assumptions of the culture in which they move; but I have also written within a framework that acknowledges the power of the wider political and economic forces that shape the cultural world. Thus I have employed a wide range of sources for this study—the official documents and pronouncements of educational experts and state authorities, the quantitative data from census and school records, teachers' representations of their lives in autobiographical writings and oral history interviews—to explore the social context of teaching, to try to understand what teaching meant to women teachers, what it provided them, how it gave them categories through which they understood and lived their lives. This attempt to understand the lives of women teachers in one local area in turn led me to explore the growth of state control over schools, the impact of powerful economic and political changes on small-town life, and the patterns of racism that have defined California from the earliest days of European settlement.

The organization of this book proceeds in concentric circles, from general to local. In Chapter 1 I explore the historical shifts in representations of the woman teacher in the broad national context of the United States. In Chapter 2 I turn to the ways assumptions about gender shaped the rise of the educational state in California. In Chapter 3 I discuss the history of Tulare and Kings Counties, the growth of their public school system, and changes in the demographic profile of the teaching population. In Chapters 4–6 I explore the lives of women teachers in the two counties through the interwar period. In Chapter 7 I consider the impact of the Second World War, the consolidation of rural schools, and the sexual politics of the immediate postwar years. Although I recognize the importance of social and economic forces in shaping the educational state, throughout I have tried to center this history on the figure of the woman teacher, to write a gendered history.

WOMEN'S HISTORY AND THE HISTORY OF WOMEN TEACHERS

Teaching became defined as women's work in the United States before the Civil War. Between the 1840s and the 1930s, women steadily moved into elementary school teaching; by 1905, according to one National Education Association (NEA) study, 97.9 percent of elementary teachers in U.S. cities were women.[1] Still today, approximately three-quarters of all elementary and secondary school teachers are women. Although the teaching of children has long been defined as "women's work," traditional histories have largely failed to address the implications of the rigid gender division in education. Even works dealing specifically with women's education frequently omit the teaching profession. In Barbara Solomon's study of women's higher education, *In the Company of Women*, for example, normal schools and teacher education are mentioned only peripherally. The last comprehensive study of women and education in the United States was Thomas Woody's *History of Women's Education in the United States*, published in 1929. Recent works exploring the history of wage work for women in the United States, such as Alice Kessler-Harris's *Out to Work*, have also tended to ignore teaching. Women's historians have generally been more interested in the domestic/paid labor debate or in the struggle of women to break into traditionally male defined jobs.[2] It is almost as though teaching has not been considered of interest to women's historians precisely because of its traditional subordinate and inferior status—it was something women fell back on and needed to escape.

In recent years, this lack of attention to teaching as women's work has begun to be redressed. Influenced by the work of social historians concerned to uncover the history of excluded and oppressed groups and of women's historians seeking to reconceptualize the past, educational historians have begun to uncover the outlines of women teachers' lives. In this chapter, therefore, I want to provide a brief discussion of the history of women teachers in the United States in the period 1850–1950. I do this to provide a context for understanding the lives of teachers in rural California; but I do it for other reasons as well. My goal in this chapter is not so much to narrate changing policies and practices as it is to analyze the shifting historical representations of the woman teacher. By "representations" I mean the discursively constructed images through which we understand the world and our lives. A focus on representation implies a struggle and contest over identity; it emphasizes the ways in which selves are unstable, constructed through both dominant conceptions and resistance to those conceptions, and suggests the incomplete and sometimes contradictory quality of our lives both in the present and as we construct our pasts in memory. This theoretical approach has led me to a number of questions: How were women teachers represented in official documents, popular works, and the authoritative studies of "experts"? Did women teachers accept as true the prescriptions of those in power? Did they resist those representations? To what extent did women teachers act in ways that bent the bars of the cage of identity in which they moved?[3]

As is true for other subordinated groups, women have been constructed in the dominant imagination as "other"—that is, in opposition to the norm, which is male. At stake in these constructs or representations are questions of power, privilege, and control. Women are constantly being rethought to incorporate changes in economic and material life, but always in ways that maintain them as subordinate/different/other. In my exploration of the shifting meaning of the woman teacher, I rely on the work of feminist historians and theorists who argue that the analysis of representations can clarify the tensions between ideology, consciousness, and material life. By examining the contradictions in the creation of an "acceptable" representation of the schoolteacher through time, we can begin to see how struggles over meanings and identities have influenced women teachers' lives.

Woman's "True" Profession

Although teaching was considered men's work in the seventeenth and eighteenth centuries, by the middle of the nineteenth century the majority of teachers in U.S. schools were women. Numerous historians have suggested explanations for this phenomenon. In the 1840s and 1850s the number of schools increased markedly, reflecting both the growing population and the rhetoric of the common school movement, which claimed that schooling for all children was necessary for the stability and health of the republic.[4] Concomitant with the common school movement and free public schooling, of course, was a need for teachers. In the antebellum period in the Northeast, the ratio of men and women teachers shifted rapidly, and by 1860 women outnumbered men as teachers in that region. While the reasons for this shift are complex, certain factors stand out. Fundamentally, women were cheaper to hire than men. Although women's literacy rates, particularly in the Northeast, were quite high,[5] the professions were closed to women. By the 1840s, moreover, factory work, which had initially been an option for native-born rural women in New England, was less well paid, more onerous, and increasingly defined as work for immigrant women.[6] At the same time, with the growth of an industrial economy and mass production, women's handwork became less essential to the maintenance of the household economy. Thus, educated women had virtually no other option for "respectable" wage work besides teaching.[7]

Susan Carter argues that "the severely limited employment opportunities for educated women set in motion a self-reinforcing cycle in which initially high levels of school attendance for young women increased the supply of female teachers, depressed teachers' wages, raised school quality and encouraged yet more women (and men) of the next generation to attend."[8] Most of these teachers seem to have come from farming and artisan families, which may very well have needed the income the daughters brought in. In a study of Mt. Holyoke graduates between 1837 and 1850, David Allmendinger estimates that over half came from farm families whose holdings were valued below the national average.[9] These young, educated, unmarried women were thus ideally situated to work as teachers for low wages: not only did they have the schooling, but it made perfect economic sense. Nevertheless, school teaching as work for "respectable" women in a society organized into rigid gender categories presented a paradox: women wage workers, at however low the wages, challenged the dominant ideology of separate spheres.

Nineteenth-century separate-sphere ideology was based on the assumption that men and women were meant to exist and move in two different spheres of activity—women in the private or domestic sphere of the home and men in the public sphere of wage work and electoral politics. As numerous historians have argued, the development of this ideology accompanied the growth of industrialization and the shift from a family economy based on agriculture to an economy of wage work. At the same time, it built upon the long ideological tradition in European culture that posited "different natures" for women and men; thus women (white, upper- and middle-class women, at least) were meant to stay in the home and the family, not because of changes in the household economic structure, but because it was their destiny as "true women" to do so. Women's historians have emphasized that this concept of separate spheres as an organizing principle of society has not been imposed by later historians, but was a constituent part of middle-class nineteenth-century society. As Carroll Smith-Rosenberg puts it, "Women and men experienced, used, and conceived of the family, religion, work and public and private space differently."[10]

Women's historians have argued that by defining the woman's private sphere as the locus of nurturance and caring, nineteenth-century separate-sphere ideology limited the parameters of the male-defined political sphere. As a result, the actions of women who worked for the social welfare were ignored. Paula Baker, in an analysis of the political sphere in the United States in the period 1780–1920, maintains not only that many women's activities were overtly political, in that they concerned the social well-being of the polity, but also that these activities were central to the smooth functioning of the male sphere of electoral politics. According to Baker, the proper sphere of women expanded in the late nineteenth century to include the social good of families and children in many settings; thus the concept of "home" expanded to include "anywhere women and children were."[11] Accompanying this expansion of the sphere of women's activities was the construction of a "cult of true womanhood."[12] According to this gender construct, because women were naturally suited to be "moral guardians," male politicians did not have to concern themselves with issues of moral and social well-being; that could be left to the women, who operated outside the state.

Increasingly, women's historians have moved from an acceptance of the separate-spheres concept as providing an accurate picture of nineteenth-century society to an examination of it as an ideological construct that only partly matched women's material lives, and then only for some women. That is, although the ideology of separate spheres was vital to the organization of social life and the maintenance of power relationships among members of the white middle class, it must be recognized as a constructed symbolic system that justified existing gender relationships for a certain group of people, not as an adequate description of all nineteenth-century society. The work and lives of people of color and white working-class and poor men and women were ignored in this construct. Even for white middle-class women, the ideological claim that they lived in a separate sphere unaffected by issues of economics, law, or politics is clearly a myth. We are increasingly aware, in the words of Joan Kelly, that

woman's place is not a separate sphere or domain of existence but a position within social existence generally. It is a subordinate position, and it supports our social institutions at the same time that it serves and services men. . . . We are moving beyond a nineteenth-century conception of society because our actual vantage point has shifted. But just as the earth and planets revolved around the sun long before Copernicus "saw" that those were the relations of the solar system, so the dialectical (or relational) unifying of our vision of the social order gives us a sounder basis for understanding society. The conception of two social spheres existing side by side simply masked this more complex social reality.[13]

In this view, separate-sphere ideology becomes significant not as a description, but as a prescription and justification for a particular social order. Historians like Kelly argue that we need to consider carefully exactly what was meant by these two spheres, and the ways in which that ideology maintained and reproduced a society in which men controlled capital, the legal system, and electoral politics. In so doing we can begin to understand the fundamental gender structure of U.S. schooling as it developed in the nineteenth century.

One of the key ways in which teaching was made acceptable for women in this early period was to define the school as a continuation of the family. The child was viewed as developing first within the maternal care of the family and then moving naturally to the care of the woman teacher.[14] This construct also may have made the schools less threatening to parents (at least to native-born white Protestant parents), who, after all, were turning over their children at a very early age to a state institution. This line of reasoning can be seen in the writings of Horace Mann, the leader of the common school movement and one of the early champions of women teachers:

Some of the arguments in favor of this change [of employing women teachers] have been, the greater intensity of the parental instinct in the female sex, their natural love of the society of children, and the superior gentleness and forbearance of their dispositions—all of which lead them to mildness rather than severity, to the use of hope rather than of fear as a motive of action, and to the various arts of encouragement rather than to annoyances and compulsion, in their management of the young.[15]

The argument that the schoolroom was a continuation of the family also could be used to justify young women teaching for a few years before marrying and beginning families of their own. Catherine Beecher, for example, argued: "The great purpose of a woman's life—the happy superintendence of a family—is accomplished all the better and easier by preliminary teaching in school."[16] By defining teaching as a nurturing behavior that was natural to women, Beecher and Mann were defining teaching as not really work in the public sphere. The result was an expansion of the private sphere to include, as Baker put it, "anywhere women and children were."

By viewing the school as an extension of the family and thus part of the private sphere, educators defined teaching as appropriate to women's own special natures. This ideological view was supported by the common assumption that human beings had both rational and spiritual parts of their natures and that these qualities were tied to gender.[17] As education came more and more to be associated with moral development, it could be argued that women, with their more finely tuned spiritual natures, *should* be the teachers of young children. The Boston Board of Education, defending the hiring of (cheaper) women teachers, stated in 1841:

That females are incomparably better teachers for young children than males, cannot admit of a doubt. Their manners are more mild and gentle, and hence more in consonance with the tenderness of childhood. They are endowed by nature with stronger parental impulses, and this makes the society of children delightful, and turns duty into pleasure. Their minds are less withdrawn from their employment, by the active scenes of life; and they are less intent and scheming for future honors or emoluments. As a class, they never look forward, as young men almost invariably do, to a period of legal emancipation from parental control, when they are to break away from the domestic circle and go abroad in the world, to build up a fortune for themselves. . . . They are also of purer morals.[18]

In the middle decades of the nineteenth century teaching was thus redefined to match existing definitions of women's "true" nature. In the process, the increasing movement of women into teaching came to be viewed as simply part of a woman's life cycle. Any threat that women teachers might have posed to the existing social order was thereby dissipated. Moreover, women were cheap. One Massachusetts school committee member put it bluntly: "As there is neither honor nor profit connected with this position, we see no reason why it should not be filled by a woman."[19]

We do not know the extent to which women schoolteachers in the mid–nineteenth century accepted the idea that teaching was "woman's true profession," but given the low wages, short school terms, and difficult living conditions (boarding with families of their students) it seems unlikely that they saw it as a desirable or even feasible long-term career. The research of Richard Bernard and Maris Vinovskis supports this view. Studying teachers in Massachusetts between 1830 and 1860, they found that the average teaching career was 2.1 years. This sample suggests that teaching was indeed but a brief interlude in women's lives, not a major life commitment.[20]

The image of young women as fulfilling their destinies in woman's "true" profession was a middle-class white construct. It could be applied to black women only with difficulty. Before the Civil War, teaching liter-

acy to a slave had been illegal; the only black schools, therefore, were the
few clandestine schools in such cities as New Orleans and Charleston. A
teacher like Miss DeaVeaux, who taught secretly for twenty-five years in
the antebellum South, cannot be understood through the domestic ideology of teaching as the work of a young woman in the brief period before marriage.[21] Given the lack of opportunities for education, there
were very few African-American women teachers, even in the North, before the late 1860s. In the period immediately after the Civil War, however, literate African-American men *and* women taught in freedmen's
schools, both schools run by local blacks and ones set up by northern
philanthropists and missionaries.[22] Such teachers as Fanny Jackson Coppin, who graduated from Oberlin College, virtually the only integrated
college in the United States at this time, and Charlotte Forten, who studied at Salem State Normal School, both of whom taught in the freedmen's schools, simply could not be understood in the context of the
dominant ideology of race and gender.[23]

Teaching may well have held deep satisfaction for the handful of
African-American women teachers who taught against all odds. Some historians have argued that white women, too, used teaching to express
themselves in ways contrary to separate-sphere ideology. The most dramatic examples of white women teachers who challenged the representation of the passive schoolmistress were those who went to teach in the
freedmen's schools in the South or established schools on the western
frontier.[24] While these women may initially have acted out of a sense of
moral or religious obligation, the experience of teaching in these extraordinary conditions empowered them to challenge male privilege and
to see themselves in a new light. While the racial attitudes of teachers
who went south were mixed, with evidence of patronizing racial superiority existing alongside deep compassion and respect for the freedmen,
they approached their job with a strong sense of social commitment that
helped them to face the hostility and physical menace of white southerners. Teachers who went to teach on the western frontier with Catherine Beecher's National Board of Popular Education, meanwhile, spoke
of their desire to be "useful" in providing moral and religious guidance,
but they also sought adventure and independence.[25]

Other historians have argued that quite ordinary women teachers also
saw teaching as a means of gaining a measure of self-expression and financial autonomy. Jo Anne Preston, for example, challenges the idea
that young women went into teaching because it confirmed them in
their "feminine natures." Letters of New England women schoolteachers
of this period examined by Preston reveal a satisfaction and pleasure in
teaching that, she argues, undermines the view that teaching was little

more than domestic work in a limited period before marriage. These teachers showed themselves to be intellectually ambitious, willing to challenge authorities, and very conscious of salaries. Moreover, their chief satisfaction in teaching did not seem to lie in a conventional maternal role in relation to their pupils. One teacher, for example, wrote that she had "as disagreeable and rebellious a set of children as fell to the lot of any teacher. . . . Some days I feel so cross I want to slap their ears. I have a class of Dunces in Arithmetic that try the life out of me." Others wrote of their desire to travel west or to continue their own intellectual development. As Preston writes, "The female teachers whose correspondence I found wanted an independent life dedicated to their own self-improvement."[26] While Preston acknowledges that these letters cannot represent the views of all teachers, they certainly present tantalizing evidence of women with ambition and a strong sense of self—women quite unlike those depicted by Mann and the common school reformers.

This view of the positive impact of teaching as work for women is supported by Geraldine Clifford, who in a number of influential articles has argued that teaching provided women with a measure of autonomy and control over their own lives. She bases this argument on her wide reading of primary sources:

I have examined hundreds of letters of nineteenth century teachers—written to family, friends, other teachers, suitors—and found expressions of assertiveness, self-determination, and ego. Some teachers voiced their enlarged sense of independence and self-worth in quiet ways—choosing, for example, not to return to a given school district but to seek a better situation. Others became more openly the "strong minded woman" so disliked and feared by conservatives. The prominent feminists, like Lucy Stone, placed a great store on their independence. But so did quite ordinary women teachers.[27]

Through her research in first-person accounts, Clifford shows that women teachers provided one another with a network of support manifested in their close friendships, their yearly coming together at institutes, and their attendance at summer courses. In addition, many women teachers came from "teaching families," with family members providing information and access to jobs.[28]

Teaching may have provided personal satisfaction and some financial independence to women teachers, but most teaching was still constructed by the powerful and by the community as appropriate women's work only so long as the school was seen as the extension of the home. The fact that the large majority of teachers were young women who taught only for a few years before marriage supported the view that teaching was not really part of the public world. With the development of large bureaucratized urban school systems in which women often taught for ten, twenty, or thirty years, however, it became more difficult not to see teaching as wage work. In this changing context the meaning of the "woman schoolteacher" became potentially more threatening and more contested.

The Changing Population of Women Teachers, 1860–1920

The idea that the schoolroom belonged to women's "proper" sphere, women's exclusion from other kinds of "respectable" work, and the large pool of educated young women with an increasing need to work combined to make teaching the logical choice for many women. Yet as the United States underwent rapid urbanization and industrialization in the late nineteenth century, the nature of teaching as work was transformed. The graded city schools that developed in late-nineteenth-century cities resembled not so much maternal families as factories. As a number of historians have pointed out, the bureaucratic school systems that arose at this time gave men administrative control, based on their accepted roles as business and civic leaders. Schools were seen as needing professional and "scientific" leadership, and education was considered necessary for the building of a modern industrial world power.[29] School reformers thus built upon dominant assumptions of men's supposed leadership abilities and women's supposed acquiescent and humble natures. Meanwhile, the bureaucratization and professionalization of teaching made it more difficult to present the school as an extension of the home. Shifting the metaphor of school from home to factory challenged the idea that teaching was not really work in the public world.

Even as these changes were occurring, the number of women teachers continued to increase; this remained true through the 1920s. Well-educated, independent women working as trained, professional teachers, many of whom made teaching a lifetime career, represented an implicit threat to separate-sphere ideology, as did the move of women into school administration. Teachers were working for longer periods; they were better educated and increasingly lived outside of family control and surveillance. As the work of teachers took on the characteristics of factory work, women teachers in cities, influenced by the suffrage movement, began to organize and to demand equal pay and better working conditions. Although the image of the woman teacher as democratic worker—evoked, for example, in such organizations as the Chicago Teachers Federation—was short lived, in the first decades of the twentieth century militant teachers challenged earlier representations of young and passive women presiding over the schoolroom in the brief years before they married. Thus the Victorian construct of the "true woman" was challenged by the image of the "new woman," who was autonomous, educated, articulate, and employed.[30] The new woman denied any special nature for women and instead demanded equal rights and opportunities to work and live in the world as an individual judged on her own merits.

As the ideological construct of the woman schoolteacher began to fracture, different images and metaphors were used to explain and control her. In large urban school systems, women elementary teachers were often pawns in struggles among male politicians in local ward politics. At the same time, to immigrant pupils the woman teacher symbolized the power and authority of America. And among women teachers themselves, the subversive vision of themselves as "new women," as feminists or activists, clearly circulated, at least in cities. In rural one- and two-room schools, the woman teacher might still be expected to symbolize moral standards and provide community cohesion, but she was also solely responsible for day-to-day practices and was accustomed to exercising considerable initiative and responsibility; in her case, there simply was no higher authority to whom decisions could be referred. Although the curriculum in these schools was generally determined by county authorities, implementation of that curriculum was left up to the teacher. She was also in charge of end-of-year exercises and programs, which called on her abilities to organize and speak in public. Thus the job of teaching in rural schools involved considerable autonomy and a public presence that challenged traditional constructs.

Focusing on ideology alone cannot capture the way teaching as work for women was transformed around the turn of the century. In the past two decades, social historians have begun to investigate the length of teaching careers, differences between rural and urban teachers, and the household and class backgrounds of teachers. As local studies of teachers accumulate, it is becoming clearer that teaching can be fully understood only in relation to changes in state structures and in the context of local school settings, communities, and families.[31]

As John Rury points out, by 1920 the possibilities for white-collar work for white women were expanding rapidly, and female labor force participation increased approximately 65 percent between 1870 and 1930.[32] Wage work for unmarried women was generally acceptable by 1920. In teaching, however, quite different career trajectories had developed for men and women and for rural and urban areas by 1900. The early pattern discussed by Bernard and Vinovskis for antebellum Massachusetts still existed, particularly in rural areas, but in urban areas another pattern had taken hold in the late nineteenth century. In urban systems, both men and women taught for longer periods, but whereas men tended to rise to well-paying administrative jobs, the large majority of women remained in the classroom.

Given the growing demands for normal school training and qualifications, it seems likely that for significant numbers of women in the later decades of the nineteenth century teaching was much more than a stopgap. In a study of teachers hired in Boston and Providence in the years 1877–81, Joel Perlman and Victoria Huntzinger discovered quite different patterns of employment from those found by Bernard and Vinovskis for the 1840s. In their study, the mean length of service for teachers hired in 1880, for example, was 19.2 years for Boston and 14.2 years for Providence. In rural Rhode Island, in contrast, teachers taught for a mean period of 5.4 years—much closer to Bernard and Vinovskis's findings.[33] The figures for Boston and Providence are similar to those from Indianapolis for 1888, where the average tenure was eight years and 27 percent of teachers had taught for more than ten years.[34] Teaching as a lifelong career was clearly a possibility in urban school systems by the late 1880s. In Perlman and Huntzinger's study, 18 percent of teachers hired in Boston in 1880 taught for between forty-one and fifty years.

While teaching provided the possibility of long-term work for women, the majority of teachers at the turn of the century still taught for a relatively brief period.[35] In 1900, women teachers in most schools were still faced by the marriage bar, which denied teaching positions to married women.[36] It seems reasonable to assume that many teachers were young women living with their parents and that they would be expected to contribute to the maintenance of the household. Clifford comments:

The ability to earn even a small wage, especially in cash-poor rural and small town America where most of the population still lived, made young women, many girls in their teens, economically important to their families. The wages of teachers, mill hands, domestics, and later, office girls, might make the difference between keeping or losing the farm in a bad year, between renting or buying a house, between sending a brother to learn telegraphy in a preparatory school or to study natural philosophy in a college.[37]

A significant number of single women teachers lived in boardinghouses, particularly in cities. Single women in their mid-thirties who lived independently, and likely had more control over both their wages and their time,[38] must have viewed teaching differently from single women in their early twenties who lived on farms with their parents, brothers, and sisters.[39]

The social characteristics of white women teachers are emerging through demographic studies, but less is known about nineteenth- and early-twentieth-century teachers of color. There were virtually no full-time Native-American or Asian-American teachers in the United States until at least the 1920s: only ten women teachers of these ethnic origins were listed in the 1890 U.S. Census, and in 1900 the 255 so categorized were virtually all Native-American women working in Bureau of Indian Affairs schools.[40]

A sizable African-American teaching force existed by the late 1800s, primarily in the segregated schools of the South, but numbers and the class and family backgrounds of these teachers are difficult to ascertain. This is partly because census statistics, particularly for the rural black South, are unreliable, and partly because careful local studies of African-American teachers are only now being undertaken. Although teachers in black schools were often white in the period immediately after Reconstruction, as segregated schools increased in number, white school boards began to hire more African-American teachers, who were cheaper.[41] By the late 1860s approximately one-third of the teachers of African-American children in the South were themselves African-American, and most were women.[42] According to the U.S. Census, women constituted 52 percent of African-American teachers in 1890, 64 percent in 1900, and 82 percent in 1920.[43] By 1920, then, the gender composition of the black and white teaching force was very similar.

Native-American and African-American women teachers have been ignored in white discourse, both in nineteenth- and early-twentieth-century constructions of the "woman schoolteacher" and in later historical studies of teaching. Discussions of the woman schoolteacher have almost always focused on white women teachers' experience. African-American women teachers, like their male colleagues, had to fight racist practices and work for "racial uplift" within the context of African-American culture, unrecognized by the dominant white world. Although they were invisible (and really unthinkable) within white racist ideology, in their own communities they occupied a place of respect and social value. From the evidence that exists, it seems clear that African-American women teachers shared the deep-seated belief in the power of literacy that characterized African-American communities generally.[44] As Linda Perkins puts it, "Education was for the entire race and its purpose was to assist in the economical, educational, and social improvement of their enslaved and later emancipated race."[45]

In African-American communities, African-American women teachers seem to have accepted a position of community leadership and prestige, often in the face of violent white opposition or blatant neglect on the part of white school trustees.[46] Mamie Fields described conditions teaching in a black rural school on the Sea Islands before the First World War:

We worked hard, knowing all the time that in the eyes of the powers that be, the Negro teachers really didn't amount to much. Neither did the pupils. When we found something more that should be done for the children, we usually had to fix it ourselves. . . . If we could have gotten the materials we needed, there is no telling what we mightn't have done with some of the children. . . . Unless the families had the money to buy the materials, we had to find donations in Charleston. Plenty of times we went on and bought the things out of our own salaries. But it never was possible to do all you could see should be done or could be done. The same white folks who went around calling the colored people "illiterates" were not letting the teachers really teach the colored children.[47]

Although the majority of African-American teachers in the segregated South, like Mamie Fields, worked quietly against racism in small ways, for others, such as Septima Clark, the experience of teaching gave them the skills they needed for leadership in later civil rights struggles.[48]

Bureaucratic Control and Women's Resistance

A number of scholars have argued that late-nineteenth-century school practices and power structures worked to discipline and exploit women classroom teachers.[49] The essence of this argument lies in the increasing bureaucratization of teaching at various levels. Centered on what Marta Danylewycz and Alison Prentice have called "male aspirations for power and social mobility," this new mode of hierarchical organization at first admitted women only to lower-level positions in the classroom. School administration was conceived of as a "natural" male occupation, one in which men had numerous advantages by virtue of their gender alone. Male school administrators, for example, could network with local business leaders and politicians in all-male clubs and political organizations.[50] In this increasingly bureaucratized structure, men "naturally" took the positions of power in large, urban school systems. Meanwhile, the percentage of women classroom teachers (particularly for the lower grades) continued to rise.[51] Control over teachers' work was expressed through new requirements for certification, compulsory institutes at which educational experts presented a scientific and modern perspective, and increased control over the content of the curriculum.[52] This "formalization" of school systems, Prentice argues, was made possible by a gendered division of work in which cheap women teachers enabled a rapidly expanding, well-paid male bureaucracy to come into being.[53]

There can be no doubt that men dominated the bureaucracy of urban schools or that many women teachers still only taught briefly in the period between schooling and marriage. But increased bureaucratization did not only lead to greater control over teachers; it also encouraged greater knowledge on the part of teachers and a potential for power and resistance. The normal schools, where women received "scientific" training, often from male experts, also encouraged an image of themselves as competent professionals. And as we have seen, a significant minority of women teachers did not marry and leave teaching, but continued to work for many years. These "quite ordinary women teachers," Clifford maintains, affected by the opportunity to work for wages in a position of public responsibility, became in turn a "large, receptive, and influential constituency for feminism."[54] David Tyack and Elisabeth Hansot have similarly noted that the period around the turn of the twentieth century was in some respects "a golden age for women school administrators." In 1905, for example, 62 percent of elementary school principals were women (compared with only 20 percent in 1972). "Of all the administrative positions held by large numbers of women," Tyack and Hansot comment, "perhaps the elementary principalship offered the greatest opportunity for autonomy and educational leadership."[55] It is important to observe, however, that these early principals tended also to be teachers. As Wayne Urban remarks, when the teaching principal was replaced by the principal as administrator, the percentage of women principals dropped sharply.[56] Nonetheless, for a time the elementary principalship provided women teachers with positions of real responsibility and decent pay. While the administrative positions held by women may have been less well paid and less prestigious than comparable positions held by men, these figures clearly challenge the argument of male bureaucratic control. And women did not work only as principals; in the Far West, they also held a number of district and state superintendencies.[57]

While the greater numbers of women in school leadership positions can be viewed as evidence of women's challenge to the ideology of separate spheres, it is also possible to see women's involvement in education as a natural extension of that ideology. Courtney Vaughn-Roberson, for example, has argued that in western states in particular, women's election to county and state superintendencies of education occurred precisely because the schoolroom was seen as part of the woman's sphere. She cites Helen Grenfell, Colorado state superintendent of education from 1898 to 1904, as arguing that education was an "outgrowth of the home or . . . the family's way of working out the best interests of the child." These early women school leaders firmly believed in the different natures and thus different spheres of men and women; but at the same time, teaching deeply affected their lives and self-consciousness: "Their jobs did, after all, gain for them social approval both in the work place and in the home. More important, these teachers, like their predecessors, capitalized on the social support that the rhetoric of domesticity granted them to demand recognition for their professional achievements and their role as community builders."[58]

The "golden age" of women school administrators and the active organizing by women teachers corresponds strikingly to the first wave of
feminism. As Margaret Gribskov observes, "The rise and fall of the
woman school administrator approximates the peaks and valleys of the
first American feminist movement of the 1800s and early 1900s, and . . .
the feminist movement was a crucial factor in producing the large number of women administrators of that period."[59] At the same time, the
combination of more advanced schooling for teachers, a sizable minority
of women who made teaching a lifelong career, and the rising cost of
city living led women teachers to challenge the idea of the teacher as an
altruistic maternal nurturer who could be paid very little. A poem in the
Woman's Journal in 1906 captures the cynical view of many women
teachers:

> Everybody's paid but teacher
> Seeking her pay above
> Everybody's paid but teacher,
> Living on ethereal love . . . [60]

This poem stands in sharp contrast to the conventional male view typified by this 1907 *New York Times* account of the graduation ceremony at a
normal school:

As the male spectator contemplates this delightful show, his uppermost thought
must be, What a shame such nice girls should have to teach school for a living:
and his final and consolatory reflection that they will not be doing it long. How
can anybody expect that they are going to take their provisional method of making a living as seriously as the male who takes it for life?[61]

It was this clash of views that led to the creation of teachers organizations
by urban women teachers.

In the rapidly growing cities, the elementary teaching population was
overwhelmingly made up of women, many of whom were second-generation Americans; it was among these women that the first teachers organizations sprang up.[62] The activities of women organizers such as Grace
Strahan in New York, Margaret Haley in Chicago, and Kate Kennedy in
San Francisco have been most closely examined by historians.[63] Under
the patronage system of the late nineteenth century, urban teachers had
no right to tenure, no pension plans, and worked under grossly unequal
pay scales. As greater numbers of single, childless women made teaching a lifelong career, the lack of a pension was obviously a major concern and one of the first to be addressed by teachers organizations.
Teachers were poorly paid in general, but the wage differential between
women and men was an increasingly urgent issue, particularly in the
cities.[64]

The "administrative progressives" of the early twentieth century did not address such inequities. These men were primarily concerned with their own position in relation to male business and political leaders; they had little interest in the needs of women classroom teachers. In a period of general labor unrest and radical political organizing, activist women teachers and principals were thus responding in part to a failure of male leadership to address the changing meaning of teaching as work for women, particularly for women who did not marry and who made teaching a career. But they were also acting in response to wider social movements of progressivism and feminism.[65] It was in this context that women organizers argued that teaching was work and demanded fair and equal pay and the opportunity to rise according to their abilities.

The "Woman Peril"

The ideological construct of the woman teacher who would fulfill her "true" nature by teaching in a school that was an extension of the home was threatened by all of these developments: the growth of a bureaucratized school system based on ideas of scientific management; additional professional training for teachers; the increasing number of women teachers who made teaching a career; articulate and capable women school administrators; and the spread of feminist ideas that directly attacked separate-sphere ideology. It was in response to these developments that the "woman peril" was posited by male experts and educators.[66] The woman peril in education was essentially an elaboration of separate-sphere ideology applied to the radically changed structure of teaching in the early twentieth century. Although some earlier male critics had worried about the growing numbers of women teachers (Harvard president Charles Eliot, for example, warned of the problem of "too many women teachers" in 1875),[67] the problem did not receive widespread attention until the turn of the twentieth century, a time of rapid social change in a number of arenas, as part of the intense debate between the new women who challenged the ideology of separate spheres and true womanhood and those who defended nineteenth-century gender ideology. The claim of a woman peril—the idea that women were inappropriate and even dangerous as teachers—represented a reactionary attempt on the part of male administrators to restore that (imaginary) past when women moved only in the separate, domestic sphere.

A common theme running through the critiques of male educators was that women lacked the intellectual capacity to prepare boys to live in the modern world. Unmarried women teachers, it was argued, stifled creativity and intellect; they were, in the words of San Francisco State presi-

dent Frederick Burk, the "withered heart" of the school.[68] Because of the
influence of women teachers, boys failed to develop a masculine character, and society as a whole suffered. This argument was set out in Admiral
F. E. Chadwick's influential article "The Woman Peril in American Education" in the *Educational Review* in 1914. Chadwick maintained that
women teachers had created

a feminized manhood, emotional, illogical, non-combative against public
evils. . . . We have in this result the cause in greatest degree, of our supineness in
municipal affairs. . . . I lay down the broad statement that no woman, whatever
her ability, is able to bring up properly a man child. . . . Men think in terms of
steamships, railways, battleships, war, finance, in a word, the greatest energies of
the world, which the woman mind never, in a practical way, really concerns itself
with, nor can it do it.[69]

This notion, that women were unable to concern themselves with "the
greatest energies of the world," was echoed by other male critics of the
time. Robert Rogers, an MIT scientist, wrote in 1929:

For a half-century now the largest part of our young people have been trained
exclusively by women teachers. The faults I have been speaking of are the faults
of women teachers: preoccupation with method, interest in details, disinclina-
tion for mathematical and political and philosophical thinking, and inclination
to insist on abstract beliefs to be accepted docilely, rather than the free give-and-
take of criticism. Fifty years of this has produced a people incompetent to think
politically and philosophically.[70]

Thus women's nurturing and maternal nature, though appropriate to
the schoolroom as an extension of the family, was not appropriate to the
training of boys in a modern, scientific state.

The idea of the woman peril rested on a belief in women's special nature—including their inability to think critically or to understand the
larger questions of politics and the economy. But if women lacked intellectual capacity, they had their own, higher calling—back in the domestic
sphere of the family. As was typical of much scientific thought of the
time, these arguments fused sexual ideology with eugenics. Not only
were white women teachers incapable of teaching boys, but in working
for wages they were avoiding their true responsibility to "the race."[71] Consider David Snedden's criticism of the practice of hiring married women
as teachers: "Does not any employer who offers tempting employment
to a married woman under forty years of age potentially contribute to
the impairment of superior stock among Americans?"[72] Other male educators worried not only about white middle-class women "doing their
duty" for the race by leaving teaching and having children, but also
about the lack of pure Anglo-Saxon women teachers, about "lower-class"

women and in particular second-generation Americans who would be unable to teach children proper patriotism and Protestantism—as in Lotus Coffman's comment in 1910: "The intellectual possessions of the race are by rather unconscious selection left to a class of people who by social and economic station, as well as by training, are not eminently fitted for their transmission."[73]

The male experts who decried the woman peril ignored the existence of women in leadership positions in the schools and teachers organizations, not to mention feminist demands for equality. Indeed, by reasserting separate-sphere ideology they implicitly called into question the whole idea of women in positions of power and responsibility. As Tyack and Hansot have pointed out, the outcry over the woman peril did not stem the numbers of women teachers, which continued to increase.[74] As part of a more general reaction to feminism, however, this rhetoric reflected a significant shift in the representation of the woman teacher.

From "True Woman" to New Woman and Beyond, 1920–50

Women educators achieved real gains in the period 1900–1920: they created teachers organizations, continued the fight for tenure and pension rights, and held significant positions as elementary principals and county superintendents, particularly in the West. In cities and towns, women teachers, particularly principals and single women who made teaching a career, were active in the suffrage movement and were sympathetic with the social feminism of the Progressive Era. Meanwhile, political, social, and ideological shifts were beginning to reframe the meaning of their work. In the interwar years especially, the material and social worlds of women were transformed. The achievement of suffrage in 1920, the move toward smaller families, the availability of household conveniences, and such technological innovations as the automobile, movies, and the radio all had a tremendous impact on women's material lives. At the same time, changing sexual standards, the greater acceptability of divorce, and increased opportunities for work outside the home redefined women's personal and sexual identities.

Movies and magazines portrayed the flapper: "Glamorous, economically independent, sexually free, and of course single, the flapper represented what a business community would have liked its young women workers to be."[75] That men retained control of business, politics, and law was rarely a matter for discussion. The social critique of feminism was replaced by a culture of consumerism and individualism; now women's freedom meant the freedom to buy and to have sexual pleasure within marriage. Instead of organizing against patriarchal attitudes and sexist practices, women were encouraged to see themselves as individuals competing in an open marketplace without regard for gender.[76] As Nancy Cott puts it, "Feminists' defiance of the sexual division of labor was swept under the rug. Establishing new formalism, these adaptations disarmed Feminism's challenges in the guise of enacting them."[77] By the 1920s many women affirmed the idea of a gender-neutral equality of opportunity. Yet the mere adoption of a language of equality does not destroy male power and control. Carroll Smith-Rosenberg notes:

Words, unallied to material sources of power, become like spirits divorced from corporeal form—shades, fantasies, brave but sad illusions. The New Women of the 1920s did not fail because they chose the wrong discourse. They failed because they lacked the real economic and institutional power with which to wrest hegemony from men and so enforce their vision of a gender-free world.[78]

Like other American women, women teachers were affected by the rapid changes of the interwar period. In some ways the gap between city and country became even more pronounced, since urban teachers lived in a world where smoking, social drinking, movies, dancing, and greater sexual freedom increasingly were accepted, while in many rural areas school boards and local communities continued to control women teachers' lives as they had in the late nineteenth century. Changing standards of morality were reflected not only in the greater number of married women teachers, but also in resistance, particularly in the cities, to the restrictions on teachers' private lives. A 1928 *Harper's* article, for example, cited the response to a demand by the Hazel Park, Michigan, school board that all teachers wear ankle-length smocks: "The one hundred and eight teachers defied the edict as a body and came to school in shorter skirts than ever; and furthermore, the state superintendent of instruction informed the worthy gentlemen of the board that the teachers had the law on their side."[79] Oral history narratives of teachers in this period contain numerous examples of resistance to social control, as in this account by a Texas teacher of the 1920s who lived in a mixed-sex teachers' boardinghouse in a small town:

If you were a teacher, you just shouldn't go off on night parties. Of course, you couldn't drink. . . . I know one night we all left. They didn't know what we were doing. So we went on a beautiful creek on a moonlight night and took our picnic supper. And we took our record player. The creek had solid rock all on one side. We were trying to dance down there too. I suppose they never did know that. But anyway, that's how strict they were a long time ago.[80]

Although smoking was still unacceptable in many settings, in the cities young women increasingly smoked. By the mid-1930s some urban schools had smoking rooms for teachers, even women teachers. Most women teachers, however, were probably like those described by Howard Beale in his 1936 study *Are American Teachers Free?*, who smoked "privately so that parents and school officials will not know it. Many others who are not forbidden just do not. . . . It might cause talk."[81] Although drinking, too, was restricted, many teachers, again primarily in the cities, did drink. The ban against going to the theater had been lifted in most places, but card playing and dancing were still mostly forbidden. Smaller infractions were targeted as well: in 1927, for example, South Carolina passed a law revoking the teaching certificate of any teacher who used profanity.[82] Cosmetics and short skirts were still forbidden in country school districts in the 1930s. Thus, despite changes in social mores, the 1930s still found many teachers treated, in David Tyack's words, as "secular nuns."

During the depression women teachers came under renewed scrutiny, salaries were cut, and the marriage bar was debated in the context of wider arguments about whether married women should work in a time of such high unemployment. In 1928 the National Education Association surveyed school systems in 1,532 cities with populations of 2,500 or greater; 29 percent of these cities still required teachers who married to resign at once, and 25 percent more forced them to resign at the end of the year.[83] A number of reasons were given for keeping the marriage bar in place: two-income families were unfair in an economic crisis, married women wouldn't pay sufficient attention to their work, these women (presumably as white Protestants) should be at home having children. But as Lois Scharf points out, married women teachers also tended to be older and have more seniority, and thus were more expensive. Just as it made economic sense to hire young unmarried women as teachers in the 1850s, so it made sense to fire married women teachers in the 1930s. But although both rhetoric and local practices during the depression discriminated against married women, demonstrating continued unease with the idea of women working in the public sphere, the percentage of married women actually increased by 1940. As Table 1 shows, the percentages of married women teachers came to approximate the numbers for all working women.

TABLE 1

Percentage of Women Workers Who Were Married, 1920–40

	1920	1930	1940
All jobs	. 23.0%	28.9%	29.6%
Teachers	9.7%	17.9%	22.0%

SOURCE: Nancy Cott, *The Grounding of Modern Feminism* (New Haven: Yale University Press, 1987), p. 183.

In many areas the acceptance of teaching as appropriate work for women still applied only to white Protestants. In his 1936 study Howard Beale found widespread discrimination against both Jews and Catholics outside of a few large cities such as New York, Chicago, and Boston. The work and lives of African-American women teachers, too, continued to be framed by racism. By 1920 African-American elementary teachers were primarily women, but their opportunities for work continued to be limited by legal and informal segregation. In the North and West, African-American teachers would almost always only be hired to teach in predominantly black schools, while in the South they could find work only in the underfunded segregated schools. As was true earlier, teachers were respected figures in the black community, and increasingly were well educated, attending segregated normal schools or state teachers colleges. Conditions in the segregated South were well known, but Beale found oppressive and discriminatory conditions for African-American teachers throughout the United States as well:

Through most of the North, Negro teachers are completely barred from the schools, because, outside of the large cities, the number of Negroes is small, and there is either one pitiful Negro segregated school taught by whites, or the Negro children are in mixed schools, where no Negro can teach. In the large Northern cities, where there is no segregation, the problem is acute. In most places, Negroes have been barred, or habitually "failed" in unfairly-graded examinations, or [were] never appointed after having qualified. In certain cities with large Negro populations they have gradually won the right to appointments in elementary schools and, in the last decade, to high schools in "black belts."[84]

Black women teachers worked hard for racial uplift. For them, the critique of sexism was less pressing than the struggle against racism. In her oral history of African-American teachers under segregation, Michele Foster documents women teachers' sense of commitment to their students and their role as leaders in their communities.[85] Nationally known African-American women educators such as Mary McLeod Bethune and Mary Church Terrell inspired ordinary classroom teachers. Mamie Fields, for example, remembered the impact of hearing Mary McLeod Bethune speak in Charleston in the 1930s:

She was a powerful speaker, but before she opened her mouth to say a word, the feeling would go around that evil couldn't prevail against her—or against us. We understood that if Mrs. Bethune said we could accomplish a certain thing, then we could. The mediocre and the scared didn't come around Mary McLeod Bethune. Or, if they did, they hushed.[86]

From the 1920s through the 1940s, organized white women teachers were remarkably silent in comparison to the generation that preceded them. The retreat of women teachers from feminist activism mirrored their embrace of the idea of professionalism and the move to consumption and entertainment as the significant arenas for women's self-expression among women in general. Women principals and superintendents continued to support the work of women teachers in many settings, particularly in the West, but an articulated feminist consciousness of the specific interests and concerns of women teachers tended to disappear. This retreat from an articulated feminist critique can be seen in the decline of teachers organizations and unions, the result in part of the red scare of 1919 and the aggressively conservative, probusiness, and antiunion climate of the early 1920s. In the reactionary climate of the day, teachers who participated in teachers organizations were persecuted or lost their jobs, and union representatives were denied access to teachers meetings or institutes. Conservative groups such as the American Legion, the Daughters of the American Revolution, and the Women's Christian Temperance Union took it upon themselves to monitor not just the lives of teachers, but the curriculum as well.

Teachers organizations suffered real losses during this time. In New York, the Interborough Association of Women Teachers successfully fought for equal pay for equal work, but following that victory the organization retreated from women's issues. The Chicago Teachers Federation was forced to end its formal alliance with organized labor in order to retain advances for teachers, and by the 1930s it, too, had lost its militant feminist stance. The American Federation of Teachers, founded in 1916 as an affiliate of the American Federation of Labor in the prolabor climate of the mid-1910s, was weak and disorganized by 1923. The one large-scale teachers organization that survived and flourished in the 1920s was the conservative National Education Association (NEA). Despite the election of the militant Ella Flagg Young in 1910 and the attempts of Margaret Haley to create a more democratic organization representative of women teachers' interests, by the early 1920s the NEA was firmly in the hands of a coalition of professional school administrators and university professors in schools of education who advocated ideas of scientific management and what Raymond Callahan called "the cult of efficiency."[87] With the rise of the NEA, no significant national organization existed any longer to represent women classroom teachers' interests. From the 1920s until the 1960s, as a consequence, gender differences in teaching were, as Wayne Urban comments, "papered over rather than solved."[88]

The Sexually Healthy Teacher

Just as in the nineteenth and early twentieth centuries the construct of the woman teacher shifted uneasily between the "true woman" of the schoolroom-as-family and the inadequate, emotional woman of the woman peril who was unfit to teach future engineers and captains of industry, so in the twentieth century did the representation of the woman teacher incorporate both idealized aspects of the liberated "new woman" and Freudian notions of sexualized femininity. As we have seen, in the period 1890–1920 the suffrage movement and the idea of the "new woman" provided the grounds for viewing women educators—school reformers, principals, and rural county superintendents especially—as educated and competent. By the 1920s, however, this representation was being challenged by new ideas of the "normal" woman and the "healthy personality," in ways that again relegated women teachers to a subordinate role. The image of the unmarried teacher subtly shifted as she became perceived as a sexual or deviant threat. Although for traditionalists, virginal "true women" or "secular nuns"—cheap, easily controlled, and symbolic of the traditional patriarchal order—still existed, a new persona now arose in the form of the sexualized heterosexual woman. This new construct was hailed by observers who could be called modernists, generally urban and politically liberal men, who defended women teachers' right to a normal life but who framed their defense in highly restrictive homophobic conceptions of mental health and wholesomeness and who did nothing to challenge either the power relations of the patriarchal family or the patriarchal structure of the school.[89]

With the advent of sexology and later the acceptance of Freudian psychology, women's sexuality became the focus of intense popular concern, becoming fused with images of the "new woman" and the flapper. Like the virginal and asexual Victorian middle-class woman, the Freudian woman was also supposedly deeply concerned with expressing her innate womanly nature, but now the ideal was heterosexual expressions of sexuality.[90] The move to a discourse in which sexual (and mental) health necessitated heterosexual relations within marriage not only privileged the married woman (whose primary allegiance was understood to be to husband and family) but also made the figure of the unmarried woman even more deviant and threatening. In teaching, this led to a revival of the nineteenth-century figure of the old maid or spinster. Consider this description of the old maid teacher on nineteenth-century comic valentines, which is reminiscent of earlier European witches and wise women living outside the patriarchal order:

Her frock was dark and shapeless; her collar tight and high; her shoes broad and unimaginative. Her nose was long and pinched at the end; her eyes small and deep set; her lips narrow and severe. Over her stomach she wore an apron of black sateen, and in her hand she held a brutal little switch, the scepter with which she ruled her kingdom of helpless children. Underneath the picture was a verse—but always doggerel that called her a crank and hurled at her the insulting epithet "Old Maid."[91]

Although the figure of the old maid teacher was not always presented in such a threatening and exaggerated way, the idea that single women teachers were oppressive and even somehow dangerous was widespread. Recall Frederick Burk's 1907 description of the unmarried woman teacher as the "withered heart" of the school. Now "spinster" teachers were seen as a threat to society as a whole, and particularly its heterosexual gender order.[92]

In the 1920s a number of liberal journalists and sociologists began to criticize the marriage bar and other restrictions on women teachers' lives. The journalist Stephen Ewing, for example, writing in *Harper's* in 1928, attacked the "petty regulations and restrictions" that marked teachers' lives: "Why are the best of our college girls giving the public schools a wide berth? Simply because no individual of spirit will choose to work in a milieu where her professional initiative will be curbed at every turn and where her personal activities will be under constant surveillance." Ewing tied the restricted and controlled life of the woman teacher to narrow thinking and a failure of imagination. He asked, "Do we want our children taught by women who know so little of the world at first hand?" By this Ewing meant more than a lack of opportunity to travel or attend concerts; rather, he worried that the social restrictions on women teachers would turn them into "sexless human beings doomed to devote all their waking hours to teaching and its attendant demands."[93] Concern about the "sexless" spinster teacher became ever more evident in popular and academic writing about teachers in the 1930s and 1940s. How could democracy flourish if children in public schools were influenced by these unhealthy women? For liberal critics, the solution lay not in undoing gender inequality, but in eliminating the marriage bar and social restrictions on teachers.

In 1930 George Counts, in *The American Road to Culture*, provided a brief discussion of the plight of women teachers. Unlike other liberal critics, Counts noted the sexism of existing power relationships in education: "Although two-thirds of the teachers in the secondary school and practically all of the teachers in the elementary school are women," he stated, "the overwhelming majority of the professorships in the universities and the important administrative positions throughout the educational system fall to men. Moreover, for the same type of work, a woman is commonly paid less than a man." Recognizing that the marriage bar undoubtedly owed its existence to "the conviction that the place of the married woman is in the home," he acknowledged that gender ideology rather than biological destiny underlay the marriage bar. But like Ewing and later observers, he also saw a danger in the reliance on unmarried women teachers who "lack the experience of both sex and motherhood."[94] By the time Counts published his influential tract *Dare the Schools*

Build a New Social Order? (1934), his concern with the sexist structure of American schools had disappeared; his call for democratic teaching left the patriarchal structure of the schools unquestioned.

Probably the most original and critical analysis of teaching in the 1930s was Willard Waller's acerbic *Sociology of Teaching*. Writing in the tradition of H. L. Mencken and Sinclair Lewis, Waller attacked what he saw as the stifling and conformist nature of American schools. Although he almost always used the masculine pronoun, particularly when expounding on individuality and freedom, he switched to the feminine pronoun when discussing the maladjusted, weak teacher who fails to challenge students to independent thought and love of learning. For example: "The teacher with a strong inferiority complex spreads inferiority complexes about her in her classroom. The teacher whose attitude toward sex is not wholesome engenders a similar maladjustment in her students." The obvious solution to Waller was the hiring of married women teachers, who were "more wholesome and normal than their unmarried sisters."[95] This recalls Stephen Ewing's observation that "there are those who assert that the married woman actually displays more professional interest than the young unmarried woman, since she has passed 'the hunting-season' and is less flighty."[96]

Waller's influence is evident in Frances Donovan's popularized sociological study *The Schoolma'am* (1938), in which she examined teaching as women's work.[97] Like Ewing and Waller, Donovan accepted the idea of "mental hygiene" and the need for a "wholesome personality." Without these things, she said, you would get the "queer teacher," with "maladjustments of sex life," who was dangerous to children and to herself. In an extended (and possibly fictitious) case study, Donovan tells the story of "Hope Grey," a rural teacher who "became mentally deranged when she was thirty years old" with "dementia praecox with systematized delusions." Here is a letter Hope Grey is supposed to have sent Donovan, packed with "the repressions of an unmarried schoolteacher":

I have lived a studious, lonely life. I've been constantly on the move, have lived, as well as taught, in many different states, and that I believe is the reason why I have never been well acquainted with any men and have never had the experience of a mutually acknowledged and returned love. Yet I wish to marry. There is nothing holy about living a life of socially enforced celibacy. It is absurd, unjust, and diabolically cruel that thousands of healthy women should have their natural passions repressed for a lifetime.

Donovan encouraged Hope to leave teaching and get a job in a factory, where she would be more likely to meet a man. As Donovan explained to Hope, "You can't expect to marry in your own class. You don't know the little tricks and wiles that entrap the sophisticated man. The working man is less complex; he'll be easier to approach." Hope then married a working man named George, but the marriage failed. She returned to live with her mother but, increasingly tormented, eventually tried to kill her mother with a pair of scissors. It was then that she was diagnosed with dementia praecox and sent to the insane asylum. For Donovan, this story represented "the typical problems of great numbers of young women, particularly of those who come from the rural groups from which she was recruited."[98] While Donovan presents other perspectives—including the suggestion that it might be better to remain single than to accept some of the inferior material available as potential husbands—underlying her discussion was an acceptance of the "normal" heterosexual woman and a striking absence of critique of existing power relations in schools.

The liberal reform campaign favoring heterosexual married women teachers had met with full success by the late 1940s, but this change was brought about at least as much by the social impact of the Second World War as by any reform movement. Faced by a severe teacher shortage, school boards and administrators eliminated the marriage bar during the war, and restrictions on teachers' private lives were to some extent lifted, particularly after the war as more and more Americans moved out of small towns or urban ethnic neighborhoods to the suburbs. Teachers during this period were at a premium, and women teachers shared in rising salaries and benefits.

In the late 1940s and 1950s, however, women teachers also faced the conservative and deeply sexist mood of postwar America. The definition of what was normal for women in 1950 was a rigid code of, in the words of Adrienne Rich, "compulsory heterosexuality" and the Freudian dictum that women's anatomy was their destiny.[99] The view that women's proper place was in a heterosexual marriage reigned, with women's work seen as supplementary to the needs of their families. This version of women's psychology, Mary Ryan comments, reached "its largest circulation after World War II, when, in keeping with the 'feminine mystique,' it celebrated a completely domesticated version of female sexuality."[100] Basic to this disciplinary discourse were ideas of "adjustment" and "the healthy personality," which explained and regulated women in subordinate positions, both sexually and professionally. The frightening alternative to the sexually healthy (and dependent) woman was the mannish lesbian or the domineering mother who destroyed her children by overprotectiveness or excessive emotional demands, as in Philip Wylie's *Generation of Vipers* (1942) or Ferdinand Lundberg and Marynia Farnham's 1947 study *Modern Woman: The Lost Sex.*

With the shift from the "true" woman of the nineteenth century to the sexualized woman of the 1940s and 1950s, the early-twentieth-century "new" woman, who had the ability to define an independent life, was effectively erased. Despite the relaxation of control over their private lives, by 1950 women teachers were firmly fixed in subordinate roles and schools were rigidly divided into gender hierarchies. Men monopolized administrative positions at all levels; indeed, by 1960 women administrators were rare. But teaching, particularly elementary school teaching, continued to be defined as women's work. In 1970, 53 percent of female college graduates who worked, taught in elementary or high schools.[101] The abandonment of a self-conscious feminist analysis of gender and power in education and the ascendancy of a disciplinary discourse of compulsory heterosexuality in society generally left women teachers without a language of critique with which to understand their subordinate role.

Conclusion

Feminist historians have emphasized the power of hegemonic ideology to obliterate past struggles—both material struggles and those over definition and meaning. This historical amnesia has marked the history of women teachers as well: both their accomplishments and the intense ideological struggles over what it meant to be a woman teacher have been neglected or forgotten. The work of a number of scholars is beginning to reveal the outline of this complex history. As is becoming apparent, ideological shifts in the meaning of the schoolteacher can be understood only in relation to larger historical movements. I have argued here that when we examine the history of women teachers in the United States we see not only evidence of women's significant participation in schooling, but conflicts over representations as well. A historical investigation of the shifting representation of the woman teacher cautions us about accepting uncritically "universal truths" about teachers and their work. Instead I have suggested that we need to employ a multifaceted approach in order to understand the world of women teachers, examining the material conditions of the work of teaching, the growth of state bureaucracy, the class and racial structures that shape schooling, but also the shifting constructs of the woman teacher. In the next chapter I use this same approach to explore the rise of the educational state in California, in order to understand the wider political and discursive currents that shaped the working lives and consciousness of rural women teachers.

GENDER AND THE GROWTH OF THE EDUCATIONAL STATE: CALIFORNIA, 1850–1940

The history of education in recent years has been approached from a variety of perspectives: in terms of national development, as a reflection of class conflict, as an aspect of state formation. More recently historians influenced by Foucault have emphasized the nexus of power/knowledge and have argued that schools, like other state institutions, discipline both minds and bodies.[1] In this study, I view the history of California education through a different lens—that of gender. The use of gender as a category of historical analysis implies a concern both with discourse—the process of creating meaning in the debates and rhetoric of historical actors—and with material circumstances—the differing life histories of men and women. It leads to questions of how the lives of women teachers were affected by the development of state institutions and how in turn that development was shaped by conceptions of gender. Ideas of gender underlie both the conflicting representations of women teachers in the discourse of educational experts and feminist reformers and struggles over material resources. An analysis of material life reveals the different access men and women enjoy to positions of power and authority, conflicts over equal pay for equal work, and struggles to maintain or challenge gender privilege for men in education. An analysis of discourse reveals tensions between the framing of images of women teachers in patriarchal authoritative discourse and the claims of counterdiscourses, often fragmentary and partial, that suggest new meanings of "woman" and "the woman teacher."

The history of state control over education in California in the nineteenth and twentieth centuries parallels developments throughout the United States. This period saw what Bruce Curtis has called the "rise of the educational state," as schools as state institutions increasingly attempted to shape the minds and bodies of children.[2] As the state gained greater knowledge and control over classroom teachers, it also gained greater power. But too great a focus on the growth of the state, on the development of ideas of science and measurement, or on the role of schools in building patriotism and a common American identity can obscure the deeply gendered nature of these discourses and practices. Just as assumptions about race have been expressed in de jure and de facto practices of segregation and in racist discrimination against teachers who are not white, beliefs about gender have shaped the fundamental organization of schools and the lives of teachers. This has been true despite the acceptance of formal civil equality, coeducation, and a "gender-neutral" curriculum. Assumptions about gender profoundly shaped the institutional structure of education, a field in which classroom teachers increasingly were women, while a disproportionate number of administrators and state officials were men.

These shifts in the gendered pattern of the teaching force in California paralleled developments in the Northeast. As was true elsewhere, the teaching force in California in the nineteenth and early twentieth centuries was almost exclusively white and predominantly Protestant. Whereas in the early days of statehood most teachers were men—which was to be expected, since the population of California in 1850 was 92 percent male—by 1900 the ratio of men and women teachers increasingly matched national figures, with women in the great majority, particularly in the case of elementary school teachers. The shift in California took place later than in New England and eastern states, but the trend was exactly the same (Table 2). Thus by 1916, approximately 90 percent of California teachers were women, matching national figures, and by 1930 almost 97 percent of elementary school teachers in the state were women.[3] In reality and in the popular imagination, then, the elementary school teacher was a woman. But the meanings associated with the woman teacher were contested, as were assumptions of male privilege

TABLE 2
California Teachers, 1860–1930

	Men	Women
1860	536	218
1876	1,167	1,983
1884	1,108	2,964
1904	926	6,871
1916	1,238	12,080
1930	750	19,504

SOURCE: California Superintendent of Public Instruction, Biennial Reports for 1860, 1876, 1884, 1904, 1916, and 1930.

and control. An examination of state policies and the discourse of academic experts concerned with education in California reveals conflicting ideas about gender, a reflection of the competing representations of women teachers circulating in society at large.

The Gendered Discourse of California School Reform

Like many western states, California based its public school system on the common schools of New England.[4] A system of common schools, to be open at least three months a year and supported by the sale of public lands, was mandated by the state constitution, although in the first fifteen years of statehood schools remained of little import to California politicians obsessed with land claims and gold.[5] In the early 1860s, however, State Superintendent of Public Instruction John Swett led a reform movement to bring schools more directly under state control. Born and educated in New England, Swett, who had been the principal of a grammar school in San Francisco before being elected state superintendent in 1862, was strongly committed to the ideas of the common school movement and attempted to rationalize regulations and procedures. State control over local schools slowly increased through the 1870s: schooling was made compulsory in 1874; six- rather than three-month schools were encouraged (although in rural areas three-month schools remained the norm); and concern was expressed over the construction of schoolhouses, adequate ventilation and grounds, and the preparation and certification of teachers.[6] With the passage of the new state constitution of 1879, responsibility for overseeing local schools was given to county and district boards of education, and control over the content of examinations passed into the hands of the local school boards. After 1879, all counties with more than twenty schools were required to hold a yearly institute as a means of encouraging and training teachers; these institutes were deemed particularly important for those who had not attended normal school.[7] The intent of these reforms was to increase control over both teachers and curriculum. The last two decades of the nineteenth century saw the development of an even more regularized system of public schooling in California, as school attendance rose, high schools expanded, and teachers became better educated and supervised.

Teaching in California, as elsewhere, was shaped by assumptions about the essential natures of men and women, which were used to justify male authority and women's limited roles as classroom teachers. Also as elsewhere, the growth of feminism and shifting patterns of work created tensions and conflicts within California education as men and women spoke and acted not only on the basis of different interests but from different assumptions as well. Both the vision of teaching as woman's "true" profession, expressed by Catherine Beecher and the common school reformers, and the later national panic over the "woman peril" were echoed in the rhetoric of California officials and university educators.

In the early days of statehood, when the school system of the state was being formed, women were encouraged to enter teaching. John Swett was a strong supporter of women teachers. Like Horace Mann and Catherine Beecher, Swett argued that the higher moral natures of women suited them for teaching: "The schools of the old world are principally taught by male teachers. I am of the opinion that one great cause of the evident superiority of our American common schools over the primary schools of Europe is this employment of female teachers." Moreover, he said, "All of the leading educators and state officials are taking strong ground in favor of a still more general employment of female teachers in the public schools."[8] Because Swett was writing at precisely the point when teaching was shifting from being predominantly men's to women's work, he may well have been trying to convince recalcitrant county superintendents and district boards to hire women. State officials such as Swett also argued that wage differentials between men and women teachers in California were less extreme than in the East. He claimed that in 1864, male teachers in California were paid $74 a month, and women $62 a month on average, as opposed to the eastern states, where men averaged $34 a month and women $20 a month. As Swett wrote, "I am proud of the fact that in this new State the rights of female teachers are thus regarded; that, when found capable of doing a man's work in school, woman is paid a compensation so nearly the same. I hope this may long continue, and that many schools now taught by men will be placed under the instruction of refined, accomplished, intelligent and enthusiastic women."[9] Swett, like later California educators, made it clear, however, that women were admirably suited to the classroom because of their emotional, not their intellectual, abilities. As he commented, "Many of our best female teachers never pass brilliant examinations. Their column of 'percentages' is always low; but a great heart, womanly tact, love and kindness, place them high upon the scale of true teachers."[10]

Swett's admiration for the "great heart" and "womanly tact" of women teachers was not necessarily shared by subsequent male educators. O. P. Fitzgerald, for example, who defeated Swett in the election of 1867 and replaced him as state superintendent, had a more suspicious view. While Fitzgerald defended the hiring of women teachers because of their "natural suitability," he was careful to make clear that he was not advocating their equality with men:

I have no sympathy whatever with any movement of the present day, looking to the dragging of woman into spheres unsuited to her nature, and contrary to the design of her creator; but the existing state of society, no less than the claims of abstract justice, demands that to those spheres of useful activity to which she is adapted she shall have free access—Woman is adapted to the school room.[11]

Fitzgerald's reference to the "movement of the present day" undoubtedly was to the women's movement and ideas of equality between men and women, ideas that were in fact circulating at least among some California women teachers. And in stating that "woman is adapted to the school room," he was simply repeating the claim of the common school reformers that women were suited to teaching because the school was part of the private, domestic sphere, an extension of the home.

Although Swett had written proudly of the smaller wage differential between men and women teachers in California as compared to the East, early women activists argued against there being any differential at all. In the 1870s, the issue of equal pay for men and women teachers became the focus for an organized protest led by Kate Kennedy, a San Francisco elementary school principal.[12] Kennedy, a well-educated Irish immigrant, was active in the suffrage movement and a member of the Knights of Labor. In 1872 she chaired a meeting of San Francisco women educators protesting a move to lower teachers' salaries; this involvement led her to argue for equal pay for men and women teachers throughout California. As a result of these protests, in 1874 legislation was passed "to prevent discrimination against female teachers." The act provided that "females employed as teachers in the public schools of this State shall, in all cases, receive the same compensation as is allowed male teachers for like services, when holding the same grade certificate."[13] By 1877, State Superintendent Ezra Carr spoke of the high wages paid California teachers, "justly, according to service rather than sex."[14]

Despite the state's formal policy of equal pay for men and women teachers, underlying assumptions of gender differences and of women's essentially moral and maternal natures persisted. Perhaps the most interesting exemplar of these attitudes was Jeanne C. Carr, deputy superintendent of public instruction and the wife of State Superintendent Ezra Carr. Probably the most influential woman educator in California in the nineteenth century, Jeanne Carr was acquainted with the ideas of European educators such as Johann Pestalozzi and Friedrich Froebel, and spoke frequently at institutes and conferences statewide. Her views of the natural superiority of women teachers can be best seen in her 1878 speech "The Industrial Education of Women," which was later published in Ezra Carr's 1879 superintendent's report.

Jeanne Carr, like Horace Mann, Catherine Beecher, and John Swett, argued that women's moral nature made them "natural" teachers; but she also insisted on equal treatment and a recognition of their valuable work: "Whether we regard women as mothers or as teachers, they are equally workers." As workers, Carr argued, women were essential to a healthy society; a woman's needs should be met through an education "devoted to the special training of woman for her work in the home, in the school, and for the right exercise of her social powers." Although Carr accepted the idea that women were suited to be mothers and teachers, and hence accepted women's difference from (and in her opinion, superiority to) men, she also argued for women's greater participation in public life: "It is doubtful whether woman will ever take her true place as educator of the race until she ceases to be a ward of the State, ceases to share its guardianship with idiots and criminals. Give her a nobler part to play on the stage of public affairs, and she will help to make education a religion, for she is essentially more religious than man."[15] Carr thus presented the well-known argument that women should be teachers because of their higher moral natures, but, like Kate Kennedy and later teachers influenced by the suffrage movement, she extended that argument to include participation on "the stage of public affairs," which implied full rights of citizenship.

As women moved in ever greater numbers into teaching, male state superintendents in the 1880s and 1890s became increasingly uneasy. In 1882, State Superintendent F. M. Campbell argued for better pay and higher standards in order to attract qualified teachers, but he couched his argument in these terms:

> When all school officers follow this course, we shall find still fewer young, trifling girls, fresh from the Grammar School studies, and who by a system of cramming are able to squeeze through an examination and secure a certificate, placed in charge of a room full of children at a most critical period of their early school life; and the better it will be for the schools, the pupils, and the State.[16]

For Superintendent Campbell, the image of the woman teacher had shifted from the pure and noble mother-teacher to the "trifling girl," who might be able to cram enough to pass an examination, but who should not be left responsible for children at this "critical period" of their school life. Although Campbell did not advocate a total return to male teachers, such comments point to a growing anxiety that would eventually develop into the "woman peril" of the early twentieth century.

The "Woman Peril" in California Education

By 1900, the ascendancy of the suffrage movement, the entry of women into universities, and the increased involvement of women in a variety of social reform activities presented a challenge to traditional male control of the public sphere. The influence of the suffrage movement and the first wave of feminism on women school administrators and teachers has just begun to be explored, but it seems clear that the greater militancy of suffrage groups and the movement of women into higher education in the Progressive Era had an impact on schoolwomen in California as well as in settings such as Chicago and New York.[17] In California and nationwide, some women were beginning to move into influential and powerful positions in education during this period. Many of these women worked in the suffrage movement and were strong supporters of equality for women in all aspects of public life. Starting in the 1890s, increasing numbers of women were elected as county superintendents of schools, particularly in the less populated mountain and rural areas of the state. In cities, teaching provided a means of financial support and a social network for single women, as well as connections with other women's organizations and reform movements. Women also held positions of authority and influence in the growing state normal schools, even though men tended to remain in the president's office. By 1900, teaching was established as women's work, women teachers were better educated than before, and teaching provided the possibility of a lifetime career, although still, in most cases, only for single women. It is doubtless no accident that the "woman question" became a matter of open debate and discussion at exactly this point, when women were beginning to challenge traditional male privileges.

Male educators reacted to women's growing presence in education with unease. This concern with the "feminization" of teaching and the potentially dangerous effect of women educators may well have contributed to the founding of the various "schoolmasters clubs" at this time in California. These associations were self-conscious attempts to further men's interests in education through the creation of networks and institutional supports.[18] The first and most influential of these clubs seems to have been the California Schoolmasters Club, founded in 1893 by Elmer Brown, professor of pedagogy at the University of California. A second influential group was the Scholia Club, founded in San Francisco in 1902.[19] These men-only clubs were made up of university professors, normal school instructors, city and county superintendents, and high school teachers. The membership of the Schoolmasters Club was limited to one hundred, and the Scholia Club seems to have been even smaller; some men belonged to both.[20] Members included such leading California schoolmen as Earl Barnes and Ellwood Cubberley of Stanford, and John Swett, the retired state superintendent of public instruction. The membership of these clubs overlapped with the leadership of the California Teachers Association (CTA); the Schoolmasters Club, for example, held its meetings at the annual CTA convention.

Many Schoolmasters and Scholia Club members were actively concerned about the problems posed by women teachers and strongly advocated bringing more men into teaching. In 1896 Stanford professor Earl Barnes, a member of the Schoolmasters Club, discussed the dangers of women teachers in a speech published in the *Biennial Report* of the state superintendent: "We live by our admirations. Our admirations are largely formed in schools. We ought not to have a generation of men who have never learned to admire the masculine qualities in the Anglo-Saxon race."[21] Here Barnes typically intertwines the themes of masculinity and racism to express his distrust of women and his concern about the well-being of "a generation of men." As was almost always the case in such discussions, girls have disappeared from his imagined school, and instead the dangerous relationship is between women teachers and boys. That the dangerous relationship might in reality be between middle-aged male professors and young women is suggested by Barnes's own career; he was dismissed from Stanford for having an affair with a student, an example of what we now would consider the sexual misuse of power, if not outright sexual harassment. Nevertheless, Barnes's anxieties about the dangers of women teachers were shared by other male leaders. In 1905, for example, Governor Pardee spoke to the state legislature of the need to pay teachers better salaries in order to attract men to the profession. Women teachers, he argued, were not serious professionals: "Young women, in too many instances, look upon teaching as an expedient which will enable them to live until something more alluring calls them from the school room."[22]

The most striking attempt to further male interests in California was the 1906 campaign for higher salaries and privileges for male educators, which paralleled a similar campaign in New York in exactly the same period.[23] In December 1906 James Barr, superintendent of schools in Oakland and former president of the California Teachers Association, circulated a questionnaire to "each County and City Superintendent of Schools in California, to the Normal Schools and Universities, and to representative men and women in other callings, including legislators, editors, clergymen, lawyers, mechanics, etc." describing the crisis of "men leaving the profession," asking for examples of how schools would be improved if more men were employed in them, and calling for suggestions for ways to induce men to "enter the profession." In a summary of the responses to this circular, Barr cited the "toboggan slide" of men leaving the teaching profession both nationwide and in California. In California, for example, between 1899 and 1906 the number of men teaching in elementary schools declined from 1,137 to 887, while the number of women increased from 5,806 to 7,195.[24] Although we do not have access to all of the responses Barr received, the sample he chose to publish certainly reveals his own views and is consistent with the attitudes of many other male educators.

According to Barr, respondents cited low salaries and the need for men to support a family as major reasons for men's departure from teaching. He reported that respondents almost unanimously stated that more male educators were needed and that one of the great questions facing California and the entire nation was the "overfeminization of the schools." He quotes some of the reasons given for the need for more men in teaching:

Outside of the home man is the dominant factor in world affairs; hence our boys and girls should view the problems of life from a man's perspective.

Other things being equal, men are better teachers; they see things in a broader way; they are not concerned with trifles; their lives are more in touch with the activities of life; the school life with them is not such a fictitious thing as with most women.

Boys need a teacher somewhere along the course of their education, who has once been a boy. This rule bars all women and some men.[25]

In response to the question of how to induce more men to enter teaching, many respondents mentioned the need for higher wages and greater respect; some made it clear that men needed to be favored over women, as in the suggestion that "more men may be induced to enter the profession by paying very radically higher salaries and differentiating definitely and openly between the salaries paid to men and salaries paid to women for what is called the same work."[26]

As further evidence of the dangers of the "overfeminization" of teaching, Barr cited the report of the Moseley Educational Commission to the United States, a commission "composed of eminent representatives" from Great Britain. According to Barr, the British were struck by the large numbers of women teachers in American public schools, and seven of the twenty-seven members of the commission "deplored the preponderance of women teachers" in the United States. Their concern was expressed most strongly by one Professor Armstrong, who deplored the plight of the American boy: "The boy in America is not being brought up to punch another boy's head or to have his own punched in a healthy and proper manner; there is a strange indefinable feminine air coming over American men, a tendency toward a common or sexless tone of thought."[27] Although this passage is somewhat extreme in its depiction of "healthy and proper" male behavior, it is typical in its assertion of an innate "masculine essence." Its direct condemnation of the ideal of a common humanity ("common or sexless tone of thought") is also interesting, since the idea that men and women possessed the same range of intellectual and moral potential was central to the more radical feminist challenges of male dominance in education. Barr concluded his account by quoting long passages by a woman, Mrs. Annie Lund Meriam of Chico, who supported the idea of male superiority and the need for male privileges in education: "In her inmost soul," wrote Meriam, "every intelligent, fair-minded woman acknowledges the superiority of the educated masculine mind over the feminine. . . . Women by nature have domestic tastes, so why should they interest themselves in civic affairs? Yet they are now expected to prepare boys for civic life."[28] Even sensible women, Barr seems to imply, recognized the natural differences between the sexes.

In response to these calls for male privilege, and probably more immediately in response to Barr's questionnaire, women teachers led by Kate Ames of Napa County held a mass meeting in December 1907, at the annual meeting of the California Teachers Association in Santa Cruz, demanding their right to equal salaries and opportunities. Although the CTA had issued a declaration supporting women's suffrage in 1904, throughout this period the organization remained firmly under the control of the alliance of male superintendents and university experts. The only woman who held a leadership position was Kate Ames herself, who was elected vice president in 1904. A graduate of San Jose Normal School and later of Stanford University, Ames had an active and successful career first as a teacher and then as county superintendent in Napa (1894–98, 1902–6). In 1906 she ran unsuccessfully against Edward Hyatt for state superintendent of public instruction. Ames was active in the CTA during this period, serving as vice president and chairing a standing committee on a state reading course for classroom teachers. Some sense of Ames's views on teaching are revealed in her reports concerning the Committee on the State Reading Course published in the *Western Journal of Education*, in which she consistently argued for the need for teacher self-education: "That a teacher may stand for something in the educational world and out of it, she should be encouraged not only to broaden her school work, but should take up some line of outside study that should stand for recreation and culture." For Ames, teaching without intellectual growth was "not entirely worth while." Instead, "the teacher must not only be creative and create, she must be free—free

to put the best of self into the work—free to be a positive, crea[
force."[29] Ames's strong belief in freedom of expression and intellec[
growth, along with her active feminism, underlay her participation and
leadership in the Santa Cruz protest.

The women's protest seems to have been ignored by male leaders of
the CTA, at least publicly. The official account of the 1907 meetings in
the *Western Journal of Education* omitted any direct reference to the
protest, though Stanford professor Ellwood Cubberley, in his editorial
on the meetings, referred obliquely to a "spur-of-the-moment and unau-
thorized nomination from the floor" and the "bad conduct" at the Santa
Cruz convention. "It is to be hoped," he stated, "that the conduct of the
State Teachers Association will in the future be such that there will never
again be need of mentioning this matter."[30] By reading the official account we would not know the content of the women's protest at all. In
September 1908, however, Kate Ames published an account of the Santa
Cruz women's meeting in the *Overland Monthly*, a popular magazine with
a large circulation in California. She reported that the schoolwomen
wanted not only equal treatment, but also recognition of the equal abilities of men and women. Rather than arguing, as Jeanne Carr had, for
the "special" qualities of women, Ames contended that men and women
received the same educational training and that "insight, industry and
skill are individual rather than sex characteristics." She also directly attacked male privilege:

Not all women have the qualities that make the good administrator; neither are
all men thus endowed. Yet practically every man in the schools to-day is holding
an administrative position. Practically every woman is holding a teaching position. When we know that eighty-eight per cent of the teachers are women, we
must, if we stop to consider, realize that the sex fallacy is not placing in many
cases the best administrators at the head of the schools.

Thus, in response to the schoolmen's arguments that they deserved further advantages because of their innate superiority, Ames sharply called
into question the privileges they already enjoyed, suggesting that women
teachers not only demonstrated intelligence and competence in their
work, but that they also often actually ran schools under—she strongly
hinted—inadequate male leadership: "Far from women exercising little
or no influence, far from women failing in control over the school in
which she is subordinate, she is in many cases the actual head, exercising enormous influence, enormous control to which limits cannot be assigned. Great as that influence now is, the recognition, in fact, would be
of still greater advantage to the school system."[31]

Ames's defense of women teachers is without question the strongest and clearest statement of feminist principles in California education in this period. Yet it does not seem to have furthered her own career, nor did her arguments significantly alter male control of the CTA. She lost the superintendency at Napa in 1906, and after her participation in the women's protest at Santa Cruz she was dropped from her leadership position in the CTA. Although women organized to elect Agnes Howe as the first woman president of the Bay Section of the CTA in 1910 (the same year Ella Flagg Young was elected president of the National Education Association), subsequent presidents and officers of the CTA were men.

Although women made some gains in this period, their progress was uneven. The role of women in education, moreover, continued to be contested, both in terms of access to positions of power and at the level of ideology. In the same period that women county school superintendents were being elected in ever greater numbers, men continued to dominate the most powerful positions in California education; and despite their largely unquestioned authority, men continued to voice concerns over the dangers of the woman peril. Writing in the *Sierra Educational News* in 1909, for example, Ellwood Cubberley argued for the need to attract talented and competent men to county superintendencies:

No one ever thinks of preparing himself, other than politically, for the office [of county superintendent]. Our normal schools to-day have almost no men students, and men in university work almost never look to county supervision as a possible field. . . . The effect of this would be in time to relegate county supervision, a work that each year calls for higher educational ability, to the poorest and most unworthy men in the work of teaching.[32]

Although Cubberley was writing at precisely the time when women were being elected county superintendent in greater numbers than ever before, in his framing of the problem he ignored the possibility that talented women teachers might make good superintendents. Instead, he made clear his contemptuous opinion of the "typical" woman educator: "It must be acknowledged that the average rural teacher of today is a mere slip of a girl, often almost too young to have formed as yet any conception of the problem of rural life and needs." This young girl, "almost entirely ignorant of the great and important fields of science" and lacking in "those qualities of leadership so essential in rural progress," needed supervision from men of "adequate preparation, deep social and professional insight, and large executive skill and personal power."[33]

Male educators worried not only about the effects of "too many women" in the schools; they also expressed concern that the men replacing these young women be, as Cubberley put it, "virile." State Super-

intendent Edward Hyatt took up the argument in 1910: "The pro
tion of male to female teachers," he remarked, "is a subject that has t
discussed quite vehemently by educational writers and speakers for a
number of years. Many school officials make strenuous efforts to obtain
male teachers, though not always with the best results. It is not only a
male teacher that is needed, but a live, red-blooded man." Hyatt hoped
that these "red-blooded men" would be filled with an ardent sense of adventure and dedication: "Possibly the cure lies in fostering a spirit of devotion to the public weal comparable to the religious zeal that drove
young men in countless thousands to the Crusades, that impels young
men to lives as missionaries or as teachers at sectarian schools."[34] Needless to say, young women who went into teaching were not compared to
Crusaders or missionaries. To the contrary, for educators like Hyatt they
were a major part of the problem. In his 1915 article "The Vanishing
Schoolmaster," Los Angeles high school teacher Roger Sterrett worried
that male teachers might someday become extinct: "The dodo, it is
noted, departed into the limbo of mere natural history largely unregret-
ted—because no one had ever found much use for a live dodo anyway.
Perhaps, under the future feministic dominance of our society, the male
school teacher will be eliminated with less regret." Significantly, Sterrett
identified "triumphant feminism" as the chief danger leading to such a
world. "To have real boys," he argued, "you must have real men," not the
"meticulous politeness and nicety of manners traditionally ascribed to
dancing masters and to school teachers."[35] Like Hyatt, Sterrett expressed
not only a hostility to "triumphant feminism," but an implicit homopho-
bia as well. In Sterrett's imagination, "real men" teachers faced both the
"meticulous politeness" of dancing masters and the potential aggression
of feminists. These feminist teachers were, moreover, neither John
Swett's women of "great heart" and "womanly tact" nor Campbell's "trifling girls," but dangerous and powerful rivals of male power.

Schoolwomen Organize

Despite the rhetoric of male educators, in the period between 1900
and 1920 women continued to move into positions of authority as
county superintendents of schools, grammar school principals, and normal school faculty. Although normal schools had been founded with an
assumption of male expert guidance of young women teachers, by 1900
women such as Margaret Schallenberger at San Jose Normal School and
Edna Orr James at Fresno Normal School were providing strong leadership and serving as model educators, serious and capable. To further
their own interests, since the CTA remained in the hands of the closed

network of male educators (still often members of the Schoolmasters and Scholia Clubs), women educators began to form organizations modeled on the women's club movement. In 1908—one year after the protest at the Santa Cruz CTA convention—the California Federation of School Women's Clubs was established. In its statement of purpose, the federation stated:

The prime reason for the formation of the School Women's Clubs, and later of the Federation, lay in the great need of co-operation among those who form the larger part of the teaching force in California. The lack of this co-operation in the past has failed to secure for them that professional recognition which other professions have. . . . Women teachers have been slow to learn this need and to seize the opportunities for that broader outlook and greater usefulness in their pedagogical, social, and civic life which, single-handed, were unattainable.[36]

During the next decade schoolwomen's clubs were founded in all the major cities of California as alternatives to the California Teachers Association. By 1912, the Federation of School Women's Clubs in the Bay Area alone had a membership of nearly 1,000.

The schoolwomen's clubs joined with other women's clubs, with mothers' clubs, and later with the early parent-teachers associations to try to influence state educational policy. A sense of these alliances and concerns is captured in an account in the *Sierra Educational News* of the 1919 meeting of the State Board of Education and leading state officials:

The women's legislative council, the various women's clubs and parent-teacher associations and various civic organizations are united with the school forces in the interest of the improvement of schools, the raising of additional moneys, and other important matters. There came in for discussion at the joint session also the necessity for improved child-labor laws, increasing compulsory school age, part-time schools, home teachers, vocational education and vocational opportunities for girls, etc. Equal educational opportunities for all children was demanded and must be had.[37]

Schoolwomen's clubs supported women's interests in a number of areas, providing social and institutional support for women teachers and working with service organizations such as the Red Cross and local mothers' clubs.[38] At the 1912 meeting of the CTA, for example, the Federation of School Women's Clubs issued a pamphlet calling on "wide awake and interested teachers" to attend the federation's annual meeting and banquet.[39] At the next year's meeting, the federation adopted a number of resolutions in favor of progressive reform, including the resolution that "efficiency, experience, and personality be considered in assigning administrative and other positions, and compensation be on the same basis irrespective of sex."[40] Although some women continued to work within the CTA, the schoolwomen's clubs provided the strongest organized support for women teachers.

The best documented of these clubs is the Oakland Schoolwomen's Club, which was founded in 1912 and was active until 1925, when it disbanded under pressure from the CTA and administrators in the Oakland school system. In 1942 Joyce Lobner, a former member and president, wrote a short history of the club. For Lobner, the club was a prime example of democratic collective education: "Surely the history of this Club proves that it is only in democratic cooperative action that teachers can achieve their best and realize professional and personal betterment. Together, under leaders elected by ourselves from our own ranks, we can go forward, 'every teacher a free and happy teacher,' to upbuild education and serve society." According to Lobner, the Oakland club was founded at a meeting called by a number of "energetic young teachers" who "liked to discuss things." "About one hundred" women teachers attended that first meeting, and within two years the membership had climbed to more than 500. The club supported a number of standing committees that furthered schoolwomen's interests by presenting recommendations to the superintendent of schools and the board of education. Various social committees were also formed, such as the Visiting Committee, composed of teachers who would "visit any teacher who was ill or in sorrow." At first, virtually all the women principals in Oakland belonged to the club, along with "a choice group" of classroom teachers; but, said Lobner, these groups soon came into conflict, and "when teachers voiced their opinions, the administrative women would 'jump and sit all over them.'" In 1916 the women administrators withdrew and joined the Principals' Club.[41]

The Oakland Schoolwomen's Club provided a variety of social outlets for the women teachers of Oakland, sponsoring automobile trips, hikes, swimming classes, rowing on Lake Merritt, and choral and drama groups. The members obtained a room in the Federal-Telegraph Building in downtown Oakland to serve as a clubroom, where tea was available in the afternoons and committee meetings were held. From 1916 to 1924 they also held an annual party called the "High Jinks," at which members wore comic costumes and presented a pageant. In 1919, for example, a "Pageant to Pensions" was performed with the theme "Motivation of Higher Salaries." At the 1921 Jinks, then-President Lobner dressed up as Professor Everyman, wearing "top hat, white tie and tails— a size too large, which permitted more buttons to show than the law allows—to the great acceleration of hilarity." Other women portrayed the superintendent and assistant superintendent of schools. As Lobner recalled, "No man ever attended these functions, unless a few, as was suspected, sneaked in disguised as ladies."[42] Over 300 schoolwomen attended the annual banquets, and in 1919 the county supervisors and city commissioners were the honored guests; Superintendent of Schools Fred Hunter gave the keynote speech and "in his usual forceful manner warned against radicalism."[43] The club also held monthly luncheons, get-acquainted teas in local schools, and occasional breakfasts to honor various members and guests. In 1922 it held "Ye Pedagogues' Prom," to which spouses and friends were also invited and which Lobner remembered as "a gorgeous affair."[44]

The club disbanded, according to Lobner, in part because of the jealousy of administrators who favored having one organization, the Oakland Teachers Association (OTA), in charge of furthering the interests of all teachers and administrators. "The more the S.W.C. accomplished, the more initiative it showed," Lobner later wrote, "the more it was opposed and feared."[45] In 1925, the Oakland Teachers Association passed an amendment stating that any local professional organization should relinquish its independent status and become a section of the OTA. Since the association had already taken over the function of representing Oakland teachers' interests in Sacramento, the Oakland Schoolwomen's Club was left with no real function except a social one. The only choices seemed to be to join the OTA, and thus the CTA; to remain simply a social club; or to disband. The executive board of the club, while regretting the "loss of opportunities for friendship gained through working in common," decided that without its political concerns the club would not be strong enough to survive. Moreover, if the club remained in existence as a separate organization, the board feared the "personal animosity, bitterness and suspicion" that would result.[46]

Whether this anticipated animosity was on the part of male administrators and teachers or other women is not made clear in the board's minutes. That the reference may be to male hostility is suggested, however, by a song written by a club member and sung at the final meeting of the Oakland Schoolwomen's Club:

> Reforms we have accomplished
> We have advanced our sex.
> But our day seems done, we're on the run
> For we got it in the necks.
> We had our jinks so clever,
> We've had our teas and sprees;
> But now we're out and put to rout
> And left in the cold to freeze.
>   · · ·
> We came to the fore, till the men made a roar
> And their guns on us they trained.[47]

The Normal School As a Women's Sphere

Another significant and overlooked site where women educators played an active role was the state normal school. By 1900 an increasing percentage of teachers had completed a normal school education, as part of the trend toward more stringent requirements. Although a small number of prospective teachers attended the University of California or Stanford, most sought normal school training, which was specifically structured to prepare them for the classroom. These normal schools, in turn, provided the talented women who served on their faculties with an excellent opportunity for intellectual and administrative work.

The first normal school in California was established in 1862 in San Francisco; ten years later the campus was moved to San Jose. Additional normal schools were founded at Los Angeles and Chico in the 1880s, and by 1913 there were eight such schools in the state. Normal schools were initially equivalent to high schools. In the 1870s, for example, students could enter a two-year normal school course at age sixteen, graduating at eighteen with a certificate to teach. By 1903 normal schools offered a two-year course for high school graduates, and a four-year course for students lacking a high school diploma. Attendance at the normal schools in this period was overwhelmingly made up of young women. In 1901, for example, the statewide normal school enrollment was 1,768 women and 214 men;[48] in 1916, 4,615 women and 382 men.[49] By this time a normal school education was increasingly desirable for teachers. In 1893, 26 percent of California teachers were graduates of normal schools; by 1920, 72 percent had graduated from normal schools, and an additional 8 percent from colleges and universities.[50] In 1921, the normal schools became state teachers colleges. In 1923–24 alone, 10,656 teaching certificates were granted in California following completion of college courses, as opposed to only 277 awarded for success in the state teachers examination.[51] Beginning in 1930, the elementary teaching credential required a four-year B.A., and although the possibility of certification via the teachers examination still existed, the exam was rarely offered.

In the period from their founding at least until 1921, the normal schools were in many respects woman-centered institutions. Although the school presidents were usually men, the faculty, particularly the heads of the training schools and instructors in pedagogy, tended to be women. And as we have seen, the student bodies of the normal schools were overwhelmingly made up of young women. San Francisco State Normal School, for example, in some years had no male students. In this world, new cultural traditions celebrating teaching as serious work for women emerged.

The de facto definition of the normal school as a woman's space was captured in the pageant "Everywoman," performed annually by San Francisco Normal students between 1908 and 1926.[52] The earliest version of the pageant, created by the school's branch of the California Educational Guild, was called "Everygirl" and was intended as a morality play to express "the attributes of woman as a teacher." Anna Wiebalk, a teacher at San Francisco Normal, described the vision of teaching that was embodied in the pageant this way: "The loving contact with little children in the school, the work of training boys and girls, and the contemplation of the ideals of the profession—all these should combine to develop womanhood in the girls attending the Normal Training School."[53] Although the president of San Francisco Normal, Frederick Burk (who in 1907 had called women teachers the "withered heart" of the school), published a later version of the pageant under the title *Guild Service and Ritual of Graduation* as though he were the author, in fact the original authors and participants were women faculty and students.[54]

In the pageant, the central character, Everygirl, undergoes a series of adventures from her first appearance, when she dances across the stage holding her high school diploma, to her maturity as a woman. Although she chooses teaching as a career "for very selfish and mercenary reasons," Everygirl soon meets the Angel of Hope and the figure Woman, who lead her to the Hall of Work in the San Francisco State Normal School; there she learns of the burdens and joys of a life of usefulness. In the last act, Everygirl is led to a room in the castle of Womanhood, where she sees Life seated at a loom:

As Everygirl stands by the loom of Life, something impels her to ask what the fabric upon the frame is. She learns it is the garment of her character, of mingled yarn, good and ill together, the design her own. A firm resolve to improve and beautify it seizes her and, as she is thus intent upon the future of her character, a chorus bursts upon her ear and there is an ensemble of Woman's court, who sing to Everygirl and promise to guard and guide her forevermore and make her life "a rhythmic psalm."[55]

Although the "Everygirl" pageant may seem stilted and naive to us now, it is interesting both in its judgment that teaching is valuable work and in its imagery of the young woman forming her own character through her work as a teacher. Thus the earlier representation of the woman teacher as maternal nurturer is combined with a sense of agency and personal responsibility—the notion that the teacher must design the "garment of her character" for herself.

The normal school as the site of a woman's culture is also revealed in the annual yearbooks. In these student-produced volumes, the importance of women faculty as models and guides is made clear. An example

of the woman-centered culture of the normal schools is provided in the
pages of *The Prospect*, the yearbook of the Fresno State Normal School
from 1912 to 1921. Fresno Normal was founded in 1911 under the
strong leadership of Fresno superintendent of schools Charles McLane.
Until that point, most teachers in the central San Joaquin Valley who
wanted normal school training had attended San Jose Normal. But San
Jose was suffering from overcrowding, and McLane argued that the valley
had a strong need for a normal school that could serve local needs, particularly of rural communities. The faculty of Fresno Normal School in
its first year comprised six men and six women. Men taught the more
manual and academic subjects, and women worked primarily in the arts
and in the primary education department. A key figure among the early
faculty was Edna Orr James, an assistant in the training department in
charge of primary work. Although she was later listed as a graduate of
Fresno Normal, she apparently began teaching in the training department without a diploma. Frequent references were made in *The Prospect*
to teas and luncheons for students held at her home. In 1912, the yearbook noted that she had spent the summer session at Berkeley: "We are
all so happy to have Mrs. James with us permanently. She has leased a
home here in Fresno and she and her mother are already established in
it." Two years later, student editors dedicated *The Prospect* to her:

> Mrs. James goes about from place to place
> Always with a joke, and a smile on her face,
> She talks too much, it is true,
> But with her one can never be blue;
> May she us with her presence ever grace.

While at Fresno Normal, Edna Orr James published thoughtful pieces
on primary teaching in rural schools in the *Educational Digest* and the
Sierra Educational News; she later became head of a rural demonstration
school in northern California.

The first class at Fresno Normal was made up of 30 women and 2
men, a ratio that remained much the same until Fresno Normal became
Fresno State Teachers College in 1921. *The Prospect* described a rich social life, with basketball and tennis clubs, theater and choral groups, luncheons, teas, dances, and parties. Typical is this account of a party in
1914: "[On] Saturday evening, January 25th, the Senior B's entertained
the Senior A's in the auditorium. The best kind of cosy, chatty time was
enjoyed. Somehow when it comes to parting time the Seniors are very
near and dear to us. It would not do to say they had never been. At any
rate, we had a jolly time." The stories and social notes in *The Prospect*'s
first few years portrayed an active social scene dominated, not surprisingly, by women students, with women faculty members such as Edna Orr

James also playing a central role. Men, however, continued to hold the positions of power on the faculty, and Charles McLane, the school's founder, was the undisputed leader. In 1915 a men's club was established "because," noted *The Prospect*, "of the fact there are so few men and because they are greatly out-numbered by the girls." Men's club activities focused on events such as debates over the size of the navy or Philippine independence. Although occasionally a man was elected to a class office, the overwhelming majority of school leaders in this period were women, and *The Prospect* was always edited by a woman.

In 1921, when the normal schools of California became state teachers colleges, Fresno Normal merged with Fresno Junior College, a two-year business-oriented school with a predominantly male student body, to become Fresno State Teachers College. Between the 1920–21 and 1921–22 school years the number of students increased from 325 (14 of whom were men) to 665 (145 men). The faculty was reorganized, and Edna Orr James, who had been such a significant figure in the preparation of primary teachers, lost her position as a faculty member and became a supervisor of the training school, one of ten women working in that capacity under the direction of male professors of pedagogy. *The Prospect* disappeared, and in its place *The Collegian* was established as the college yearbook. The editor of *The Collegian* was a man, as were all officials of student government with the exception of the secretary and the women's athletic manager. In the introduction to the first *Collegian*, the editor wrote of the difficulties he faced, since "there were no traditions to follow, in composing the annual"[56]—this despite the fact that *The Collegian* was modeled very closely on *The Prospect*. In the early 1920s fraternities and sororities arrived at Fresno State, and, perhaps most significant for defining social life and values, male varsity athletic teams, particularly football and baseball, were established and soon became the focus of college identity. Thus the woman-centered world of the normal school was transformed into the male-dominated culture of the state college, even though women students continued to predominate in number.

The County Superintendents

In the early 1900s women educators achieved positions of authority and responsibility as school principals and normal school instructors and created supportive institutions in schoolwomen's clubs and associations. They also sought power in the public sphere through electoral politics. In 1918 the first four women were elected to the California legislature, and in the 1920s women began to be appointed to state boards and were elected to local office in a number of counties.[57] The period 1900–1920

TABLE 3
California School Superintendents, 1880–1947

	Men	Women		Men	Women
1880–83	50	2	1915–19	32	25
1883–87	48	4	1919–23	26	31
1887–91	45	7	1923–27	34	23
1891–95	41	11	1927–31	31	26
1895–99	44	13	1931–35	30	27
1899–1903	40	17	1935–39	34	23
1903–7	35	22	1939–43	33	24
1907–11	34	23	1943–47	36	21
1911–15	36	21			

SOURCE: Roy Cloud, *Education in California* (Stanford: Stanford University Press, 1952), pp. 272–84.

is also striking for the marked increase in the numbers of elected women county superintendents of schools (Table 3). Although it has been argued that the county superintendencies held by women were less well compensated and less prestigious than comparable positions held by men, nonetheless the numbers of women county superintendents clearly represent a challenge to the ideology of male dominance in education.

The figures shown in Table 3 raise several interesting points. First, of course, is the shift from overwhelmingly male superintendents to a more equal number of men and women superintendents. This change reflects both the increase in the percentage of women teachers and the increase in years of training needed for certification. The year 1914, the first year in which women could vote in California, saw a rise in the numbers of women county superintendents, and in 1919 women outnumbered men 31 to 26 in the position. The 1918 election in which they were elected was the second state election held after women had gained suffrage in California in 1912 and took place only two years before women gained national suffrage in 1920. In many ways this was the high point of the first wave of feminism in the state. Although women county superintendents were never again in the majority, they continued to be elected in sizable numbers; it is striking that as late as 1947 there were still 21 elected women county superintendents in California. After this point, however, the percentage of women county superintendents dropped steadily; in 1970 there was one woman county superintendent in California, and it was not until the 1980s that women again began to be elected to county superintendencies.

In addition to numbers, it is important to consider the nature of the counties that elected women superintendents, most of which were lightly populated and rural. San Francisco, Alameda, and Los Angeles Counties, for example, never elected a woman superintendent. Women superintendents were particularly concentrated in the mountainous northern counties. Alpine County in the Sierra Nevada, for one, elected a woman to the school superintendency every year from 1883 to 1947. Relatively prosperous and densely settled rural counties are somewhat more difficult to categorize. Such counties as Napa, Santa Barbara, and Kings, for example, elected women superintendents repeatedly over a period of decades; yet very similar areas, such as Fresno and Tulare Counties, never elected a woman superintendent.

Overall, the pattern in California supports David Tyack and Elisabeth Hansot's observation that elected women educators nationwide have held the least desirable and least powerful positions.[58] We can speculate on the reasons for this pattern. One obvious factor is the small population and hence small number of schools in rural counties; the county superintendent simply did not control significant resources in such settings, and so posed little threat to the traditional power structure. Moreover, there were probably few educated men available, much less willing, to seek the job. Whatever the reasons for their success, women county superintendents held positions of at least nominal power in these rural counties, and must have learned to negotiate between the world of women classroom teachers from which they had emerged and the male-dominated school boards and the local business leaders who dominated politics at the county level.

Women in the Educational State

In California as elsewhere, the first two decades of the twentieth century were marked by an expansion of state bureaucracy and by the impact of the Progressive movement. The problems facing California educators were similar to those faced by educational leaders nationwide: rapid population growth, the rise of the automobile and mass culture, immigration, and social unrest. The 1910 election of the Progressive candidate Hiram Johnson as governor marked the beginning of a period of political reform in California.

In education, the reform impetus led to a reorganized state board of education and gave new support to the demand for more centralized control of education through stricter regulations and increased supervision by state officials. In 1914, the state educational bureaucracy was expanded with the creation of three new appointive positions: commissioners for elementary, secondary, and vocational schools. The three commissioners, who worked directly under the state superintendent for public instruction, were expected to visit schools statewide, investigate existing courses of study, and report their findings and make recommendations to the appointed board of education. From the beginning, the commissioners of secondary and vocational education were men, while the commissioner of elementary education was a woman. This gendered pattern continued until the positions were eliminated in the early 1960s. In a sense, the appointment of a woman as commissioner of elementary education was a way of containing women's demands for greater participation. From its inception, the position provided an opportunity for women's leadership and the furthering of women teachers' interests, but in an arena—the lives of young children—that did not really challenge assumptions about woman's proper sphere.

The organization of the educational state in California rested on unstated assumptions about gender. It is important to note, however, that struggles over men's and women's roles in education did not always completely follow the social identities of gender. That is, because an educator was a woman did not necessarily mean she self-consciously spoke for the interests of other women or presented herself as gendered in her writing or work. Margaret Schallenberger McNaught, the first commissioner of elementary education, for example, was a woman educator who admired the male model of efficient and scientific school administration while supporting women's rights and suffrage. When she was appointed commissioner, she already had achieved a distinguished career in California education. As head of the training school at San Jose Normal School, the oldest and most important of California normal schools, she was well connected to the world of university educators.

Born in 1862, one of five children of Moses Schallenberger of Santa Clara, a well-known rancher and pioneer who had come to California in 1844, Margaret was educated in the public schools of San Jose. She entered San Jose Normal School at the age of fourteen, graduating three years later, in 1880.[59] She taught for five years in the public schools of San Jose, and in 1889–90 taught as a critic teacher in the training school at San Jose Normal.[60] Between 1893 and 1898 she was an instructor in the newly formed department of education at Stanford under Earl Barnes and Ellwood Cubberley, during which time she completed the work for her B.A. She then went on to Cornell, receiving her Ph.D. in 1902 at the age of forty. The next year she was named principal of the training school at San Jose Normal, where she remained until she was named California commissioner of elementary education in 1914.[61]

In many ways McNaught was typical of the professional educators who were shaping schooling in the United States in this period. She accepted the authority of "scientific experts," was deeply concerned with order, cleanliness, and good manners, and was profoundly patriotic. Together with other state officials, she attempted to provide guidance for teachers by means of speeches at county institutes, visits to local schools, and the publication of widely disseminated state educational journals and official *Reports*.[62] Like other educational administrators of the Progressive Era, McNaught supported the introduction of widespread student testing, increased standards for teacher certification, and closer classroom supervision. One "problem" that particularly concerned her was immigrant children and the responsibility of the schools to further Americanization. Typically, she tied American identity with cleanliness. As she argued in the *Blue Bulletin*, a journal sent to all California schools: "The lessons of *patriotism*, of *hygiene*, of *sanitation*, and of *democracy*, must first be taught the immigrant child and by him spread through the entire family circle."[63]

McNaught was quick to accept the claims of scientific authority concerning the need to test children's mental ability. The measurement and classification of children through the use of standardized intelligence tests only became widespread in California in the 1920s and 1930s, but even before the First World War university professors, especially in the newly established School of Education at Stanford, began to advocate intelligence testing as the best way to identify "backward" children and to separate children according to their innate abilities. In 1918, influenced by this growing movement, McNaught advocated courses in testing and measurement at the state's normal schools, enthusiastically citing research on "backward" children being conducted at Stanford and Berkeley.[64]

With the 1917 entry of the United States into the First World War, the attention of California educators turned to the need to support the war effort and encourage patriotism. A sense of McNaught's deep patriotism is captured in this call for patriotic education for elementary schoolchildren:

Children should be permitted to share the thrill of drum and flag; to feel the pride of the pomp and parades that accompany military affairs; to take their part in assemblies and public spectacles. . . . Youth can never be too early instructed in public duties as well as in patriotic devotion; and it behooves the teachers of elementary schools to be diligent and fervent in giving that instruction to the children that are under their charge in this time of national exaltation of our flag and our arms on land and sea, in both the new world and the old.[65]

Her patriotic sentiment can be seen as well in her support of the campaign against the ground squirrels. In her article "The Squirrel Is a Hun," McNaught cites G. H. Hecke, state commissioner of horticulture, who exhorted "the boys and girls of the public schools to be 'School Soldiers' in a war to the death against ground squirrels," offering an award of $50 to the grammar school that killed the largest number of squirrels.

(Poison could be acquired from county agriculture agents.) According to Hecke, ground squirrels destroyed "about $30,000,000 worth of food-stuffs every year." Killing squirrels would help conserve the food supply and thus support the war effort. McNaught explained: "By destroying our food, the squirrels help the Huns; by killing the squirrels we help to save food for the soldiers in the battle line whom the Huns are trying to kill. It is therefore for patriotism as well as for profit, that the boys and girls of the schools are asked to assist in ridding California of squirrels."[66] While this is one of the more colorful examples of schooling being shaped by patriotism (as well as by profit), it was typical of McNaught's approach. She wrote numerous articles urging children to plant gardens, to write to Belgian schoolchildren, and to work hard in school for the good of the nation in its fight against "the Hun."

McNaught's patriotism and deep respect for state authority led her to support the rhetoric of State Superintendent of Public Instruction Will Wood during the Red Scare of 1919–20. In the *California Blue Bulletin* of December 1919, Wood urged school officials to be vigilant lest subversive literature find its way into the schools. He had earlier sent a letter to all school officials asking them to investigate such a possibility:

I was pleased to receive reports from practically every high school principal, that no radical or revolutionary literature is being distributed in his school. Most of them report also that it is not being circulated among the students so far as they can find out. In one of the Bay city high schools, however, the principal reports that some of the students are in possession of the radical pamphlets including the detestable I.W.W. songbook. . . . Every effort will be made to check any attempt to spread red propaganda in the public schools.[67]

In 1919, the California legislature passed a law forbidding the distribution of "bulletins, circulars or other propaganda" in the schools. Wood commented in the 1919 *Annual Report*: "This office has been especially zealous in preventing the spread of dangerous propaganda in the schools of the state. An investigation revealing improper activities on the part of several teachers resulted in the revocation of their credentials by the State Board of Education." Furthermore, he continued, in the future all teachers would be required to swear an oath of allegiance to the United States.[68]

Despite her patriotism and respect for authority and expert opinion, qualities she shared with most male educators of the time, McNaught was also committed to furthering women's participation in public life. After California women won the vote in 1912, for example, she affirmed that women teachers who had played an important part in the fight for suffrage could look forward to a new age of active and responsible citizenship:

Through the teaching of independent women, all women of open minds learned to take an intelligent interest in the practical affairs of the community in which they lived. . . . A demand for the franchise followed, made by clear sighted, wisely discerning women who were also in large numbers self supporting and independent. It was conceded. Woman suffrage came therefore not as a gift to ignorance but as an imperative call to intelligence to assist in the government of city and county, state and nation. It is then a sure conclusion that since the woman teacher has had the will to gain the right of suffrage, she may be counted upon to have the will to use it rightly.[69]

McNaught supported the educational work of the California Federation of School Women's Clubs and suggested that teachers should work closely with women's organizations such as the California Congress of Mothers and the Daughters of the American Revolution.[70] She also helped build a network of women educators by encouraging meetings among women leaders at the annual State Convention of County and City Superintendents, where she hosted dinners for women superintendents.[71]

Although McNaught was an advocate of women's participation in public life, at the same time she accepted existing authority relationships and insisted that women should not challenge men, but rather should work with them to build an orderly world. In her initial message as commissioner to California teachers in 1914, for example, she made clear her vision of the cooperation that was desirable between boys and girls, and implicitly assured her readers that the equal education of girls would not challenge the privileges of boys: "We shall teach both boys and girls . . . that they are interdependent companions and not rivals in the world's work. And we shall not forget to give them much opportunity throughout childhood to feel the great joy there is in being useful."[72] The contradictions in McNaught's views can be seen in her celebration of the strengths of women teachers even as she argued for greater expert control over their work.[73] Underlying the latter argument was a view of women teachers as somewhat helpless and in need of professional guidance, as reflected in this passage:

Who has not wondered at the pluck of the optimistic young normal graduate who goes, as a rule, for the first few years of her teaching life to the rural school. Far removed from all social relationship that would tend to stimulate or inspire her, unrewarded, unencouraged, unnoticed, she spends day after day, week after week, month after month, trying to do what she thinks she is paid for doing. No wonder should she lose her standards, no wonder should she become disheartened. We have no other analogous condition. Our army, our railroads, our banks, our churches, all our great political and industrial organizations are planned according to some method of oversight of the rank and file by the superior officer. In the rural school only, does the worker go about her task unchecked by superior criticism, uncheered by superior approval.[74]

This passage reveals not only McNaught's vision of the "disheartened" and isolated young teacher, but also her confidence in the superiority of the methods of efficiency and business management, beliefs typical of progressive educational administrators in this period.[75]

At other times, McNaught applauded the competence and initiative of country teachers, as in her description of Annie Smith, a graduate of Chico Normal School, who taught a one-room school of six children in an isolated canyon in Humboldt County:

She is a good example of what county superintendents mean when they say, "Give us teachers who have strong personalities." Not all persons attract in the same way; not all show strength in the same manner. Miss Smith has succeeded because she has made the best of Annie Smith. Physically she is small in stature, lithe and graceful and the embodiment of health. In disposition she is fun-loving and courageous, gentle and sympathetic. . . . It must have been a lonely winter for a young girl who had never before been away from home, yet not a murmur has been heard, and the little group of children, as the writer, who visited the school, can testify, has been well taught.[76]

Annie Smith represents an independent and capable rural "new woman," healthy and optimistic, who is able to flourish in the isolated conditions of a one-room country school. She stands in striking contrast to the disheartened young normal school graduate, in need of direction from a superior officer. McNaught's image of rural woman teachers thus drew upon, but did not reconcile, the conflicting representations of the woman teacher that marked this period.

Women and Rural School Supervision

Margaret Schallenberger McNaught's concerns reflected a wider national anxiety over what was called the "rural school problem." Worry over the perceived decline in traditional rural values, fears about urbanization and immigration, and a general uneasiness with rapid social and economic transformation all contributed to this anxiety. The first two decades of the twentieth century saw the publication of a number of expert studies and impassioned polemics condemning the existing system of locally controlled one-room district schools and attributing to it a wide range of presumed social ills.[77] Although the concern with rural schools was part of the movement to rescue the agrarian values of traditional American society in a period of social change, it also clearly reflects the demand for greater state and expert control over the work of teachers, as well as a belief that rural teachers were not benefiting from the methods of business efficiency that were transforming urban school systems.[78] This emphasis on discipline and control was typical of school officials and ed-

ucational experts in the Progressive period, who were attempting to re-
cast the educational bureaucracy on the model of business efficiency. Because the overwhelming majority of rural teachers were women, whereas
reformers tended to be men in positions of authority, the gendered sub-
text of this reform movement is not difficult to see. Rural schools were
described at various times as unscientific, backward, out of touch with
the needs of rural society, unclean, disorganized, and, significantly,
presided over by untrained and ignorant young women teachers.[79]

The two solutions most frequently proposed to solve the "rural school
problem" were consolidation and rural supervision. With consolidation,
rural schools were to be reorganized into a more centralized, bureaucratic system under the control of professional school administrators.[80]
In 1900, the California Educational Commission, made up of forty-five
"prominent Californians," had suggested as a priority the "concentration
or consolidation of rural schools and transportation of pupils." Despite
the support of state officials, however, local resistance to expanded state
bureaucracy and the desire of local districts to retain control over their
schools prevailed. In 1917, McNaught complained that although she had
been urging rural school consolidation for three years, there were still
only 28 cases of school consolidation in the state. She compared California unfavorably to "cold, bleak, frozen North Dakota" and Louisiana,
"which California regards as slow in everything," both of which had hundreds of consolidated schools.[81] As one exasperated official noted in
1918, consolidation efforts faced the "conservatism of rural folk . . . deep
rooted sentiment toward the little red schoolhouse on the hill; scene of
my childhood, etc."[82]

State officials continued to urge consolidation, but they also began to
look to rural supervision as an alternative means of controlling the work of
teachers.[83] In 1915 a special committee of the California Council of Education recommended that legislation be enacted to create a fund for rural
supervisors.[84] Editorials in the *Sierra Educational News* throughout 1916
and 1917 strongly endorsed supervision, along with proper teacher training and consolidation, as the solution to the rural school problem. Given
the popular resistance to consolidation, rural supervision seemed a politically easier path, promising greater control of rural teachers at a relatively
low price and with much less disruption of local institutions. In 1920, after
a concerted campaign by the California Teachers Association and their
supporters, California voters passed Proposition 16, which called for a
minimum salary of $1,200 for all teachers, more equitable support for
high schools, the appointment of a state attendance officer, and the allo-
cation of county funds for the appointment of rural school supervisors.[85]

Proponents of rural school supervision presented two quite distinct views of rural schools and teachers. On the one hand was a view of rural supervisors working with teachers to encourage their creativity and professional mastery; on the other was a vision of control by experts over incompetent, virtually helpless (and implicitly women) teachers. Although these political views do not always follow gender lines, a close examination of the issues at stake in rural school reform in California reveals a close correlation between people's social experiences and subjectivities as men and women and the arguments they presented and even the language they used.

The view of rural supervision as supporting and enriching the work of capable rural teachers was almost always put forward by women rural teachers and supervisors, who argued for teachers' autonomy and their potential for personal and intellectual growth. These arguments echoed those of such turn-of-the-century school reformers as Mabel Carney and Ina Barnes, who had celebrated the capabilities of rural women teachers and argued for a Deweyan vision of progressive education, with teaching seen as a creative and imaginative process grounded in the natural and social world of children and community.[86] The view of supervision as a means of measuring and gathering information about rural education, of providing expert oversight of the work of teachers, and of offering new administrative positions, in contrast, was most commonly put forward by university professors (including Ellwood Cubberley of Stanford), school board members, county superintendents, and state education officials—in most cases, men.

Although the hiring of rural supervisors was mandated by the state, individual appointments were left to local superintendents. In a 1921 article State Superintendent Will Wood recognized that some counties might have trouble finding trained educators for this work. He therefore suggested three possible sources for rural supervisors: "borrowed" faculty from normal schools, who might take one-year leaves; "university graduates of maturity, who have some experience in elementary school work and who have specialized in recent years in problems of elementary education"; and finally, rural teachers themselves. Wood urged caution in hiring this last group, however: "There may be strong outstanding elementary school teachers in your own county. Provided they have had normal training and are progressive in their attitudes, these teachers may prepare for supervision by taking summer courses at our Universities or state normal schools, specializing in rural and elementary school problems."[87] Since the vast majority of rural school teachers were women, whereas a much higher percentage of normal school teachers and university graduates and specialists were men, it seems clear that Wood's imagined "expert supervisors" were likewise men. As for rural teachers, they would be acceptable only if they were "progressive in their attitudes." In any event, the number of such men was inadequate to the need, and when rural supervision was formally established, most rural school supervisors selected were experienced rural women teachers.

Not everyone agreed on what rural supervision should entail, or even whether it was necessary. An anonymous teacher writing in the *Sierra Educational News* in 1915, for example, argued that the real problems of the rural school had to do with inadequate support and difficult teaching conditions, not insufficient supervision. She wondered what would happen to a young teacher if she were sent "to some of the schools I have taught, where she will have to board as I have boarded, living in cold, unsanitary places, eating course, ill-cooked food, and encountering some of the wild and awful things I have encountered in some California districts, and then see how long it is before your 'finished product' is just a 'mediocre teacher.'" The solutions suggested by this teacher included decent schoolhouses and grounds and, in particular, "wages that afford a decent living."[88]

There is some evidence of resistance to the idea of supervision, or "snoopervision" as it was occasionally called, but this evidence is fragmentary; the rural teachers who wrote articles about their teaching experience tended to present a positive and often romantic view of their work. An exception to the lack of overt criticism was a letter to the *Sierra Educational News* in 1922, supposedly from a "crack city teacher" who went to teach in a rural school. The letter was submitted for publication by Frederic Burk, head of San Francisco State College, who felt "it is something which other teachers, in these modern days of centralized and supervising authority," ought to see.[89] The anonymous (and probably fictitious) teacher described the numerous supervisors of her work:

Dear ———,

I write probably for the last time. I am thinking seriously of taking up my abode at Napa or Stockton [state mental hospitals]—not temporarily but permanently. I envy the little old lady who believes she is a little black-bird and spends her days in the branches of a tree. I'm going to be a turkey hen and have less brains than any living being.

The Superintendent of Schools—the assistant "sup"—visiting "sups" (three in number), the county nurse and other official visitors have been popping in on me so many times the last week and a half that I lock my bedroom door at night so that I can at least sleep in peace.[90]

This humorous account of the dangers of supervision elicited an impassioned response from Meta Neal Footman, a rural supervisor from Madera County. Dr. Burk, she declared, did not take into account the real work of rural supervisors, "the newest born of us, educationally speaking; those who sprang into existence by reason of Amendment 16; drawn into the teeming, bickering, hopeful, hopeless, tempestuous cataclysm of 'snoopervising.'" Footman describes the difficulties and successes of what she describes as this "pioneering work":

It is a strange, many sided existence in which nursing a Ford over mountain roads, being pulled from mud holes by irate farmers, riding in the dark of the early morning with frosted wind shield; shouldering the burdens of the isolated young teacher, green or fresh, as you like, from the Normal, who has seen little of life and less of good teaching methods . . . or, greatest task of all, convincing the pitiful old gentleman, charming in himself but invincible in the determination that the three R's are to be taught and they alone; in getting the idea across that the curriculum really has enlarged, and that music, art, physical education, health nursing, sanitation and interest stirring devices are not fol-do-rols, but real honest-to-goodness, tried and proven educational principles.[91]

Footman's account, in which she presents herself as the bearer of progressive educational reform to the "pitiful old gentleman" committed to the three R's, puts forward an image of the forward-looking woman supervisor in a position of power over the traditional male teacher, an image that may well have fueled male hostility toward women rural supervisors.

Positive views of rural supervision were expressed in numerous articles in the *Sierra Educational News* by teachers celebrating the richness of their work but also stating the need for recognition and increased support, both through better normal school courses and through supervision.[92] But whereas early rural supervisors saw their work as supporting teachers by means of personal contact, a different vision was put forth during this period as well, most frequently by male university professors and administrators. In this view, similar to that of school reformers like Ellwood Cubberley, rural supervision was intended to help schools function more efficiently and scientifically, in the mode of modern business. A typical example of this perspective can be seen in an article by Sam Cohn, of the State Department of Instruction in Sacramento:

No thinking person would hold that any other business, so great in extent as is that of the schools, should be conducted without proper supervision. Our railroads, mines, post offices, express companies, ranches, and lumbering interests have their superintendents and foremen whose business it is to unify and coordinate the work of the individual units into a smooth working whole. In this business of the schools it must be remembered that unless there is good and competent supervision the work of the machine will be far from efficient.[93]

Other writers saw supervision as part of a more general movement to measure and gather information about rural education. Eugene Irwin of the Board of Education of Colusa County, for example, argued for more extensive supervision along with a more standardized system of examinations for student promotion, consistent methods of accreditation, and continuous record keeping. These more efficient methods of measurement and control would not only make the schools more effective, they would also provide opportunities "for the most capable [teachers] to use to advantage every bit of administrative skill available. It is an opportunity for leadership. It opens as well a great field for research."[94] Since Irwin cites the Men's Teachers Clubs in northern California as a model of the organization and energy of ambitious teachers, it seems he had specifically male administration in mind for these reforms. Supervision and administration as careers for men continued to be pressed in this period. Male educators continued to argue that education as a career for men did not imply only classroom teaching, but the opportunity for leadership and scholarship as well as public service in the community.[95]

One of the clearest examples of the "scientific" model of supervision was presented by John Almack, from the School of Education at Stanford. In a 1927 article, "The Supervisory Program," Almack applies the methods of standardization and scientific management to the work of supervision. He begins by posing the engineer's approach to problem solving as a model for educators: "Engineers distinguish two types of planning: (1) the empirical, and (2) the scientific. The first is the hit and miss type, usually based upon personal opinion and individual experience; the second is based upon recorded data. The empirical is better than none; the scientific type is more comprehensive and reliable."[96] Almack recommends that the supervisor proceed by observing, tabulating results, and identifying problems, citing a 1925 study by Charles Bursch that lists 175 problems of beginning teachers. Once the problems of the teacher (who is assumed to be a woman) are identified, they should be classified. Almack suggests the following approach:

A two-way table may be prepared, the names of the teachers at the side of the sheet, the problems at the top. A check is then placed under the problem of a given teacher and opposite her name. Such a table will show what teachers need help in making assignments, directing study, preparing in advance for teaching, project teaching, enlisting cooperation, maintaining order, and so on. The table will show that certain matters may be taken up with groups; certain others are for individual conference. As a rule, all ordinary instructional problems may be discussed with those teachers who stand in need of help of the particular kind; all personal problems such as dress, neatness, mannerisms, where an open discussion would prove embarrassing, should be taken up individually, regardless of the number in need of guidance.[97]

Almack is confident of the ability of supervisors to identify and correct the faults of teachers in a scientific and measured fashion. Nevertheless, he also calls supervisors themselves to task. The supervisor (who is assumed to be male) should be concerned with his own self-improvement and should use "one or more of the many self-rating devices on the market, and after rating set himself to the improvement of any elements which are too low." One aid to self-improvement was the timetable, in which the supervisor should note "(1) the order in which things will be attempted, and (2) the total time given to any factor."[98] Almack suggests a four-year plan in which teachers are to be observed and their problems identified and ranked in order of seriousness; the supervisor then should discuss the problems with the teacher, after which time the problems are expected to be corrected. The supervisor himself should also be constantly monitoring his own progress and efficiency. It is not clear to what extent schemes like Almack's were actually put into effect by rural supervisors, but there is no doubt that sharply different conceptions of the nature and possibilities of rural supervision and rural teaching—divided between university professors and educational experts following a model of scientific efficiency, on the one hand, and rural teachers and supervisors following Deweyan progressive ideas, on the other—marked the introduction of rural supervision in this period.

Georgiana Carden: A Woman Reformer in the Service of the State

The passage of Proposition 16 in 1920, which established the system of rural school supervisors, also called for the credentials of teachers and social welfare workers to be strengthened. This parallel move toward greater state control continued throughout the 1920s. For example, the truant officer was replaced by the "social worker, a person with definite educational requirements and special training for the work who could be employed only when granted a special credential for this service by the state board of education."[99] The spread of new ideas of mental health and the movement to measure intelligence led to greater surveillance of children. Counties were encouraged to institute standardized IQ tests, and in 1928 the California Bureau of Mental Hygiene was established with the goal of "*prevention* and not cure; prevention of delinquency and of crime; of nervous disorders and of insanity; and of failures and maladjustments in general."[100] School authorities were then encouraged to "work on their own initiative" to identify and cure the maladjusted, using the techniques of the mental hygiene movement and the standardized intelligence tests being developed at such institutions as Stanford and the University of California.[101]

As was frequently the case, these policies were carried out by women, who were assumed to have a special and natural concern with issues concerning children and the family. But such women officials did not speak with one voice. An example of the complex motivations of these women can be seen in the career of Georgiana Carden, who served as the first state attendance officer from 1919 to 1926, working in the Division of Rural and Elementary Education. Carden, the daughter of a northern California Presbyterian minister, attended Chico Normal School and the University of California at Berkeley and later taught at Chico Normal.[102] As state attendance officer, Carden traveled throughout California, visiting schools and labor camps and encouraging local officials to provide adequate schooling for migrant children. As the state representative for Indian education, she also visited reservation schools and saw herself as the champion of Indian interests. Carden accepted the need for state involvement in local communities and schools and for greater control over what she often presented as different and sometimes inferior groups of children.

One of Carden's first goals as state attendance officer was to convince the owners of California's immense ranches to build schools to provide some schooling for the children of their workers. Carden seems often to have succeeded in these efforts, in part because of her own sympathetic view of the ranchers. As one of her supporters wrote later, "Through her courtesy, tact, and understanding, she had been able to win over to an attitude of friendship, the farmers and business men who were originally greatly opposed to the State's insistence upon the enforcement of the school law."[103] Her respectful comments about ranchers in her diary are in striking contrast to her general acceptance of racist stereotypes. Consider, for example, her summary of lunch with Frederick Stegmeyer and his wife, owners of the Boston Land Company in Fresno County: "Mrs. Ayers takes Miss Henderson and me to the Boston Land Company. Find Frederick Stegmeyer in the geographic center of 42,000 acres. He will arrange a school building, largely because certain workers have asked for schools. Lunch at his home. Mrs. S. a Washington woman with attitudes toward darkies carried over to Mexicans."[104] The schools she negotiated with the ranchers were often minimal, as this description of the school built in the labor camp on the Hoover Farm in Kern County demonstrates: "There is no building available nor will the fund at our disposal permit an elaborate structure. The plan is to build a platform, 32' x 36', and use a large tent on this. Mr. Kilburn [the owner of Hoover Farm] said he would furnish the tent. Later, we may add screen and canvas flap sides."[105] Both Carden and local teachers displayed racist attitudes toward Mexican and black children. For example, Carden describes the "excellent" work of Miss Shea, the first teacher at the Hoover Farm school, who "[is] working very hard against big odds. Still cheerful although she would like to dispense of the darkies."[106]

One of the first issues raised for the California Department of Education was whether migrant children should be taught in separate schools or included in local public schools. In 1924 Carden reported that experimental classes for migrant children had been established in some agricultural counties, particularly those producing walnuts, cotton, and asparagus. She concluded from these schools "that for the school attendance of the children of migratory laborers a separate system of state schools is neither necessary nor desirable."[107] By 1926, however, Carden had reversed her position:

The first policy toward the migratory child was that he should be blended into the regular school as much as possible, but the increasing numbers have tended toward a swamping of the regular with benefit to neither the temporary children and decided detriment to the residents. One instance may be given. The school at Isleton, Sacramento County, was within six weeks of the end of the term, and the climax of promotions and graduation was approaching. An arky [sic] of migratory children appeared with the ripening asparagus. The whole school underwent adjustment in receiving them. A migratory family developed measles, an epidemic ensued, the schools were closed for four weeks, with consequent disruption of the year's work. For the following year, the district of Isleton provided a separate school building for the migratory children, and this arrangement has been maintained ever since.[108]

These themes and the language of Carden's 1926 report are repeated over and over again in local and state discussions of the education of migrant children: fears of "swamping" the "regular" children, the possibility of "epidemics," the "disruption" of work (implicitly the work of the "regular" children), and the familiar solution: to place the migrant children in separate buildings. Carden's language and acceptance of the segregation of migrant children rested on an acceptance of their dangerous difference. These ideas of "difference," which were first applied to African-American and Mexican children, were later applied as well to the white children of the southwestern migrant farm workers who began to appear in California in the late 1920s. Carden seemed even more dismayed by these new migrants than she had been by Mexican children or "darkies." In her private diary for 1925 she wrote:

Tulare County is receiving also the problem of the cotton picker from the Southern States including those coming from Texas via Oklahoma, than which no poorer human material has yet been encountered. It is hoped that a special study of the group may be made next season leading to a definite program for their instruction and control in matters related to the public health and to the care of children. . . . There were other evidences in Tulare County of the growers' willingness to help in the enforcement of school attendance, in fact, the only real difficulties lay with the school directors and the "pore Whites."[109]

Carden's description of the "poor human material" of the South stands in sharp contrast to her defense of California Indian children. In 1924, Indians throughout the United States were finally enfranchised. At the same time, they were to be included in public schools. Carden accepted the inclusion of Indian children in public schools, noting the inferior conditions of reservation schools: "Racial prejudice has at times demanded a separate school allowed under the law for Indian children and district finances in these instances have not been adequate for two schools of equally good equipment. The education has been generally perfunctory, characterized at best by a condescending kindliness and at worst by well-nigh criminal neglect."[110] Carden's views of Indian children rested on beliefs about their essential natures. Unlike Mexican, African-American, or white migrant children, she saw Indian children as physically skilled and close to nature. The Indian girl, for example, had acquired "deftness of hand through generations of basket making. Her coolheadedness, and her patience promise development into excellent nurses." "Coolheadedness" was also a quality she saw in Indian boys, as well as physical prowess: "The qualities that have made the Indian boys such renowned football players could be turned to many expressions. Their mechanical sense is strong, and as engineers they are coolheaded, accurate and reliable."[111]

Carden presents a fascinating example of a woman reformer. While she believed in the power of the state to redress social problems, her vision of reform rested on essentialist and racist categories that led her to see Indian children as destined to useful futures based on their innate abilities and migrant children as "problems" needing to be contained. Thus, although she spoke the language of social reform, she advocated a segregated and unequal education for children she considered different from the norm. In 1926, Carden resigned her position and moved to San Francisco, for reasons that are not clear.[112] Her replacement was Lillian Hill, who subsequently worked closely with Helen Heffernan, the new commissioner of elementary schools. The appointment of Helen Heffernan in 1926 added a powerful new voice to California education.

Helen Heffernan and Rural Women Teachers

Margaret Schallenberger McNaught retired as commissioner of elementary schools in 1923. Her successor, Grace Stanley, served until 1925, and was replaced by Mamie Lang.[113] When Mamie Lang was drowned in a car ferry accident the next year, Helen Heffernan, then a rural supervisor in Kings County, was appointed to her post, and a new era in California education began. In her forty-year career as commissioner, Heffernan was strongly influenced by the progressive education movement and worked tirelessly to bring this approach to California schools.[114] She became the central figure in a network of progressive women educators, principals, supervisors, and state officials.

Helen Heffernan had taught in one- and two-room schools in Nevada, Idaho, and Utah before she came to California to complete her B.A. and M.A. at the University of California. From 1923 to 1926 she worked as a rural supervisor in Kings County, one of the first group of rural supervisors appointed after the reforms of 1921. There she worked under County Superintendent Miss M. L. Richmond, a respected and progressive leader, who had gathered together an outstanding staff of women educators.[115] At the time of her appointment as commissioner of elementary schools, Heffernan's talents were already widely recognized. As the *Sierra Educational News* commented, "Her work in Kings County has been such that it has brought her prominently before educators in the West."[116] Her appointment was greeted enthusiastically by attendees of the 1926 California Rural Supervisors Conference at Lake Tahoe: "We have met Miss Heffernan at all meetings of the association in which she has taken an active part and have come to know her. Supervisors throughout the state rejoiced to have one of 'their own' chosen for this high honor."[117]

In her first address as state commissioner to the Rural Supervisors Association, Heffernan set out her agenda for reform. She encouraged the founding of local rural supervisors groups, supported the better rural schools conferences, argued for the appointment of a legislative committee to lobby for rural school interests, and urged increased publicity.[118] Heffernan saw publications as a particularly valuable means of communicating her ideas and building support for her projects. One of her first acts as commissioner was to launch a journal. As she wrote in the first issue: "Note the title: CALIFORNIA EXCHANGE BULLETIN IN RURAL EDUCATION! The significant word in the title is 'exchange.' This bulletin is to be the responsibility of every one who has a vision of better rural schools for California. You have *your* contribution to make to the realization of a rural school that means opportunity."[119] The pages of the *Bulletin* were filled with accounts of progressive experiments in rural schools and admonitions to rural supervisors to inspire teachers to see the advantages of the one- and two-room school for a progressive approach:

It has become so customary for us to think of the handicaps and obstacles to effective educational opportunity existing in rural schools, that for the most part we have not taken advantage of the inherent conditions which make the rural schools an ideal place to coordinate educational theory and practice. Modern educational ideals come nearer to being realized in the rural school where it is administratively possible to arrange a flexible program suited to individual differences in capacity and interest.

With all the opportunity for flexible adaptation to individual needs, with freedom to develop initiative and originality through activities, with no administrative need for formality, who will say that the progressive rural school cannot satisfy the demands of an education which develops individual potentialities and raises the level of human excellence?[120]

In expressing her vision, Heffernan frequently cited Fannie Dunn and Marcia Everett's *Four Years in a Country School* and other accounts of progressive practices in rural schools.[121]

Rural supervision provided women with well-paid positions that encouraged autonomy and leadership. Still, wage discrimination continued: in 1924–25 there were 33 male supervisors earning $3,139 and 75 female supervisors earning $2,738, on average; the next year there were 37 men earning $3,583 and 85 women earning $2,687, on average. Nevertheless, these salaries were double those of classroom teachers, and the work was intellectually challenging and responsible. The Rural Supervisors Association, moreover, provided a network and institutional space where women's work was respected and valued and where friendships and support could develop.

Women dominated the rural supervisors' conferences. Although the Rural Supervisors Association included both men and women, women tended to make up the majority of the membership and to hold most leadership positions. In 1926, for example, the president of the organization was Mrs. Ethel Ward, and eleven of twelve speakers at the annual conference were women. The next year, Ethel Ward was reelected president, and seventeen of twenty-four conference speakers were women. The male speakers were predominantly university professors. By comparison, the board of directors of the CTA in the same years comprised nine men and one woman, and the annual conventions were heavily dominated by male university professors and superintendents.[122] During the late 1920s through 1936 there were between 100 and 150 members in the Rural Supervisors Association in any one year. The group was thus small enough for personal friendships and alliances to be formed, and Heffernan herself knew most of the members.[123]

Heffernan advocated what she called "democratic supervision," a system committed to child-centered progressive education in which supervisor, teacher, and pupils cooperated in solving problems. She actively recruited as rural supervisors teachers who she felt would carry out progressive ideals, and frequently suggested specific individuals to local superintendents. In San Bernardino County in the early 1930s, for example, she helped Ruth Goodman, a young widow and a graduate of Teachers College, Columbia, attain a position as rural supervisor. Goodman subsequently was an articulate and active supporter of Heffernan's progressive views.[124] In numerous reports and bulletins, Heffernan cited what she considered the valuable work done by rural supervisors. In a 1933 *Department of Education Bulletin*, for instance, she pulled examples from the annual reports of the 150 rural supervisors, citing such achievements as the institution of hot lunches, physical and dental examinations for all children, and milk for undernourished children provided by local organizations, as well as more subjective accomplishments such as changes in teachers' attitudes, increased initiative, and cooperation.[125]

The vision of rural teaching as intellectually challenging and important work undertaken by rural teachers in collaboration with supervisors and state officials underlay the establishment of rural teachers clubs and groups. The Napa Rural Teachers Club, for example, was founded in 1923 under the direction of the newly elected county superintendent of schools, Eva Holmes. The club met once a month at scenic local resorts such as Stag's Leap. These meetings, which were attended by the county superintendent, librarian, and attendance officer as well as rural supervisors and teachers, provided an opportunity for both friendship and discussion of formal educational questions. According to one club member, "We transact what necessary business we have on hand, and then indulge in a discussion upon one or many subjects, and enjoy a friendly pow-wow."[126] Activities included occasional outside speakers and planning for the annual wildflower show and play day. In San Joaquin County, supervisors and rural teachers organized their meetings around specific professional interests. Supervisor (and former Fresno Normal School instructor) Edna Orr James described the benefit of these meetings:

Group meetings are important in many ways. It is important that the members of a large group realize their procedure as a part of the whole school system. Cooperation results from group discussion. Rural teachers have profitable social contacts with one another. A supervisor's work is made more efficient and definite by teachers coming together for discussion, for group planning, and for necessary instruction.[127]

Comments like these clearly reveal the influence of the progressive education movement. In a 1927 article in the *California Exchange Bulletin in Rural Education*, Ada York, San Diego County superintendent of schools, stated that the teacher in the one-room school had a "favored opportunity to keep school by the modern method known sometimes as the Creative or Progressive Education." York argued that rural teachers were active professionals who could and should immerse themselves in progressive educational theory:

Just as the artist, the musician, the physician, the lawyer, the churchman, find it imperative to read regularly the literature of their profession, so should teachers be taught to feel the need of frequent and regular contact with the advanced thinkers among the educators. A taste for such reading should be developed until it becomes an urge. Thus, and thus only, will the teacher keep the light of her inspiration aglow.

To prepare rural teachers in these methods, she said, educators should stress this "new viewpoint in the free education of children" based on "the writings of Dr. Dewey, Evelyn Dewey, Dr. Kilpatrick, Harold Rugg, and others."[128]

Ideas of progressive and democratic education were also spread by means of the rural demonstration schools. These schools were first established under Helen Heffernan's direction in the late 1920s and continued to exist through the 1930s. By 1930 there were twenty such schools, ranging from one- to five-room schools, designed "to bring new ideas, inspiration, and higher professional ideals to scattered rural teachers, to give them a concrete picture of what a progressive school should be."[129] Probably the best known of the rural demonstration schools was the Woods school at Woodbridge in San Joaquin County. Heffernan was particularly proud of this school, which was under the leadership of Edna Orr James and Tene Cameron, two rural supervisors who were deeply committed to Heffernan's progressive ideals. Describing the Woods school and the Escalon school, the other rural demonstration school in San Joaquin County, Heffernan wrote:

These schools have been visited by nearly five hundred superintendents, supervisors, and teachers during the school year, and have provided an opportunity for showing a program of progressive education to many. One elementary school principal of many years' experience, when reporting at the state department after a visit to Woods and Escalon, said: "They are the nearest approximation of my ideal of what an elementary school should be of anything I have ever seen."[130]

The Woods school was located on a five-acre site, with five classrooms, a library, principal's office, auditorium, playground, and school garden. The school offered nutrition education, health examinations, and free medical care for those unable to pay. Children underweight 10 percent or more were given daily eggnogs to bring up their weight. In terms of curriculum, the project method was used, and social activities such as gardening, folk dancing, and club participation were encouraged. A great emphasis was placed on individual development and progress, and testing was used to establish the specific achievement level and needs of each child. A better sense of the curriculum and organization of the school can be gathered from this description by Heffernan:

The old-type recitation method has disappeared from these demonstration schools. It is replaced by socialized conferences which permit of adjustments to individual differences. The individual method is used almost entirely in the formal subjects. Each child is allowed to grow in his own way, progress at his own rate, and toward his own goals. . . . Mass instruction is never suited to each child's needs; injustice is done by neglecting the wide range of differences in ability. Much later mental maladjustment may result from the attempt to keep all children doing the same thing at the same time.[131]

In her pamphlet "Information to Visitors Concerning California's State Rural Demonstration School," Heffernan described what she saw as the goal of the Woods school as a model for all rural and progressive schools:

We are trying to view education as *development from within* rather than the mere acquisition of knowledge and skill. We value *creative activities* more than those that merely conform to existing patterns. We transfer responsibility from the teachers to the children as completely as possible. We value above all things *the individual*. We realize that children differ so completely in physical, mental, social, and educational capacities, experiences, achievements, and rates of growth that no mechanistic organization of education will serve to develop the distinctive personality of each child.

These goals of course reflect very closely the Deweyan ideal of beginning education with the individual child and of establishing a stimulating educational environment within which creative development can take place.

Throughout the 1930s, Heffernan promoted progressive ideas through both articles and public appearances. Between 1928 and 1930 she edited a monthly section on rural education in the *Western Journal of Education*, which gave her an additional forum in which to articulate and disseminate her ideas. In 1931 she established the *California Journal of Elementary Education*, which was published through 1963. Here she continued to present the ideas of Dewey, Kilpatrick, and other progressive educators in articles such as "The Reconstruction of the Elementary School Program" (November 1932), "Supervision Appropriate for Progressive Schools" (August 1937), and "How Can We Make a Rural School Democratic for Children, Teachers, and Parents?" (May 1940).[132] She spoke frequently to prospective teachers on college campuses, encouraging them to use progressive approaches.

Depression-Era Challenges to Progressive Rural Education

The world of progressive women educators shaped and led by Helen Heffernan was deeply affected by the crisis of the depression. California in these years experienced widespread labor unrest and sharpened political divisions between right and left. Perhaps the most dramatic instance of this discord was the gubernatorial campaign of 1934, when Upton Sinclair, a socialist, won the Democratic nomination for governor. Although he eventually lost to Republican Frank Merriman, the polarization exemplified by the campaign continued to mark state politics for years.[133] As historian James Gregory comments, California in these years became a "political battleground between frightened conservatives and frustrated liberals."[134]

Education was politicized in this period as well. Unlike many other states, California succeeded in guaranteeing financial support for education throughout the depression years. In the early 1930s, the California Taxpayers Association (heavily supported by California utilities companies) led a movement to cut funding for education and other human services. In response, the California Teachers Association successfully mobilized local and legislative backing for education. Despite threats of cutbacks in 1932 and 1933, schools continued to be funded and teachers continued to be able to find work in California.[135] In 1933, an initiative to increase state support for schools passed and the legislature instituted a sales tax to raise revenues.[136] As well as aiding all public schools, this legislation continued support for migratory or "emergency" schools and funding for the salaries of teachers in districts that experienced a large influx of migratory families.

For a brief period in the early 1930s, even leaders like Vierling Kersey, the cautious state superintendent of public instruction, spoke favorably of the progressive social reconstructionist theories of George Counts and Harold Rugg.[137] By the mid-1930s, however, these ideas in education were coming under increasing suspicion, fueled in part by the financial crisis. As the progressive education movement became associated with more critical and politically radical ideas, all aspects of progressive education came under attack. Controversies developed over textbooks and curriculum; in California as elsewhere, the social reconstructionist social studies materials developed by Rugg were attacked as biased and "socialistic." Rural supervision also was viewed with suspicion, owing to both financial constraints and conservative distrust of the supervisors' progressive approach.[138] By the mid-1930s Heffernan's vision of rural supervisors as encouraging the work of progressive teachers in rural schools had come into conflict with some county superintendents, who had their own agendas and who wanted rural supervisors to be under their direct control, not that of the state commissioner. This dispute became particularly sharp after 1933, when the state took over responsibility for funding rural school supervision. Conservative taxpayer associations and legislators began to argue that rural supervision was not only costly but unnecessary. In 1933, a bill was presented in the state legislature calling for the elimination of funds for rural supervision. Thanks to an organized campaign of the California Department of Education, as well as sympathetic legislators, the PTA, and favorable public opinion, this bill was defeated.

Although rural supervision had been saved, conservative superintendents, who saw Heffernan as dangerous and threatening to local values and autonomy, continued their attack on her progressive policies. Superintendent Kersey, while he cautiously supported Heffernan's views, seemed unwilling to enter into conflict with local superintendents or local interests. By 1934 some county superintendents were reducing support for rural supervisors, in contravention of existing legislation. Kersey complained of this practice in a letter to the county superintendents:

We have been advised . . . that in a number of areas considerable reductions have been effected in the programs of rural supervision despite the fact that adequate funds are available for the performance of this service. In a number of cases considerable portions of the funds granted by the state for rural supervision have remained unexpended and have been transferred to the unapportioned county elementary school funds as unnecessary surpluses. At the same time it is obvious that in these same counties rural school service has been materially reduced and the object of the state apportionment for rural supervision has therefore not been attained.[139]

Kersey set out the nature of the conflict in an internal memo to Helen Heffernan. On the one side stood rural supervisors controlled by the county superintendents for their own political goals. In these cases, the function of the supervisors had "come to be nothing more than supplemental support to the activities of one sort and another of the country superintendent. In some instances these activities are entirely educational and in some instances they are not." On the other side stood "a body of rural supervisors rather intimately tied to the State Department of Education, primarily through your own office. These people conduct their responsibilities in terms of a developed program."[140] Although the rural supervisors were paid by the state and overseen by Helen Heffernan, they were appointed by the county superintendents and worked out of county departments of education. The state education department, moreover, did not have the legal authority to appoint rural supervisors, even though after 1934 it was providing the funds for the positions.

In a letter to Kersey, Heffernan estimated that only 25 percent of rural supervisors were "closely identified with the political interests of local county school superintendents." But, she wrote, "I should estimate that two-thirds of the rural supervisors are very intimately connected with the state department of education and are accepting state department leadership in the formulation of their programs. Probably no professional group in the entire state is tied in its interests more closely to our program." Heffernan felt she was able to work well with a number of county superintendents, who had appointed rural supervisors "on the basis of professional qualifications and my recommendation. The extent to which [our program] may be accomplished depends upon the personal attitudes of the superintendent." Other county superintendents, however, were hostile toward her, either because they wanted greater control over local education or because they were opposed to her progressive ideas, and often for both reasons.[141]

Kersey, although he recognized that the funding for rural supervisors came from the state, refused to confront county superintendents on this issue. Eventually, in 1936, the continuing attacks on rural supervisors as a liberal group influenced by the progressive ideas of Helen Heffernan led to the dissolution of the Rural Supervisors Association, after which it was reorganized to include "all school supervisors and directors of instruction, whether urban or rural," and changed its name to the California School Supervisors Association.[142] Heffernan, despite losing the smaller woman-dominated rural supervisors organization, continued to support and influence this new group.

During the depression Heffernan focused increasingly on the need to provide migrant children with adequate health and employment services through the schools. Both Heffernan and her chief assistant in the Division of Elementary Education, Gladys Potter, spoke against growers and local districts that, they argued, failed to give these children a basic education. At a 1938 Fresno conference on migrant education, Heffernan argued:

If facts are to be faced realistically, we must admit that there is frequently discrimination against migratory children. Such children and their parents are wanted only as a solution to a labor problem. They are not considered an integral part of the community life; the children are not wanted in the regular schools because of considerations of cleanliness, health or social status; and some socially myopic adults who would decry long hours of labor as barbarous for their own children, actually advocate labor rather than education for the migratory child.

The policy of the California Department of Education toward migrant children, said Heffernan, "may be briefly stated in these words: Wherever there are children of school age, it is the responsibility of the constituted educational authorities to establish and maintain schools of a quality equal to that of schools provided for the permanent residents of the community."[143]

Speeches like this doubtless contributed to the growing animosity toward Heffernan shown by local politicians, business leaders, and conservative groups throughout the state. Heffernan's conception of an adequate education for migrant children included "proper school buildings with standard classrooms and proper sanitary facilities"; showers, which were often not available in the labor camps; a noonday meal of "nourishing meat, fruits, vegetables, and milk"; and physical examinations and other health services. Gladys Potter elaborated on the state's vision of migratory or emergency schools: They should be clean, with books and materials. The teacher should welcome the children and make them feel wanted. "If he is a stranger your responsibility is even greater. The room may be already filled to overflowing but that is not the fault of the child. Through no decision or desire of his has he come to an overcrowded school. . . . This is *his* school and he has as much right to consideration as the early comers."[144] Potter recommended organizing the emergency school like a one-room school, without strict grades—a sensible suggestion for children whose education was often disrupted by moves. Like Heffernan, she suggested a Deweyan curriculum, emphasizing nature study, projects, and what she called "dramatic play."[145]

Helen Heffernan continued to encourage and lead like-minded women educators throughout her career. After 1940, she built a network of followers in summer sessions for elementary school supervisors at UCLA run jointly with Corinne Seeds of the UCLA Laboratory School, which continued until 1956. Although this network never made a formal statement of feminist goals, it provided a comfortable space where women in California education could find encouragement and express their shared conception of women's equal abilities with men.[146]

Conclusion

In the period between statehood and the outbreak of the Second World War, a bureaucratic state system of education emerged in California. Conceptions of gender, representations of men and women teachers, and direct struggles between men and women in education over issues of power and authority are central to that history. Gender was significant in the organization of the California State Department of Public Instruction, schoolmasters and schoolwomen's clubs, and both the formal organizations and informal networks of supervisors, teachers, and administrators associated with Helen Heffernan. Although women never controlled key educational organizations such as the California Teachers Association and no woman was ever elected as state superintendent of public instruction, a women's sphere in education emerged from a complex interaction among early-twentieth-century feminism, demands for the reform of rural education, ideas about progressive education, and the activism of a significant number of key women educators in positions of power and influence.

Schoolwomen in the period before 1920 framed educational issues in terms of women's rights, and the place of women teachers was openly debated. At the same time, the idea of professionalization in education was often framed in gendered terms as embodying male authority, privilege, and control over women's work in teaching.[147] Male teachers and administrators sought to retain their positions of privilege by means of this rhetoric of professionalism, on the one hand, and the moral panic of the woman peril, on the other, arguing in both cases for the need for male expert authority over untutored women classroom teachers.

The interwar years continued to be marked by these competing visions of the work of women teachers. Rural school reform, which emerged from a movement for greater scientific and state control over women teachers, ironically gave women access to positions of leadership and allowed the rise of an organized network of educated women. Nevertheless, despite these gains, the patriarchal representation of male leaders was never completely erased; as a result, the feminist representation of the strong and capable teacher failed to be firmly secured by women reformers. Without the constant articulation of their interests and identities, women in education remained vulnerable to the redefinitions and appropriations of what it means to be a woman teacher.

Teachers lived and worked in a world defined by these struggles over meaning and power. A major concern of this study is the way in which political and discursive struggles in the public sphere shaped the consciousness and material lives of actors at the local level. This requires a shift from the authoritative discourse of state and public officials to the ground of the everyday. In the next chapter, the social and economic history of Kings and Tulare Counties will be explored, to provide the local context in which one group of women teachers lived. Only then can we consider how women teachers worked within the confines of state regulations, and how they constructed themselves through or against the gendered discourses of the powerful.

CULTURE, SCHOOLS, AND COMMUNITY: TULARE AND KINGS COUNTIES

The story of women teachers in rural California is part of the story of the American West. In the century between 1850 and 1950, interior central California—which had been relatively untouched by the native peoples who had lived there, by some accounts, for almost ten thousand years—was transformed, the culture of the native Californians all but destroyed, the land itself leveled and plowed, native oaks and chaparral cut down and replaced first with wheat and then with irrigated orchards and fields. In the place of the original oak savannah, a mechanized, industrial landscape was imposed. At the same time, human society was remade. The rural communities established in Tulare and Kings Counties in the nineteenth and early twentieth centuries reflected the rapid social and economic transformation of the West, shaped both by the eventual ascendancy of large corporate agriculture and by the mores of small towns and family farms.

Although this rural culture claimed a specific frontier identity, in fact it replicated the existing gender, racial, and class structures of the United States. In rapidly developing rural areas in the West, however, class tended to be obscured by the ethos of frontier individualism; what defined western rural culture instead was race and religion: the hegemony of white and predominantly Protestant knowledge and values, transmitted by means of the schools among other institutions, and shared across class lines by the dominant white English-speaking population. Just as the lives of the women who taught in these schools were shaped by the rise of the educational state, so were they influenced by small-town culture and by the social and economic development of the rural West. At the same time, as teachers they played a key role in the maintenance and reproduction of this world. Before turning to accounts of the lives of these women, I will first examine the social and economic forces that defined their lives and the schools in which they worked.

Tulare and Kings Counties, 1852–1940

Tulare and Kings Counties lie in the San Joaquin Valley in the heart of California, stretching from the oil-rich hills of the Coast Range to the wilderness of the Sierra Nevada. The counties include the Tulare Lake Basin with its rich soils, once the bed of a shallow inland sea hundreds of square miles in area formed by the runoff of Sierra rivers and streams.[1] When the first European Americans arrived, the area was inhabited by native peoples who fished and hunted waterfowl in the lake marshes and gathered acorns from the abundant native oaks. John Muir described the San Joaquin Valley in 1868 before it was put under cultivation:

Making your way through the mazes of the Coast Range to the summit of any of the inner peaks or passes opposite San Francisco, in the clear springtime, the grandest and most telling of all California landscapes is outspread before you. At your feet lies the great Central Valley glowing golden in the sunshine, extending north and south farther than the eye can reach, one smooth, flowery, lake-like bed of fertile soil. Along its eastern margin rises the mighty Sierra, miles in height, reposing like a smooth, cumulus cloud in the sunny sky, and so gloriously colored, and so luminous, it seems to be not clothed with light, but wholly composed of it, like some celestial city.[2]

Once the valley was settled by Americans, its fertile soil was exploited, first as grazing land for sheep and cattle, then as wheat fields; finally, with irrigation, it became one of the most productive and diverse agricultural regions in the world.

The first whites settled Tulare County at the time of the gold rush, when a group of miners moved south into the area (then known as the Four Creeks) from Mariposa County, built a stockade, which they called Fort Visalia, and petitioned the state legislature to establish a county. Although California had been settled by the Spanish in the late 1700s, the relatively small Spanish and Mexican populations were more or less confined to the Pacific coast. In 1852, when Tulare County was founded,[3] the resident population was almost exclusively native Yokuts and coastal Indians who had fled inland to escape the Spanish missionaries and Mexican rancheros.[4]

In 1856, the growing number of white settlers turned on the native Indians in what was known as the Tule River War. The "war" began when an Indian was accused of cattle rustling. Sixty white men formed a vigilante posse, and 400 soldiers were called up from Fort Tejón to the south. The number of Indian deaths in the six weeks of the war was not recorded, but one eyewitness described soldiers "[riding] over women and children, killing some, cutting down their jerky lines, burning their tule huts that they lived in."[5] After the Tule River Indian Reservation was established in 1857, all subsequent native claims to land in the county were ignored. According to the U.S. Census of 1860, the county had a white population of 3,191 and an Indian population of 1,175 men and 165 women. Given the racial and gender attitudes of the census takers, who were local whites, these figures for the Indian population are, needless to say, suspect.[6] But it is clear that by 1860 Indian resistance to white settlement had been broken, and the native Californians were being driven either further into the foothills or onto the Tule River reservation.

White settlement occurred mainly at the base of the Sierra Nevada foothills. Visalia became Tulare County's leading town and a terminus for the Butterfield Stage and Overland Mail in 1858 and the Pony Express and telegraph in 1860. By 1859 the *Visalia Weekly Delta* boasted of the town's Methodist brick church, courthouse and jail, and "a frame school which, with some few needed improvements, will become a comfortable place for the instruction of the young."[7] Other observers were less impressed by the charms of the area. A visitor in 1861 described Visalia as "little more than a labyrinth of crooked streets, ditches, fences, brush, weeds, etc. A quarter mile out of town one is in the wilderness to all intents and purposes. Streets are straight and square as far as they go, but they don't go, and it takes a very uncommon owl to get to his regular roost in the burg after dark."[8]

The history of the county during this period was characterized by violence, not only against the native Indians but among the white settlers as well. Tulare County, like California generally, was divided by the Civil War. Half of the white population of Tulare County in 1860 had been born in the South,[9] and pro-Confederacy sentiment was so strong among these Southerners (who were called Pikes after Pike County, Missouri) that the federal government maintained troops at Visalia throughout the war. The two local weekly newspapers were filled with accounts of shootings, vigilante lynchings, and brawls. In one noted case the editors of the two newspapers, one a Republican and one a Democrat, fought a duel, which led to the death of the Democratic editor. (His opponent was discharged on grounds of justifiable homicide.)[10]

The county's white population increased from 3,191 in 1860 to 4,391 in 1870, and a few more towns were established. The economic basis of the county continued to be raising stock—cattle and sheep—on unfenced range land. With the coming of the Southern Pacific Railroad in 1872, however, the county turned rapidly to wheat farming. Not only could wheat be dry farmed in this area with very low rainfall, but it was also the only crop that, before the introduction of the refrigerated railroad car in the late 1880s, could be successfully transported to wider markets.[11] In 1874 the shift to wheat farming was accelerated by the "no fence law," which made stockmen responsible for the damage done by their animals and led to the fencing in of the open range. Settlement now began to increase rapidly; the population of the county almost tripled between 1870 and 1880, to 11,281. The mid-1880s were the high point for wheat, with more than 90 percent of cropland planted in wheat in 1884.[12] The southern San Joaquin Valley was now one of the most productive wheat farming areas in the nation.

The coming of the railroad encouraged the creation of these vast wheat farms, which could be worked by steam combines and groups of landless men, but it also opened the area up to homesteading and smaller farms. To encourage the building of the railroad, the U.S. government had granted the Southern Pacific twenty sections (12,800 acres) for every mile of track it built. This land was then later sold by the railroad to private bidders. In Tulare County farmers were invited to settle on Southern Pacific land, which they improved, hoping to buy it for the $2.50-an-acre-and-up price promised by the railroad. When the Southern Pacific eventually demanded from $17 to $40 an acre, the farmers, naturally, resisted. The resulting conflict led to the deaths of seven men in 1880 in what became known as the Mussel Slough Massacre.[13] Mussel Slough left a heritage of distrust of the Southern Pacific Railroad, which found expression later in widespread support of populist parties in the county and in sympathy for the bandits John Sontag and Chris Evans, who specialized in robbing Southern Pacific trains.

The agricultural base of the county began to shift in the late 1880s as large wheat farms were replaced by mixed-crop farming and orchards, methods of husbandry more feasible for small farmers. This shift in the organization of agriculture reflected the integration of the area's economy into national and world markets and the effects of technological and demographic changes. The introduction of refrigerated railroad cars and the growth of nearby urban markets in southern California and the San Francisco Bay Area meant that orchard fruits, citrus, and dairy products could be more profitably grown than wheat. Moreover, wheat experienced a sharp decline in price in the early 1890s owing to Canadian and Russian competition.[14] An equally important factor in the shift to mixed-crop farming was the development of widespread irrigation from the diversion of the Kings and Kaweah Rivers running down from the Sierra, artesian wells, and deep well pumping. The Wright Act of 1887 authorized state taxes and bonds for the creation of local irrigation districts. By 1890, Tulare County led all other counties in California with

168,455 acres dependent on irrigation.[15] The population of the county continued to climb, reaching 24,547 in 1890; as agricultural production shifted to smaller farms, a more settled rural community developed, with stronger ties to the land and the district.

In 1893, after years of political maneuvering by local businessmen, the western third of Tulare County was removed to form Kings County.[16] The major focus of population and agriculture in the new jurisdiction was the Kings River Delta, also known as the Lucerne District after the alfalfa and dairying that had come to characterize the delta.[17] Hanford, a railroad town in the Lucerne District, was made the county seat. In the southern part of the new county lay Tulare Lake, at this time a vast, shallow expanse of water whose area depended on the amount of runoff from the Sierra each year. The western portion of the county was much less desirable land, farther from the Kings River and with inferior soils. One early settler in the Kettleman Hills remembered, "The only neighbors we had were desert squirrels or chipmunks, rattlesnakes, antelope, coyotes, horned toads, lizards, north winds, and sandstorms."[18] The land on the West Side, as it was known, was not subdivided into small family farms, as was true of the Lucerne District, but was held in large tracts. Tulare County retained the rich farmland of the eastern San Joaquin Valley, the foothills, and the high Sierra.

In the early 1900s Tulare and Kings Counties were linked more closely to urban areas by the coming of the automobile and the expansion of oiled roads. In 1915 the major highway between Los Angeles and San Francisco was completed, running close to the boundary between the two counties.[19] The economic base for the region remained farming, which from the beginning was organized as a capitalist business. Tulare and Kings County farmers did not for the most part even consider being self-sufficient, but continued to raise specialized cash crops. Increasingly, the population of the two counties comprised smaller farmers who could make a living raising citrus, fruits, and vegetables. These small farmers shared both a dependence on national markets and a distrust of the monopolies that controlled those markets, particularly the Southern Pacific Railroad. In the early 1890s in Tulare County the populist Tulare County People's Party gained widespread support among small farmers. In the 1892 elections, the People's Party won from 38 to 75 percent of the vote cast in eleven rural precincts in Tulare County.[20]

Cultural institutions in the area were defined and dominated by the prosperous Protestant, Anglo-American small farmers who made up the large majority of property owners. Of 109 churches and meetings in Tulare County in 1914, 95 were Protestant.[21] Protestant churches, particularly Methodist, Presbyterian, and Baptist, were important social institutions throughout the county, especially for farming families. Eulalia Dunn described the founding of the Presbyterian Church in Dinuba in her poem "On Christmas Eve in 1892" thus:

> Dinuba's two churches, in eighteen ninety-four
> Were the Methodist and Baptist, "and there should be one more."
> So thought some people, who long had been
> Associated with the Presbyter-i-an.
> So the Cochrans and Fields, and Mrs. Elam, too,
> Got together to organize this Church, new.[22]

Although Eulalia Dunn may not be remembered as a major poet, her account of the central role of the Protestant churches in small-town culture is typical of stories in the pages of local papers and the memoirs of nineteenth- and early-twentieth-century Tulare and Kings County settlers.

The dominant vision of a prosperous, cohesive community was frequently represented in local newspaper articles and broadsides citing the advantages of the area. Typical, for example, is the description of Hanford, the seat of Kings County, in a Southern Pacific pamphlet from 1908 as a town filled with "vines and palms, and a variety of ornamental trees" and boasting "an opera-house, a free library, good hotels, schools and churches, a creamery, packing houses, condensed-milk cannery, fruit cannery and winery, and solid business blocks."[23] Or consider the inscriptions on the arches in the town park of Stratford in Kings County: "Yearly: One Million Pounds of Butter / One Million Sacks of Grain."[24] With prosperity, the radical critique of the People's Party was increasingly lost in the celebration of the benefits of individual hard work, speculation, and profit.

In the U.S. censuses through 1930, the populations of Tulare and Kings Counties were recorded as being well over 90 percent white, and the dominant churches were Protestant. But from their founding, the counties included other racial and religious groups. There was a small black population in Tulare County from the 1870s onward (80 in 1880, 73 in 1900, 253 in 1920), and Kings County was similar, with 76 "Negroes" listed in the 1900 census, and 180 in 1920.[25] Other ethnic groups established settlements in the area as well. Mexicans and Mexican Americans lived and worked in both Tulare and Kings Counties from the beginning; their numbers, however, are difficult to estimate, since people with Spanish surnames were not counted as separate groups in the early censuses.

Many Chinese workers came to the area to work on the railroad and stayed on, primarily as farm laborers and servants. Most Chinese in Tulare County lived either as servants in households or in all-male boardinghouses, although in Hanford in Kings County there was a somewhat larger Chinese population, including families who owned restaurants and laundries. Hanford became the center of Chinese institutions in the southern San Joaquin Valley. In 1893 the Sam Yup Association, a Chinese fraternal organization, established a Taoist temple in Hanford that provided a community center, meals, and housing for association members and a worship space for Buddhists, Taoists, and Confucians.[26] During the economic depression of the 1890s there were several forced deportations of Chinese from the area.[27] Thus, although in 1880 Tulare County had a Chinese population of 326 (out of 11,281 total), by 1910 the figure had dropped to 257 (out of 35,440). The story in Kings County was similar: 417 Chinese were listed in 1900 (out of 9,871 total), and although twenty years later the number of Chinese was roughly the same—451— the overall population of Kings County had more than doubled, to 22,031. Japanese settlers began to arrive in the first decade of the twentieth century: Tulare County had 48 Japanese in 1900, and 1,602 in 1920; Kings County had 156 and 594 in the same years, respectively.

In 1915 the Presbyterian Mission commissioned a social survey of Tulare County. Conducted initially by sociologist O. F. Wisner and then completed and published by Hermann N. Morse, the study documented both the prosperity and the instability of society in Tulare County in the years immediately prior to the United States' entry into the First World War. While Morse noted the prosperity of the county's farmers and townspeople, he was also struck by their competitive capitalist ethos, a characteristic that he considered typical of California as a whole. As he remarked, "Everything in the state—farms, mountains, forests, parks and all—is on the counter, price-marked and for sale. . . . There is something rather irritating about this to the disinterested spectator who longs to discover one beautiful thing in the state whose charms have not been flaunted at him from every bulletin board, and which he has not been persistently urged to inspect, rent, purchase or otherwise enjoy." Morse also noted a certain degree of social instability:

A rapidly growing community, a shifting community, a community of diverse racial elements might be expected to show many marks of instability. Add to this a large annual influx of population at certain seasons of the year, made up in part of itinerant, seasonal workers, in part by property owners having their permanent residences elsewhere and in part of tourists, and you have a situation that would make the acquisition of community stability a slow and difficult process.

Although there was little evidence of class conflict, Morse did note strong religious and ethnic boundaries between immigrant groups. When these

groups fit in the category "white," they experienced little social or economic discrimination; such was not the case, however, for those categorized as racially "other." Morse commented, "The northern European
groups are being quite rapidly assimilated in language and customs,
though the German and Swedish people still use their own language to a
considerable extent in their homes and churches. The Southern Euro-
peans, Mexicans, and Orientals are mostly colonized or segregated and
are not being assimilated."[28]

Racism, particularly against Native Americans and Chinese, defined
social relationships in Tulare and Kings Counties from the earliest days
of Euro-American settlement. Native peoples, referred to derogatorily as
"diggers," were considered generally to be racially inferior savages. In the
decades surrounding the turn of the twentieth century, Indian families
lived a marginal existence, working during the growing season as fruit
pickers or farm laborers in the valley and returning for part of the year
to the foothills or the Tule River reservation.

Violence against the Chinese was widespread not just in Tulare and
Kings Counties but throughout California in the 1870s and 1880s, with
racist attitudes acceptable even among the "best" of white society. In
1880, for example, George Stewart, editor of the *Visalia Weekly Delta* and
one of the wealthiest and most influential Tulare County businessmen,
published a poem called "Our Chinaman." It began:

> A Chinaman our cook was born
> Our country's ways he holds in scorn
> He still is faithful to his land
> That cook of ours—John Chinaman.
> His fingernails are long and black,
> His pigtail hangs way down his back
> His face is ugly and he looks
> Like 'rang o tangs in picture books.[29]

Anti-Chinese hostility and accounts of racial attacks were common in the
pages of local newspapers during this time. A typical article from the *Tulare County Business Directory* reveals the economic motive behind some of
this racist sentiment:

Market gardening pays in Tulare county, but nobody knows how much. There
must be nearly a hundred Chinese vegetable wagons running in the county, for
no neighborhood is without one. Five dollars each per day would be a low estimate of their gross receipts, and their expenses are next to nothing. Five hundred dollars per day, 365 days in the year, makes $182,500 that these fellows pick
up in the course of the year from the "Melican" man. This would support in comfort not less than 100 white families, and how much better that would be for the
county.

Chinese vegetable farmers, according to this article, exhausted the land, caring only for profit, and worked twice as hard as even the Portuguese (who "by courtesy are called white"). The only answer was to curtail all immigration for Chinese and "wait for death and departure to China to do the rest."[30]

One response to racist attitudes and practices was for groups to establish separate colonies or communities. Japanese immigrants, for example, tended to cluster together for mutual cultural and economic support. An example of an early Japanese settlement in the San Joaquin Valley is the unincorporated town of Del Rey, in Fresno County, directly adjacent to Tulare County. As one Japanese settler remembered Del Rey: "We had about four or five boardinghouses; we had three pool halls; two or three chop suey houses. We had a *tofuya* (tofu shop) and a *sakanaya* (fish store). One man came in 1922 I think and even started an auto repair shop."[31] The town provided amenities for the large numbers of Japanese men who worked as farm laborers and who were in the United States without their families. Another early Del Rey resident remembers life in his family's boardinghouse, where Japanese farm laborers would stay during the winter. The men "didn't want to stay out in the farm camps so they came into town. Our place had a bath house in back and a great big dining room where everyone ate. My mom cooked all Japanese food. Just like an old time Japanese hotel."[32] In 1919 a Japanese Community Hall was built, which housed a language school for the children and sponsored both Buddhist and Japanese Congregational services.

Other ethnic groups followed similar patterns. Armenian immigrants arrived in northern Tulare County in 1901, settling around the town of Churchill. In 1905 they successfully petitioned to have the name of the town changed to Yettem ("Garden of Eden" in Armenian) and established a church and community center. In the Lucerne District in Kings County, meanwhile, Catholic Portuguese settlers established themselves as dairymen. The localized nature of these settlements is revealed in the 1920 U.S. Census, which lists 435 Armenian-born residents in Tulare County, while adjacent Kings County has only 63; and 715 Portuguese-born residents in Kings County, versus only 4 in adjacent Tulare County. In the Presbyterian Mission survey, Morse remarked on the tendency of these groups to form successful separate communities: "Each of the various foreign communities, such as the German Lutheran community at Deer Creek, the Mennonite community west of Dinuba, the Swedish community near Kingsburg, the Armenian community at Yettem, is, in the main, of a single economic and social level. Elsewhere the people very generally fraternize together, without many hard and fast lines being drawn, except on the basis of racial differences."[33]

Nevertheless, the lines drawn "on the basis of racial differences" could be very powerful, as in the account of Norvin Powell, a black high school graduate from Colorado, who recalled trying to find work in Tulare County in the period around 1920:

Upon arrival in Allensworth I immediately started looking for a job. Alpaugh, Earlimart, Corcoran, Terra Bella, Porterville, wherever I went the reception was the same. Until this day the signs which almost seemed to come at me from the windows, business after business, are still graphic and humiliating:

NO   negroes
        filipinos
        mexicans
        dogs[34]

Such examples of racism were hardly unique to Tulare and Kings Counties, of course, but it is important to remember that they were an integral part of the rural culture that defined the dominant institutions of the area. These racist attitudes and practices, as well as people's particular cultural identities, doubtless encouraged groups such as the Armenians and Japanese to settle together and to establish their own churches and social organizations.

The best-known example of a racially separate settlement in Tulare and Kings Counties was the all-black town of Allensworth, which was founded in 1909 by a group of urban African Americans from Southern California. Influenced by the ideas of Booker T. Washington and encouraged by the success of black towns of the Midwest, Col. Allen Allensworth (after whom the town was named) and William Payne, a teacher and graduate of Denison University in Granville, Ohio, conceived a plan for a race colony in California.[35] In 1908, a site for the colony was located in southern Tulare County adjacent to the Santa Fe Railroad line and the station of Solito. This land was owned by a consortium of white land speculators, Pacific Farming Company, which described it as fertile land blessed with abundant water, located on the main railway line from Los Angeles to San Francisco. Subsequently all of these claims were called into question, particularly that concerning water. At the time, though, Allensworth, Payne, and their associates were pleased to have found what seemed to be a promising site for their colony. By 1909 the first settlers arrived and a post office was established. In 1912 Allensworth was made into a voting district and a school district, and the two-room public school was built; in 1914 it was made a judicial district, with Oscar Overr becoming the first African-American justice of the peace in California.

Officials in Tulare County seemed willing to accept the black settlement so long as it remained a separate community. By 1914 more than 2,000 acres had been sold, supporting a small but flourishing community. It is difficult to determine the precise numbers of residents in Allensworth at any one time. In her study of the colony, Eleanor Ramsay estimates the population in the period 1908–20 at between 120 and 200.[36] An early settler, Henry Singleton, later estimated that in 1914 and 1915, the high point of the colony, some 300 people lived at Allensworth, although he also noted that this was a "floating" population of people who would stay for three or four months and then leave to seek work elsewhere.[37]

Allensworth was founded with high hopes, but it faced profound obstacles to survival: the hostility of the Santa Fe Railroad, which refused to establish a station at Allensworth; the highly alkaline nature of much of the land; and most important, the lack of water.[38] The colony flourished between 1913 and 1918, but inadequate water, along with the failure of a campaign to establish a state-supported vocational school at Allensworth, ultimately led to its inevitable collapse. By 1920 the colony's leading families were leaving, and by the 1930s it had become a campground for migrants seeking work in the fields of the San Joaquin Valley.[39] Allensworth was a significant attempt by African Americans to establish an alternative to the racist culture in which they lived. Nevertheless, their contributions were never acknowledged in the dominant images of valley culture, any more than those of Chinese and Japanese vegetable farmers or Armenian fruit growers.

By 1920 the days of the "pioneers" began to be mythologized in the newspapers of Tulare and Kings Counties. Interviews with early settlers were published, framed as accounts of the courageous conquerors of the frontier. Picnics for pioneers and their descendants, along with presentations at local women's clubs and fraternal organizations, helped to establish a past that included the glorification of the early days of settlement and the assertion of a common culture based squarely on frontier values. Yet as Morse commented in his social survey of Tulare County, "Most of the substantial progress [in the county] is of recent occurrence, and what remains of the pioneer spirit is reactionary in tendency. These communities have had to be re-created."[40] This process of the re-creation of a pioneer past continued throughout the 1920s.

But even if the identity of these communities was being constantly re-created, the residents' sense of complacency rested on real economic prosperity. William Preston, in his study of the Tulare Lake Basin, describes the area in 1920 thus:

Farming had never been so lucrative: urbanization and industrial growth in Europe and America brought an expanding market for agricultural commodities, and prices for farm products of all types actually rose faster than prices for other commodities. Farm prices rose more than 89 percent from 1899 to 1910, and jumped another 140 percent with the eruption of hostilities in Europe at the beginning of World War I.[41]

Tulare and Kings County farmers responded to the favorable agricultural markets of the early twentieth century by adopting new and more efficient technology and by diversifying crops. These trends, in turn, made smaller farms possible. In the period 1900–1925, the average farm size in Kings and Tulare Counties fell from 460 acres to 159 acres; at the same time, the number of farms increased from 3,144 to 9,465.[42]

Although the prices of agricultural products were high in the period between 1900 and 1920, the price of land was also high, driven up by large-scale land speculation and local boosterism. By the mid-1920s, half of the farms in Kings and Tulare Counties were mortgaged.[43] At about the same time, overproduction, the collapse of world prices for agriculture, and high operating expenses led to the loss of many small family farms and to an increase in the number of large corporate farms.[44] Thus when the Great Depression of the 1930s began, Tulare and Kings Counties were already in economic crisis. The influx of displaced farmers from the south-central United States—Oklahoma, Texas, Missouri, and Arkansas—only exacerbated the situation. By the mid-1930s, white Dust Bowl evacuees made up the majority of the migrant labor force in California, although Mexican and some African-American families continued to work in the fields as well.[45]

The small-town culture of 1920s and 1930s rural California remained under the sway of conservative and frequently racist attitudes. The Ku Klux Klan was active in both Tulare and Kings County in the 1920s. As early as 1922, the Klan in the small town of Orosi in Tulare County sent letters to Japanese farmers demanding that they give up their land and leave the area, and in the same year it was estimated that "around 100" residents of Hanford, including "many prominent citizens," belonged to the Klan.[46] In 1931 the Klan Klorero, the California Klan's annual conference, was held in Visalia, with over 500 in attendance. On that occasion the Klan held a public parade through the streets of Visalia and performed a "dramatic pageant." Although some local citizens worried about potential violence, the convention passed without incident.

The racist attitudes typified by the Ku Klux Klan with regard to Mexicans and Mexican Americans, African Americans, and Japanese Americans were applied in turn to the Dust Bowl migrants of the depression era. Although the extent of migration to California in the 1930s was in fact less than in the 1920s or 1940s, the large number of destitute families seeking any kind of agricultural work, camping along ditches, living in tents, and concentrated in a small number of rural counties created a kind of panic among local residents. Alarmed editorials, letters in local newspapers, and statements by local officials in both Tulare and Kings Counties warned of the threat of migrant farm workers, both Mexicans and white southwesterners. Joan Pratt, the Tulare County welfare department director, for example, made her contempt clear when she stated: "You can't change the habits of primitive people from the Southern and Middle Western States. You can't force them to bathe or to eat vegetables."[47] These sentiments were surpassed by a resident of Porterville in Tulare County, who wrote to President Roosevelt protesting the establishment of a federal migratory camp in Porterville:

These "share croppers" are not a noble people looking for a home and seeking an education for their children. They are unprincipled degenerates looking for something for nothing. The fact that they are leaving their native land unfit for human habitation is not surprising. Their ignorance and maliciousness in caring for trees, crops, vines, and the land is such that California will be ruined if farming is left to them.[48]

The ultimate source of local communities' hostility toward migrants was ideological, but it was also grounded in economic hard times: the destitute Dust Bowl families were seen as threatening not only to local community life, but also to economic well-being.[49]

When attempts were made to organize the migrants to strike for better wages and more humane working conditions, violence tended to be the result, often instigated by growers and condoned by local police.[50] During the October 1933 Pixley cotton strike in Tulare County, for example, two men were shot and killed and several others wounded as they stood listening to a speech by Pat Chambers, a labor organizer. Although five ranchers were arrested for the murder, they were later released without being charged. In the same month, cotton workers—both Mexicans and Dust Bowl refugees—near Corcoran in Kings County banded together to create a tent city and struck for better working conditions and wages. The threat of the forcible breakup of the camp by county and state law enforcement officers, however, caused the strike to be called off and the camp disbanded three weeks later.

Hostility to migrants and fear of union organizing led to the founding of such groups as the Associated Farmers of California and the California Citizens Association. In 1938, another year of labor unrest, Tulare County supervisors officially condemned the "crooks coming into our county from the Dust Bowl."[51] Outrage at the conditions the migrants were forced to endure culminated in the publication, both in 1939, of John Steinbeck's *The Grapes of Wrath* and Carey McWilliams's *Factories in the Field*. By 1940, however, the economic crisis was beginning to abate in California. Both left-wing anger and right-wing hostility evaporated with the coming of the Second World War, as migrant families moved from Tulare and Kings Counties to southern California and the Bay Area to work in the war industries, and new enemies and new heroes appeared in the country's imagination.

Schools in Tulare and Kings Counties, 1852–1900

A number of works have argued for the positive historical role of rural schools in building a sense of community and a common American culture.[52] This occurred in a variety of ways: local country schools served as symbols of a coherent identity; they were frequently built through common labor, and teachers boarded in local homes; the school buildings themselves served as sites of celebrations and gatherings. In terms of the knowledge and traditions they taught and validated, they helped to create a myth of a common culture. These assertions of a common rural culture, however, need to be examined in relation to the gender, race, and class composition of these communities and the influence on these communities of larger social and economic structures.

In the 1850s the majority of Euro-Americans came to Tulare County, as to other parts of California, as gold seekers or adventurers, not as settlers. The establishment of schools was far from their minds. In this early period, moreover, the county superintendent of schools was also the county assessor, and so the yearly reports sent to the state superintendent of public instruction tended to be sketchy at best.[53] Until the coming of the railroad in 1872, Tulare County was lightly populated and, with the exception of the town of Visalia, the population was very mobile. There is little evidence that schools were perceived at this time as state institutions under the direct control of a central authority. Even though schools were established in part as a response to the legal obligation to provide schooling, they tended to reflect the concerns of local families rather than state mandates. The first record of a school in Visalia occurs in 1855, when a Presbyterian minister, Reverend Kennedy, held school in his house for thirteen children.[54] In 1857 the county board of supervisors established a school at Elbow Creek (it still exists as a country grammar school) and donated a block of city land for a schoolhouse in Visalia; this became the "little white schoolhouse," which served as the Visalia public school until 1872. In 1858 two more schools, at Elbow and Woodville, were established.[55] All these small country schools were open for only three to six months a year. In 1859, according to the report of the county superintendent of schools, the county still had only four schools.

The number of schools increased slowly but steadily throughout the

1860s. In 1864 there were thirteen schools in Tulare, five held for three months or less, six held for three to six months, and two in session for nine months of the year. By 1871 the number of schools had more than doubled, to twenty-nine. This increase reflects both the growth of population in the county and the influx of families as opposed to single men. The report of the Tulare County superintendent of schools for 1870–71 gives some sense of the state of schools in this early period:

The schools of this county are in their infancy. The county is new and the population migratory. The deltas of the streams are constantly changing the face of the country by filling up old channels and opening new ones. The arable land is only formed in strips along the water courses and over old creek beds. This renders it very difficult at times for the patrons to send [their children] when the streams are full. As the inhabitants settle down to a more fixed and permanent mode of life these difficulties will disappear and the schools grow better. There is considerable interest manifested in the subject of public schools and many localities are laying the foundations for first class schools. There are many things that I might address as reasons for our want of progress, but I am not nor do I propose to be a grumble, but a worker.[56]

The schools in Tulare County in this early period were usually one-room log, adobe, or wood-frame buildings. In the superintendent's report for 1862–63, all ten of the schools in the county were placed in the category "would disgrace the state."[57] Often instruction was conducted in a farmhouse or outbuilding. Antelope School, for example, was first held in a small frame building that had been used to shelter sheep. Some of the solutions to the problem of inadequate facilities were ingenious. At Fountain Springs, for instance, "they had a system of building the school on skids which could be moved by teams of horses. The idea was that when there was a large family located on a ranch the school could be moved close to them."[58]

In isolated communities the school was frequently established on the initiative of local families. Cottonwood School in the foothills of the Sierra was held in a small building built by Hudson Barton, a local rancher, who also became the schoolteacher. His daughter later recalled:

My father helped build the schoolhouse in which he taught—a very small room, with desks and seats that he made himself. His teacher's desk was a work of art of which he was very proud. There was no money available for the windows— besides it was still quite warm fall weather. So a large opening—in fact several boards were left off the side of the building for light and air. This soon became the exit for small boys and girls. . . . I asked him what he did for school books in those days, for I knew there was no railroad in this valley at that time. Everything was hauled from Stockton by team. He had just odds and ends of books that had been brought "across the plains" by wagon train.[59]

This school was built and maintained by the community and the Barton family. The curriculum was also decided by the local families. At Cottonwood School, "generally the subjects taught were those the child or his parents desired. A term varied from three to six months and pupils were admitted from five to twenty-five years of age."[60]

In this rural frontier society, the laws and regulations of the state of California were lightly felt, if at all. Early schools such as these reflected and reproduced the literate knowledge and social needs of the settlers. One early settler recalled:

The homesteaders were far apart, the roads were just tracks across the desert, there were no electric lights, no telephones, no automobiles, yet there was no lack of social life for the people. Artesian wells were rather common and trees were planted by these wells to furnish shade. Here, as well as at the "Free Ranch" and Elk Bayou, school picnics, watermelon feeds, church socials, birthday parties and anniversary celebrations were held in the summer. In the winter the schoolhouse was the center of social life. Entertainments, literary societies, programs and box socials were enjoyed. The adults would play such games as Miller Boy, Musical Chairs, and Skip-to-my-Lou.[61]

With the coming of the railroad in 1872 and the transition from stock raising to wheat farming, the population of the county increased rapidly and the number of schools rose correspondingly, from twenty-nine in 1871 to seventy in 1879. Of those seventy, only three were held for three months or less; sixty met for three to eight months, and seven for eight months or more. Conditions in country schools were still primitive, but the county superintendent in 1875 was optimistic that improvement would occur, "from the fact that the county is settling up rapidly with families from other and older counties and also from the East; these families appreciate good schools."[62] Three years later, however, the new superintendent, William Kirkland, felt that much still needed to be done. As he commented in his annual report to the state superintendent: "The school buildings in most districts are but little better than cow sheds, and the furniture corresponds with the buildings. Some of the seats are instruments of torture. The schools houses, furniture, grounds and outhouses are a disgrace to the county, state and civilized community."[63]

Although material conditions were still primitive in the late 1870s, the idea of schooling was by now well established. The county had small rural one-room schools, larger graded schools in towns such as Visalia, and private secondary schools such as the Visalia Select Seminary and the Visalia Normal School. After the passage of the new state constitution in 1879, teachers and schools in Tulare County came under the direct control of the county school board, which oversaw the examination, observation, and training of teachers. While there may have been some abuses statewide in the granting of certificates through local examinations, in Tulare County this seems not to have been the case: there the examination was conducted openly, with the results (including percentage scores) published in the local newspapers. The examination was apparently quite difficult. In 1883, for example, only twenty-three of fifty-three applicants passed.[64] In the two decades following 1880, the school system became more centralized at the county level, new and improved schoolhouses were built in rural areas, and the schools themselves became symbols of a prosperous and settled society.[65] Tulare County Superintendent of Schools J. E. Buckman saw the 1880s as a time of "wonderful development in the organization of new school districts, adoption of regularly organized courses of study and the extension of the school term to seven and sometimes eight months."[66]

By the mid-1880s the county was engaged in a wave of school building. The early sheds and rough cabins were replaced by substantial schoolhouses with cloakrooms, adequate heating and ventilation, and stagelike platforms at the front of the schoolroom. County Superintendent Charles Murphy wrote in 1886:

The advance made in school property the past three years has been more than surpassed the present year. The schools were never so well provided with suitable buildings as at present and there is a growing disposition on the part of the people to supply the necessary accommodations. More than a score of good substantial and commodious school edifices have been erected the past year at a cost from one thousand to twenty thousand dollars each. They are not merely "four walls," but handsome structures after modern designs. In almost every town, village and neighborhood the best and more attractive edifice is the schoolhouse.[67]

By 1890, Murphy noted the "strong public sentiment for better support as is evidenced by the laudable enterprise in voting special taxes to extend school facilities, and bonds to build costly and substantial school edifices."[68]

Tulare County had no public secondary schools until 1888. In the years prior to that, secondary education was provided by a series of private schools established in Visalia. In 1859, Miss Keziah Clapp advertised the opening of a high school in Visalia at a tuition of $5 per week (in advance) in the *Delta*; this school, however, apparently never saw the light of day. That same year, Rev. and Mrs. Taylor, who had come to Visalia from Texas, opened the Visalia Select Seminary, a day and boarding school that continued through the 1870s. The Select Seminary charged $8 a week for "tuition, board and room, with the use of bedsteads, tables and chairs." Instruction in languages and higher branches of mathematics cost another $2 a week, with cultural subjects available at additional "reasonable" cost. The seminary was advertised as providing a "moral and intellectual" atmosphere for the children of Visalia's more prosperous citizens, both boys and girls.[69] A second private school, the Academy of the Nativity, opened in 1861. This school, which existed for only a decade, was founded by Father Dade, the first Catholic priest in Tulare County.[70] Tuition was $5 a week, and the students—also, doubtless, from prosperous Visalia families—were largely non-Catholics, reflecting the population of the county, which was overwhelmingly Protestant.

The third private school was the Visalia Normal School, which provided teacher training, general secondary education, and a model elementary school. It was founded in 1876 by two entrepreneurs, S. J. McPhail and A. R. Orr, and provided the equivalent of a secondary education along with courses in pedagogy. After the Select Seminary closed, the Visalia Normal School offered the only secondary schooling in the county until the first high schools were built. It also apparently trained a significant number of teachers for the county's schools in the 1880s.[71] The school's bulletin presented the aim of the school as "to give general culture and liberal education; to qualify students for the practical duties of life, as well as for the teacher's profession."[72]

The school offered study in the following departments: professional studies; pure and applied mathematics; language and literature; natural science; art; and commercial studies. The professional course, which prepared students for teaching, lasted four years, but, the bulletin advised, "by devoting his entire time to professional work, a teacher with the necessary scholarship may complete this course in a single year. As a means of culture and of preparation for the practical duties of life, the completion of the course in this Department is an education within itself." Tuition for the school was to be paid in "United States gold coin." The school also provided cultural and social events, including school picnics to Rocky Hill, a "normal lyceum" that met every Friday evening with "singing, select and dramatic reading, essays, papers and debates," and a Normal Literary Society.[73]

While many of the normal school students planned to go into teaching, others (particularly, it seems, boys) wished simply to gain a more advanced secondary education. In 1883, forty-two boys and thirty girls attended the Visalia Normal School. Some families enrolled all of their children in the school. The Pogue family of Lemon Cove, for example, sent two boys, Earl and Tom, and two girls, Genie and Eva. Only the girls entered teaching.

The Visalia Normal School closed in 1888, the same year that a high school was established in nearby Lemoore. Between 1888 and the opening of the state normal school in Fresno in 1911, prospective teachers in Tulare and Kings Counties gained certification either by passing the county teachers examination or by attending the state normal school in San Jose. Of these two options, the latter was increasingly favored by the end of the 1800s. In 1900, of 143 teachers in the counties, 38 (27 percent) were graduates of California normal schools; 11 (8 percent) had graduated from normal schools in other states; and 7 (5 percent) were graduates of either the University of California or Stanford University. Thus, 40 percent of the teachers in the county had received advanced teacher training.

During this time, in California as elsewhere in the nation, local attempts to oversee and control the preparation of teachers were focused in teachers institutes. After 1879, all counties with more than twenty schools were required to hold a yearly institute as a means of encouraging and training teachers. Attendance was deemed particularly important for those who had not attended normal schools. The first teachers institute was held in Tulare County in 1868, its purpose, the founding constitution stated, being "the improvement of its members in the science of teaching and in the most approved practice; the diffusing of information upon the system of Common School Education among the people, and promoting harmony of feeling; and the greatest possible advancement in scientific and general information."[74]

By the mid-1880s the institute was required of all teachers, and the general public could participate as well. The 1890 institute lasted for three days, with attendance at evening sessions, according to the county superintendent of schools, numbering fourteen or fifteen hundred. Some sense of the topics and tenor of the institutes is given in this description of the 1885 institute, which was attended by 107 of the 109 teachers in the county:

Three very interesting entertaining and instructive addresses were delivered during the evening sessions by Dr. Stratton, President of the University of the Pacific, and Prof. Allen, Principal of the San Jose State Normal School. The subjects of the former lecture were "Some of the dangers which threaten our Country and their remedies." The latter subject was "Industrial Education." An unusual interest prevailed throughout the session. The presence of two such prominent educators gave us a new impetus in the work. Each teacher felt greatly benefited and returned to labor with renewed vim and energy and a determination to do better work in the future.[75]

Although we might question whether everyone in the audience was filled with such "vim and energy," the institutes certainly did serve to bring teachers together, often from distant and isolated country one-room schools, and to solidify their sense of the value and importance of their work. One teacher's recollections of the 1908 institute capture the positive nature of these meetings:

Teachers' Institute came in March and lasted a week. We traveled on the train to Tulare. . . . The program was inspiring and instructive. Mrs. George of San Jose told about a trip to India and said that riding elephants was like eating olives, an acquired taste. The discussions on teaching methods that went on each evening at the home where a half dozen of us roomed and boarded were as helpful as a course at teachers' college.[76]

Schooling the "Other Children"

The public school systems of Tulare and Kings Counties grew in size and complexity during the first two decades of the twentieth centuries, and the numbers of students and teachers rose markedly, reflecting the prosperity and rapid population growth of both counties. Between 1901 and 1920, school districts in the two counties increased in number from 134 to 172, and the number of teachers listed in school records rose from 205 to 463.[77] According to Morse's 1915 survey, most rural schools in Tulare County had slate blackboards, some form of music (piano, organ, or phonograph), globes and maps, and framed pictures; almost half had potted plants or window boxes. Virtually all of the schools had a supply of drinking water, either from a school well or spring or piped in. Although only six schools had inside toilets (the rest had outhouses), Morse was pleased to note that "there was quite a noticeable absence of writings and markings on the toilet walls."[78] In the conclusion to his survey he wrote, "The average of these schools as to buildings, grounds and equipment is very high. Commendable progress is being made. Definite steps have already been taken, and bonds voted to supplant some of the poorest buildings by adequate structures. Many of the newer buildings would do credit to any locality."[79] A similar story of progress and growth was given by Kings County observers, for both the graded town schools of Hanford and Lemoore and the rural one-, two-, and three-room schools.

Accounts like Morse's reinforce the image of schools as providing a common cultural identity, much as Horace Mann and the other common school reformers had desired. But emphasizing schools as sites for the transmission and production of a collective social identity can obscure the fact that they denied the culture or even existence of subordinate groups.[80] The exclusion of African-American, Chinese, and Indian children from schools throughout the West in the nineteenth century was a powerful means of maintaining a cohesive, monocultural world.[81] In California, provision for the education of African-American children, as well as Indian and "Mongolian" children, was not made until the 1860s, when communities were required by law to provide separate schools in cases where there were "more than ten colored children" in a district.[82] The call for separate facilities reflected widespread concern about the impact of "inferior races" in the public schools.[83]

This segregated system seems to have been erratically enforced, however. Some public schools admitted children of color, others ignored them, and in some places separate schools were established. In 1871, a statewide conference of African-American leaders called for a petition to the legislature and if necessary a court case to ban "caste schools" and enforce integration. The appeal to the legislature failed; then in 1874, in the case *Ward v. Flood*, the California State Supreme Court ruled that although all children must be provided with schooling, it could take place under the principle of separate but equal. The African-American community took this as but a temporary defeat and continued to fight at the local level. By 1875 the schools of Sacramento, Oakland, Vallejo, and San Francisco were integrated, and beginning with the school law of 1880 no further mention was made of separate schools. Nevertheless, the struggle for integrated schools in California was by no means won. Although a 1907 attempt to establish segregated schools for Japanese children in San Francisco failed (after creating a diplomatic crisis between the United States and Japan), separate schools for Mexican, Chinese, and Indian children continued to exist in many local areas of California.[84]

Tulare County had only small African-American and Mexican populations in the nineteenth century, but the response of the white community and of local officials to the issue of their children's schooling reveals the power of race in structuring educational practices. The clearest case of segregation was in Visalia, a town where southern influence remained strong. Between 1873 and 1890, African-American children attended the Visalia Colored School, which was originally set up as a private school but was later taken over by the city as a segregated public school. The school was originally begun in much the way that rural schools for white children were. First, a local African-American farmer, Tom Hinds, hired a teacher in 1871 to tutor his children; then, two years later, the teacher, "an elderly cultured negro" named Daniel Scott, established his own school.[85] Scott was described by a Visalia writer, Mervyn Shippey, as "an educated negro from the northeastern United States. . . . The gentleman was at this time quite an elderly man, with snowy white hair, a most pleasing and genial personality according to the information gathered from interviews with several persons who had been acquainted with him."[86] After teaching Hinds's children and other African-American children on the Hinds ranch, Scott purchased a lot in Visalia and built a small school, which he called the Visalia Colored School.

When Scott moved away in 1875, the school continued as a private school until 1878, at which point the city of Visalia built a small segregated school just outside the city limits. Other school districts sent African-American children to this school as well. According to Shippey, the school was not well supported by the city of Visalia: "I should say here that the school never did gain much distinction firstly because of the method of treatment by the City Board of Education and secondly the quality of the pupils was never very high. . . . It was difficult to obtain a colored teacher and few persons other than negroes would accept such a position. . . . The buildings were not kept in good repair compared to other schools."[87] The Visalia Colored School was finally closed in 1890 after an African-American student, Arthur Wysinger, demanded admission to Visalia High School. When the city refused him admission, his parents sued the school system. The case eventually went to the California Supreme Court, which forced the integration of Visalia schools in 1890.[88] Surprisingly, given the strong southern heritage of the county, school integration seems to have been accepted without white resistance, possibly because of the very small African-American population in Tulare County at this time.

The legacy of the Visalia Colored School may help explain the willingness of Tulare County officials to establish the segregated black school at Allensworth, which had all African-American teachers (the only African-American teachers in Tulare or Kings County at the time). The African-American historian Delilah Beasley, writing in 1919, noted the racist tradition of Tulare County, which, she pointed out, had fought "against the admission of colored children into the public schools long after other counties throughout the state had admitted them."[89] The first school at Allensworth was established in 1910, one year after the first colonists arrived, and the modern two-room schoolhouse built in 1912 was by far the largest and most imposing building at Allensworth.[90]

In 1912 Allensworth was made a county school district with the right to elect its own school board, which could then appoint teachers. An African-American school board was immediately voted in, with Mrs. Allensworth as chair, Mrs. Overr as clerk, and Mr. Hall as the third member. While the state of California supported only one teacher for a school of Allensworth's size, in September 1912 the Allensworth school trustees levied an extra tax to pay for an additional teacher, thus demonstrating the colony's willingness to support education to the best of their means (which were by no means extensive). The black community of Allensworth received county support for the school and library on an equal basis with other communities, and for a brief period the teachers and librarians of Allensworth participated with white colleagues in county organizations and institutes. But in the end, even the most sympathetic whites viewed the Allensworth library and school paternalistically as segregated institutions for, in the words of Mrs. Twaddle, the county librarian, these "hard working, ambitious, and self-respecting colored people."[91]

For the educated African Americans who settled in Allensworth, schooling was a central concern. Nimrod Rainbow, who had attended normal school himself, came to Allensworth in 1911 because of what he saw as improved educational opportunities for his children and because he could put his own education to use in the colony. His daughter recalled the value the family placed on education: "Nightly Papa would diligently hear our lessons. When we lived in Kansas they would report every month in the newspaper the children that got 'E' for excellent. And our names, Alma's, Charlotte's and mine, were in the paper each time. A learned man himself, our father had been trained in Ohio as a teacher. Papa was always studying and reading."[92]

The importance of education for the colony was symbolically expressed in the schoolhouse itself. The first school in the colony was held in the unused house of J. A. Hackett. After the petition to make Allensworth a separate school district was approved in 1912, the colonists voted a $5,500 bond to construct a larger school. The resulting impressive and well-built structure served as the center of intellectual and social life for the colony.[93] Helatha Smith, who was a pupil in the school, remembered a globe that could be pulled down from the ceiling to study geography. Several other former pupils remembered the portrait of Colonel Allensworth, with a map of the town of Allensworth emerging from his head, that hung in the schoolroom.[94] A number of clubs for schoolchildren and for adults met in the schoolhouse. The Theater Club, which included both older schoolchildren and adults, performed three plays a year for a number of years.

Both the *California Eagle* and the *Los Angeles New Age*, Los Angeles–based black newspapers, carried accounts of the elementary school graduations at Allensworth in the late 1910s and early 1920s. These events were preceded by "Education Week," featuring exhibitions, contests, concerts, speeches, and an alumni reunion.[95] In 1917 the graduation ceremony at Allensworth school was attended by Will Wood, later state superintendent of public instruction. Wood was impressed by the pride the settlers showed in the school and its graduates:

How these colored settlers appreciate the benefits of a free American school! They regard it as the sanctuary of their long-deferred hopes. Here their children will have the opportunity to become the men and women that the Almighty intended them to be. . . . Many communities in California, composed only of white people, and abundantly able to provide better advantages for their children, haven't the faith of these colored people in the efficacy of education. It seems that men who were born upon heavy handicap are the ones who appreciate to the fullest the value of the American school.

Despite Wood's praise of the attitude of the settlers at Allensworth, his patronizing and racist assumptions about the supposed inferiority of the Allensworth settlers is also striking:

Commencement was a great event in the lives of these young people, and it was a season of joy for the entire colony. Fathers, mothers, and neighbors, all of the negro race, many of whom had never been to school, rejoiced that their children had mastered the rudiments of human culture which to them is a forecast of the final redemption of their people.[96]

In fact, not only were the Allensworth colonists literate beyond the "rudiments of human culture," but as normal school and Tuskegee graduates, several of them were better educated than the majority of white farmers in surrounding communities.

Although Indian, Mexican, and Asian children in Tulare and Kings Counties continued to experience discrimination in different forms, by the turn of the century they had been largely accepted into local public schools. The major exception was the children of the Tule River Indian Reservation in Tulare County and the Ramona Rancheria in Kings County. The U.S. Bureau of Indian Affairs established and ran a school on the Tule River reservation from 1866 until 1932, when control was passed to Tulare County.[97] Conditions at reservation schools were apparently dismal. Georgiana Carden, the state attendance officer, described the Ramona Rancheria school in the 1920s thus:

On to Hanford and go with Mrs. Ayes to two schools—the Mussel Slough and the Ramona (Indian). Clear up understanding of compulsory law at the first and go with the teacher to see the equipment at the latter, it being rather late in the day. This school is just a wreck and the worst, by far, of any yet seen. The teacher [is] a unique little person, a German who has just finished U.C. The building is tottering, there is but one toilet, the water supply is from an 8 ft. well which stands 40 ft. from the toilet—17 children in all. Stopped at one Indian home on the Rancheria and talked to the girls—a hapless place—[98]

Carden, who saw herself as an advocate of Indian interests, complained to Dr. Taylor, the Indian agent in Porterville, who promised a new schoolhouse. The Ramona school was eventually closed, and the Indian children from the rancheria integrated into the county schools.

When the school on the Tule River reservation was run by the Bureau of Indian Affairs, it was used to teach Indian children what were considered healthy habits and to prepare them for menial work.[99] According to one early newspaper account, "Girls receive instruction in all kinds of housework, and the boys in general work. The boys are required to work at least three hours a day."[100] Further education was obtained at Indian boarding schools, which for Tule River reservation children usually meant Sherman Institute in Riverside. Indian children who lived off the reservation apparently attended local schools, although public school districts in California were still allowed to provide segregated schools for Indian children if they wished until 1935.

Some Mexican children in Tulare County attended the Visalia Colored School before it closed in 1890; from 1861 to 1871 others were given free tuition at Father Dade's early Academy of the Nativity.[101] By the early twentieth century Mexican children seem to have been accepted into the local public schools.

There were very few Chinese children in Tulare County in the nineteenth century, since discriminatory immigration policies made it difficult for Chinese women and children to enter the United States. As we have seen, however, Hanford in Kings County did have a small Chinese community. These children attended both the Hanford public schools and an after-school Chinese class held in the back room of the Taoist temple, which started up in 1922. According to Richard Wing, who grew up in Hanford, the Chinese school was autonomous and under the control of the local Chinese community, subsidized by the gambling houses and merchants of China Alley. Wing quoted a former superintendent's description of the school: "It was run by the Chinese, run by the Tongs. They would go to school. Let's see, we would get out, the public school, at 3:30. And they would go to the Chinese schools. There were also Japanese schools. And they had their own teachers and educational system. Nobody knew much about what they did because it was a foreign language." Wing, who attended the Chinese School for seven years, noted: "Before the Second World War, the Chinese born here in Hanford, they all could speak and write the Chinese language fluently."[102] He also mentioned that the teachers at the Chinese school in Hanford were well-known scholars from China. The Chinese school apparently closed during the Second World War.

Japanese children, too, attended family-supported Saturday schools for Japanese language and culture, such as the Japanese school on the Uota ranch near Farmersville in Tulare County.[103] Japanese children in Tulare and Kings Counties were accepted in the public schools from the beginning, although after-school and Saturday Japanese schools remained common, particularly during the 1920s and 1930s. A similar pattern emerged in the Armenian community, where children attended regular public schools but learned Armenian language and culture in a special Armenian school, the first of which was established at Yettem in 1912.

The Teaching Population of Tulare and
Kings Counties

Since California did not have a system of rural school inspectors or
supervisors until 1921, there are no records of official visits from which
descriptions of individual teachers or classrooms can be gleaned.[104] Nevertheless, other valuable sources do exist from which certain types of information can be obtained. The U.S. manuscript censuses undertaken
during the period 1870–1920, for example, provide considerable statistical information about the teaching population of Tulare and Kings
Counties.[105] Indeed, this source is the closest thing we have to accurate
evidence of the changing composition of the teaching population.[106]
Census records can be augmented by school records, though in the case
of Tulare and Kings Counties, unfortunately, only fragmentary school
records survive. The numbers of men and women teachers for some
years between 1852 and 1932 appear in the biennial reports of the California Superintendent of Public Instruction, and a handwritten list of
teachers' names from Tulare County for the period 1880–91 is available
on microfilm in the California State Archives. Otherwise, it is impossible
to trace specific teachers' careers in Tulare and Kings Counties before
1910, when school directories began to be published.

As was typical of other Western frontier areas, Tulare and Kings Counties had predominantly male populations well into the first decades of
the twentieth century. In 1890, Tulare County was 58 percent male, with
12,805 men and 9,127 women; in 1920, there were 25,711 men (53 percent of the total population) and 22,865 women. Similarly, in 1900 Kings
County had 5,672 men (57 percent) and 4,199 women; and in 1920,
12,131 men (55 percent) and 9,900 women. This continued gender dis-
crepancy likely reflects the large number of single male farm laborers.
But men held virtually all the political and economic power as well and
owned most of the property. And violence, including racist violence, was
the province of men, the legacy to some extent of the early frontier but
also reflecting generally accepted social norms.

Although women contributed their labor to household and ranch
economies and held some jobs in towns, they were not seen as working
in the public sphere.[107] Of course, women always did work—as servants,
laundresses, boardinghouse keepers, waitresses, barmaids, and prosti-
tutes. And a small number of women in the West found work in untradi-
tional fields, such as photography.[108] By 1900, women began to find work
as typists and stenographers and as clerks in stores.[109] Nevertheless,
throughout the period 1850–1920 in Tulare and Kings Counties, teach-

ing provided what was probably the most acceptable form of paid work for educated women—although of course, like office or sales work, it was open only to white women.

As elsewhere in the United States, the number of women teachers in Tulare County increased over the course of the nineteenth century. Early on, most teachers were men; in 1865, for example, there were thirteen men and two women teaching in the county. When the population began to climb following the arrival of the Southern Pacific in 1872, the schools followed suit, increasing in number from 31 in 1872 to 73 in 1878, to 101 in 1883. As the number of schools grew, the percentage of women teachers increased as well, from 42 percent in 1870 to a peak of 92 percent in 1920. What is striking about the numbers in Table 4 is not just the shift in percentages, but the shift in actual numbers of teachers. Over the forty years from 1880 to 1920, the number of male elementary school teachers dropped from 41 to 34, while the number of women teachers increased tenfold, from 40 to 429. The resurgence of male teachers by 1940 doubtless reflects the impact of the depression, but it also reflects the trend toward specialization. Many of these men taught vocational education, music, or physical education in the larger graded schools or taught the upper elementary grades (seventh and eighth).

School reports are probably fairly accurate in terms of the numbers of men and women teachers, but they provide no clues about teachers' ages or household composition. That information may be found in the U.S. manuscript censuses. This source, however, presents a different set of problems, particularly for the nineteenth century, when far fewer

TABLE 4

*Teachers in Tulare and Kings Counties
by Gender, 1870–1940*

	Men	Women
1870[a]	15 (58%)	11 (42%)
1880[a]	41 (51%)	40 (49%)
1890[a]	50 (34%)	97 (66%)
1900[ac]	57 (28%)	148 (72%)
1910[bc]	37 (14%)	234 (86%)
1920[bc]	34 (7%)	429 (93%)
1930[bc]	44 (7%)	563 (93%)
1940[bc]	128 (18%)	598 (82%)

SOURCE: California Superintendent of Public Instruction, Biennial Reports for 1870, 1880, 1890, 1900, 1910, 1920, 1930, and 1940.

[a] All schools.
[b] Elementary schools only.
[c] Includes Kings County.

TABLE 5
Residence of Tulare and Kings County Teachers, 1880–1920

	Women			
	Boarder	Dependent	Head	Married
1880[a]	4 (24%)	13 (76%)	0	0
1900[b]	13 (18%)	65 (73%)	3 (3%)	6 (6%)
1910[b]	72 (32%)	115 (51%)	14 (6%)	24 (11%)
1920[b]	104 (26%)	189 (47%)	41 (10%)	66 (17%)
	Men			
	Boarder	Dependent	Head	Married
1880[a]	10 (29%)	7 (20%)	17 (50%)	15 (44%)
1900[b]	7 (19%)	7 (19%)	23 (62%)	21 (56%)
1910[b]	9 (22%)	5 (12%)	27 (66%)	23 (56%)
1920[b]	4 (6%)	8 (13%)	49 (78%)	47 (77%)

SOURCE: U.S. Bureau of the Census, Manuscript Censuses for 1880, 1900, 1910, and 1920.

[a]All schools.
[b]Elementary schools only.

TABLE 6
Mean Age of Tulare and Kings County Teachers, 1880–1920

	Women			
	Boarder	Dependent	Head	Married
1880[a]	31.0	21.6	n/a	n/a
1900[b]	29.0	26.3	31.0	41.3
1910[b]	28.7	26.1	40.7	35.7
1920[b]	28.0	26.9	37.7	36.0
	Men			
	Boarder	Dependent	Head	Married
1880[a]	31.6	24.0	31.5	31.7
1900[b]	32.2	24.8	37.9	38.0
1910[b]	28.8	23.0	39.9	39.3
1920[b]	27.8	26.9	34.5	34.4

SOURCE: U.S. Bureau of the Census, Manuscript Censuses for 1880, 1900, 1910, and 1920.

[a]All schools.
[b]Elementary schools only.

teachers are listed for Kings and Tulare Counties than are included in school records. (For instance, for 1880 the census includes only fifty-one teachers, whereas the school records list eighty-one.) Nevertheless, if we take the census as a kind of sample of the teaching population, rather than a precise record, it does provide an invaluable source of demographic information (Tables 5 and 6).[110]

Although according to the school records, the Tulare County teaching population in 1880 was evenly divided between men and women (41 to 40), the fifty-one people who identified themselves as teachers in the 1880 manuscript census are more skewed: 34 men to 17 women. This may reveal the bias of the census takers, who perhaps assumed that women would not work, or it might indicate a reluctance on the part of women to state that they were employed. In any case, the 1880 census reveals three different groupings. The first is composed of older (mean age 31), exclusively male teachers, typically married and heads of households. For these men, teaching in winter three-month schools may have been a way to supplement their income as farmers; it may have been a temporary way of making a living before acquiring land or more lucrative work; or it may have served as a long-term career. The second group consists of unmarried, younger teachers—both men and women, typically in their early twenties—who lived with relatives or parents. These younger teachers were likely contributing to the household economy by bringing in a cash income, thus continuing an earlier conception of a household economy in which men and women, young and old, were expected to contribute. The third group comprises either boarders in all-male boardinghouses (six men) or lodgers in family households (four women and four men).

The average career length for some of the teachers listed in the 1880 census can be ascertained for the period 1880–90 by means of county school records.[111] Men listed in both sources taught for an average of 2.8 years, women for 2.6 years. These figures are strikingly similar to those published in a 1910 survey by Lotus Coffman, *The Social Composition of the Teaching Population*, whose rural respondents averaged two years' teaching experience. Averages like these, however, obscure individual career trajectories. Among the men listed as heads of household in 1880, for example, were two single men, W. F. Dean and J. M. Brooks, whose careers as rural one- and two-room school teachers can be traced continuously from 1880 at least through 1900; and among the women one finds such exceptional teachers as Anna Mills Johnston, who made a significant career of teaching. On the other hand, six men who list their occupation as teacher in the 1880 census do not appear at all in the 1880–90 school records, and none of the women in the 1880 census taught continuously between 1880 and 1890. Of the seventeen women listed, fourteen taught between two and four years. Most likely these young women married after teaching a few years, in keeping with general assumptions about women teachers of the common school era.

Discrepancies between school records and the manuscript census still exist in 1900: whereas the Tulare County school records list 107 women and 37 men, the census lists only 74 women and 32 men; meanwhile, the school records for Kings County, formed in 1893 and still very lightly populated, list 45 women and 11 men, compared to 16 women and 5 men in the census. Despite these inconsistencies, it is notable that the ratio of men and women teachers in the census (71 percent women, 29 percent men) is very similar to that of the school records (76 percent women, 24 percent men). Male teachers in 1900 tended to be somewhat older than women, and more than half of them were married. Only 7 percent of women teachers in the 1900 Kings and Tulare County censuses were married. These statistics are typical of national figures, reflecting as they do the customary if not statutory bar on married women teachers.

The most striking difference between the census figures of 1900 and those of 1880 is the much larger group of women compared to men teachers, a shift consistent with trends nationwide. Patterns of household composition for men and women remained fairly consistent, however. In 1900 as in 1880, the largest group of women teachers were in their twenties and lived with their parents. By 1900, this group had become the largest category of teachers in Tulare and Kings Counties. Seventy-three percent of women teachers lived as dependents in families, compared to only 19 percent of men. In contrast, 62 percent of men teachers were heads of households, and virtually all of them (21 out of 23) were married. In 1880 no married women teachers were employed in the county; in 1900, however, six women teachers were married. In 1900, moreover, three women listed themselves as heads of households. One of them was Carrie Barnett, a thirty-two-year-old single woman who owned her own home in Visalia, supported her sister and nephew, and later became principal of the Visalia graded school.

In terms of the age of teachers in various categories, the most significant change in the period 1880–1900 is the mean age of dependent women, which increased from 21.6 to 26.3, and which may indicate longer teaching careers. Single men living as dependents were approximately the same age in 1900 as in 1880 (24 to 25 years old). This almost certainly reflects a situation in which young men worked for a time as teachers before setting up independent households of their own. The mean ages of men who were heads of households, in contrast, rose markedly between 1800 and 1900, from 31.5 to 37.9. It seems a reasonable assumption that these older men who were heads of households in 1900 had made teaching a career.

In 1910, the data in the manuscript census and school records are in closer agreement, the former listing under the category "teacher" 225 women and 42 men, the latter listing 234 women and 37 men. The most striking change relative to 1900 is in the number of women boarders, who increase from 14 percent of women teachers generally to 32 percent. This increase doubtless reflects changing cultural expectations of women and their move from domestic to wage work. An upward trend occurs also in the employment of women as teachers. According to the census, in 1910, 81 percent of those who identified themselves as teachers were women, as opposed to 70 percent in 1900.

In the 1920 census, although the percentage of women teachers who lived as boarders fell somewhat (to 26 percent of all women teachers), now 11 percent of women teachers list themselves as heads of households, and 16 percent are married. The percentage of women living with their parents or other relatives is still fairly high at 47 percent—but considerably lower than the 1880 figure of 77 percent. Men, for their part, are increasingly married and heads of households—78 percent as of 1920. By that year, clearly, teaching for both men and women was a viable career path.

The Growth of the Educational State, 1900–1930

The first three decades of the twentieth century saw an expansion of state control over education. At the same time, local community interests continued to shape school practices. Mediating community and the state were the elected county superintendents. Tulare and Kings County superintendents, like other education professionals throughout the United States in the early twentieth century, respected efficiency and business values. David Tyack and Elisabeth Hansot call these educators "administrative progressives," eager to introduce order and progress into the schools by means of such innovations as a longer school year, improved sanitation, modern school buildings and equipment, and more careful monitoring of curriculum.[112] These officials reflected community pride in local schools—a pride that contrasts strikingly with the anxieties over the "rural school problem" expressed by state and national officials.

One of the most successful of these early-twentieth-century administrators was J. E. Buckman of Tulare County, who served as county superintendent of schools between 1911 and 1935. The son of early settlers, Buckman graduated from the Visalia normal school in 1882 at the age of eighteen and worked in Tulare County schools for the rest of his life. A friend to leading business and professional men of the county, he was proud that, as he put it, "many of our most prominent people have been closely identified, either as trustees or teachers, with the educational system of our county."[113] Buckman's pride in the schools is captured in this celebratory account:

From 1912 to 1923 our schools were engulfed in a tremendous building wave; old buildings everywhere were razed or abandoned and new modern, up-to-date buildings took their places, so that today our county is one of the foremost counties of the state in regard to value and convenience of its buildings, modern light, modern sanitary conditions, modern heating, and modern ventilating systems. Curriculums have been reorganized, teachers have been better trained, school terms have been extended to full nine months, and it may be truthfully said that Tulare County is the peer of any county in California in the support and care of its children.[114]

Buckman followed a conservative and traditional approach to education. Although innovations such as testing and rural supervision were introduced during Buckman's tenure, he did not champion these changes himself, but instead looked back to an earlier model of the county superintendent as both representative and defender of small-town community and culture.

In Kings County the period 1902–34 saw the election of three women school superintendents: Nannie Davidson, M. L. (Lee) Richmond, and Elsie Bozeman. The reasons for their election are not entirely clear. Perhaps the very definition of the position was unstable in this period, reflecting the contradictory views of women educators in general. Kings County did tend to characterize itself as "prosperous and forward looking," however, and so may simply have considered women equal to the task, whereas Tulare County, which prided itself on its frontier individualism and traditional ways, may have been more resistant. In any event, from 1902 to 1914 the Kings County superintendent of schools was Nannie Davidson, mother of nine and widow of a well-known local physician. While Davidson often called upon her experience as a mother in defending her suitability for the position, she also emphasized her "progressive" views and the advances Kings County schools had made during her terms as superintendent.[115] Davidson was succeeded by Joe Meadows, a longtime teacher and administrator who, in more typical male fashion, pointed to his business experience and contacts as qualification for the post of superintendent.[116]

In 1918, however, another woman, Lee Richmond, was elected superintendent. Serving until 1926, she was seen as one of the more "forward-looking" educators not only in the Valley but in the state as a whole. In

one article, Richmond described how Kings County's "progressive program [was] putting into practice the principles upon which modern education should be based."[117] Richmond's staff was made up entirely of
women, including for three years the young Helen Heffernan.

In 1926 Richmond was defeated in her bid for reelection by Elsie
Bozeman. Bozeman was a member of the Daughters of the American
Revolution (DAR), the Women's Christian Temperance Union (WCTU),
and the First Christian Church—factors that may have contributed to her
win. By the late 1920s these organizations, particularly the DAR and the
WCTU, exemplified "traditional" small-town society and culture. But
while Elsie Bozeman was conservative in a social sense, she was nevertheless up-to-date in her embrace of "scientific" methods of educational
management.

The attitudes of both superintendents and classroom teachers in this
period were influenced by such state-supported periodicals as the *Western
Journal of Education* and *Sierra Educational News,* the official publications
of the California Teachers Association. Between 1915 and 1921 the state
published the *California Blue Bulletin* as well, in which state officials presented their vision of modern and efficient schools and provided tips
and suggestions for teachers. Other educational journals were put out
by the normal schools, such as Fresno Normal School's *Educational Digest* (1914–16), with articles of particular interest to San Joaquin Valley
teachers. All of these periodicals made the editorial point that they were
concerned to address issues of classroom practice and method in a language that teachers could understand. Typical is this editorial in the first
issue of the *Educational Digest*:

The main feature is the digests—brief, crisp, to the point—tabloids of articles
that are likely to prove too abstruse, or too lengthy for the busy teacher to spare
the time for. . . . One feature that cannot be overestimated by local teachers will
be the letters each month from the Valley Counties' Superintendents to their
corps. Thanks to the cordial support of these, the valley teachers are to find
within easy access their necessary and authoritative instructions.[118]

Educational journals were widely disseminated to Tulare and Kings
County teachers, their pages filled with the concerns of state officials and
university experts—over patriotism, hygiene and sanitation, good manners, the construction of modern school buildings, and the beginnings
of the movement to test and classify children.[119] Descriptions of model
rural schoolhouses and even architectural plans were often included as
well.

A major concern of state officials and educational experts in this period was the "problem" of immigrant children and the need for what was
called "Americanization." Although Americanization programs were fo-

cused largely on the cities, educators in rural areas like the San Joaquin Valley also became caught up in the need to Americanize immigrant and non-English-speaking children.

An example of the ways in which ethnicity, gender, and class and class assumptions shaped these efforts can be seen in the description in the *Blue Bulletin* of an Americanization program that was set up in Bakersfield in the southern San Joaquin Valley for Mexican teenage girls. The program involved a special class emphasizing both instruction in English and homemaking skills, such "that they may improve their homes, and become self-supporting. By the same efforts they are mastering their English and more rapidly acquiring knowledge in the common school subjects." It was assumed that these teenagers not only attended classes but worked for wages as well: "Seven of the girls contribute to the support of their families by working in local homes on Saturdays, and from 3 P.M. until 7 P.M. on school days. The women employing these girls phone frequent reports of their work to the school and thus assist in their training." The girls were also expected to "prepare and serve lunch for 14 teachers, and also a free lunch for 30 under-nourished children in a school nearby."[120] It is not clear from this account whether this course of study would lead to high school diplomas or whether it was intended simply to prepare these girls to become servants for the middle-class families of Bakersfield. In any event, it is a striking example of the way in which "Americanization," conceived in ethnic, gender, and class terms, worked to preserve existing structures of power.

With the entry of the United States into the First World War in 1917, the attention of California educators turned to the need to support the war effort and to encourage patriotism. The Department of Education published pamphlets for teachers with such titles as "Guard the Schools as Well as the Trenches," "The Safeguard of Democracy," and "War Citizenship Lessons for the Elementary Schools." Tulare County Superintendent Buckman shared this enthusiastic patriotism. In an article in the *Educational Digest* he reminded teachers that "the law requires the flag to be displayed over each building and in each class room. The flag outside should be run up in the morning and lowered at night. To leave the flag up over night indicates that the school is besieged by enemies."[121] In the spring of 1917, a supplement was added to the Tulare County school manual that included the American's Creed and paragraphs supporting the Red Cross, war gardens, and the flag. These sentiments were then incorporated into subsequent manuals, in which the inculcation of patriotism was presented as a major responsibility of teachers. In 1924, as the result of a campaign by the Americanism Commission of the American Legion, the Pledge of Allegiance was required in schools throughout California. The Tulare County school manual included directions to teachers on how the pledge should be recited: "Standing thus, all repeat together slowly, the Flag salute. At the words 'to the Flag,' the right hand is extended gracefully, palm upward, towards the Flag, and remains in this gesture till the end of the affirmation, whereupon all hands immediately drop to the side." The same manual states that "the chief object of our public schools should be to teach our boys and girls to become good American citizens."[122] This emphasis on patriotic symbolism (the salute to the flag, for example) differed from the ideas of "citizenship" in earlier school manuals. Rather than focusing on the need for children to become responsible participants in democracy, the later manuals emphasized obedience and uncritical love of country.

Patriotism was also encouraged through increasingly elaborate end-of-year school programs and pageants.[123] School graduation ceremonies in Tulare County had always celebrated the glories of the state, with addresses such as "A Tribute to Father Serra" and "Pastoral Days in California," the presentation of the bear flag, the singing of the state song, and regional poems and recitations.[124] With the coming of the First World War, however, such programs evolved into major performances, such as the "Patriotic Pageant 'Triumph of Democracy'" performed at an elementary school graduation in Visalia in 1918. In this pageant, the history of U.S. involvement in the war was presented as a kind of morality play: first "the Spirit of the Sea arouses peaceful America with the reality of European war"; after the successful intervention of American troops, "despondent America is aroused by news of victory. Her troops return. The Allies express their gratitude. The Spirit of Democracy states the new ideals that must govern the world." In the performance, children played roles such as Uncle Sam, Railroad Magnate, Laborer, Red Cross Worker, and countries like Costa Rica and Guatemala.[125]

Perhaps the most dramatic example of a local pageant in these years was the Valley of the Sun pageant, presented in the foothills near Woodlake in Tulare County on May Day, 1926. The pageant, in which both schoolchildren and local residents participated, was written by Virginia Stapp, a well-known teacher and principal. It was the focus of activities in the schools around Woodlake during the school year of 1925–26. In her autobiography, local resident Grace Pogue provided a description of the pageant, which portrayed the history of the San Joaquin Valley from a mythical time, before the Indians came, down to the time of its presentation, May 1, 1926.

There were more than seven hundred in the cast, all appropriately costumed. Every school in the Woodlake Union High School district was represented. It was presented in a lovely natural bowl on the Sentinel Butte Ranch. More than ten thousand people came from far and near to witness its presentation. Spectators and neighboring newspapers were generous in their praise. The Fox News and Pathe News men were on hand to film the pageant. Harry Goldman was chairman of the Pageant Committee. He had forty men of the community working on the stage, concessions and booths as well as seats for the spectators. Jeff Davis and Lon Calvin arranged a true-to-life Indian village with the Indians, themselves, on hand to make acorn bread, weave baskets, and reproduce the old Indian dances. . . . The woodland scene with its flowers and butterflies, bluebirds and bees, its Sun Maidens and Clouds was a beautiful fantasia. The Indians, the Spaniards, the cowboys, the ranchers, the tourists made the history of our valley live in the minds of their audience. Education and Religion played their part.

The Indian Spirit told the story of Creation in the first episode. In the last scene, he reviewed the sharing of this land, its birds and flowers and fruits with the white people. Summing it all up and looking down the long vista of the future he concluded, "And everywhere there shall be Peace."[126]

In the Valley of the Sun pageant, the racism, violence, and greed that marked the county's development were erased, and the history of the valley was reshaped as one of peaceful cooperation between Spaniards, Indians, and "the white people." Even the attitude toward the natural world, which in reality had involved destruction of the natural landscape for profit, was transformed into a celebration of "sharing of this land, its birds and flowers and fruits." The response of the local Indians, "on hand to make acorn bread, weave baskets, and reproduce the old Indian dances," has not been recorded. And the contributions of Chinese and Japanese immigrants, among others, were not even acknowledged. Pageants like this one, involving the active reconstruction of a past history, were common in California in the early decades of the twentieth century. The history told in the Valley of the Sun pageant in a sense defined the imagined identity of the white Protestants who held power in the valley. We can only speculate about the impact participation in such a spectacle had on children, the sense of excitement and drama that must have made a strong impression on children, and probably adults as well.

Through celebrations of a nostalgic history such as the Valley of the Sun pageant, schools helped to create and maintain an imaginary community. Beginning in the 1920s, however, schools began to serve a different function: that of categorizing and sorting children by means of standardized testing. This emphasis on quantification and measurement, which has become synonymous with public schools, was foreign to the nineteenth-century conception of the local school.

In areas like Tulare and Kings Counties, schooling in the nineteenth and early twentieth centuries was framed by the ideological assumptions of the common school movement, in which citizenship and the acquisition of literacy and numeracy skills were emphasized for all students. Although racist assumptions profoundly limited this ideal (as did class differences), in the relatively homogeneous public schools of Tulare and Kings Counties the task of teachers in the nineteenth and early twentieth centuries seemed comparatively straightforward. Children were assumed to be able to learn a common curriculum through the eighth grade that would prepare them for life.

The teachers manuals that guided rural teachers demonstrate these assumptions. According to the Kings County school manual for 1908, for example, the aim of arithmetic instruction was to enable children to solve "such problems as are likely to occur in practical life"; reading meant not only "accurate comprehension" but also "the cultivation of a taste for pure, wholesome literature." Perhaps the most important subject (at least judging from the extensive discussion in the school manuals) was U.S. history and civics. "The cost of the public schools of the state is returned in the product of the schools—the citizens of the state." Only a thorough grounding in U.S. history and a strong knowledge of government would prepare these pupils to be responsible citizens.[127] The Tulare County school manual for 1911 presents a similar picture of the connection between school subjects and the practical life of the community. Here, however, the moral dimension of schooling takes on an added weight. In terms of civics, for example, the Tulare County manual emphasized the "aim to inspire in all of the pupils the desire to become self-governing individuals"; to this end it called for "Ethical Training":

The teacher is frequently the sole inspiration to the pupil whose home surroundings are unfortunate, so we should be very careful to be what we are trying to teach him to be. Practical morals and manners depend more upon habit than upon knowledge. It is not sufficient to know what is right, but one must also habitually do what is right. A teacher's attention should be directed rather to the formation of the habit of right thinking, right speaking and right acting on the part of the pupils than the formal teaching of the subject by set lessons.[128]

Striking in both of these teachers manuals is the assumption not only that schooling should have practical, political, and moral dimensions, but also that the course of study would be mastered by all students.

Beginning in the early twentieth century, both Tulare and Kings Counties began to employ a form of achievement assessment—a test on the Constitution that students had to pass in order to graduate from the eighth grade. In 1926 standardized IQ testing was introduced in Tulare County. In the same period, Elsie Bozeman wrote enthusiastically about centralized planning and the use of standardized tests in her summary of her work as Kings County superintendent of schools in the *Sierra Educational News*:

The county board of education took two advanced steps in curriculum-making by (1) correlating the social studies in all grades, following the Bagley-Kyte curriculum study; and (2) by adopting a reading course comprising five types of readers: (a) method reader, (b) a work-type reader, (c) a science reader, (d) character reader, (e) literature readers.

An educational guidance study of all the eighth grade pupils' of the county has been made, including (1) intelligence tests, (2) standard achievement test, (3) character trait rating, (4) case study of the family as to factors affecting further study, special abilities, disabilities and inhibitions. These studies were passed on to the high schools for their information. Classification is in accordance with these studies.

Through the use of work-books and outlines, all the one- and two-teacher schools of the county are conducted on the "individual instruction" plan, within grades. The county course of study is followed, the grades are preserved, and promotions are made much as usual. Individual records, progress, and achievement profiles are kept.[129]

Testing was well established by the mid-1930s. Teachers were now required to give both intelligence and reading tests to their pupils twice a year and were encouraged to read children's previous year's tests and make graphs to follow their progress.[130] Although country teachers continued to have greater day-to-day autonomy than teachers in graded town schools, they were increasingly held accountable for their students' work, through both the surveillance of supervisors and these standardized measures.

The Great Depression

In the prosperous early 1920s, as population increased in both Tulare and Kings Counties, local communities supported the building of new schools and greater spending on education in general. In 1922, for example, when the town of Dinuba in Tulare County needed a new school, the school bond issue passed by a vote of 318 to 29.[131] By the late 1920s, however, the earlier sense of prosperity was rapidly being eroded. With the agricultural depression, schools were faced with a shrinking tax base and smaller budgets. Some towns in the eastern part of the two counties actually lost population in the early years of the depression. In Dinuba, for example, average daily school attendance dropped from 940 to 662 between 1923 and 1934.[132] By 1932, school budgets had been cut throughout the two counties; teachers' salaries were reduced, construction of new schools ceased, orders for new school buses were rescinded, and classroom supplies became scarce.[133] Fortunately, the passage in 1933 of the public schools funding initiative provided a secure base of support throughout the depression.

The intense political climate of the early 1930s also affected school politics in Tulare and Kings Counties. In 1934, Elsie Bozeman was defeated by Joe Meadows, who had previously served as county superintendent for one term between 1914 and 1918. Supported by local businessmen, Meadows served until 1942. Meanwhile, when J. E. Buckman retired in 1934 after twenty-four years as Tulare County superintendent of schools, Roy Driggers, a more liberal educator sympathetic to the ideas of Helen Heffernan and her followers in the California Department of Education, was elected in his place. Driggers gave enthusiastic descriptions of Tulare County schools in articles in both the *Sierra Educational News* and the *Western Journal of Education*.[134] The revised Tulare County school manual of 1936 clearly reveals the impact of Driggers's progressive ideas. In a section called "Transition from Old to New," for example, the "traditional school" is juxtaposed to the "modern school." In the traditional school "the teacher is a taskmaster," whereas in the modern school "the teacher is a guide and counselor." Instead of "conformity," the school should emphasize "creative self-expression." Instead of "formal desks and seats screwed to the floor and arranged in fixed rows," there will be "informal table and chairs arranged conveniently for group activity."[135] In 1936 Driggers also established the *Tulare County Schools Bulletin*, a newsletter published every month during the school year for classroom teachers and administrators that served as a conduit for Driggers's progressive ideas. Driggers began the first *Bulletin* with this quotation from Dewey: "What the best and wisest parent wants for his own child, that must the community want for all its children. Any other ideal for our schools is narrow and unlovely."[136] In another early *Bulletin* Driggers included the following excerpt from an address by Grayson Kefauver, dean of the School of Education at Stanford:

The freedom of the teachers to work with students in a study of all aspects of contemporary life and all problems should be guaranteed. Individuals and minority groups in the community should not be allowed to force avoidance of consideration of important problems in order to create public ignorance of important issues so as to serve the personal interests or to humor the prejudices of those exerting the pressure.[137]

Given the generally conservative climate of Tulare County, Driggers may well simply have been defending his own liberal and progressive ideas.

One difficult problem with which school officials in both Tulare and Kings Counties were faced during the depression years was the schooling of the children of migrant agricultural workers. In 1927, the state counted 36,891 children as migratory, and this figure seems to have remained fairly constant through the 1930s.[138] By the mid-1930s, many of these workers were white refugees from the Dust Bowl. Although the familiar image of these migrant children, as photographed by Dorothea Lange and depicted in the novel and film *The Grapes of Wrath*, has come to define migrant farm labor in depression-era California, the first migrant children were those of Mexican, and later African-American, families, groups that continued to work as migrant farm laborers throughout the depression and later.[139]

Beginning in the late 1920s, emergency schools were established in labor camps for the children of these migratory farm workers. Lack of equipment, books, and adequately trained teachers was common in these schools. Clara Coldwell, a rural supervisor from Kings County, commented in 1927:

Teaching the children of seasonal workers is a difficult school problem in California today. This is so because of the short period of time some children are able to spend in the same school, because of the different ages and different grades of the pupils, because of the lack of equipment in most of the seasonal schools, because of the shortage of suitable textbooks for the type of pupil in the seasonal school and because of the lack of training of the teachers in the seasonal school in this highly specialized work.[140]

Some communities provided charity to support the migrant children in the emergency schools. In nearby Fresno County in 1929, for example, a check for $7.50 was given by the local chapter of the DAR for the migratory schools in the county. Frances Averill, a Fresno County rural supervisor, reported:

We purchased canned milk, chocolate, oranges, and graham crackers, and served a mid-morning lunch to six of the children whom the nurse felt would be particularly benefited. At the end of a week and a half the two underweight children had gained eight to ten pounds each. Two large boxes of used clothing were also donated by the same chapter of the Daughters of the American Revolution.[141]

Occasionally, ranchers themselves provided free lunches for children in their labor camps. Clinton Merritt, the owner of Tagus Ranch in Tulare County, was one such benefactor; for many years he sponsored a hot lunch program at the "model" emergency school for migrant workers on his ranch.[142]

Both state and federal agencies attempted to meet the needs of migrant children. The Works Progress Administration (WPA) established various projects in Tulare and Kings County schools. In Tulare County in the mid-1930s, for example, the WPA provided hot lunches in nine schools, employing twenty cooks and assistants. Hazel Ledbetter, a long-time rural principal, was appointed by the WPA as supervisor of the Tulare County Recreation Project, which operated twelve centers.[143] In the early 1930s, a Doctor Gifford from the State Bureau of Child Hygiene held a monthly clinic at a selected Tulare County school for first-grade and preschool children from six or seven adjacent school districts. Two other local doctors held monthly clinics in schools "where the children seemed below par, either in weight or vitality."[144]

Although state and federal programs sought to provide health and educational services to migrant children, local growers continued to see these children primarily as potential workers. During the October 1933 Pixley cotton strike, for example, growers argued for a school holiday so children could act as strike breakers and pick the cotton. Sociologist Paul Taylor reported:

Children were picking on a number of ranches, while on two west of Tulare there were several crews of twenty or more students taking advantage of the opportunity to assist the farmers and at the same time earn a few extra dollars spending money. Meanwhile businessmen and growers gathered in groups today and discussed the situation, urging that a general meeting be called at which time a formal request would be made to citizens and students for a school holiday in order that all who could would be enabled to reap part of the $6,000 per day paid out in labor in this district for cotton picking.[145]

This proposal to replace education with fieldwork was protested by liberal observers, who raised the issue with President Roosevelt and used it as an example of local growers' callousness. Although the proposal was never put into effect, school officials in agricultural counties often cooperated with ranchers in other ways. State Attendance Officer Georgiana Carden, a strong supporter of the interests of the growers, described the migratory schools at Corcoran in Kings County in the 1920s thus:

It is essential that the financing of school provisions for migratory children be determined in a way to meet the demand of the initial year. Such demands, for instance, as arose in the district of Corcoran when with the coming of the cotton, the numerical need for teachers arose from ten to nineteen. The story of meeting this need is one that redowns [sic] to the glory of that town's sense of civic responsibility. Growers, townspeople, high-school districts, and teachers all helped. Three additional schools were set up in the cotton fields. A special supervisor of attendance was employed and every child was provided for educationally during the cotton season.[146]

In an interview, a former Kings County administrator recalled the 1930s:

The people lived in labor camps out in the field, housed at first in Army tents, later in one-room buildings. With hundreds of children in scattered school districts, it was a problem at first to get a migrant school organized and then to get the children to the school. Classes were held in barns and tents. . . . Desks were the old-fashioned two to a bench type. There were no lights at first and the rooms were heated by a coal stove. . . . Some days there were fifty children, and other days there were ten, depending on the weather. All children picked cotton when they could. The teacher often had to round up the children.

According to this official: "We looked the other way sometimes in the sense that the kids would pick cotton on certain times, well they'd do it after school and before school. So they'd arrange their school time so that they could get maybe 3 or 4 hours of cotton picking in to supplement the family income." Although the state clearly required children to attend school and the county had appointed school attendance officers to enforce compulsory education laws, Kings County education officials seemed to listen more to the demands of the growers than to the laws of the state:

We had nurses and attendance people. But the attendance people didn't do anything except [to] the flagrant offenders. . . . Because, so what, what can you do with them? And the thing the school was interested in those days was your average daily attendance, you got your money from the state on that. So, you tried to get the kids in as long as you could. And what you did, you adjusted the day to the minimum day and you'd get them there and then let them go out and work. We never had any problems that way, and the enforcement was leaning towards the growers rather than to the kids.

Both this official and Superintendent Roy Driggers in Tulare County were sympathetic to the needs of migrant children, but the power of local ranchers clearly shaped depression-era school policies in these rural counties as well.[147] By the late 1930s, the political climate in rural California was becoming increasingly conservative—a trend that probably led to Driggers's defeat in 1938, after having served only one term, by Theo Nickel, who continued as Tulare County superintendent of schools until 1949.[148]

Schools in Tulare and Kings Counties in the interwar years took on many of the characteristics that mark them still today. The reform legislation of 1921 mandating rural supervisors and the active and energetic involvement of Helen Heffernan as commissioner of rural and elementary education led to the introduction of progressive ideas in county institutes, teachers' magazines, and summer workshops and college courses, including those at Fresno State Teachers College, where a large number of Tulare and Kings County teachers were educated. At the same time, ideas of scientific measurement and accountability increasingly shaped both the curriculum and classroom practices. By 1940, children were routinely tested on their academic achievements and supposed innate abilities. But as the treatment of migrant children illustrates, local superintendents shaped educational practices not only in response to the dictates of the state, but also in response to the interests of local communities and elites.

Conclusion

As in other rural areas of the West, Tulare and Kings Counties experienced rapid increases in population and immigration and improved means of communication and production during the first several decades of the twentieth century. Although the vision of a homogeneous frontier society founded by "pioneers" persisted through the 1930s, in fact the two counties had the same racial and ethnic divisions that typified the United States as a whole. A key institution in the maintenance and reproduction of this social world was the school, in which citizenship, patriotism, manners, and morals were taught to all children in an attempt to forge a common culture. That this culture reflected the small-town and rural values of the majority of the population is hardly surprising.

In Tulare and Kings Counties, schools were viewed as symbols of progress and as the proud expression of local culture. Powerful as these assertions of a common rural culture were, they need to be examined in relation to the race and class composition of local communities and the way these communities reflected larger social and economic structures.[149] If this society was marked by assumptions of center and margin in terms of race, class and ethnicity, it was at least as profoundly shaped by conceptions of gender. By 1900 the teachers of the schools of Tulare and Kings Counties—the individuals who mediated this social and cultural world—were overwhelmingly women. Underlying both common schooling and progressive reform were assumptions about gender that justified continued male control of women teachers' work. But the growing bureaucratization and professionalization of teaching also provided women with the possibility for a new sense of autonomy. How were these ideological and institutional tensions played out in the lives of country women teachers? What was the role of these women in the rural society of Tulare and Kings Counties? How did ideological representations of them as women and as teachers shape their choices and understanding of their lives?

SUBJUGATED KNOWLEDGE: LIVES OF WOMEN TEACHERS, 1860-1920

In the years between 1860 and 1920, the work of teachers in California was gradually transformed. A longer school year, better pay, and higher standards of education and qualifications created both new definitions of teaching as women's work and new anxieties about women teachers. In cities, normal schools and schoolwomen's clubs provided sites for a separate women's culture. More generally, the suffrage movement raised challenges to patriarchal control of the public sphere, while new opportunities in clerical work, sales, and other fields arose. In rural California, by 1920 even small farming communities felt the impact of these changes to some degree, especially in increased job opportunities in the larger towns. The big-city struggles over gender and power, in education as well as other areas, remained relatively muted, however, surfacing most clearly in the campaigns for county superintendencies. Unlike Kate Ames of Napa County, for example, Tulare and Kings County teachers did not directly challenge what we today would call patriarchal practices or ideology. Although assumptions about gender in fact profoundly shaped their lives, these discursive categories were so fundamental to these women's construction of themselves that they were not remarked upon.

The lives of women teachers were shaped not only by conceptions of gender, but also by the power of race and class.[1] In the nineteenth century and well into the twentieth, in virtually all schools in California, only white teachers were hired. Clearly, race shaped the lives of teachers of color much more overtly than did gender. The same was in fact true for white teachers; however, their race privilege was so accepted as natural that it was not even mentioned.[2] Class also was an important element in the lives of teachers, since the work required a high degree of literacy and a culturally acceptable presentation of the self. Nonetheless, it is difficult to place teachers, particularly women teachers, within the class divisions of rural California. For many if not most of those women who became teachers, their work was a necessary source of income, for themselves or their families. Thus, by the criteria of wages alone, which were equivalent to those of skilled laborers, they would be considered part of the established working class. But they were not named as such, nor did they represent working-class values. Although women teachers did not control productive resources or wealth, they often spoke and represented themselves as what we would call middle class, as the conservers and defenders of the moral order. As a result, women teachers are represented in contemporary accounts and represent themselves as respected and respectable.

One of the limits to writing a history of rural teachers is the documentary evidence—or lack thereof. First, as we saw in Chapter 3, there is the quantitative evidence—the manuscript censuses and school records—which can establish numbers of teachers, along with their gender, age, marital status, and household structure. However, such records cannot capture individual life histories—the different ways women teachers used teaching to shape their identities, or the meaning the profession held for them. Understanding the subjective significance of teaching requires the examination of more impressionistic texts: letters, scrapbooks, and school manuals; newspaper columns celebrating "pioneer times"; memoirs included in locally published town histories; and autobiographical essays.[3] Between 1936 and 1940, the California Retired Teachers Association annually published collections in which teachers, looking back to pioneer times from the perspective of the increasingly bureaucratized, professionalized 1930s, recounted their experiences and created images of themselves and their work.[4]

For Tulare and Kings Counties in these early years, only a handful of extended teachers' narratives exist. Outstanding teachers and principals are described in memoirs of former pupils or in newspaper accounts of retirement ceremonies, and a few teachers left privately published autobiographies or newspaper articles summarizing their lives, but otherwise only fragmentary evidence remains for understanding what it meant to be a woman teacher in an early rural classroom. In the rest of this chapter, I attempt a reading of this evidence. In so doing, I speculate on the ways these women used teaching to construct themselves and consider some of the ways they were constructed in the accounts of others. These women followed a number of different paths; I have organized them into three basic groups: "seekers of power," "outsiders," and, by far the most common, "country schoolmarms." In each of the examples presented be-

low, the women's own accounts and those of observers draw upon various conventional images of the woman teacher to make sense of the possibilities and meaning of their lives. By examining these specific lives, we
can begin to explore the ways in which ideologies, material constraints,
and personal understandings shaped these women—both as women and
as teachers.

Seekers of Power

Although many women teachers in Tulare and Kings Counties in the
nineteenth and early twentieth centuries seem to have followed the pattern of teaching briefly before marriage while contributing to a household income, others used teaching to build lasting careers and to gain
independence, power, or adventure. As we have seen, in the period
1890–1920 women in California were elected as county superintendents,
found careers as normal school instructors, and began to create a
woman-defined culture in the cities. These women were frequently supporters of the suffrage and temperance movements and members of
women's clubs. In rural areas, such ambitious women tended to live in
the largest towns—in Tulare County, Visalia; and in Kings County, Hanford. They sought positions of leadership in education as principals of
graded town schools, as county school superintendents, and in one case,
that of Nannie Davidson of Kings County, as state superintendent of public instruction. Opportunities for self-expression and leadership existed
for women in small country schools as well. Hazel Ledbetter, my mother's
first principal, worked in Tulare County schools for fifty years, between
1909 and 1959, serving in leadership roles in county and state organizations and speaking about school questions at conferences and meetings.
The position of principal allowed her to use her considerable talents in a
way that seemed to give her deep satisfaction. Accounts of women school
leaders such as these build upon traditional notions of women as moral
guardians, but also on less conventional, gender-neutral conceptions of
women as adventurers and strong leaders.

In this section I focus on three women leaders, Carrie Barnett and
Anna Mills Johnston of Visalia and Nannie Davidson of Hanford. All of
these women achieved success and recognition as educators, and some
documentation has survived of the lives of all three. These women all
spoke in terms of moral guardianship, standing up for the good of the
community in their role as ethical guide, but at the same time we can see
that teaching offered them an opportunity for adventure, material comfort, and personal pleasure.

Of these three women, we know least about Carrie Barnett, a teacher and for many years principal of Visalia's Tipton Lindsay Grammar School. She was born in California in 1868 and began teaching in a rural one-room school at the age of seventeen in 1885. She is listed in both the 1900 and 1910 censuses as head of household (one of three women teachers so listed in the 1900 Tulare County manuscript census), supporting her older sister and nephew. Her name is frequently mentioned in the social columns of the *Visalia Delta* and in accounts by school leaders. She never married. After her death in 1921 at the age of fifty-three, a new school in Visalia was named in her honor. Although Carrie Barnett was clearly a respected schoolwoman and powerful voice during her lifetime, she left no evidence of her personal life, and we know little else about her.

We know much more about Anna Mills Johnston, a well-known educator who taught in Tulare County schools between 1877 and 1901.[5] One of the five women teachers listed as boarders in the 1880 Tulare County census, Anna Mills was at this time an independent woman of twenty-six who supported herself through her teaching. Like Carrie Barnett, she became well connected to the "best" Visalia society, particularly through her friendship with George Stewart, the wealthy owner of the *Visalia Delta*. In 1914 she unsuccessfully ran for the office of Tulare County superintendent of schools. She died in 1921, the same year as Carrie Barnett.

The third woman, Nannie Davidson, had taught in country one-room schools as a young woman before her marriage in 1876 at the age of twenty-four. After her physician husband's death she returned to teach in the Hanford public schools before being elected Kings County superintendent of schools for the first of three times in 1902. In 1914 she ran for the position of state superintendent of public instruction but was defeated, whereupon she retired from public life.[6] She died twelve years later, in 1926.

These three women shared certain privileges. First of all, there was the unremarked power associated with their whiteness and Protestantism, characteristics they shared with the vast majority of public school teachers in Tulare and Kings Counties. Class was also a powerful, if unnamed, factor in their lives. All three women had connections through family or friendship with the most powerful local social and business leaders. Carrie Barnett, for example, owned her own house on the same block as Ben Maddox, the editor of one of Visalia's two newspapers and a well-known local leader. This choice location indicates both high social status in Visalia and the probability of some inherited wealth.

Anna Mills moved in the same circles. She moved to Visalia in 1881, after having taught in country schools near Porterville in southern Tulare County for four years. From newspaper accounts, it seems that she quickly succeeded in associating herself with the social and business elites of Visalia. Her name frequently appears in accounts of local social events, concerts, and pageants; she even played the Goddess of Virtue in the benefit spectacle "The Triumph of Love." There is some evidence that Anna Mills hoped to encourage a romantic interest in George Stewart, but their relationship did not develop.[7] George Stewart married another woman, and Anna Mills herself, at the age of thirty-two, married Robert "Tombstone" Johnston, a stonecutter and owner of the local gravestone works, in 1886. She then left teaching for six years. As a married woman she could not teach in the city schools of Visalia, so when she returned to teaching in 1892 she went instead to the country one- and two-room schools where married women were sometimes allowed to teach—first, from 1892 to 1896, at Ivanhoe, and then, from 1896 to 1900, at Elbow Creek. She finally retired from teaching in 1901; her last school was a one-room school at Eschom Valley in the foothills of the Sierra. In her years of retirement she traveled, making trips to Alaska and Europe, and involved herself with women's clubs and Visalia society.[8] Accounts of her luncheons and dinner parties appeared frequently in the society pages of the local Visalia newspapers; for example:

Mrs. Wilbur of San Francisco was honored most delightfully on Tuesday afternoon at a luncheon given by Mrs. Anna Mills Johnston. The living room was artistically decorated with immense yellow chrysanthemums, while the dining room had been converted into a perfect bower of French marigolds and it was in this room that the delicious luncheon was served. Pretty hand-painted place cards in the form of China tea cups, each with a clever little verse distinctive of the person, marked the places.[9]

The guests at these luncheons and dinners included the "best" families of Visalia.

Nannie Davidson also moved in socially respectable circles. Born Nannie Ellis in Texas in 1852, she came to the San Joaquin Valley with her family when she was a child. Her father, T. O. Ellis, was appointed school superintendent for Tulare County in 1860 and 1861 and later served in the same capacity in Merced County. As a teenager, Nannie worked in her father's office and thus became acquainted with the politics of local schooling. In 1876 she married Dr. J. A. Davidson, an Englishman who was a graduate of the Royal College of Surgery and Medicine in London.[10] Through her father and her husband, Nannie Davidson was connected to the most powerful families in Kings County. Later, as a widow with nine children, she used her own talents to expand these connections and to build her career as a teacher and county superintendent of schools.

All three of these women were described as outstanding teachers. Both Anna Mills and Nannie Davidson attended well-known and progressive normal schools—something that in the 1870s and 1880s only a small percentage of rural California teachers did. Anna Mills was educated at the Oswego Normal School in New York State, a center of Pestalozzian pedagogy and home of the progressive "Oswego method," one of the most advanced teaching methods of the time.[11] Nannie Davidson attended San Jose Normal School, at that time the only state-supported normal school in California.[12] Although Carrie Barnett passed the Tulare County teachers examination and had no further formal schooling, she was frequently mentioned in memoirs and contemporary newspaper accounts as an inspirational teacher.

Unfortunately, few descriptions of the teaching methods of these women have survived. When Anna Mills decided to leave New York for California in 1877 at the age of twenty-three, a newspaper account described her this way:

Miss Anna Mills, who has been teacher of our village school the past two terms, leaves May first for California where she will engage in teaching. She will make her home there with Mrs. Redfield (formerly Miss Jennie Hudson, of Mannsville). Miss Mills has been one of the most successful teachers in this part of the state, and the school commissioners, as well as the various localities where she has taught, give her highest praise.[13]

We know nothing of the qualities that led to this praise, but she seems to have been equally successful in her teaching in California. One of her pupils later remembered her as "an especially outstanding teacher. Intelligent, widely traveled, interesting and inspiring to her pupils."[14] Like a number of white women teachers of the time, Anna Mills became deeply interested in the culture and lives of the local Yokut Indians, and another former pupil remembered how she brought "Indian lore" to her teaching as well.[15]

These qualities of imagination and intellectual engagement seem to have been accompanied by considerable energy and organizational ability. Probably because of her social connections to the editors, both Visalia newspapers carried descriptions of school programs and ceremonies in her classrooms at Ivanhoe and Elbow Creek. An example is a *Visalia Times* account of "Bird Day" at Elbow Creek School: "Mrs. Anna M. Johnston, backed by a progressive board of trustees and a live school, has placed Elbow Creek at the very head of the procession in this particular exercise, for this is the first time in the history of the county that 'bird day' has been given recognition." People from all over the district attended the celebration, including the teacher and pupils of nearby Ivanhoe School. The *Times* reporter gave a detailed description of the decorations:

The interior of the room was a veritable bower of greenery. Ropes of evergreen extended across the room, and the walls were almost covered with palm leaves, branches of pepper tree, wreaths of ivy and other decorations. In the corners of the room were placed large branches cut from trees in which the nests just as built by the birds were still hanging. On one side of the room was a cage containing two live quails, while a number of stuffed ducks, quails, meadow larks and other birds adorned the blackboards, and several apt quotations from prominent authors were written thereon quite neatly.[16]

Although programs like this were common in country schools in the 1890s and into the twentieth century, Anna Mills Johnston's classrooms were apparently unusually elaborate and recall the descriptions of her luncheon and dinner parties for the best Visalia society.

No descriptions survive of Carrie Barnett's classrooms, but references to her teaching celebrate her intellectual and moral stature. In her eulogy upon Carrie Barnett's death, Elsie Crowley, herself later a respected principal in Visalia, recalled her time as a student in Carrie Barnett's classroom as one that "brought to me, as it did to many another, rich treasures; not only a very clear understanding of what was taught us from our textbooks, but also those greater and more important lessons in character building—optimism, determination to stand for the right, and ambition to do the very best possible." This emphasis on character and "standing for the right" is typical of accounts of Carrie Barnett. Elsie Crowley returns to Barnett's moral commitment in her description of her teaching: "It was not until I became principal of the Lincoln School, and we talked over together the general school problems, that I fully appreciated how very broad her views were, what a deep love for humanity she possessed, how staunch she was to stand for what she thought was right, and how carefully she considered every problem so that everyone would receive justice."[17]

Carrie Barnett's conception of universal justice and her belief that everyone should strive to be "the very best possible" echo the language of male school leaders of the time. Indeed, contemporary accounts present all three of these women as intelligent and inspirational teachers, rather than as the maternal nurturers so touted by common school reformers. Nevertheless, in their public involvement with social and political issues, all of them drew on representations of women's higher moral natures to justify their claim to speak for the common good.[18]

Women's claim to moral authority can be seen in Nannie Davidson's 1914 campaign for state superintendent of public instruction, where she used the traditional association of morality and motherhood to redefine the job of state superintendent and to challenge the business and professional model of school administration that dominated urban and university education. In her campaign statements Davidson consistently emphasized not only her experience as a school administrator but also, and more pointedly, her advantages as a woman and a mother. In the *Sierra Educational News*, for example, she wrote: "The trend of the times is progressive, and as the office of State Superintendent of Schools deals primarily with the education of the youth, woman is especially fitted for that position."[19] In her campaign statement issued to newspapers across the state, she argued that the superintendent of public instruction should do more than manage a large bureaucracy; she must also be "the friend and advocate of the children."

As a mother, a teacher, a County Superintendent of Schools, a co-worker with the other superintendents of the state in educational conventions and congresses, I have always kept in mind and worked to further the one maxim: First, last and always, the schools are for the children: give them the best possible teaching. Knowing my intention, I hope you will not deem me pretentious when I ask you, fathers and mothers, to support me in my endeavor to secure the nomination for Superintendent of Public Instruction of the State of California.[20]

The claim of women's moral authority can also be seen in these women's involvement in the temperance movement. Both Carrie Barnett and Anna Mills Johnston were active in the WCTU in Visalia, speaking out as women and educators for the good of the community and in particular of the children (though neither had children of her own). An example can be seen in a 1914 letter to the *Visalia Times* in which Barnett defended Visalia's benefits as a dry town. Two years earlier, the temperance forces had achieved the prohibition of saloons in Visalia; however, a large and vocal group continued to argue in favor of legalized drinking. One of their arguments was that prohibition led to the establishment of illegal and unregulated drinking places, called "blind pigs"; these were widely frequented by young men, who then fell into delinquent and violent behavior. Barnett was unswayed. Did any mother or father really believe, she asked, that "the best regulated saloon in the world is or can be a good place for children, for men, for women, for anybody? The seamy side of a number of lives has been revealed to me here in this little town through my school work, and I know whereof I speak." Barnett presents herself as an authority on the "seamy side" precisely because of her role as a teacher and principal. She goes on to challenge the citizens of Visalia to look to their moral responsibility to children, rather than to selfish pleasures:

If the citizens of Visalia (and I am one of them) took as much interest in the children of the community as they do in automobile races, citrus fairs and baseball they could have the cleanest, fairest city in the state. You can't just close up pool rooms, saloons, blind pigs, and questionable joints and hope to succeed unless you substitute clean, wholesome places. Stop being moral cowards. Make it so hot for those contributing to the delinquency of your children that they will be glad to stop. You can do it.[21]

In February 1914, 350 women marched through the streets of Visalia to demonstrate the strength of the women's auxiliary of the Good Government League, which supported prohibition. Both Carrie Barnett and Anna Mills Johnston spoke at a rally later that day in favor of keeping Visalia dry. According to a report in the *Visalia Times*, in her speech Johnston charged that "men and boys were being systematically plied with liquor to create sentiment in favor of the saloon as an improvement over existing conditions. 'It is part of the game,' she said, 'and the women of Visalia will not be deceived by the wild stories emanating from the "wet" agencies.'"[22]

Although these women did not hesitate to call on women's moral authority to defend the traditional ideals of their community, they actively challenged traditional gender ideology when it came to personal goals. Anna Mills Johnston, for example, was deeply committed to the temperance movement as a moral crusade in a way that is consistent with images of women's altruistic concern with children and community. But descriptions of Johnston's teaching and social life, and her own presentation of herself, highlight her ambition and use of teaching as a means to find personal pleasure and adventure. She moved to California as a young single woman of twenty-three, leaving her family behind in New York State. In 1878, the year after she arrived in Porterville, she became the first woman to climb Mt. Whitney, the highest mountain in the continental United States. She recalled this adventure vividly in an article she wrote for the *Mt. Whitney Club Journal* in 1902:

As no ladies had yet made the ascent of the real Mt. Whitney, we determined to be the first to stand on its lofty summit. So anxious was I to begin climbing, that I left Porterville two weeks ahead of the party, going as far as Dillon's Mill. There I spent two weeks peering into nature's beauties, enjoying the invigorating mountain air and the breath of the pines, which seemed to put new blood in my veins, and nothing I did in the way of climbing or walking did I consider too difficult to undertake.[23]

Johnston's narrative of the climb up Mt. Whitney is filled with adventure, danger, and obstacles overcome. For example, she describes her determination to climb the mountain thus: "Having been lame from early childhood" (a subject that, curiously, is mentioned nowhere else in the accounts of her life and accomplishments), "everybody said it would be utterly impossible for me to climb to the summit of Mt. Whitney. But I was not easily discouraged, and had always held to the idea that I could do what other people could—my surplus of determination making up for what I lacked in the power of locomotion."[24]

Anna Mills Johnston's narrative of the Mt. Whitney climb is the most extensive text she left. It is similar to other accounts of women travelers and adventurers, which tended to be written in an active voice that challenged dominant stereotypes of passive, domestic women. Like those women adventurers, Johnston does not speak of herself as a nurturer or moral guardian, but as a kind of pioneer; since "no ladies had yet made the ascent," she was determined to be the first, despite her lameness. A reporter for the local newspaper of Jefferson County, New York, noted the receipt of "a fine specimen of granulated rock picked up by [Anna Mills] on the top of Mount Whitney, Sierra Nevada Mountains, the highest peak in the United States, for our private mineral cabinet"[25]—a gift surely indicative of her pride in her accomplishment. In 1901 Anna Mills Johnston helped organize the Mt. Whitney Club, an organization made up of people who had climbed the mountain, over which George Stewart presided as president and in which the only women were Johnston herself and Mrs. Stewart.

In 1897 and 1898 Anna Mills Johnston served on the county board of education, to which she was elected president in 1898. A newspaper account of her unanimous election commented, "For many years she has stood among the leading educators of Tulare County, teaching some of the best schools and drawing a larger salary for her services than is usually allowed a woman."[26] That same year, she traveled back to her childhood home in Jefferson County, where she was received as something of a celebrity. The *Jefferson County Journal* reported:

Mrs. Johnston is one of the self made women of the times. By her own unaided efforts she obtained a thorough education, became one of California's most celebrated teachers, made money in wise business transactions, and has seen much of her own country, last year visiting the Yosemite, this year the Worlds Fair and next year she proposes to visit Alaska and later a trip to Europe is on her program.[27]

On this trip to Jefferson County Johnston also stopped to see her old friend Marietta Holley, then one of the nation's best-known satirical novelists and author of the popular feminist "Samantha" series. Although we do not know Johnston's views about Holley's books, her continued friendship certainly suggests an openness to Holley's strongly pro-suffrage, pro-feminist stance.

In 1914, at the age of sixty, Anna Mills Johnston decided to run for Tulare County superintendent of schools. Women had won the vote in California in 1912, and women throughout California were increasingly running for school superintendencies in rural counties; in this sense, her campaign was not unusual. In Tulare County, though, it was also framed in the context of the intense debate over prohibition, which added a controversial edge to the race. Johnston's public association with the temperance movement was not universally approved in the county. Moreover, she hoped to seize the Republican nomination from the incumbent, J. E. Buckman, a popular superintendent with strong family and business ties in the county. Although Anna Mills Johnston was also well acquainted with local business and professional leaders, the guests listed at her luncheons and dinners were primarily women, and her club memberships were in women's organizations. Whether because of her gender or her politics, Johnston was soundly defeated in the primary, receiving 3,202 votes to Buckman's 4,821. This campaign was her final involvement with the schools of Tulare County.

In Kings County, meanwhile, Nannie Davidson succeeded in being elected county superintendent for three terms. Yet despite the success she enjoyed early on as an educator and administrator, we know relatively little about her, relying for information primarily on newspaper accounts of her unsuccessful campaign for state superintendent of public instruction in 1914. Davidson's 1902 election as county superintendent of schools marked a clear departure from the pattern in Tulare County, of which Kings County had been a part until a decade before. There, the school superintendency was always held by a man, and the superintendent was a key figure in the political maneuvering and power brokering in the county.

As we have seen, the movement to elect women county superintendents was gaining momentum throughout the state in this period. In 1902, the year Davidson was first elected in Kings County, for example, twenty-two women and thirty-five men were voted in as county superintendents of schools statewide. Davidson's election, therefore, came at a time of changing views about the county superintendency and the role of women educators generally. But two local factors may help explain Davidson's election as well. First was the self-conscious image of Hanford, the county seat of Kings County, as a modern and "progressive" town in a forward-looking county; it distinguished itself sharply from Visalia, the county seat of Tulare County and one of the oldest towns in the Valley, which was viewed in the early twentieth century as conservative and set in its ways. As part of their attempt to solidify the town's identity as modern and broad-minded, local leaders in Hanford may have seen the innovation of a woman superintendent as beneficial. The second factor that doubtless led to her electoral success was the character and position of Davidson herself, not only as a respected teacher, but also as a woman connected to powerful men through her father and husband.

Davidson became actively involved in educational leadership during her third term as county superintendent of schools. In 1912–13 she was president of the Central California Teachers Association, a role that suggests both her interest to seek wider influence in education and her considerable energy and ability to expand her professional life. In the summer of 1914, when Nannie Davidson filed to run for the office of state superintendent of public instruction in the September primary, she made use of her contacts with both women educational leaders and women's clubs statewide.

In the newspaper accounts of her campaign, Davidson's appeal to women is frequently mentioned, as in this comment in the *Hanford Morning Journal*:

Hearing that she was making talks in San Francisco, Los Angeles women have assured her their enthusiastic support and have asked that she visit them. San Jose women's organizations have also asked for a visit from Mrs. Davidson, but it is not likely that she can make these trips, as she is now busy with her annual report for the supervisors and other pressing office work.[28]

A subsequent report of a trip she made to Santa Cruz, Pacific Grove, and Watsonville noted: "There are four men running against her for the nomination, she being the only woman, and the women of the coast cities are loyally coming forward in the support of 'their candidate' as they regard Mrs. Davidson."[29] Davidson herself cited the support of women as key to her chances. In her statement the night before the primary, she said: "If I win out tomorrow it will be largely due to the good work done in my behalf by the women's clubs in this state."[30]

Kings County and the San Joaquin Valley were not ideal locations from which to make a run for state office, since both population and political power in the state were centered in the cities of San Francisco and Los Angeles. But despite the disadvantage of being from a rural county, Davidson came in second in the primary. She thus faced the incumbent, Edward Hyatt, in the November election. In her campaign Davidson emphasized her qualifications as a woman and a mother, while Hyatt relied on his experience and contacts with male business leaders and educators throughout the state. This was the first California election in which women could vote, and although Davidson made a respectable showing, she nonetheless lost. While she easily carried Kings County, she lost in Tulare County 6,923 to 6,564. (This, by the way, was the same year that Anna Mills Johnston lost the Tulare County superintendency to J. E. Buckman.) Davidson retired from public life after this defeat.

In the life stories of Nannie Davidson, Carrie Barnett, and Anna Mills Johnston we can see an opening of possibilities for women school leaders that marked the early twentieth century and enabled such women to shape independent and active lives. Unlike more militant leaders such as Kate Ames, these women did not directly name gender oppression; instead they relied on their abilities and their class position to seek pleasure and power, using their high moral calling as women to justify their ambitions. Through marriage and friendships, they used their connections to local male elites to further their goals. Carrie Barnett, an active temperance advocate, supported her sister and nephew in a comfortable house through her work as a school principal. Independent, strong-willed, and adventurous, Anna Mills Johnston used teaching to create an exceptional life. Nannie Davidson, who emphasized her womanly and maternal qualities, was in many ways the most successful of these three women. We can only speculate about the energy and determination of a widow with nine children who not only returned to teaching to support her family and then three times sought election to the county school superintendency in a period when women were only beginning to aspire to such positions, but who also ran a hard campaign for state office at the age of sixty-two. All of these women used the privileges of their race and class and the opportunities provided by teaching to gain access to the public world and to seek both personal and social power.

Outsiders

Education in California in the nineteenth and early twentieth centuries was defined by race. Although segregated schools had been officially eliminated in most of the state by 1900, teachers remained almost exclusively white. In 1900, for example, the U.S. Census listed only two teachers in the category "Indian, Negro, or Mongolian" for all of California.[31] In 1910, sixteen "Negro" and twenty "Indian, Chinese, or Japanese" teachers were listed.[32] When segregated schools existed, such as the colored schools of the 1800s, black teachers would be hired to teach black children. But when those schools were closed, the possibilities of employment for black teachers disappeared. So long as white children were in a classroom, even an integrated classroom, schools hired only white teachers.

Tulare and Kings Counties were white-dominated societies, and as elsewhere, only Euro-Americans were hired to teach in white or integrated schools. In this period, however, Tulare County also had two segregated schools, which provided a limited opportunity for African Americans to find teaching jobs. These schools were the Visalia Colored School (1873–90) and the school at Allensworth, which was founded as a black school in 1912 and remained a school for black and Mexican children at least through the 1930s.

The first teacher of the Visalia Colored School, in the early 1870s, was an African American, Daniel Scott. In the 1880s we have references to four women teachers at the Visalia Colored School, at least three of whom were African-American women. A Miss Hinds of San Francisco is mentioned as teaching at the school in 1880; her race is not clear, but she may have been related to the African-American farmer Tom Hinds, who founded the school for his own children. She was replaced by Mary Dickson of Vallejo, who taught at the school until 1884.

A detailed description of Dickson exists in an article from the *Visalia Delta*. In December 1881, fourteen prospective teachers took the Tulare County teachers examination in Visalia. Six passed, but only one received a first-grade certificate. This was Mary Dickson, then teaching at the Visalia Colored School. According to the *Delta*, Mary Dickson then was "about twenty-three" and had come to Visalia from the colored school in Vallejo.

The *Visalia Delta* article is as interesting in its portrayal of Mary Dickson as it is in its narration of her accomplishments. The reporter, after describing the results of the teachers examination, including Dickson's outstanding performance, then provided a "pen picture" of her. This description is striking in its presentation of Dickson as an exotic figure outside the white norm.[33] The reporter (whom I assume to be a man) seems fascinated by Mary Dickson's physical presence and describes her body in great detail:

She belongs to the race properly termed "colored" and this fact adds interest to the subject in view of her remarkable success. She has the medium height of women; her form is full, straight, rounded and symmetrical, and as near perfect as the form of a handsome woman can well be; her hands and feet are narrow, and her fingers denote artistic taste, her hair is remarkably abundant, is straight with occasional graceful waves, and of course is black as night.

He goes on to describe her

large, black, intelligent eyes, . . . more expressive than which there are none. Negatively, the cheek-bones have not the prominence noticeable in the black race, and the chin, though prominent, betrays no evidence of African blood. Her mouth is almost faultless, the lips inclining to fullness, but only agreeably. The *tout ensemble* of the face is a slight rounding of the cheeks and the elongation that belongs to the Caucasian race; and perhaps handsomer features, altogether, are not to be found in California.[34]

Although Mary Dickson is "colored," the reporter emphasizes the "Caucasian" quality of her features. It is almost as though she represents to him a white woman trapped inside a black body.

The reporter seems to have been present at the teachers' oral examination. He comments not only on Mary Dickson's intelligence and beauty, but also on her delicacy in not presuming familiarity with "the white ladies present":

The most strongly marked feature of her deportment during the examination was her retiring modesty, as she seemed to fear that voluntary intercourse with the white ladies present would be looked upon as intrusion, on account of her color. She is an unusually good reader, having a clear strong voice that denotes the complete physical woman. She has an extensive knowledge of general literature, and is what may be termed a bright and ready conversationalist. She employs the choicest language, which is free from those numerous violations of grammar that daily custom almost sanctions. She is fluent and animated, though reserved in manner.[35]

The fact that Mary Dickson gained the only first-grade certificate among the fourteen applicants suggests that she was an unusually well educated woman. Unfortunately, we have no testimony from Dickson herself to counter the exotic representation of the *Visalia Delta* reporter. What did she feel when she was awarded her first grade certificate? What did her "retiring modesty" conceal? According to Tulare County records, she stayed at the Visalia Colored School for only four years. I have found no further reference to her.

The next teacher who we know taught at the Visalia Colored School is, surprisingly, the young Ida B. Wells, who worked there briefly in 1886 before going on to become a well-known anti-lynching activist and journalist. Wells's aunt Fanny had come to Visalia from Tennessee the previous year, bringing her own children and two of Wells's sisters with her. Fanny Wells, finding life in Visalia lonely, then convinced her niece Ida, who had been teaching in Memphis, to come west. Wells's description of life in Visalia was not positive: "Not a dozen colored families lived there, and although there was plenty of work, it was very dull and lonely for my aunt and the five youngsters in the family. There was good work and good wages for her, and better health than back in Memphis, but no companionship, so I decided to stay with her. I regretted it almost as soon as I sold my ticket."[36]

Wells was soon offered the teaching position at the Visalia Colored School, which she described as "a makeshift one-room building." She became immediately despondent. Although "the separation of the races in school had been asked for by the colored people themselves," she was angry that she was "helping to perpetuate this odious state of things by staying and teaching at the school. I spent an unhappy day [her first day of teaching] as these thoughts kept occurring to me."[37] Fortunately for Wells, her letters asking for help to return east resulted in the offer of another teaching post in Memphis. So after only a week Wells took the train back to Tennessee, taking one of her sisters with her. We do not know who filled the position she left vacant.

The last, brief reference to a teacher at the Visalia Colored School is found in Delilah Beasley's history *Negro Trailblazers of California* (1919), an invaluable source for African-American life in the state. According to Beasley, Sara Sanderson, the daughter of Jeremiah Sanderson, taught in Visalia in the late 1880s.[38] Jeremiah Sanderson, who came to California from New Bedford, Massachusetts, in 1860, was probably the most significant African-American educator in California in the nineteenth century. He taught at the colored school at Stockton and later became principal of the San Francisco Colored School. His daughter Sara thus came from a well-educated family that certainly valued schooling.

Black women like Dickson, Wells, and Sanderson used teaching as a means of support, and it was probably the best possibility for the expression of their considerable talents, just as it was for white women. But racist hiring practices and underfunded schools meant that only a small number of black women were able to teach at all in California. When the Visalia Colored School closed in 1890, no further employment opportunities for black teachers presented themselves in Tulare or Kings County until 1912, when a public segregated school for African-American children was opened at Allensworth Colony.

The life of Margaret Prince Hubert, who taught at the all-black school in Allensworth between 1914 and 1919,[39] provides a striking example of what it meant to be a black woman teacher in the early years of the twentieth century. Her life is documented in newspaper accounts and in an oral history interview conducted toward the end of her life in the 1970s. Black newspapers in Los Angeles and Oakland closely followed events at Allensworth between 1912 and 1920 and included reports of school events and teachers' activities. When Allensworth was made a California state historic park in 1976, several oral histories were conducted with former colonists; these, too, contain descriptions of the teachers and school. A number of African-American scholars have conducted research on Allensworth, including Eleanor Ramsay, who completed her Ph.D. dissertation on Allensworth in 1977.[40]

Margaret Prince was the daughter of Harald and Ruby Williams Prince of Pasadena. Both of her parents valued education; her mother had graduated from elementary school in Pasadena, and her father, although he had only attended school through the third grade, was a well-read man. Prince remembered her parents' support of her own schooling: "It seemed only natural, although urgent, to my family that I go on to high school."[41] In 1911 she finished Pasadena High School—the only African

American in the graduating class—and, along with one other African American, entered the California State Normal School in Los Angeles. Prince later remembered the separation from her family as painful: "Often now I think about times and remember moments when I got so lonesome that I wished I would die." Upon graduating from normal school, Prince faced the realities of racism in California:

> Here is where I had my first real setback, for I rudely discovered that my ability to control and direct my professional career virtually ended with the completion of my formal training. . . . At the time, the only Los Angeles school hiring Black teachers, Home Street School, had only two staff positions. The school served Furlong Tract, the Black section located just outside Los Angeles City Limits. Home Street School certainly did not offer serious employment opportunities for the many Black teachers resident in the Los Angeles area.

Then, in the summer of 1914, William Payne, who was a friend of the Prince family in Pasadena, offered Margaret the position as primary school teacher at Allensworth, the colony he had cofounded two years earlier in Tulare County.[42]

As Margaret Prince remembered her first teaching position, then, it was as a forced choice within a racist structure that her parents and grandparents knew only too well. Her grandmother had been compelled to work as a maid, traveling with rich white families, separated from her own children and family.

> My parents too well knew that the only employment locally available to our people was in the service industry. Thus, they quietly accepted the fact I would be separated from the family nest. As I now remember my parents' beaming faces at my graduation—twenty strong in the fourth row in the Pasadena High School auditorium—they must have known then about my destiny. For their own reasons, my parents chose not to tell me then, that to break the occupational pattern of the Prince family, I would have to leave home, just as my grandmother had done twenty-six years before. Continuously though, they reminded me, "To have an education is to be somebody."

Prince describes the journey from Los Angeles to Allensworth in vivid images: sleeping in a Pullman, waking to sunrise as the train left the mountains to enter the hot, flat valley. At Bakersfield Mrs. Russell and Mrs. Winters, friends of her parents, met the train at seven o'clock in the morning. Margaret then took the local train, which arrived at Allensworth at eight; there William Payne met her and took her to meet the chair of the school board, Mrs. Allensworth.

The detail in her account of this journey to Allensworth is typical of teachers' narratives of their first school. Yet Margaret Prince did not teach in an isolated setting faced with physical danger, but in a supportive community. She spent the summers in Pasadena with her family, and members of her family made frequent trips to Allensworth, particularly during her first year. Her brother Harald, for example, spent Thanksgiving of that year with her; after a Thanksgiving service at the school, Mr. and Mrs. Payne hosted a dinner that was attended by the Overrs, Margaret and Harald, and another friend from Pasadena.[43] In May 1915 her mother came with her brothers and sisters to spend four weeks at Allensworth.[44] The Allensworth columns of both the *California Eagle* and the *Los Angeles New Age* mention Prince frequently as a dinner guest at the homes of the Paynes and other Allensworth colonists. Typical is the tone of this account:

A surprise Valentine party was tendered Miss Margaret Prince the evening of Feb. 15th. The surprise was cleverly carried out as a rebuke to the school marm for a boast recently made that a surprise party, pure and simple, was an impossibility if the surprisee had gumption enough to note what was going on around him. She thinks differently now. The young ladies had arranged a number of interesting games and these with the usual entertainment of such occasions made an evening enjoyable to all.[45]

Prince was also a musician; she accompanied the school glee club on piano and often performed "piano and vocal selections" at graduation ceremonies and other community celebrations.[46]

All accounts of life at Allensworth mention the importance of education and the respect with which the teachers were held. That the school board and teacher at Allensworth were African Americans and that the school was a regular county school were treated as a matter of pride in the black press. The *Oakland Sunshine*, for example, wrote in 1913:

Allensworth is blessed with a splendid educational system and has had it from the very beginning. It possesses not a Jim Crow school, with an insufficient amount of money to run it and an indifferent and incompetent crew of teachers, but a regular state school, under the supervision of the State and County Superintendent, with district trustees elected by the people and receiving its share of state and county money with the other schools of the state. . . . With teachers graduates from Eastern universities, holding California High School [teaching] certificates, there should be no reason why the schools should not be the very best.[47]

Former colonists emphasized the excellent teaching at Allensworth School. One remembered both William Payne and Margaret Prince: "The people that lived there and went to school to [Payne] have often remarked that it was more like a private school, because he and Miss Prince . . . were well qualified in music and in the arts and they gave those children opportunities and things that they wouldn't have known ordinarily."[48] In the few years they taught at Allensworth, Payne and Prince both attended county institutes and professional meetings with other Tulare County teachers. Such trips were of interest to the whole community. In April 1915, for example, the *Los Angeles New Age* reported that "Miss Prince and Mr. Payne, who attended the California Teachers Association which convened in Fresno, made a brief of their observations while away, at a public meeting Sunday."[49]

In 1919 Margaret Prince married Tom Hubert, who had been a teacher in Texas, and left Allensworth. Unable to find teaching jobs in California, the couple moved back to Texas, where they taught in segregated schools until 1924. William Payne left the struggling Allensworth colony in 1920 to accept the principalship of the new segregated school in El Centro, established for the children of the African-American farm workers who came to the area to work in the cotton fields.[50] In 1924, Payne invited Tom and Margaret Hubert to join him at that school. Margaret later summed up this move, and in a sense her own life and that of other African-American teachers: "Once again, I moved in pursuit of occupational opportunity, relocating closer to home this time than the previous move, but nevertheless still without the option of returning to my family's hearth. It just so happened that I was a Black teacher unwilling to do domestic work; thus, I could not go home again."[51]

Margaret Prince Hubert's narrative expresses both pride in her work and her bitterness at the racism that shaped her life. Teaching was a profession for which she had been educated and to which she felt a deep commitment. But it was only at black schools like those of Allensworth and El Centro that she could find work employing her skills as a teacher. Like Mary Dickson, Ida Wells, and Sara Sanderson, she would not be hired in white or integrated schools because of the racism of the white community; but in teaching in a separate black school, she was forced to participate in a segregated structure. As was true for white women teachers, teaching offered Margaret Prince the opportunity to use her talents and to support herself. Yet as someone defined by the dominant society as Other, she had but limited options. Her life reveals the complex choices for African-American women teachers, struggling to create a meaningful life for themselves and others in a hostile world.

Country Schoolmarms

The great majority of teachers listed in the Tulare and Kings County censuses between 1880 and 1920 were young, unmarried white women, living in their parents' households or, by 1920, as boarders with families or in boardinghouses. Few of these teachers left written accounts of their lives, and country teachers were seldom mentioned in newspaper accounts. However, evidence does exist of three Tulare County rural schoolteachers: Nevada Porch Hastings, Grace Canan Pogue, and Ethel Hall Besquette.

In many ways these three women are typical of the teachers listed in the manuscript censuses of 1900 and 1910. All had come to California as young children, the daughters of ranching families. Nevada Porch was born in Iowa in 1870, Ethel Hall in Kentucky in 1882, Grace Canan in Ohio in 1888. They were white, Protestant, and of English descent. They did not attend normal school or college, but passed the county teachers examination. They began teaching in one-room mountain schools at the ages of eighteen or nineteen, and they all married; Ethel Hall and Grace Canan had children of their own, and Nevada Porch cared for stepchildren and nieces. Their lives come closest to both statistical norms and conventional images of country teachers: they were not highly educated; they taught in small rural schools and lived in small country towns. And yet as their stories attest, they reflected on the world through which they moved according to needs and desires that were at once conventional and, in Emily Dickinson's phrase, aslant.

When Nevada Porch began teaching in 1889 at the age of nineteen, she was typical of the women teachers represented in the census that had been taken nine years earlier.[52] Of the seventeen women teachers in the 1880 group, twelve were living at home with their parents or siblings, and their mean age was 21.4. Like those other young women teachers, Nevada Porch grew up in a farming family. Her father, Robert Porch, an Englishman, was a farmer in the village of Plano, near Terra Bella. In a typical pattern of migration, he had first farmed in the Midwest, and then moved to California in 1886, together with his wife and their three children, when cheap land became available.[53]

Nevada Porch's early education is unknown. She attended the village school at Plano in 1887 and 1888, then enrolled in Visalia Grammar School in September 1889, when she was nineteen. (Visalia High School did not open until 1891.) That November she passed the county teachers examination for her primary certificate, and immediately began teaching at the small mountain school at Xenia. The next year she moved to the small school at Salem, near her home. After two years there she spent a term in the new high school in Visalia in preparation for the county examination for the grammar school certificate, which she passed in 1893. She taught at Wheatland from 1894 to 1898, at Salem through 1902, and at Vandalia through 1906—all near the village of Plano, where her parents farmed. Between 1895 and 1897 she also taught in the summer school held at Grapevine in the southern Sierra. The 1900 census finds Nevada Porch at the age of thirty living with her parents, who at that time were seventy-five and seventy-two; the other two children were no longer living at home. We can assume that during the school term Nevada Porch either boarded or lived at home and drove a buggy to school; in any case, she considered her parents' home her own and lived there during school breaks. She probably helped care for her parents during these years and may have contributed part of her salary to the household income.

According to the county school records, Nevada Porch stopped teaching in 1906; three years later, at the age of thirty-nine, she married William Hastings, a widower with five children;[54] she was also, according to another account, "like a mother" to her three nieces. After her marriage, she must have been busy caring for these children. In 1914, however, Nevada, then forty-four, turned to teaching once again, first at Hope and then, from 1917 to 1934, as principal of the two-room school in Terra Bella. In 1917 she was appointed to the county school board, which by law had to include two teachers; she served in that capacity until 1934, when she moved back to the Hope school, teaching there until her retirement in 1942 at the age of seventy-two. It seems clear from her appointment to the school board and from the affectionate tributes to her upon her retirement that Nevada Porch Hastings was a respected teacher. However, in her reminiscences about her teaching life, she says very little about the content of her work, her methods or goals. In one interview in 1949, when asked what gave her the most satisfaction, she said it was often what was "outside the curriculum. . . . If I had taught only what was between the lids of a book I'd have been an utter failure."[55] For Nevada Porch Hastings, success seems to have been defined by the respect she won from her community and, by implication at least (teaching what was "not between the lids of a book"), by her relationship with her students. Altogether, she taught in Tulare County schools for forty-eight years.

Grace Canan Pogue is the only early Tulare or Kings County teacher to have left a published autobiography. For many years she also contributed a column in the *Woodlake Echo*, and in addition to her autobiography, *The Swift Seasons*, she published a history of the town of Woodlake. Both her family of birth, the Canans, and her husband's family, the Pogues, were early settlers in the towns along the foothills of the Sierra and appear frequently in local newspaper accounts and local histories. Grace was deeply involved with the Presbyterian church; she taught Sunday school and was a member of the Christian Endeavor, a Presbyterian social group, and her books contain frequent references to religion. She was also a fervent supporter of temperance.[56] Unlike Anna Mills Johnston, who presented herself as an adventurer of determination and will, or Ida Wells, who portrayed herself as actively shaping her life by the choices she made, Grace Canan Pogue speaks of her life in terms of womanly self-sacrifice and self-abnegation and often seems absent as an actor in her own life history. Both of her books are optimistic narratives of frontier settlement and progress, even when harsh or tragic events are described.[57]

Grace Canan was born in Ohio in 1888. Her father was a farmer and the township assessor. The picture she paints of her childhood in Ohio is one of comfort and family harmony, full of cherry and apple trees, flower beds, and "wide blue grass lawns." The family, she writes, had a "bobsled and a sleigh, a phaeton and a spring wagon"; "husking bees and quilting parties were a happy combination of work and fun."[58] She was five when the family left for California. Her account of the trip by train from Ohio is typical of her cheery style. Although the whole family had to sit up for the 2,500-mile trip, "When you have a big family to raise, you take a reclining chair and talk about how comfortable it is and how you don't sleep well on a train anyway. Personally, I'd rather be part of a big family and economize. It makes life a gay adventure." Once in California, the family bought a farm in Tulare County, near her uncles, who had settled there earlier. In Grace Canan Pogue's memory, "Life in California was one continuous adventure,—riding horses, herding cattle, raising turkeys, feeding pigs, growing wide fields of grain,—every season of the year had its special diversions."[59]

Grace Canan Pogue's idyllic picture of California rural life includes only people like herself: white, Christian farmers and small-town residents. Those beyond that circle are outsiders, exotic and suspicious, as in this description of the first Chinese men the family sees on their arrival in California:

We rode from Goshen junction to Visalia with a whole carload of pig tailed, sandal-footed Chinamen who chattered constantly. . . . Grandpa Jake, who had been an officer in the Civil War and liked to have things go his way, spluttered vehemently about the indignity of crowding us in with a gang of almond-eyed Orientals. We youngsters wouldn't have missed the experience for anything. Roy had paid fifty cents to see a Chinaman in a sideshow at Upper Sandusky; and here we were seeing a whole carload for free.[60]

This exoticizing of the Chinese, who are likened to exhibits in a carnival sideshow, recalls George Stewart's racist poem in the *Visalia Delta* in which he compared Chinese to orangutans.[61] Pogue later describes local Chinese vegetable farmers as "numerous opium smoking Chinese."[62]

Grace Canan's family supported her education, moving from their country ranch into the town of Visalia so she could attend high school (a not uncommon practice among ranching families). Grace met with much success in high school, winning an essay contest on "The California Fruit Ranch" and graduating as valedictorian. Once she graduated, though, she faced the realities of her family's limited resources:

A period of mental adjustment followed High School graduation. For four years, dreams of Stanford University had taken shape. A girl needed more units to enter Stanford than were required of a boy. I had the units. Also my recommendation said, "Rank in class, distinguished." But my financial backer married the girl of his dreams and I found my hopes of a college career dissipated. The idea of working my way through college didn't appeal to my family.[63]

This passage is interesting on a number of counts. First, she mentions Stanford's different entrance requirements for boys and girls without comment. Although she met the higher requirements for girls and had outstanding success in high school, she also presents without further comment her family's decision that she should not work her way through school, which in effect killed her chances of attending college. Then there is the obscure reference to her "financial backer," which is never explained, and, finally, her use of the phrase "mental adjustment" to describe her emotions, which one would expect would include deep disappointment if not anger at this lost opportunity.

Following her graduation from high school, therefore, Grace Canan had little option but to take the county teachers examination. Like Nevada Porch, she first taught in a small mountain school, then moved to a school near her family's farm. In 1910, when she was twenty-two, Grace Canan married John Pogue, the son of a well-known local family that had come to California in 1857, among the first white settlers to arrive in Tulare County. Several of John Pogue's aunts had attended the Visalia Normal School in the 1880s and had been early teachers. Grace Pogue's description of her marriage is somewhat ambivalent. Although she was attracted to John Pogue ("When Prince, the splendid bay trotter, began stopping in front of our house," she wrote, "funny little thrills would chase each other up and down my spine; and my heart would skip a few beats"), at the same time, she seems to have resisted marriage: "I had never considered a man necessary to my happiness. I still intended to finish college, but I seemed to be as far from it as when I started teaching."[64] As was typical of the day, she stopped teaching upon her marriage, but—and again, this was not uncommon—after a few years she returned to the classroom and continued to teach as a married woman until her retirement in 1950 at the age of sixty-two.

Ethel Hall Besquette taught in country schools off and on between 1900 and 1926. Like Nevada Porch Hastings and Grace Canan Pogue, she was in many respects typical of the teachers described in the 1900 census. We know something of her life from two brief memoirs of her teaching career in collections published by the California Retired Teachers Association. In the first, "Pleasant Valley School," Besquette recounts her experiences at her first school (in actuality Drum Valley School), a small country school in Tulare County, "about twenty miles back in the hills," where she taught for a year. In the second, "School Near Mt. Shasta's Grandeur," she tells the story of her year in a rural school in northern California, living with her two children and her sister. Both accounts are filled with details about conditions in rural one-room schools, but even more, they reveal what Ethel Hall Besquette saw as important and how she chose to present herself to the world. These accounts are virtually the only evidence we have of her life.

Ethel Hall did not settle down in Tulare County but "wandered teaching over much of California."[65] She also married (though apparently unsuccessfully) and had two children. Her retirement was not celebrated with picnics, speeches, and newspaper accounts, as was true of Nevada Porch Hastings, and she did not leave an extensive autobiography, as did Grace Canan Pogue; nonetheless, her two brief narratives provide a fascinating glimpse into the consciousness of a country schoolteacher.

Besquette states that she began teaching "at the turn of the new century," having just passed the county teachers examination, an assertion corroborated by Tulare County school records, which cite Ethel Hall as the teacher at Drum Valley in 1900–1901. According to the manuscript census taken in the spring of 1900, Ethel Hall, eighteen years old, was a boarder in Los Angeles and a student. She therefore must have returned to Tulare County that summer in search of a teaching job. Since she took the teachers examination, she probably did not complete her course of study in Los Angeles. She recounts that her mother "came in from the ranch" and drove her up to the mountains of Drum Valley to see the trustees and ask about the position at the school. That she came from a farming or ranching family is typical of the young women teachers in the 1900 Tulare County census, although it was unusual that her mother and not her father drove the wagon to the mountains. We know nothing about her marriage or whether she quit teaching when her children were born, though in her second narrative she does mention being the single mother of two young children when she taught near Mt. Shasta. How she spent the next few years is likewise unknown, but in "Pleasant Valley School" she describes her return to teach at Drum Valley for one last year in 1926:

More than twenty-five years later after I had wandered teaching over much of California I came again to Pleasant Valley. I was old and struggling desperately for each successive school to add just that much more to the pension I was determined to get. A San Francisco Agency secured my school without telling the name of the district. The school was in Tulare county and they wanted a teacher who would supply furniture for the teacherage. I agreed and when at last the name of the district came it was Pleasant Valley. So like Alice in Wonderland, I had run as hard as I could only to find myself in the same place.[66]

It is worth noting that when she described herself as "old and struggling desperately," she was forty-four. We do not know whether she finally collected her hard-earned pension.

The narratives of Nevada Porch Hastings, Grace Canan Pogue, and Ethel Hall Besquette reveal sensibilities that, although different in detail, suggest a common world. All of these women began teaching in late adolescence before they married, with teaching marking the transition between childhood and adulthood. The narratives of Hastings and Besquette in particular emphasize adventure and coming of age, themes that recall Anna Mills Johnston's journey to California and ascent of Mt. Whitney and Margaret Prince Hubert's account of the train journey from Los Angeles to her first school at Allensworth. Indeed, women teachers' stories tend to emphasize "the first school." The first teaching job often was a woman's first time away from home and brought in her first real wages; even if the young teacher contributed a good deal of her income to her family, she still had something of her own for her own pleasure. Similarly, accounts of teaching at one-room country or mountain schools often feature physical dangers overcome. In the narratives of California teachers, for example, rattlesnakes are not uncommon, and the teacher's "dispatch" of the snake is a mark of her competence and courage.[67]

These accounts have a great affinity with nineteenth-century narratives of women travelers, in which images of the brave adventuress counter the conventional vision of the maternal and self-sacrificing "true woman." Consider Nevada Porch Hastings's account of her arrival at her first school, told fifty-seven years later, at a picnic held in her honor by her former pupils:

[That] morning, we left all haste to try to make the early passenger train at Pixley. Just as we came to the railroad track and turned for the last one half mile, the train whistle blew and the mud flew as my brother Austin applied the buggy whip to the horses. There was no time for the hitching rack as we reached the station; no purchase of a ticket from the genial Mr. Kelly, the station agent. I rushed across the platform and climbed the steps of the coach as the train conductor called, "All aboard." At Tulare, I boarded the train for Visalia—a narrow gauge which many of you will remember. That same day on arrival in Visalia, I reported at the Superintendent's office in the Court House, engaged passage on the stage for the trip next day, made sundry purchases at Sweet's Store, and then retired feeling I had had a very full day. . . . The last part of my journey was by stage from Visalia to Aukland, a distance of around 30 miles. The stage driver wore hip length rubber boots; the streets were a perfect loblolly. . . . Sunday morning, I was conveyed over a steep mountain road full of gullies, stones, etc. to the home of the clerk, Bishop Brown, where I boarded.[68]

The drama of Austin whipping the horses to catch the train and of Nevada rushing, ticketless, to catch the train; the curiously attired stage driver; the steep, rough mountain road—all provide the details of a story of which the nineteen-year-old Nevada Porch is the heroine. Compare this story with Ethel Hall Besquette's account of her trip to her first school in the mountains: "The team was a pair of mustangs that needed a strong hand. They were hitched to the buckboard with chain harness that made a merry jingle. I held onto the iron arm of the high seat for dear life as we dashed down the rough mountain roads. I got a thrill when we reached the unbridged streams which the horses tried to cross by a lap from bank to bank."[69]

In these accounts, the teacher successfully faces physical challenge and hardship; but she is also very young. The intensity of the experience of living in an isolated community outside the care of her family is revealed in this description by Nevada Porch Hastings:

I was surprised by a visit from my father and mother who had written me previously they would not make the trip on account of the rain; but later, they changed their minds throwing me entirely off my guard. As they halted at the gate, the people saw them before I did and someone said, "It's an old man and lady. I never saw them before." I noted the horse and then all I could say was, "That's General." I was completely overcome and behaved like a child, crying and sobbing.[70]

The months spent teaching at Xenia are presented as a transition to adulthood for Nevada Porch. The actual job of teaching in her first one-room school, in contrast, gets but vague attention. We do know that she had in her charge eleven pupils from three mountain families. Although she describes the schoolhouse as having a fireplace against the winter chill of the mountains, she does not explain what went on inside the schoolhouse. Instead she describes her own adventures in the mountains; the "delicious sour dough bread" made by the grandmother of the family with whom she boarded; the quail, wild hog, and deer they had for dinner; and the "long winter evenings, entertained by Mr. Brown's violin, Mrs. Brown's second violin or dulcimer as it was known then, and by the daughter Isabelle's playing the bass viol."[71]

Ethel Hall Besquette's account of her first school is similar. There were only three families in the Drum Valley district, she says, the school was very small, and teachers were hard to come by. Besquette remembered that the trustees (who were also the three ranchers with children in the school) liked her and hired her on the spot. "In those days, all applications and contracts, as far as I know, were verbal. The school law was a wafer-thin book and there was a minimum of reports and other red tape."[72]

As was the custom in isolated country schools until the 1920s, she boarded with the family of one of her pupils. Her accommodations were simple: "My room had a homemade bedstead, a small commode, a chair and my trunk. There were a few nails on which I hung garments. I had at that time never heard of such a convenience as a coat hanger."[73] From this last comment we get some sense of the simple living conditions to which she was accustomed and the probable importance of teaching as a means of making a living for the eighteen-year-old young woman.

The school was a typical one-room school of that period: one large room, with "many openings at the floor, the ceiling and around the windows that would admit small birds, lizards, mice and snakes." Books were kept in a "heavy mouse-and-rat proof bookcase with a good lock"; furnishings included "double golden oak desks, a box stove, a desk and chair for teacher, a clock and handbell, a water pail and dipper."[74] All the students were boys, and Ethel Hall Besquette presents herself as capable of dealing with them or any of the various problems that arose. During the program preceding the end-of-term picnic dinner, for example, a snake interrupted by "appearing above the window sticking his tongue out at us. I disposed of him amid great applause. The boys behaved beautifully and passed the ice cream and cake to everyone. And so ended my first school."[75] This story of her dispatching of the wayward snake "to great applause" provides a fitting conclusion to Ethel's account of her first teaching job—and her initiation into adulthood.

Descriptions of the first teaching job are also filled with incidents involving physical risk. Nevada Porch Hastings, for example, recounts the time bloodhounds treed a wild cat and her horse became frightened and bolted with her. Another time, when the wagon broke down and she approached what she thought was a deserted ranch house, she was surprised by a rancher who took her for a thief. Ethel Hall Besquette describes similar perils. At that time mountain lions and wild hogs still were seen in the hills; rattlesnakes were always present, as were other snakes. Sometimes she presents these dangers as challenges to be vanquished, other times simply as strange features of the natural world, as in this account:

One bleak wintry day, I noticed a strange bundle or growth in a willow. I gave it a punch with a stick. It let go and such a shower of snakes as rained down upon me! From a safe distance I watched what seemed to be hundreds of them glide away down the creek. They were water snakes I was told later. I saw snakes at later times, but never more than a dozen in the tree again.[76]

Here Besquette displays no fear or anxiety (though she must have been startled when snakes started to rain down upon her!); instead she is merely an interested witness of the workings of nature. She often gives detailed observations of the plants and animals around her—for example, frogs' eggs: "I had seen strings of toad eggs in the ponds and puddles of the grain fields but seeing frog's eggs was something new." When it snowed, she studied the tracks left behind: "Birds made tracks as dainty as the snow crystals themselves. Rabbits made dots and dashes, while pigs and cows dragged along. Mice made the loveliest of all, like a lace net over the snow." She watched the nest that a pair of canyon wrens built in an empty desk in the schoolhouse, "a nest of grass and hair in which soon appeared six bluish eggs."[77]

While both Nevada Porch Hastings and Ethel Hall Besquette present themselves as heroines, there is a certain ambiguity in these accounts between their curious, adventurous nature and their awareness of the dangers around them. Besquette, for example, who presents herself as competent and fearless, is also conscious of the potential violence of the male world, as in her account of two first-graders, Mack and Mark Kingman, who lived with their one-armed grandmother:

Through sympathy for grandmother, I punished Mark for sitting in the mud while making miniature irrigation ditches. Mack mounted his horse and dashed for his shot gun to shoot me. I waited for dark for him to come with the gun, but his grandmother prevented his return. However, she showed no appreciation for the concern I had shown to save her [having to do] washing.[78]

The potential for violence here is presented without comment ("I waited for dark for him to come with his gun"); meanwhile, Besquette's final ironic comment that the old woman didn't appreciate her attempt to keep Mark clean is surely an attempt to place herself in a detached and competent position.

Ethel Hall Besquette's sensitivity to both male violence and the potential dangers of the natural world is clear in her story of a visit she made to an eagle's nest. Larry, the head of the family with which she was boarding, told her "that every year for as long as he could remember, the eagles had used the same nest on the top of an oak and that every year he had killed the young before they could fly, but in no disguise had they been able to get within rifle range of the old ones." Because Besquette loved the eagles, however, Larry allowed the two chicks to live.

When the weather warmed I resumed watching the eagle's nest. Mother eagle was now sitting. She sat still and blinked her eyes at me as I sat on the hillside. I had a good look at her brown body, her own gold head and neck and her large deepset, intelligent, fearless eyes. I wanted to see if there were baby chicks and threw some sticks at the nest. Mother eagle raised herself slightly and snapped her bill at me and then I realized that she was not getting ready to fly away but to come down and settle things with me. I sneaked away through the manzanita bushes too cowardly to leave by the trail. Mother eagle remained on the nest. She knew me for what I was—the variety of human who wore dresses and did not carry a gun and was no more to be feared than a sheep.[79]

There is a deep ambivalence in Besquette's self-presentation in this account: on the one hand, she is as fearless as the mother eagle; on the other, as a woman, she is as harmless as a sheep.

The narratives of Ethel Hall Besquette and Nevada Porch Hastings are framed in images of adventure and physical danger, but there is a third logic to these stories as well: that of material need and caring for others. Of the three women under discussion, Grace Canan Pogue most fully fulfills the stereotypical image of the self-sacrificing, nurturing "true woman" that was so often used to characterize nineteenth-century teachers.[80] Indeed, Pogue uses this representation herself to explain and justify her life. But in her and other women's cases, it was more than an abstract construction; rather, it revealed a pattern of caring that in fact frequently marked women teachers' relationships. Consider, for example, Sarah Goodin, who as a single woman taught in Tulare County schools for over thirty years. Her niece portrayed her thus: "Her entire life was devoted to a labor of love in her home, her school, and her church. She took care of her father during his declining years and helped rear her brother's four children when their mother died."[81] This passage not only constructs Sarah Goodin in an ideal image of self-sacrifice (her life "a labor of love") but also describes the *reality* of her caring for others.

This intertwining of ideological construct and material practice also characterizes Grace Canan Pogue's narrative, as in this explanation of her desire to teach:

It was decided that Sister and Mother and Dad and I would live at Yokohl and Sister would be one of my pupils. My ambition to teach was about to be realized. When I was a little girl, I had declared my intention to be a matron of an orphans' home; then came a dream of being a missionary. But my love for children and my yearning for an opportunity to guide them in the right paths could be realized in the teaching profession. And so, by the time I reached my teens, I was determined that a teaching career was what I wanted.

Here Pogue ignores her earlier ambition to attend Stanford and instead presents as her life's ambition the desire to serve others as a moral guide, speaking in the accepted discourse of the woman teacher as altruistic, virtuous exemplar. She does suggest satisfactions from teaching other than guiding children on the correct path, however: "I had bought a watch with half of my first month's salary, a seventeen jewel Elgin that was my pride and joy."[82]

Personal indulgences were probably rare for these women, however. All three of these country teachers came from farming families in which a teacher's wages no doubt contributed significantly to the household income. Both Grace Canan Pogue and Ethel Hall Besquette also mention working in canneries in the summers, which was typical for girls from ranching or farming families: cannery work provided extra income and it was considered respectable work.[83]

Teachers' wages in the late nineteenth and early twentieth centuries were apparently at least double those of farm laborers. And like farm laborers, teachers received pay only for the time they spent actually teaching. At Drum Valley, for example, Ethel Hall received $60 a month, of which she paid $15 a month for room and board. She mentions that her brother earned a dollar a day working "in the harvest fields from dawn to dusk." At the one-room Yokohl school, nineteen-year-old Grace Canan received $70 a month for an eight-month term and rented a vacant house about a half mile from the school for $8 a month. Her parents, meanwhile, leased their ranch and accompanied her to the mountains (whether to protect and support her or to be supported by her is not clear).

In "School Near Mt. Shasta's Grandeur," Ethel Hall Besquette explains that she returned to teaching in 1915 out of necessity. She was then living in Healdsburg in northern California with her two children. A friend suggested that she take a position at an isolated mountain school in Siskiyou County, so she loaded "five boxes of household goods, three suitcases, and the children" onto the train. She was accompanied by her twenty-year-old sister, who was studying for her teachers examination and who helped with the children. Her description of her life in Siskiyou County reveals the difficulties faced by a single-parent woman teacher at a small country school:

The schoolhouse was just across a ten-acre hay field from the cottage. As it grew colder, I braided [daughter] Alice's stubby braids and sent her across to make the fire in the schoolhouse while I washed the dishes and fixed the lunches. It was never easy to get to school on time, and when anything special like scrubbing the kitchen floor had to be done, sister covered for me by reading the school their morning story from James Willard Schultz.[84]

As is typical of teachers' narratives, Ethel Besquette gives no information about her classroom or the actual work of teaching.

The narratives by and about these women reveal the importance of teachers' wages even after marriage. Although it is often assumed that the marriage bar prevented married women from teaching, this was not universally the case. Unfortunately, the custom of taking the husband's name makes it difficult to follow the careers of many women teachers; nevertheless, we do know from biographical and autobiographical accounts that a good number of women did in fact return to teaching after marriage or children. We know, too, that the percentage of teachers who were married rose significantly between 1900 and 1920—from 6.6 percent to 16.3 percent in Tulare and Kings Counties.

Ethel Hall Besquette, Nevada Porch Hastings, and Grace Canan Pogue all returned to teaching sometime after marriage. Pogue continued to work, though not in teaching, after she married. Her husband was overseeing the grading of the streets of the new town of Woodlake; meanwhile, she maintained the house, cooked for the teamster crew, and contributed to the household income by caring for chickens. "The men got a dollar a day and their board and room," she wrote. "I added to the care of the chickens and incubators and brooders, keeping a house of eight rooms and five porches in order and cooking three meals a day for eight hungry men."[85] She rose at 4:00 A.M., prepared breakfast for her husband and the crew, fed the chickens four times a day, crated fresh eggs for market, and kept house. Although John Pogue owned a fairly large amount of land, the family could always use more income. For several years, therefore, Grace and John boarded teachers from the Wood-lake school at $20 a month each:

Hazel and Georgina Brown had stayed at our home and taught at Woodlake in 1911 and 1912. The following year Georgiana and Myrtle Woodard were with us. All three were old time friends. Now it looked as if our place was to be a permanent refuge for teachers. Naomi Heiskell, Lillian Rush and Fannie Lazarus came next. The following term, Naomi stayed and Helen Shake came to join our family circle.[86]

In 1922, when Grace's son Richard was six years old, County Superintendent of Schools J. E. Buckman "drove into our yard one March morning and asked me to teach the Ash Springs school the remaining three months of that school term. My first question was 'What will I do with my son?' Mr. Buckman said, 'Take him with you. They need him. The district will lapse if the attendance continues to dwindle.'" Grace and John Pogue apparently needed the income; thus, "after a family conference, it was decided that Richard and I would go to this lovely place in the hills for the remainder of the term." It is interesting that Buckman had no aversion to asking a married mother to teach in a country school some twenty-five miles away from home, even if it meant leaving her husband behind. So, as Grace Pogue put it, "As simply as that, I entered the teaching field for another twenty-seven years."[87]

The accounts of these country teachers reveal tensions about what it meant to be a woman and a teacher. When Nevada Porch began teaching at the age of nineteen in 1889, she was in a sense the stereotypical country teacher who lived at home and contributed cash to the household for a period before marriage. After marrying, however, Nevada, like many other women, supported not only herself, but her husband and her stepchildren as well. She returned to teaching in 1914 at the age of forty-four, and remained active as a principal until she retired in 1942 at the age of seventy-two. For Nevada Porch Hastings, teaching was not preparation for life as a wife and mother; rather, it came to define the very meaning and value of her life.

Grace Canan Pogue uses the imagery of the nurturing and self-sacrificing woman to portray teaching as an occupation suitable for a moral Christian woman and something she had always wanted. Yet this representation of the teacher as an altruistic moral guide (like the missionary or the matron of an orphans' home) stands in uneasy juxtaposition with the material world she describes. The family could not afford to send her to Stanford; they would not allow her to work her way through college. Instead she went to work and helped support her parents, husband, and son with her salary as a teacher.

For Ethel Hall Besquette, the decision to teach was shaped strongly by material need: after the failure of her marriage, as a single mother she had few options for supporting herself and her children. Nevertheless, her narratives are striking in the absence of representations of the self-sacrificing nurturer or moral guardian. Instead, Besquette presents herself as the close observer of a world filled with wonders. Her intense interest in nature, her matter-of-fact recounting of dangers and obstacles, and her intelligence and curiosity suggest a person of strong independence and keen sensitivity. Telling of her year in the school near Mt. Shasta when she was a young mother raising two children alone, she does not list her obligations or piety, but instead remembers the pleasure of a mountain evening: "After dinner on the first night in my new home, the other guests and I watched the harvest moon rise over Shasta. The sight was so beautiful we forgot to talk, but sat in the garden by the box trees, each with his own dream of beauty."[88]

As country women, these women had few respectable choices open to them other than teaching. Yet in their memories, teaching allowed them to find personal satisfaction even as they cared for and supported the needs of others.

Conclusion

Teaching afforded women in Tulare County in the nineteenth century, as elsewhere in the West, a number of life trajectories. These paths, revealed to us in sources such as school and census records, as well as in memoirs, biographies, and newspaper accounts, reflect both ideological and material constraints: men were assumed to be heads of households, while women were expected to live as dependents within families; married women, moreover, were frequently denied the opportunity to teach. But as the life stories discussed in this chapter demonstrate, individual women in fact constructed lives and met personal needs in specific and often unexpected ways. Through their engagement with existing practices and ideology, they forged new meanings and possibilities for themselves.

These women's lives mediated both ideology and actual material constraints. Rather than allowing themselves to be defined by an ideological construct of what they "should" be, women in fact actively negotiated expectations, both societal and internalized, in the context of material needs and desires. In this sense they engaged in the construction of their own subjectivities within the arena of existing practices, discourses, and institutions. Only by examining teachers' individual lives in a social context can we begin to speculate on the ways in which they constructed meaning—the reasons decisions were made, the possible rewards and limitations of different paths. In this light, we can begin to see teaching as contradictory, allowing new possibilities for the meaning of "the woman schoolteacher" and of "woman," even as it served to reproduce an existing vision of the world.

The early economic development of Tulare County was based on wheat farming. This photograph of a twenty-four-mule team harvester dates from around 1910. Thomas Wrought, one of the men operating the harvester, was the author's grandfather. (Property of the author.)

LaMotte School, Pleasant Valley. LaMotte was a typical one-room schoolhouse in the foothills of the Sierra Nevada. This photograph reveals both the extreme simplicity of the building and the isolated setting in the middle of a cattle range. This school was later moved to the Tulare County Museum in Visalia, where it can still be seen. (Edwards Studio, Porterville, California)

Anna Mills Johnston. One of the best-educated early teachers in Tulare County, Anna Mills came to Tulare County from New York State in the 1870s. She had been educated at the Oswego Normal School and introduced nature study and other progressive practices to her classes. She was the first woman to climb Mt. Whitney. (Edwards Studio, Porterville, California)

This photograph of Ailila School, a typical four-teacher school, shows the relatively ornate architecture of schools of this period. Schools were frequently the largest and most imposing buildings in rural areas, representing the prosperity of these communities, and were used as meeting places. (Edwards Studio, Porterville, California)

Nevada Porch Hastings and children of Vandalia School, 1906. Vandalia was a two-teacher school near Porterville in the San Joaquin Valley. In the years before rural supervision, principal Nevada Porch Hastings and a second teacher would have conducted this school with relatively little oversight from county or state officials. (Edwards Studio, Porterville, California)

Between 1900 and 1920 the number of single women teachers who boarded in hotels and boarding houses increased markedly. Hotels like the Orosi, shown here in about 1905, would have separate floors for women teachers. This stylized photograph captures small-town culture just before the introduction of automobiles. (Property of the author.)

One of the few existing photographs of the interior of a country school, this 1920s depiction of Deer Creek School shows children of different grades sitting in separate rows. (Edwards Studio, Porterville, California)

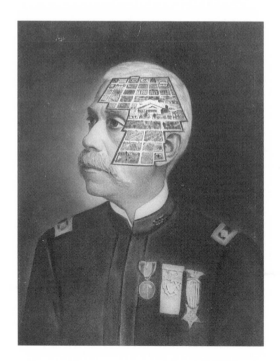

This portrait of Colonel Allen Allensworth, with the superimposed image of his dream of the town of Allensworth, hung in the local school. Note that in his vision the school is by far the largest building and center of the colony. (California Department of Parks and Recreation)

Children were the hope of Allensworth. This picture of the children of the two-room Allensworth school shows a typical range of ages. (California Department of Parks and Recreation)

Children of the Tule River Reservation School salute the flag. In the 1930s, a county school was operated on the reservation as part of the "new deal for Indians." Under later changes of policy, children from the reservation attended schools in local towns. (Edwards Studio, Porterville, California)

The 1920s saw numerous pageants, fairs, and parades in celebration of local culture. This photograph from 1921 of the Armistice Day parade float of Porterville's Burton School shows the intersection of images of patriotism, economic prosperity based on agriculture, and white children as the future of a homogeneous rural society. (Edwards Studio, Porterville, California)

Helen Heffernan was appointed chief of rural education when she was just thirty years old. As a former rural school supervisor from Kings County, she was well acquainted with the conditions of rural teaching. The introduction of progressive methods into rural one- and two-room schools was one of her earliest projects. (Special Collections, Tomas Rivera Library, University of California, Riverside)

After the Second World War, the bar against married women teachers was eliminated and rural schools were consolidated. This acceptance of married women teachers was accompanied by an expectation of heterosexual behavior and dress by teachers. Young male veterans entered the newly consolidated schools after studying on the GI bill. It is interesting to compare this photograph of teachers of the Terra Bella School, taken in the late 1940s, with that of Nevada Porch Hastings and the Vandalia school from only forty years earlier. (Edwards Studio, Porterville, California)

MEMORY AND IDENTITY: LIVES OF WOMEN TEACHERS, 1920-1940

Teaching provided both a means of support and the opportunity for personal validation for women in Tulare and Kings Counties in the late nineteenth and early twentieth centuries. Although teaching continued to be a relatively well paid and respectable job for rural women after the 1910s, the cultural context within which teaching existed now began to change. In the 1920s and 1930s, the growth of consumer culture, new definitions of women's sexuality, changes in state education policies, and the economic turmoil of the depression all increasingly shaped the lives of women teachers. Yet even as rural women came in closer contact with a commercialized urban culture that offered new images and possibilities, local communities fought to maintain their traditional control over the private lives of teachers, particularly women teachers. Control at the state level increased as well, as more extensive professional education and training became the norm.

In teachers' accounts of this time we can read the ways in which they constructed meaning from their lives and used teaching to meet personal needs and desires. But lives are defined by more than individual understandings. The spaces in which we move are shaped by struggles over resources and power that may be far from the sphere of our own lives. The very language used to describe rural teachers, the various ways in which control over their work was maintained, and the resources that were made available to them all reflected political contests that encompassed more than education alone. The accounts of women teachers from this period are striking in their silence about women's issues and the barriers they faced because of their gender.[1] Nonetheless, discursive constructions of what it meant to be a woman, cultural expectations of them as women teachers, and gendered social practices continued to shape their lives.

The evidence from which to construct a history of these rural women teachers is found in a number of sources. As in the period 1860–1920, school records and census data provide valuable statistical information about the changing patterns of work; for the period 1920–1950, too, we have at our disposal state documents and the pronouncements of state officials like Helen Heffernan, which provide examples of official authoritative discourse, the guiding ideas that shaped policy. But as we saw in the last chapter, the consciousness of women teachers themselves can be revealed only through their own words. I have been unable to find any collections of letters or diaries of teachers in Tulare and Kings Counties. Instead, the evidence from which I construct a history of these teachers' lives is shaped through memory—as expressed either in published memoirs written in later life or in narrative accounts provided in interviews.

The oral accounts on which I base the following are taken primarily from thirty interviews I conducted in Tulare and Kings County between 1987 and 1992. Twenty-three of these interviews were with retired teachers who were born between 1899 and 1913 and who taught in the schools of Tulare and Kings Counties in the period from the 1920s through the 1950s. Additional interviews were conducted with former students or later administrators or school officials.[2] I located retired teachers in one of three ways: either they responded to a query I placed in the county retired teachers association newsletter, their names were suggested to me by other teachers in the course of interviews, or their names appeared in newspaper accounts or on membership lists of retired teachers organizations. They thus represent a very small, arbitrary, and random sample of the retired teachers in the county. All of the teachers I interviewed were white, Protestant, and of northern European descent; twenty-one were women, two were men. (The latter two later worked as administrators: as a school principal and county superintendent of schools.) Of the twenty-three teachers I interviewed, fifteen were born in California, and thirteen had grown up in Tulare or Kings County. Ten of the twenty-three had attended Fresno State (the local teachers college), one attended San Jose State, eight attended private colleges or state universities, and four took the local teachers examination. Of the eleven who attended Fresno or San Jose State, eight came from farming or ranching families; all four of those who took the teachers examination came from farming families. Of the remaining eight, only two came from farming or ranching families. Thus, of the twenty-three retired teachers I interviewed, over half grew up on family farms, and most of them attended the local teachers college or took the teachers examination.[3] In the following two chapters, I explore the lives and work of the rural teachers of Tulare and Kings Counties in the interwar years primarily by means of these oral history interviews, augmented by the small number of written life histories found in newspaper interviews, collections of teachers' memoirs, and privately published autobiographies.

Personal Narratives and Popular Memory

I have based my analysis of the personal narratives of teachers on the work of a number of oral historians and feminist scholars.[4] My approach here is similar to that described by the British social historian Raphael Samuel:

We wanted to break down the opposition between the imaginary and the real, and to show for personal life narratives as for anywhere else, that no statement that is made about one's past individually, is in any way innocent of ideology or of imaginative complexes. We wanted to break down the differences between the public and the private, and the personal and the political, by showing that the same kinds of imaginative paradigms which structure ideology and which structure politics, also structure the ways in which people understand their own lives.[5]

While this approach opposes an empiricist view of the past as something unchangeable and "there" to be discovered, it does not reject the idea that the past existed and exists, and thus can in some ways be known. That is, it does not imply a denial of material reality, but instead recognizes the constructed quality of memory itself.

This reading of memory suggests ways of conceptualizing the relationship of ideology, consciousness, and material life. As Luisa Passerini puts it, "Interpretation should be able to recognize the various levels of expression and eventually find through other sources, as well, the historical contexts wherein they make sense. The guiding principle could be that all autobiographical memory is true; it is up to the interpreter to discover in which sense, where, and for which purpose."[6] The popular memory approach reveals the past not as a set of facts uncovered through the interrogation of eyewitnesses, but as a discursive construct expressing power conflicts and competing meanings. It emphasizes that ordinary people's memories are deeply affected by the ways in which the past is represented in what I call the dominant memory. This notion of dominant memory recalls Bakhtin's "authoritative discourse," which offers (or imposes) a language in which to frame our past and present selves; but it stresses as well the heteroglossic instability of memory—the ways in which memories can be subversive, invoking Gramsci's "good sense" or what Bakhtin called "internally persuasive discourse."[7]

Reading personal narratives, whether written or oral, from this vantage point calls into question the transparency of these texts as evidence

and makes self-conscious the act of reading or interpreting them. The
Popular Memory Group usefully suggests two approaches to the analysis
of personal stories: reading for structure and reading for culture. Both
readings rest on what the group calls the "social individual," one who
"speak[s] out of particular positions in the complex of social relations
characteristic of particular societies at particular historical times."[8] In
reading for structure, the focus is on the "experience" of the material
world as contained in memories, which in turn can reveal the workings
of that world—for example, the organization of work or solutions to material needs such as food, housing, clothing, and child care. In reading
for culture, the focus is on the ways in which memory makes sense of
events and experiences. Because personal narratives are constructed
within specific cultural and social contexts, they can be read and in a
sense decoded to reveal underlying structuring processes:

> It is plain, reading such accounts, that they are the products of thought, artifice,
> verbal and literary skills, always involving authorship in this sense, having (like
> all "sources") an active presence in the world. . . . So information about the past
> comes completely [sic] with evaluations, explanations and theories which often
> constitute a principal value of the account and are intrinsic to its representations
> of reality.[9]

Feminist historians have suggested additional valuable approaches to
the analysis of personal narratives, arguing that such narratives can be
read to reveal the constant struggle to create gendered selves.[10] Sandra
Frieden, for example, suggests that by "focusing on the construction of
subjectivity, especially the contradictions individuals are unable or unwilling to repress, feminists have used the 'bad fit' of imposed social
roles as an impetus for social transformation."[11] Central to feminist
analysis of women's narratives is the concept of hegemony, in particular
patriarchal hegemony, through which an unequal gender structure is
taken to be in some sense "true." As the Personal Narratives Group
points out, "Women's personal narratives . . . are especially helpful in
understanding androcentric hegemony because they document a variety of responses to it."[12] Thus, whereas some women's narratives express
acceptance of patriarchal norms and reveal the ways in which those
norms are reproduced by women themselves, others can in fact be seen
as "counternarratives" to a hegemonic vision, in that they defy the rules
defining social relationships or present alternatives to accepted views of
what is appropriate or true. Still others present a contradictory sense of
negotiation and construction of self. This range recalls Luisa Passerini's
argument that oral accounts are not shaped simply by the questions of
the interviewer (though the interviewing process has an important ef-

fect); rather, "when someone is asked for his life-story, his memory draws on pre-existing story-lines and ways of telling stories, even if these are in part modified by the circumstances [of the interview]."[13] In constructing their life stories, women avail themselves of different discourses; but in all of them, the dominant discourse is evident—either by being incorporated or by being resisted.

The following discussion of the lives and work of Tulare and Kings County women teachers in the interwar period builds on these theoretical concerns, particularly what Samuel refers to as the "imaginative paradigms which structure ideology[,] . . . politics . . . [and] the ways in which people understand their own lives" and Frieden's "'bad fit' of imposed social roles" in women's self-presentations. My examination of these teachers' narratives is concerned with the ways in which unconscious assumptions and imaginative paradigms organize and shape teachers' understanding of the world and of their actions in it. In their stories, teachers present themselves and their life choices in ways that challenge hegemonic definitions of women teachers as mothering, self-sacrificing, and passive; at the same time, the narratives contain unacknowledged contradictions and a kind of dissonance with regard to accepted conceptions of society and gender. I have read these stories for both structure and culture, on the one hand documenting the materiality of these teachers' lives—the organization of families, of schooling, and of the social world—on the other hand examining the selective quality of memory, the ways in which the past is framed as narrative, the representations through which value is given to lives.

Growing Up in Rural California

In discussing their childhoods, the teachers with whom I spoke tended to remember themselves as part of working households, particularly those who were raised on farms or ranches. The world they described is one in which girls as well as boys were expected to be useful and competent. The years before the First World War were what William Prescott, in *Vanishing Landscapes*, has referred to as the "golden age" of California agriculture, marked by a sense of coherent community among white, Protestant, English-speaking farmers. Even if that community was of recent origins, short-lived, or illusory, teachers remembered a stable and solid world of Protestant church membership, hard work on the farm or ranch, and community activities.

This sense of community and of trust is particularly striking in the accounts of women who grew up in Tulare and Kings Counties in the early years of the twentieth century. Three women described driving a horse and buggy to school when they were young children; although their fathers or older brothers would harness the horse, they would drive alone to school. Here is Jane W.'s account:

Jane W.: I drove my pony from in the field on the west side of 99 highway down to the gate, took down the old wire gate, led the pony through 'cause she wouldn't stand still and then put the gate back up . . .
K.W.: How old were you?
Jane W.: Six. And then drove across 99 highway and down the highway to the school. And the eighth-grade boys gloried that they could feed and unharness and take care of him. . . . So the eighth grade took care of him, but I drove him.

The expectation that a six-year-old girl was competent to drive a horse and buggy to school was part of a rural world in which girls contributed physical work not only in accepted women's activities such as cooking, cleaning, and gardening, but also in activities traditionally defined as men's.

Several women remembered themselves as tomboys—an accepted role in the strongly patriarchal world of the early twentieth century. I asked Evelyn B. what exactly it meant to be a tomboy.

Evelyn B.: You played with the boys, and I guess if anybody dared you to do something, you just went ahead and did it. You know, I'd walk on the top of the ridge pole on the barn, and I was the fastest runner in school over here except for the man principal.
K.W.: Did you play sports?
Evelyn B.: Oh, yes. I was on the boy's baseball team. Third base.

For Beatrice H., being a tomboy was a more conscious choice. She did not have sisters or brothers, and her father encouraged her to do and be whatever she liked. When she was about nine years old she overheard some girls at school talking about the advantages boys had:

These girls were angry because the boys got the best of everything, and boys were top class citizens and girls were shoved behind, and the people would rather have boys when they had new babies. . . . I took this all in. Something like this never occurred to me up until then.

After hearing this, Beatrice H. wanted the advantages of being a boy too. The handyman on the ranch told her that if she kissed her elbow she would become a boy, but try as she might, she couldn't manage to kiss her elbow. When her father came home, she told him what she had overheard:

After I told him all my troubles he patted me on the head and he said, "You just don't worry a thing about it. You're my boy and we won't care what other people say." And from that time forward he would, whenever he introduced me to people, he'd say, "This is my boy.". . . He taught me to hunt and ride and whatever he was doing, working on the cars or anything: I always had my nose stuck in everything. I remember going with the neighbors for raccoon hunting at night, we'd take our dogs and go raccoon hunting around through the swamps. . . . Back in those days, of course, it wasn't settled like it is now. Out around the rivers and all the swampy land and open country, we'd go hunting and they'd take me along—along with the men and the boys. So I just grew up that way. He always, he stuck to his word and he always just treated me like he would a boy.

After that Beatrice H. no longer wanted to *be* a boy; instead, supported by her father, she just dressed and acted like a boy, "much to my mother's disgust." For Beatrice H. there was no contradiction between being a tomboy as a child and becoming a teacher:

K.W.: Why did you become a teacher?
Beatrice H.: I always liked children. When we moved over into town . . . there I started babysitting for people around the neighborhood. I went on into high school and I babysat all the time. I enjoyed small children. I recall, I guess my junior year teachers would help us decide what we wanted to do. I remember my counselor, talking to her, and she'd ask me various questions, and I said I thought I would like to work with small children. And she said, "I think you're right. I think you'd make a good kindergarten or primary teacher." Back in those days you could go to Fresno, I could go three years and get a credential for kindergarten or primary in just three years' time. So that's what I did.

Dressing like a boy as a child, going hunting, and being addressed by her father as "my boy" did not contradict Beatrice H.'s liking for children and her adolescent vision of herself as a schoolteacher. Although Beatrice H. does not tie her adoption of boys' clothes and her movement in the male sphere of hunting and cars to sexuality, her account is a sharp challenge to conventional views of what it means to be a girl. The seeming contradiction between the tomboy and the nurturing schoolteacher are unreconciled in her narrative. Like Evelyn B., Beatrice H. did not imagine teaching as "women's work," or as something to fill the time between girlhood and marriage; instead teaching was a way to earn a living and to express her own abilities. She later married but continued to work, becoming a teacher of blind children, member of the school board, and well-known spokesperson for education in her town.

Beatrice H.'s account is similar to that of Jane W., another only child, who also remembered herself as a tomboy and her father's companion. When Jane W. became a teacher in a two-room school, her competence in the male world was shown in the way she worked with boys:

Jane W.: We would take our cars full of kids and go places and show them things. I taught my boys how to shoot up on Rocky Hill. How to shoot a gun and how to handle a gun and how to be safe with a gun.

K.W.: How did you know that?
Jane W.: My dad taught me. Like I said, my dad didn't think there was anything that he couldn't teach me, and he did.

Evelyn B., Beatrice H., and Jane W. put forward a way of "being a teacher" that builds on the strength of "being a tomboy." As tomboys, these three rebelled against conventional roles for girls, but none of them moved from their remembered strengths as unconventional rebels against traditional girls' roles to a critique of patriarchal assumptions, whether about teaching as women's work or about the social limitations they confronted when it came time to find a job. These contradictions are left unaddressed and unintegrated.

Becoming a Teacher

Retired teachers presented various reasons for their choice of teaching as a means of earning a living. One obvious issue was economic need; another was the desire for meaningful and productive engagement in the world. The reasons given differed somewhat according to the class location of their families. Although the teachers I interviewed never identified themselves according to class, both the livelihoods and wealth of their families varied. Over half of the teachers I spoke with came from farming or ranching families, but these families also differed according to the resources they controlled, some apparently owning substantial amounts of land, others leading only a marginal existence, particularly during the depression. All of the teachers recounted their expectation or need to work. In many farming families, it was understood that daughters would contribute to work in the household or on the farm; when they became teachers, much of their earnings was transferred directly into the household. Three teaching sisters, for example, were left fatherless when they were quite young, at which point their mother found work as a school janitor and rented out the family farm. One sister recalled: "Oh, yes, we all did very menial work, mother too. Like working in canneries and cutting fruit, picking prunes out in an old hot field. All that sort of thing, we all worked in that type of thing. We got through." In this family, the three daughters immediately contributed to the family income when they became teachers.

Women whose fathers were businessmen or in the professions recounted their family's expectation that they would attend college. Polly O., for example, was the daughter of a Methodist minister; her parents "had always talked from the time I was a little kid, they talked about my going to college. I always took it as a matter of course that I would." Although her mother did not go beyond high school, Polly O. remembers that "she was always reading." After college, it was assumed, these young women would work if they did not immediately marry. But the possibilities for respectable work for these middle-class women were limited, with teaching as the obvious choice.

For the ten teachers who attended Fresno State, all the daughters of ranchers or farmers, the economic need to work was central. Almost all of these women worked even while attending school. Although many of their parents supported the idea of college education, few families had the resources to provide full board and tuition. In the 1920s and 1930s, the most inexpensive teacher education available to residents of Tulare and Kings Counties was at Fresno State, the only public four-year college in the San Joaquin Valley. It was in their accounts of their experiences in Fresno, the valley's largest city, that these country teachers positioned themselves in something approaching class terms.

Several of the women who attended Fresno State lived as household help in families. Rachel B. lived with a professor's family. "The first year I walked to and from their home to save bus fare," she recalled. "As I look back on it, I don't think I saved anything, because you had to buy shoes more often." Later, after moving to the YWCA, she worked as a typist and took on extra work on the weekends: "There were a lot of girls in the Y who went to beauty school. They used to give me ten cents for each uniform that I ironed for them. I spent all day Saturday doing my own washing and laundering and ironing for them. I got through."

Evelyn B. also lived with a family during her years at Fresno State:

Well, I was used to work. It didn't hurt me to work. And we didn't have very much. So I didn't expect very much. You took care of what you had. You changed your clothes when you came home from school, and I'd always done that. So, I did it when I went to college, too. I think I wore . . . I guess I had two pretty good dresses—outfits that I wore for two years—maybe even three years. Otherwise, except for coats, we made our own clothes. When you start in the seventh grade to make your own clothes because your mother doesn't have time to do it as nice as you want, you learned how to sew.

For these country women, teaching was the most accessible and acceptable work available. Ellen A., who was raised by her uncle and aunt after her parents' divorce, gave vague reasons for going into teaching.

K.W.: When did you decide to go to college and become a teacher?
Ellen A.: I can't remember a time I didn't think I was going to. It was always there that I was going. My father put me through school.
K.W.: Where do you think you got the idea to become a teacher?
Ellen A.: I have no idea. Just that I wanted to be a teacher. There were no other jobs open. You either became a telephone girl or you could work in a packing house—There were no girls working in banks—That was it.

Here, Ellen A. begins by saying she has "no idea" why she decided on her profession, she "just . . . wanted to be a teacher." She presents this choice as freely made. But she then elaborates, saying there were very few options for women, not even working in banks. In this short passage, then, she asserts her free choice—thus presenting the dominant American vision of isolated individuals acting of their own volition—and then immediately presents the commonsense reality of the restrictions that she as a woman faced. Although she constructs her past through the hegemonic discourse of free choice, the limits of a patriarchal society break through her narrative to create unreconciled contradictions.

In Evelyn B.'s account, by contrast, the limited choices available to her as the daughter of a struggling farmer were clear:

I was not about to work out in the fields, packing grapes and picking figs, and I was not about to do that all my life. And I wanted to help my parents. Here I was, the oldest one in the family now because my sister was married. So when I did graduate, I went to the bank and borrowed fifty dollars—one of the first things I did when I graduated from Fresno State. Because I had a contract, and they would give you money on a contract. So I borrowed fifty dollars and got my mother a washing machine. Oh boy! If you don't think that helped out!

Evelyn B., like many of the other teachers with whom I spoke, did not allude to the intrinsic appeal of teaching; rather, she needed to work and saw only limited options. For Evelyn B., teaching was not stereotypical "women's work," an occupation that appealed because of its traditional qualities of nurturance and motherliness. Instead, it was a profession that offered relatively decent working conditions and pay and brought material advantages, in this case, a washing machine for her mother.

Four teachers I interviewed could not afford to attend Fresno State, but received their teaching certificates after taking the county teachers examination in the 1920s. Hannah A., for example, was married with a young son:

Hannah A.: I went four years to high school. I started going with my husband when I was a junior. By the time I was through high school, we decided to get married. So I graduated in May and we were married in October. About a year and half later, we had a son. After we'd been married about five years, I decided that I wanted to go back and I wanted to teach school. So I went over to Visalia. My sister was living over there then and I stayed a week with her, took the county examinations, and passed.
K.W.: What did your husband think of this?
Hannah A.: He didn't think much of it, but then . . .
K.W.: You mean, he didn't approve of it, or . . .
Hannah A.: Not exactly, but . . .
K.W.: Did you need the money?

Hannah A.: We needed the money. He was driving a school bus at that time. Up until that time, he worked with his father in the cattle business. Of course, you may think the cattle business is something wonderful, but there's not, unless you have a big operation, there's not much profit.

In this account, both the economic need to work and tensions with her husband over her decision to become a teacher are evident. The teachers exam provided Hannah A. with the opportunity to work, even in the face of her husband's disapproval.

For the women I spoke with, passing the teachers examination was a significant achievement, one they described in detail. Teresa D., who came to California as a young woman from the Midwest after having completed one year of college, took the exam in Tulare County in the late 1920s:

I had no studying for it or anything, and I went in and I passed. I remember at that time the superintendent was Mr. J. E. Buckman—I don't know if you've heard of him. I can't remember exactly, there must have been fourteen or fifteen applicants, and they kept dropping out because they took too low on something, especially on math. They had science, and I had physics in my high school work, almost no chemistry, and the exam was on chemistry instead of physics. I remember I guessed a lot. I used a little judgment! I passed. I don't know if there's anyone left living that took the test when I did.

Veva Blunt, who taught in Tulare County for over thirty years (a Visalia elementary school was later named in her honor), took the teachers exam after graduating from high school in the early 1920s. She was an inspiration to Irene Rivers, who took the exam the next year:

Irene Rivers: A friend of ours, Veva Blunt, was my oldest sister's chum all through school, and I was Veva's sister's chum. Mother said, Well, Veva did it, you can do it. . . . The only thing that I didn't know anything about was school law and procedures. So I went in and talked with Mr. Montgomery, who was superintendent [of Visalia schools] at that time. And he gave me some books and I studied those a little bit on my own.
K.W.: Because other people would have been to college? To normal school?
Irene Rivers: I was the only one who hadn't been. The others had one or two years. I never saw so much cheating in my life! They had answers written all over everywhere. I was too dumb to cheat.

The examination took all week. Each day the names of those who had failed the previous day were announced. Irene Rivers recalled the anxieties of taking this test:

There were thirty-some-odd started, and each day they would call out those who would get up and leave. I think there were eight of us who finished. The numbers were called out early in the morning. And on that particular morning, I think it was the third morning, my mother took me in and she waited, so if my number was called she'd be there to take me home. But they hadn't finished checking all the papers. Said they would not call off the numbers until after lunch. So I went down to tell my mother, and her face was just white when she saw me coming. She knew I'd failed. But it was just to tell her everything was okay as far as I knew.

Irene passed the test. And although she did not say so, her sister later told me that she achieved the highest results of all the applicants that year.

The First Job

Once a young women had attained a teaching credential, she was faced with the task of finding a job. In the 1920s, young teachers could use agencies or college placement offices to learn what positions were open, but the process of interviewing was still quite informal. Karen R., for example, told this story:

I went to Miss Porter—she was the appointment secretary at UCLA—after I graduated to get possibilities of vacancies. I wrote to all of them, but I didn't hear from them. Finally, I got a letter from L. J. Williams [who] said that he had an uncle that lived in Whittier and he was going to be down there to visit his mother and sister and wanted to have an interview with me. That interview was funny. He said that he would telephone to me when he got down and we could settle on a place for the interview. Dad had this stand, he was selling watermelons and fruit of all kinds from the ranch. I was waiting on trade, and this fellow came up and asked, "Are you Miss R——?" And I said, "Yes." And he said, "I'm Mr. Williams. I'll just wait until you are through with your customer." Well, you know how that would make me feel: flustered. . . . I finished waiting on that customer. I made a 360-degree circle looking for that fellow, and I could not see him. One of the fellows that worked for Dad, Charley, was there. And I asked him, "Where the devil did that man go?" And right at my shoulder was Mr. Williams. I had gone to town and got new clothes and shoes. And here I was interviewed in my working clothes. That was my interview. I laugh every time I think about it.

This story is interesting not only for what it reveals about the informal practices of hiring teachers, but also for its description of the work Karen R. contributed to the family farm. Although Karen R.'s father was a successful farmer, and although she was able to attend Los Angeles Normal School (later UCLA) without having to work to support herself, she still contributed to the family business by working summers at the farm stand.

Several of the teachers found their first job through family members or through contacts in their hometowns. Jane W.'s first teaching job in the early 1930s, for example, was in the school she had attended as a child, though she had applied "up in the mountains and all over. There weren't many vacancies, but what there were were difficult ones. They were out-of-the-way places, up in the foothills. . . . At the last minute, the trustees here decided to establish that fourth classroom, and I received it." She "probably" got the job, she remarked, because the trustees knew her and her family.

Church and lodge membership also helped young teachers find jobs. Polly O.'s father was a minister, and a member of his congregation told him of an open position. Ellen A. thought she got her first job in 1931 because of her uncle: "The [school] board members were all Odd Fellows. I think they belonged to the Odd Fellows lodge or the Presbyterian Church. And because they knew Uncle Jimmy, I got the job. The principal had already picked another teacher, but I got the job." When Evelyn B. finished Fresno State, she was unable to find a teaching job and finally returned home:

It was the last place I applied because I didn't think I should be teaching here. It just wasn't the right thing to do, to teach in your own neighborhood. That's what I thought. But I wasn't getting any response from anyplace else. So right next to where we lived was one of the trustees, who I had known from the time I started school over here in the sixth grade, and the other one, we went to the same church. So it wasn't any problem to go interview. I had worked for him before I ever started to college. I was working in the emperors [grapes], packing them, and I did such a good job and he didn't have to check up on me. He said, "If you ever want a job, be sure you come back." Now, that's the last thing he said to me. Then I was up at college all the rest of the time. When I applied, he said, "I thought you would never come to apply. Don't you remember I told you?" It made me feel good.

In other cases, young teachers wrote or contacted the local trustees, often in small or isolated districts. Teachers were often hired for what seemed like whimsical reasons. Teresa D. was told by a trustee that she got the job because he thought she could help his son, a seventh-grader, learn phonics. Rachel B. told this story:

The trustee told me later, "Do you wonder how you got this job?" I said, "No. I just know I got it." He said, "Well, at the time you got that job there were fifty teachers that applied for it. I didn't know which one to take. So I would sic them on to my girl that was going to be in the class and see how they took to her. She said to you, 'Do you want to go out and see my baby chickens?' And you said, 'Of course I do, I love baby animals.' And you walked through the chicken pen to see the chickens. That made up my mind that you were the teacher." You get jobs in queer ways.

The power of trustees and the ways young teachers could employ family and community networks in getting jobs are clear in Beatrice H.'s vivid account of her first job. She heard of an opening in Earlimart, a small town in southern Tulare County:

I fortunately had a car and so I drove down there. When I got down to Earlimart I inquired where to find the chairman of the board, and was directed over to his house, Mr. Howard. His wife came to the door and she says, "Well, he has the chicken pox, but if you've had it already and you're not afraid of it, you're welcome to go in and talk to him." Well, like most all kids through school I'd had chicken pox and mumps and measles. Of course, I needed the job bad enough I probably would have said I wasn't afraid even if I had never had them. So she took me into his bedroom, and because a lot of times chicken pox will bother your eyes, they had the blinds all closed. But he was there in bed, and she told me that she and her daughter were on their way to some sort of a social thing, and so they took off. It wasn't very long after that he of course asked me where I was from and where I lived and so on, and as soon as I began to tell him where I was from, we very quickly found out that his wife's sister was Mrs. Stapp Waddle up at Badger, and I had known them for years, and Luenna Waddle had lived with Mother in Exeter when she was going to high school. . . . Well, he talked to me for a while. I had told him that I would like to have a first grade, so he reached alongside of his bed and picked up a notebook, and he said, "I think you'd make a good first-grade teacher." And he rubbed out a name that was there and put my name down. So after I talked to him awhile, I said, "You know"—you know, sometimes when I think back on the things we do, it seems so strange—"if I come to teach and work for you, you'll have a good first-grade teacher, but my roommate needs a job, and if we both came down you'd have a good team." I started telling him all about my roommate. After he listened a little while he said, "Well, I'll put [in] a position for her. I'm going to be in Dinuba the following Wednesday"—this Mr. Howard, he was in the pump business. Pumps in wells, you know, and this sort of thing. So he had a business in Dinuba as well as down there at Earlimart. So he was going to be over here at his business in Dinuba the following Wednesday. He said, "You two girls come to Dinuba on such and such a date. And I'll have your contracts made."

This story raises a number of fascinating issues. There is Beatrice H.'s distinct memory of the wife and daughter "taking off" and leaving her there in the intimacy of the bedroom with the trustee, a middle-aged man with a pump business and the power to give the young teacher a job simply by "rubbing out a name" and writing hers down instead. But even though the man with the pump business is a man with power, Beatrice H., the tomboy whose father called her "my boy," presents herself here as fearless, bold, and with the power of her wits. She drove down to the town alone in her car, asking directions of strangers. She negotiated alone in the bedroom, using common acquaintances to establish a personal connection. And when she got the job, she pushed further to get a job for her friend, saying, "You'd have a good team . . . " In Beatrice H.'s narrative, the arbitrary power of the school trustee is not questioned, but at the same time, her own power to manipulate the situation to her own ends is also emphasized. What is not questioned, of course, is her own advantage as a member of this culture and community or the implications these networks have for the maintenance of racial and cultural privilege.

Community and Social Control

The rural schools young women teachers entered in the 1920s were central to the maintenance and reproduction of a common cultural identity. In Tulare and Kings Counties in the interwar years, schools were still centers of local community, and teachers served a significant role in organizing this common culture.[14] Probably the most dramatic example of the creation and enactment of a common history in these years was the Valley of the Sun pageant, written by local teacher Virginia Stapp and held in the hills above Woodlake in 1926 (see Chapter 3). But the same forces of cultural construction were at work on the small stage of the rural school, which continued to reinforce a white Protestant hegemony, even when children of many different cultural and linguistic backgrounds were present. Margaret C., for example, who taught in the same two-room school for thirty-five years, described the close-knit Portuguese community in Kings County:

Eighty percent of the people owned their homes. It was before the Dust Bowl. Great people. Eighty percent were Portuguese, but they sent their kids to school for one purpose—to learn the English language and become Americans. . . . They never asked for Portuguese history or bilingual Portuguese; they wanted them to be Americans. And the little kids worked hard, up at three o'clock in the morning to milk cows—they had dairies out there—then they'd come to school. If they'd fall sleep in the middle of the day, I'd let them sleep. I figured that'd do more good than to make them stay awake.

Margaret C. told this story in the late 1980s, when concerns over bilingual education were widespread. Margaret C., like many other retired teachers, looked back nostalgically to this school as the site of a common desire to create and celebrate an American identity, and she implicitly contrasted this picture with the conflicted present. As she remembered it, this school served as the center for social life as well as the means of Americanization for Portuguese-American children. Margaret C. described holiday celebrations in which both children and parents participated. May Day, which was a major school holiday in Tulare and Kings

Counties in these years, was marked by a maypole, dancing, and a May festival. "The parents came and we sat out underneath the umbrella trees with tables, and they'd bring fried chicken and potato salad, and home-made ice cream and cake. The kids would put on a May festival. We al-ways wound the maypole." Margaret C. also described family nights held once a month during the school year:

Every month we'd have a family night and they'd come and we'd move back the desks and have games—relay races, carrying peanuts, anything we could think of. Then the parents would bring cakes or pies, and one of the neighbors would make, because we didn't have a kitchen in the old building, make a big pot of coffee. Around ten o'clock we'd stop and then they had a big time.

Similarly, Irma R. remembered the importance of school programs in the isolated mountain community of Badger:

Irma R.: You used to have to have elaborate Christmas programs. I had one mother, whose three children were in my school up at Badger, and she will still mention things about my programs.
K.W.: And you were responsible for organizing them . . .
Irma R.: Organizing them, practicing, seeing to the costumes, and everything! Parents would do some of it, but most of it was up to the teacher—the scenery, the stage management . . . Even the last year I was at Goshen, my sister and I each had a third grade, and we worked out our program so that they would all have some part in it.

Many teachers described this sense of a coherent community with shared values and culture. Hazel Fowler described her first job in the small Kings County town of Stratford in 1920: "There was good commu-nity spirit—the parents, teachers and community worked for the benefit of the children. In the spring, the entire community packed a picnic lunch and went to the West Side for a picnic among the wildflowers, which were so plentiful then. Dances and parties included everyone, and the feeling was good."[15] Ruth G. described teaching in a school at which a community dramatic and musical club met once a month. The club put on plays and musical performances or simply brought families together for community singing and refreshments. Then there was the all-county track meet for elementary schoolchildren, a major event in the lives of rural children and their families. As Grace Canan Pogue told it:

One of the big events of the school year was the Mooney Grove picnic and County Track baseball throw and the big ball game. There was a preliminary try-out on the home grounds, when parents and patrons of the school were invited. Even the primaries, who were not qualified to take part in the County event, had their races and won ribbons. The day before the big event, the tiny tots were loaded into a gaily decorated bus, the older ones were lined up in marching array, carrying the blue and gold school banner, and there was a Big Parade through the business section of the town. On the Big Day, parents loaded the ice cream freezer and the baskets of fried chicken and salad and lemon pie and chocolate cake and all the delectable food imaginable into their cars and took a day off for the school picnic.[16]

Yet even as young teachers in rural communities were helping to maintain a sense of common cultural identity through these school-centered activities, they were living under the close surveillance and control of their communities. By the 1920s, most young rural schoolteachers had attended normal schools or teachers colleges, institutions that encouraged them to see themselves as educated practitioners with specialized training. The communities in which they lived and worked, however, saw them as young women first, and expected them to meet strict standards of behavior. Margaret Nelson, in her study of rural teachers in Vermont, argues that single women teachers posed a p⸗ ⸗ential threat to the social order as examples of autonomous women in the public sphere. Rigid social rules and surveillance in a sense "contained" the danger that these young women represented.[17] The formal and informal rules of behavior for teachers are well documented for this period. By the 1930s liberal social commentators were beginning to condemn the restrictions on women teachers, but in the countryside, women teachers continued to be subjected to close observation as both communities and school boards judged their private as well as professional lives.

Many women teachers in Tulare and Kings Counties lived with their family for the few years before they married. Others lived in a hotel or boardinghouse until marrying. A small number of teachers in isolated districts in the 1920s and 1930s boarded with local families in conditions similar to those described by Nevada Porch Hastings and Ethel Hall Besquette at the turn of the century. Margaret C., for example, came to Tulare County from southern California and boarded with a local farming family during her first year of teaching:

I had never lived on a farm or a ranch. I roomed and boarded with the Stahl family. They had a dairy and they had grapes and had some fruit trees. And they had this Elmer. He was in the third grade and school was about a quarter of mile from the ranch, and you had to walk that lane and down the road to go to school. And hot! I had never been in such hot weather. I had a bicycle, so I said, "Elmer, let me ride you on the handlebars to school." So I did. Then coming home, it would be so hot so we'd take off our shoes and stockings and wade in the irrigation ditch on the way home.

In this story, Margaret C. presents herself as a companion to the third-grader, and by implication part of the family, rather than a professional authority. Irma R. described a similar relationship in her first school in the mountains when she was nineteen. Although she describes herself as being fully in control, she was also treated like a daughter by the mountain community.

Irma R.: Here I was teaching a one-graded school and the oldest boy in school was fifteen.
K.W.: Was that any trouble?
Irma R.: Not at all. I was the teacher, and that was it. The week before school was to open, I tore all the ligaments loose in my knee. So they postponed the opening of school for one week. And they arranged where I was to board, with one of the homes up there. The grandmother lived with them, and every day when I would come home from school, my knee was so swollen, and she would work putting hot packs . . . they were just lovely to me. They arranged for another neighbor to pick me up and bring me to school and to bring me back home in a car. Everybody was so friendly up there. They more or less adopted my family and all my friends. Occasionally in the spring, they'd have big fish fries and my gang would all come up. They were all so good to me.
K.W.: How long were you up there?
Irma R.: Just the one year. Then I put an application in at Oak Grove because it was just a couple of miles from home.

Virginia B.'s first teaching position was at Aukland School in the foothills when she was eighteen. At first she boarded with the clerk of the school board, but it was too expensive, so after two months she rented a little house by the school. Since she didn't want to stay there alone, she brought her younger brother (he was ten or eleven) to live with her. When her brother returned home, she asked various friends to come and stay with her for a few days during the week. Every Friday she went home to spend the weekend. Virginia B., like Margaret C., Irma R., and many other young women teachers, stayed only one year in this isolated school. She then moved back to her parents' ranch and taught in a nearby school.

The social restrictions faced by teachers in Tulare and Kings Counties in the interwar period varied from town to town. In rural school districts, where trustees could hire and fire teachers at will, these young women lived under close scrutiny. Even when the rules were not articulated by school trustees or town principals, community expectations were clearly understood. One teacher described a landlady who would go through her belongings while she was at school teaching. Another told the story of a friend who taught in Porterville, in southern Tulare County: "Where she lived there was a woman on the other side of her who watched her wash that hung out on the line. And one Saturday, she hung up six pair of underpanties instead of seven. That women came over and asked her, 'What happened to you? You didn't have seven pair of underpants on the line this week.'"

Although there was somewhat greater anonymity in larger towns, teachers there were closely watched as well. In the Kings County town of Stratford in 1920, Hazel Fowler recalled, "Teachers were expected to attend and participate in the church and all local affairs. Skirts could be only so short and teachers were to wear bloomers. The boy friends were closely watched as well as the teachers."[18] Gerald Jacobus, who was later Kings County superintendent of schools, described an annual parade in Hanford, the county seat, in the 1930s: "All of the elementary students and teachers marched in the parade. The children thought it was great, but the teachers fought it all the way! They had to march with their charges going down the street two by two, carrying small American flags. This was a chance for the public to eye the teachers."[19]

As Hazel Fowler noted, one form of social control in these rural towns centered on religion. It was generally assumed that teachers would attend church on Sunday and would participate in church activities. "We were expected to attend choir practice every Wednesday evening and church service every Sunday morning," recalled Wellabelle Maloney. "The school principal picked us up to insure that we did."[20] In Woodlake, Beatrice H. remarked, "most of the, of what you might say the leaders belonged to the Presbyterian church," and teachers were expected to attend one of the several churches in town, preferably the Presbyterian. Ellen A. recalled feeling "pressured" to go to church; she had "sort of a feeling" that "if you don't do this you might not get your job back next year." In Tulare County virtually all of the teachers in this period seem to have been white Protestants. But in Kings County, with its large Portuguese population, schools also hired some Portuguese teachers who were Catholic. One such teacher, Jo Semas, remembered: "When I first taught, we couldn't, when applying for a position, say we were Catholic; we had to say we were Christians."[21]

In the interwar period, drinking, smoking, and even dancing were considered inappropriate for country women teachers. Beatrice H., for example, commented: "When you had your interview they would say, We don't approve of smoking—especially women, I don't know if they said this to the men. We don't approve of your smoking, and of course, as far as the men were concerned it was the same thing as far as drinking. They didn't approve of the use of liquor. They let us know that they didn't." Beth Friend of Kings County remembered a time when she and her sister Grace boarded with "an elderly lady": "One Sunday, she came home and found us dancing to phonograph recordings. . . . She scolded us, and I cried on Cecil's shoulder. Teachers were not supposed to dance!"[22]

In their accounts, teachers describe the ways in which local communities exerted control, often citing rigid social expectations but at the same time accepting these restrictions as "natural." Ruth G., for example, at first denied there were standards of behavior for teachers, but then provided specific examples:

K.W.: Were there standards for teachers?
Ruth G.: No, not really. Well, certainly, you didn't wear shorts in those days. But the only thing, be a little careful about your clothes, not bizarre in any way. And very little makeup. They never said anything. They hired me so I guess I looked all right. No, I didn't find it a problem at all. But I had a friend that had to be very careful. She was out near Lemon Cove and she couldn't wear a sleeveless dress, had a lot of limitations put on.

George J. noted the economic reasons underlying some of these expectations: "They were particular about you buying your cars in town, the town that you taught. I don't know what the pressure was, I just did it. I didn't buck the system." Teresa D. took a similar attitude: "There were always some that watched and there were people on the board that watched, trustees that watched . . . but it never did make much difference to me 'cause I worked quite hard anyway, and it didn't make much difference."

Autonomy, Contestation, and Consumer Culture

Women teachers in the interwar years were caught between nineteenth-century middle-class standards of behavior and an expanding mass consumer culture that was mounting a strong challenge to the old mores. Now images in films and magazines were presenting a new, sexually and socially "liberated" woman, who was not constrained as to the clothes, hairstyle, and makeup she wore and who had the freedom to smoke, drink, or dance as she pleased. In this rapidly shifting cultural world, many women teachers rejected the conventional representation of the proper, dowdy, repressed schoolmarm. Christine McCready described a job interview in the 1920s: "The principal looked me up and down and said he'd hire me because I didn't look like a 'flapper.' I felt crushed. Everyone wanted to look like a 'flapper' in those days."[23]
Some teachers told of actively resisting or negotiating social expectations and regulations. Evelyn B., for example, described being part of a group of women teachers who went up to Fresno and experimented at a friend's house with smoking. In Hanford, one male teacher remembered: "Of course, [the community] was strongly anti-cigarettes and booze. The silly part was teachers, men, would always go to the furnace room to smoke, and then the fumes would be picked up by the ceiling and blow all through the hallways. It was so darn silly." Margaret C., who had grown up in southern California and attended the University

of California at Berkeley, recalled job interviews in which trustees would ask personal questions. But Margaret C. was not intimidated by the questioning:

Margaret C.: Oh, they asked you all kinds of questions that they wouldn't dare ask now. If you played cards. What church did you go to—you're supposed to go to church. I'd always supported the church, but I was not one to go to church. We've always, my mother says she thinks that all of us were born with a deck of cards in our hand because we all played cards.
K.W.: Did you tell them when they asked if you played cards?
Margaret C.: Oh, I said, "Yes. I play cards." Nobody played cards out there then.

Despite declining to attend church and confirming that she played cards, Margaret C. was hired. Thus, even when community standards of behavior seemed fixed, they could be challenged in this period of cultural instability.

The social anxiety over women's bodies can be seen in particular in responses to the new practice of short or "bobbed" hair. Jo Semas, for example, remembered when "we, the women, were told not to cut our hair."[24] In one highly publicized California case in 1924, the school board of Santa Paula dismissed a teacher because she had bobbed her hair.[25] Urban liberal observers decried this infringement of women teachers' rights: "Never was there greater need for calm, dispassionate thinking than now," wrote one editorialist in 1924. "It is to be regretted that here and there, principals of schools, superintendents, teachers and board members have so far lost control of themselves as to join in the hue and cry against bobbed hair."[26]

Bobbed hair provides a classic example of the ways in which teachers negotiated and resisted the control of school boards and communities. Margaret C. told the following story with great enjoyment:

In Tulare, we all went up to the Big Game. We were about divided, Cal and Stanford. But we always went up. And went to the sorority for tea. . . . The first year we went up, we still had long hair. And everybody [else] had their hair cut. So the sorority sisters said, "We can tell you're from the country." Well, that just rubbed us the wrong way. So we went down after the tea and got our hair cut. . . . Then we got scared. We had to go back. Nobody in Tulare had their hair cut. So we thought, what on earth shall we do? Well, in those days they had teachers institute—Monday, Tuesday, and Wednesday and then Thanksgiving Thursday and Friday. And we always had to go to Visalia [for it]. Most of the time you stayed over there in the hotel in Visalia. But we didn't tell them we had our hair cut; we got some hair nets and ratted our hair and bought two big hats. And so we got ready and went to the institute and we sat down there and a couple of the sorority sisters spotted us. And they came down the aisle and looked right at us and said, "How do you like your short hair by now?" Well, we about died. Another one said, "What short hair? What short hair?" They said, "You're going to lose your job, you won't have a job come next week. Soon as your people out there find out you have short hair, they'll just fire you." Well, that didn't set too well, and so . . . we worried about that and so we went to Grandma Middleton. And she said, "Why do you worry about such things? It's all right if you wanted to cut your hair. Whose hair is it? It's your own. Now stop ratting it, take that net off, and go have short hair. . . . If you want short hair, that's all right." So we did. And I think within the next two weeks we cut about, oh I guess we cut about three dozen people's hair. We didn't know how to cut hair, but we cut it off anyway.

K.W.: And nobody said anything?

Margaret C.: Nope. Isn't that something?

In this story, bobbed hair symbolizes a cultural shift from a nineteenth-century representation of femininity to a twentieth-century image of modernity and freedom. Margaret C., who had attended the University of California and who frequently visited Berkeley, in a sense brought this new image home to Tulare by cutting her own hair. Movies and magazines had already spread the figure of the flapper throughout society, urban as well as rural, which made it more likely that the community would accept such rebelliousness on the part of the young teacher. Grandma Middleton, who is not identified further, is presented by Margaret C. as a voice of older women's authority in the community. Her comment "Whose hair is it? It's your own" echoes the earlier feminist and suffragist discourse of women's rights. Community resistance to bobbed hair was short-lived, probably because its symbolic assertion of women's freedom posed no real threat to power over resources or hegemonic authority.

Increasingly in the 1920s and 1930s, single women teachers lived in hotels or boardinghouses in towns, places where they could find companionship and amusement. Polly O., for example, lived in a hotel in which the third floor was occupied almost exclusively by teachers. Each teacher had a private room with a bathroom down the hall. "We got together. We had a room that was a kitchen and we got together for our meals. We each did our own meal and did our separate cooking. But we'd often eat together. We had quite a good time. Practically all of us were first- or second-'year teachers except this one teacher . . . who had been there a number of years. We would do things together." Karen R. described a similar situation in the early 1920s. The small town she lived in had only one hotel, and six women teachers boarded there:

Karen R.: There were six of we schoolmarms, as they referred to us, that lived there. We didn't have any transportation, we didn't have automobiles. We schoolmarms weren't rich enough. My first-year salary was one hundred twenty-five dollars a month, and it was only for nine months—they only paid for the months that we taught. So, we made our own enjoyment, fun. There was a drugstore with the old-fashioned fountain. There was a couple that owned that, and they were very good to us. We used to go over there when we didn't find anything to do and couldn't do anything else; we would go behind the counter and make our own sodas, ice cream sodas.

K.W.: They didn't mind that you lived in the hotel?

Karen R.: No. Well, they knew that the hotel had a very good reputation, and there was a group of young fellows down there that boarded there also. Mr. and Mrs. Conkey were reputable people. . . . The fellows all stayed upstairs. We took the east house, that was where the schoolmarms stayed. Those Conkeys were so tolerant, as I look back on it now, I don't know why they didn't knock our knuckles against the wall. Maybe at night we decided we wanted to make some fudge. The heaters were these old kerosene heaters that stand up. So, we had a pan and put it on top of the heater. We didn't have any sugar, so we'd just go down and empty all the sugar bowls on the dining room tables. You know, people don't like to put up with that kind of thing. We would make our fudge or maybe sometimes when we had dinner we wouldn't want to eat our dessert right away, so we would take that on down there. Poor Conkeys, sometimes they'd have to come down and resurrect their dishes. . . . Oh gosh, those were the days. . . . Sometimes, we decided that we wanted a piece of pie or something, we would go down into the dining room, and there was a serving room and a kitchen; off the kitchen was a screened porch, and in those days they had a icebox and put it in there, and Joe had his room off the kitchen. This icebox had a heavy lid and it was on a pulley and you would lift it up and the pulley would make it stay open. We would go in there and take a pie, and just at the time when we were getting it, old Joe was saying, "Ssssss." We would jump! It's a wonder we didn't have some broken wrists or something.

Karen R. was a respected retired teacher of ninety at the time of this interview. Accounts of her life had appeared in local newspapers, and the story of the Conkeys' hotel had been told frequently. Here, Karen R. describes a supportive and domestic world of wholesome amusements—making fudge, taking some pie from the icebox in the evenings. She makes a point of affirming the hotel's good reputation and notes that "the fellows all stayed upstairs." The young women teachers in her narrative are presented almost as children, who certainly posed no threat to the community and were themselves in no danger.

Karen R.'s picture of the upstanding world of the Conkeys' hotel may have exemplified the lives of other young women teachers as well. Her statement that she was "not rich enough" to have a car is interesting. In fact, by the late 1920s many schoolteachers owned cars in Tulare and Kings Counties. Having a car gave them much more independence, both in their work and in their private lives. Beatrice H. described the freedom the car brought for her:

I always had a car, but I was more fortunate than many of my peers, because I had no brothers and sisters in the family [whom I had] to help. I had some money of my own and I worked the whole time. So I had money to put into things, that I could spend. Like, back in those days you could get a secondhand Ford for a couple, three hundred dollars. They didn't cost nearly as much as they do now. I remember I had a car from the time I went to Earlimart, in fact I was the only one of the four of us [who] roomed together [who had a car]. We'd all pile in, I especially remember after we got the DeSoto—it was just a little coupe, you know. We'd all pile into there, three or four of us. One would sit on somebody else. We didn't [just] stay down there.

Margaret C. remembered the pleasure of her first Model T, which she bought in 1924 for $585: "Oh, that Ford just went all over the country, and we thought we had the world by the tail. It was a Ford coupe." Evelyn B., who lived on the family ranch until she married, remembered trips and outings that the car made possible: "When we went up to the mountains, and we were going to be a foursome, it was always my car! 'Cause it was a four-door. And we went over to the coast a couple of times, went to summer school at Huntington." Polly O. recalled:

People were getting to do things [thanks to the car]. There wasn't too much danger. Back when I was at Parlier in my early years, I thought nothing of starting off at ten o'clock at night and driv[ing] till two in the morning if I wanted to. I very frequently used to go down over the ridge and down to my brother's. For instance, maybe we'd have a program at school, at Parlier, and I would start up after the program was over.

Having a car also gave the teacher the power to distance herself from a hostile community. Rita M., for example, taught at Harmony School but lived in a nearby town:

K.W.: What happened when you went out there to teach at Harmony?
Rita M.: Several people told me not to go because the children were all out of control and it would be such a hard place. Even the teacher who had taught there before me, I don't remember who she was, told me that the night or daytime of graduation she had to hide her car behind a haystack to keep them from damaging it.

Although Rita M. claimed she had no trouble at the school, it is interesting that the disliked teacher's car was the focus of vandalism; perhaps it was seen as a symbol of privilege or independence.

Living in hotels or boardinghouses, driving their own cars, young women teachers had considerable freedom to live outside the bounds of their families or the local community. Most women married after a few years of this independence, but a minority of women teachers remained single. Of the twenty-three women teachers I interviewed, five never married, and three of these continued to live with their parents. Jane W.'s father was a successful farmer and may not have needed her income, but she continued to help him with his accounts. Teresa D. described her mother's death from tuberculosis and her sister's long illness, during which time Teresa D. helped both with nursing care and by contributing to the family income. Polly O. lived alone, first in a boarding hotel and later in her own home. Another woman lived with a close woman companion who was also a teacher. These two had met in college; they then worked and lived together for over fifty years, owning a house in town and a cabin in the mountains. Referred to in newspaper accounts as "the girls," they were greatly respected and beloved by the community. Although such a close, long-term association would probably now be seen as a lesbian relationship, neither the teacher I interviewed nor others who knew the two women described it as such. This reticence may reflect an understandable lack of trust of me as a stranger, or it may simply suggest a different cultural framing of close women's relationships.

Overt sexuality was rarely mentioned in the interviews. Evelyn B. spoke more freely on this subject than most teachers. In one school, the male principal, who was married and had children in the school, was attentive in a way that made her uncomfortable. He would make a point of coming into her room in the late afternoon when she was working alone. She also told about a teacher who had an affair with a married man:

K.W.: You couldn't get away with that out in the country schools, do you think?
Evelyn B.: It was a country school at Travor, but she didn't do any of her monkey business in Travor. She'd leave, you know. . . . I guess she must have lived there in the community, but to sneak around . . . what a life . . . sneak[ing] around with this married man . . .

The only direct reference to lesbianism in the interviews I conducted was when a widowed teacher described an incident that had happened over fifty years earlier. Mary C. told this story after I asked her about her acquaintance with Helen Heffernan:

Mary C.: I'm going to shock you with what I'm going to tell you, because that's what makes it so interesting. This woman one time suggested that we go down to Carmel.
K.W.: Was this Helen Heffernan or was this your friend?
Mary C.: No, this was not Helen Heffernan, I haven't said the friend's name. When we got there, we went into the hotel lobby, and she said, "I'll make the arrangements." She came back and she said, "I got us a double bed." It could have been twins, you know. So when we got in bed, why, she said, she just wanted to love me. I said, "Oh, I'm through with that, I can't do that." And this lovely woman, sweet and kind and all, that was her . . .
K.W.: And you didn't have any idea?

Mary C.: No, I didn't know. You can't tell exactly, I didn't know what pain I was causing. Anyway, she got from Helen Heffernan that there was a supervision of music job down in Hanford. So she wanted to know if I would like to have it, and I said yes. I had been frantically seeking a certificate to be a supervisor.

This story was told as I was questioning Mary C. about her professional life and the means by which she obtained her first position as a rural supervisor. Although at first I assumed she was telling this story because it was a shocking incident, in fact Mary C. wanted to make the point that, as the object of unwanted desire, she saw herself as responsible for causing suffering. But she did not present this desire as unnatural or negative. The teacher is referred to as a "lovely women, sweet and kind and all," and Mary C.'s comment "Oh, I'm through with all that" may imply earlier sexual experiences with women. Since Mary C. had been educated and had worked in suburban towns close to San Francisco, areas where all-women social groups were much more widespread than they were in the rural towns of the San Joaquin Valley, her narrative may reflect an accepted world of romantic relationships between women.

The Marriage Bar

One of the best-known examples of control over women teachers is the marriage bar. The stricture that women teachers could not be married was never officially made into law in California, as it was, for example, in Pennsylvania, but the bar was widely practiced in California nevertheless. In Tulare and Kings Counties, the marriage bar varied from place to place. Although the 1880 U.S. Census did not list any married women teachers in Tulare County, by the 1890s some districts were hiring married women, and their numbers continued to rise slowly in the early twentieth century. But even though the numbers of married women teachers continued to rise, most women teachers in Tulare and Kings Counties in the 1920s were single. According to the 1920 U.S. manuscript census, 16 percent of women teachers were married, 1 percent divorced, and 4 percent widowed; of the remaining 79 percent who were single, a significant number lived as boarders, and an increasing number listed themselves as head of household. As for men teachers, 78 percent were married, none divorced, and 2 percent widowed.[27] Because manuscript census data for the years after 1920 have not been released, we do not have a detailed picture of the households of later teachers; however, an analysis of women teachers using a married name (Mrs.) in the 1930 and 1940 school manuals for Tulare and Kings Counties shows a marked increase in the percentages of married teachers. In 1930 and

1940, respectively, 47 percent and 48 percent of women teachers in the two counties used their married name. While these figures are somewhat suspect—they may include widows, and some married teachers may not have admitted to being married—they are evidence of a clear trend toward hiring married women. Even so, the marriage bar was still enforced in many districts up until the Second World War. The retired teachers I interviewed all mentioned the existence of the marriage bar in the interwar years.

Women teachers who faced the marriage bar responded in a variety of ways. Some gave up teaching, either to take up other work to supplement their husband's wages or to stay at home. Leah Smith, who began teaching in Angiola in Tulare County in 1915, left her job in 1919 when she married: "I fell in love with a farmer, married him and lived in a cookhouse out on Tulare Lake for three years, cooking for eight men and doing roustabouting. I had a wood stove and we ate, slept and fed the men in the one-room cookhouse."[28] She returned to teaching in the 1940s, after her children were raised and her husband developed valley fever and could no longer work.

Others found school districts that would hire married women. When Evelyn B. married in 1935, she was forced to give up her teaching job in Ivanhoe, so she found another position in nearby Woodlake and drove to the new job in her car. Miriam J. mentioned that she quit teaching when she married because "it was the thing to do in those days. When you got married you weren't supposed to have a career, you were supposed to stay home and keep house. I guess you know that. I suppose you can become interested in keeping house. It's just a little boring. I persuaded my husband to let me go back and teach." Thus Miriam J. at first accepted the societal interpretation of a married woman's place, but then changed her mind and sought out a school that would accept married women teachers. Others resorted to various subterfuges to keep their jobs. Ellen A. recalled a women she knew who was teaching in a school near hers: "She told me, 'Don't call me by name.' I don't know whether she went by her maiden name or her married name. I never did find out. I just called her by her first name."

Although many rural districts maintained the bar against married women teachers until the Second World War, others, usually small rural or mountain school districts, had hired married women beginning in the late nineteenth century and continued to do so. Some districts would even hire women with small children. Grace Canan Pogue, for example, was hired for the mountain school of Yokohl as a married woman with a small child; as was fairly common, her mother lived with her and cared for her child. Once teachers had proved themselves in a job, moreover, they could negotiate with school boards to keep their jobs if they married. Karen R., who began teaching in a small town in Tulare County in 1920, recalled:

When I came here, they wouldn't hire a married woman. When Carl and I decided to be married, I'd taught three years. They gave me my contract. The contracts came out in April or May—April, I guess. They gave me my contract, and we were planning on being married that summer. So I didn't feel right in signing it and giving it back to them. So I went to the president of the trustees, Mr. Wilkins, and I told him that I was planning on being married. And I said, "Now, if that isn't agreeable with the board, I want you to know I'll just take back my contract." Well, in a week he came back and he said it was all right, but I don't know what you want to get married for. Later he apologized for that remark!

Accounts from the 1930s reveal a growing acceptance of teachers marrying, even in the face of the depression. Evelyn Burke Huffman described getting her first job in Lemoore in Kings County in 1932, where being single "was a requirement." After she had taught for one year, however, the board of trustees gave her permission to marry, and she continued teaching for three more years before becoming pregnant with her first child.[29]

Even when school boards hired married women teachers, they still sometimes maintained control over their private lives:

George J.: My wife and I were engaged when we came here and she taught a year, and then we got married the day after school started. She continued to teach there, but we couldn't live together.
K.W.: So they let you get married, but you couldn't live together?
George J.: That's right. Well, I guess you could live together, but [only] if you were working someplace else, if you were commuting or that sort of thing.

Stories like this are common, but in some towns it was perfectly acceptable for teachers to marry. Beatrice H., for example, was teaching in Woodlake in Tulare County when she married in 1935. When I asked why she was not required to resign, she said, "They had several married teachers there. Apparently, [it] didn't make a bit of difference at all to them. My roommate got married about the same time, a few days apart, but they never said a word to us about it." Virginia B., too, continued to teach after her marriage in 1932. In 1939, when she was pregnant with her first child, she asked for maternity leave. Although the board had never heard of such a thing, they agreed to give her six months off. Of course, Virginia B. had been teaching for fourteen years when she became pregnant and was well respected in the community. Her father, moreover, was a well-known local rancher, and her mother also was a teacher, facts that doubtless made a difference in how the board treated her.

Although the marriage bar was more or less a fact of life for Tulare and Kings County teachers until the early 1940s, retired teachers interpreted it in different ways. When I asked Ellen A., for example, why she thought school boards refused to hire married women, she said: "They just wanted to be dictatorial. Husbands were supposed to provide for you." Other teachers expressed more contradictory attitudes. Ruth G., who left teaching when she married in the 1930s, provided the following account:

Ruth G.: I got married and they weren't hiring married teachers. But I didn't want to teach then anyways.

K.W.: That's interesting too. Once you got married at Thermal they wouldn't have kept you on?

Ruth G.: No, they wouldn't have over at Oakland Colony either, that's the school out by Tulare. The principal *was* married, but she had been there quite a while. A woman. Well, she taught it as a one-teacher school. But they wouldn't hire married teachers after that. There weren't enough jobs really.

K.W.: Did they give reasons?

Ruth G.: No, except there were, there was a surplus of teachers, and that was one way of not hiring. Married teachers, their husbands could support them. Other than that I don't know.

K.W.: Wasn't that kind of hard on you, to give up your job in the depression?

Ruth G.: Well, he was working. He made enough. Ninety-eight dollars a month, and it was ample compared to now. I subbed some, quite a bit. No, that amount seemed to go as far as, a great deal more than nowadays. I can remember, on our honeymoon, in September, and we'd drive by these schools with people in them and I'd sit there and cry and he'd say, This is a heck of a honeymoon.

K.W.: You were crying because . . .

Ruth G.: I wanted to teach.

Ruth G. begins by saying she didn't want to teach once she married, but then contradictorily tells about how she cried when she passed a school on her honeymoon, a story that seems almost to escape from the logic of her narrative. Note the break in the story between discussing her husband's $98 a month ("that amount seemed to go as far as, a great deal more than nowadays") and the next sentence that begins, "I can remember, on our honeymoon. . . . " Although Ruth G.'s husband could support her, teaching was clearly an important part of her self-definition; financial need or no, she "wanted to teach."

Conclusion

What do these narratives contribute to an understanding of the lives of women teachers? Competing representations of women and of teachers, the force of material need, the ways individual women negotiated a rapidly changing social world are all revealed here. In their accounts, these women teachers challenge accepted notions of teaching as a means of expressing an "essential" womanly nature.[30] The reasons they put forth for becoming teachers are not presented in terms of the dominant images and assumptions about women teachers—that they are nurturing, self-sacrificing, only seeking a smooth transition between father and husband. Instead, they present themselves as free agents who deliberately chose teaching as work; in this they speak through the authoritative discourse that sees the United States as a society composed of individuals free to shape their lives without impediment.

This depiction of themselves as free agents does not, however, call into question the gender segregation and patriarchal privilege of the world in which they lived, nor does it address hegemonic assumptions that teaching is "naturally" women's work. These narratives are contradictory, both confirming and implicitly challenging dominant ideas. Thus, the limited number of job choices for women is not a limitation, the rebel tomboy is not rebelling, the way the world is arranged is natural and inevitable, what was done does not negate the dominant view of what *should* be done. As we read these accounts "for structure," the material conditions in which these women lived and worked and the economic and personal reasons for their decisions to become teachers become clearer. As we read "for culture," we begin to see the complexity of the imaginative paradigms that organize their memories. These narratives thus provide the possibility of imagining and understanding a past world, both in terms of the material world in which these women moved and in terms of the categories through which they created their own selves.

THE WORK OF TEACHING IN RURAL SCHOOLS, 1920–1940

In their narratives, rural teachers describe a world in which shifting social expectations led to representations of both women and teachers that were both unstable and contested. Yet despite ongoing attempts by community and, as we shall see, the educational state to control teachers' lives, the interwar period was in many ways a positive time for women teachers. The key role of women in positions of power at the county and state levels led to the creation of a women's sphere in education, even if this sphere was not publicly acknowledged. In California, rural supervisors influenced by the progressive ideas of Helen Heffernan encouraged and respected the work of elementary school teachers, the vast majority of whom were women. In rural two- and three-room schools, women held responsible positions as school principals and were encouraged to see themselves as capable professionals. And women continued to be elected as county superintendents in many rural California counties until the end of the Second World War.

The interwar years were also a time of social conflict. In Tulare and Kings Counties, changes in agricultural production, in particular the introduction of cotton and the consequent need for cotton pickers, brought in new populations, which heightened the racial tensions of Valley society. In the 1930s, the depression called into question the earlier belief in a homogeneous and cohesive rural culture. Government responses to the depression brought both state and federal programs into rural communities, thus challenging local autonomy and inciting political and social conflicts between conservative and radical forces.

In their work in the schools, rural women teachers mediated the tensions created by these social and economic changes. Although they may have entered the profession for reasons of material need and personal satisfaction, they nevertheless found themselves participating in a state institution that in many ways reproduced the racial, class, and gender inequalities of the wider society. As white women, they shared in the privileges of white identity, understanding the world through the categories of center and margin that marked the culture as a whole. As rural teachers in the depression, they taught the children of migrant workers—Mexican, African-American, and white southwestern American—who were often seen as dangerous outsiders by the communities of which these teachers were a part.

The work of women teachers in rural California schools in the interwar period was thus complex and contradictory. It offered women opportunities for leadership and personal satisfaction, even as the labeling of students by language, ethnicity, and ability continued to be elaborated by the educational state. How did the growth of state control and the crisis of the depression affect the lives of rural women teachers? How did they come to define themselves through their work?

Teaching in Rural Schools

Retired teachers' accounts of their work in rural schools in the first three decades of the twentieth century recall the conditions described in nineteenth-century memoirs. Maria Hayden Miller's description of her first school in Kings County, for example, presents a familiar picture of the duties of the country teacher:

In 1917, when not yet 19 years old, I did my first year of teaching at the King School in Kings County. This was a small, one-room school with all grades in one room. The school was located four miles east and three miles south of Hanford. At this time, the country roads were definitely not highways, and many of them not even oiled in places. Many of the country roads became very deep in mud in spots. Consequently, through the wet winter there were several times that my car had to be pulled through the mud by a kindly farmer's team of horses. The neighbors in the area were very kind and helpful to the young "school marm." The district was not exactly rich. The teacher's salary was $75 per month. Her duties were not only teaching but included sweeping out each night, dusting, and seeing that wood was in ready for the morning fire.[1]

In many respects, this could have been written fifty years earlier, except for the significant mention of the car, which meant that this young teacher could live in town and drive out to work in the countryside.

Margaret C.'s account of her first school in 1922 likewise raises themes common in rural teachers' memoirs. Margaret C. had grown up in San Diego, and she recalled both the anxiety of running a country schoolroom and her shock at what seemed to her unsanitary and primitive conditions:

K. W.: What was it like when you first walked in the door to that school?

Margaret C.: Scared to death. There was one large room and a great big, old woodstove right in the center. Coal oil lamps along here. A little raised platform about six by eight. A teacher's desk and a chair, that if you leaned back in it the springs would go way back. Then an anteroom for the girls to put their coats up, and one for the boys. There was a bell with a rope. And I was supposed to ring the bell at eight-thirty every morning. And one o'clock. If they ever set their clocks by that bell, they'd [have] been off I don't know how many times. Of course, they had a well and a hand pump and a tin cup with a chain. I about died. The toilet out there scared me to death. And here was everybody drinking out of this one tin cup.

The unsanitary "tin cup," which was frequently cited by reformers in their attacks on the backwardness of the one-room school, was mentioned by other teachers. Discipline, too, was a common issue. Margaret C., for example, emphasized her ability to maintain order, even though when she started out she was not much older than her oldest pupil.

K. W.: Did you ever have to strike a child?

Margaret C.: Oh, yes, I used a small cane, we called it "the board of education." I'd tell them to lean over—the boys especially—pop and make a lot of noise on their jeans, you know. But it didn't hurt. But I never did that unless they knew that they were supposed to have it. I never punished a youngster if they felt they didn't deserve it.

K. W.: What would you do then?

Margaret C.: Talk with them.

K. W.: When you were a young teacher, you were teaching fairly big boys . . .

Margaret C.: Well, I started teaching at nineteen and the oldest one I had was seventeen. They never gave me any trouble.

The multigraded classroom, of course, had its challenges, as the teacher catered to children of widely different ages and abilities. Beatrice H. described teaching in a one-room school:

I'd have a group reading, and I'd usually have about two groups in their seats. These children would be working on their names or numbers or colors or whatever I had made up for them that day. Just like a four-ring circus, you know, one group would come up to read, and the group at the blackboard would go their seat, and one of those [who were seated] would go to the board. We just switched around this way. And used what facilities we had.

Margaret C. provided a similar account, even using the same metaphor of the circus:

I think, I've always said that teachers really miss a lot that never taught in a multigraded room.

K. W.: Why? What was it that was good about it?

Margaret C.: The first thing, it's like a three-ring circus. You'd have a group at the board, [one] back in the corner, the reading circle, you'd have a group studying whatever. And you had all grades you had to take care of. They learned to concentrate. Older ones helped the younger ones. We never had any discipline problems.

As a matter of course, teachers in country schools were completely responsible for their students from the time they arrived at school in the morning until they left in the afternoon. This meant directing and overseeing children at lunch and recess as well as inside the classroom. Polly O. described dealing with the children on the school grounds:

The school grounds were covered with [the spiny weed] puncture vine. We had, as I recall, two pieces of athletic equipment, one was a volleyball or soccer ball and one was a baseball and bat. Not hardball—softball. We had to keep that equipment in good shape. The soccer ball was always getting in the puncture vine, which was not too good. The baseball—we played baseball practically year round—the backstop had a big hole in it. So I told the clerk of the board that it made it a little difficult for the catcher. He said, "You should have a catcher who can catch the ball." So I made his son the catcher. We would go out and we were supposed to play other schools too some of the time. That was an interesting thing because we really hardly had enough to make a team. We had an irrigation ditch that ran across the street and one of their pet stunts was that they would hit the ball so it went into the irrigation ditch when it was full of water, and because we had only one ball we had to get it back. So one or two of them would be commissioned to go chase the ball, and I found out that what they were doing was throwing clods at the ball so that it would go as far downstream as possible, and that would give them half, three-quarters of an hour chasing the ball. After this had happened two or three times I decided we needed to do something about it, so I got a long piece of bamboo and made a little net and every time we went to play baseball I would march out with my net [to be ready to rescue the ball]. It was amazing how much more accurate they became.

In this account, Polly O. touches on several common themes: the need to respond to the school trustee about the smallest detail of school life (a catcher who could catch the ball), her own ingenuity in making a net to fish out the errant softball, and her sense of authority and responsibility for classroom decisions.

The difficulties of teaching in country schools were similar nationwide. But one unusual theme in the memories of California rural teachers was the problem of rattlesnakes. Hannah A. remembered one vivid incident at Rural School:

We had those down-the-hill rest rooms, if that's what you want to call them. One morning as soon as recess was over, I made a beeline down there to get ahead of the kids and get out of the way. When I opened the door to come out, there was a rattlesnake coiled right in the door. Well, there was only one way out and I jumped over the thing and hollered for the boys to bring the baseball bat down there. [One boy] hit it, but that didn't even hurt it. So it went under, and every time anybody would go down there, you'd hear it rattle. The kids kept telling me—they'd get there to school before I did—about this snake that was down around the pump house. So one afternoon when school was out, the kids made a dash down to the pump house for some reason or other, I don't know what, and then I heard them send up a yell, "Come here, come here!" So I got the shovel and went down there and the thing had stretched across—they'd gone in over it into the pump house and they'd turned around to come out . . . here the thing was stretched across the door. So we got the thing out, chopped its head off, and buried it in a squirrel hole.

This account, in its description of both danger and the competence of the country teacher, recalls Ethel Hall Besquette's published accounts of teaching in mountain schools in Tulare County two decades earlier. Esther Edes also mentions the threat of snakes at her first school, in Calabasas in 1923:

At our interview the clerk of the Board informed me that three teachers had been "run out" the previous year. They just could not stand the mice, lizards, snakes and other surprises when desk drawers were opened. I assured him that nothing like that would affect me. That I'd had several courses in biology, had been raised on a ranch, and loved animals and people. . . . One snake episode occurred but, when I took the snake, the pranks ended.[2]

Although the details of these narratives of teaching in rural schools echo earlier accounts, teachers who started teaching in the 1920s and 1930s often also emphasized the opportunities for creative teaching provided by small rural schools as opposed to the graded town schools. In country schools, teachers followed the guidelines set out in the county school manuals, which defined both instructional goals and subjects to be covered. Written by the staff of the county office, the school manual was given to each teacher. Rachel B. described the manual: "The county office had a big black binder about twelve inches long and eighteen inches wide. The pages you had to cover were in it when I first started teaching. You had to know that you were going to cover a certain amount during the year, that the children had to know so much at the end of the year. And the state had readers that you had to go through." Teresa D. added: "You see, the manual or the board of education would include certain requirements for a grade level, and you had enough [time] to cover it in general . . . enough to do what you needed to do if you worked on it." Evelyn B. also described the manual: "It stayed in the schoolroom, and then the next teacher had it until that one was expendable and we got another one . . . or else you took it home, and you [either] liked what it was or you modified it and adjusted it to your own program." It was this opportunity to adjust the county goals to a teacher's "own program" that allowed country teachers to experiment with different approaches.

The graded town schools were more hierarchical in structure, and the work of classroom teachers more closely supervised by principals. Teresa D., in distinguishing between teaching in town and rural schools, commented that in the graded school, "if your principal is real strict and real close on discipline or on the course of study, the curriculum, you know, you follow that very closely. Whereas if you were out in the country, you still would follow a plan but it wouldn't always be quite as close." Teachers in the graded town schools sometimes had more resources than did the one- or two-room teachers, but teaching conditions were still not easy. Beatrice H. described teaching in the graded school at Earlimart during the late 1920s:

Well, we were young and it was our first experience and we didn't have a lot of other things to compare it to, and so I think most of us enjoyed it. But we had no equipment back in those days. . . . We had no duplicators, so if you wanted to make an extra picture, like for art or something, you used these old gelatin pads. They'd be about nine by twelve, the size of a regular piece of art paper. And you put your picture up with your duplicating ink on it, and smacked it down on there, and that soaked in and took that off. And then you could make—you got ten good copies, from there on they kept getting lighter and lighter—so if you wanted to make more than twenty copies or so you had to make another one of those, you couldn't put the ink back on.
K.W.: You had to pour that gelatin out and put more in?
Beatrice H.: Yes. You had to start all over and wait for it to get cool, you know. Of course, if you anticipated this ahead of time, if you were going to make some kind of art pictures for children, then you'd probably make more than one of those to begin with. . . . But practically all of our work was put on the board. At the beginning of the year I made copies, hand copies for the children with their names and numbers and colors and this sort of thing.

Principals in town schools monitored everything from teaching practices to supplies. Rachel B., who taught in both one-room schools and graded town schools, described the close control that was exerted in the town schools at Orosi and Woodlake:

We had restrictions. For instance, a pencil had to last a child for a month. A ruler lasted a whole year. And scissors lasted a whole year. My. At Orosi, I was in a situation where we had a scissors rack, and that rack was filled with scissors when school started. At the end of the year the rack was supposed to be full of scissors [too]. So I collected them every day. I had different people help me during the week, and they did it for a whole week. Before they went home we checked to see if all those were full. Out at Woodlake, if they didn't have the ruler that the child had used it had to be paid for. Scissors that were missing had to be paid for.

Some teachers left the town schools for smaller country schools precisely because the smaller schools offered more freedom for innovation and autonomy. Miriam J. described her move from the graded school in Dinuba:

Miriam J.: My aunt, who was Mrs. Perkins, I don't know if you know her, she had been teaching out at East Orosi, a little school. She had such a good [time] teaching out there with the art work and the craft work. So I changed and moved over. When she quit teaching I went out there . . .
K.W.: That was a two-teacher school.
Miriam J.: It was a two-teacher school. We did a lot. We could do things that you couldn't do at a large school.
K.W.: Why?
Miriam J.: Well, you could do what you wanted to do. I taught the older children—I think I was better teaching older children. We did all kinds of things. We did clay work, and they never had anything like that. Different kinds of art work. Then I always had to teach the music, too. Every school I taught, I had to teach the music. I don't think I'm musical in any way. I can play the piano. So we put on little programs. And the clay work we did, well we got our picture in the state, I don't know what you call it, textbook or report. It was a book. We got our picture in it.

Irma R.'s description of the mountain school at Badger indicates the opportunities for innovation and flexibility for an imaginative teacher, as well as the greater freedom that existed to challenge gender expectations for boys and girls:

Irma R.: The last year I was there, everybody took cooking, including the boys. And on cooking day, as soon as the bus arrived, the mothers would come, each group would make part of the menu, and I would check with the mothers ahead of time, and anything that was lacking the mothers would bring, and they would stay, set the table according to 4-H, we would eat. And then the mothers would go home and we'd go back to school.
One little girl, when she came to the story about the little red hen that found the seeds . . . I took her into the kitchen and we made two loaves of bread. And they were just out of the oven when the milkman brought our milk. [He said,] "I'll give you a pound of butter if you'll give me two slices of that bread." So the little girl had me cut off two slices for him and he gave us the butter. When it was cool enough I sliced it and she buttered it and took it in to treat all the children back in the classroom. From that time on, she just whizzed through her reading book because she wanted to see if there was anything else in any other book that she could find that she could go cook!
K.W.: When you taught in the one-room school, you really had the freedom to do things like that.

Irma R.: Yes. Up there at Badger, it doesn't snow very much and by noon the snow is all very slushy. We'd have P.E. first thing in the morning. We'd go up by the teacherage, there was a good slope and everybody would play in the snow. Some had sleds, some just had pieces of cardboard. But they would all bring a change of clothing. By the time we had half an hour of P.E. out there in the snow they would be wet. We'd go back in and they would all change clothes and we would stay inside the rest of the day. We could just rearrange things to suit ourselves. When jump rope season came—the boys all thought jump rope was sissy. So I got a film one time of prize fight training. I never had any trouble after that, those boys learned to jump rope right along with the girls. And the girls learned how to play baseball right along with the boys.

Responsibility, Power, and Control

Teaching in a rural one-room school challenged young teachers to make decisions and take responsibility for the well-being of both their students and themselves. Two- and three-room schools also offered the possibility for leadership, since one of the teachers would simultaneously act as principal. Although these principalships were less prestigious than administrative positions in cities held by men, they did offer opportunity for decision making and the exercise of authority.[3] Hazel Ledbetter, for example, a teacher and principal in Tulare County for over fifty years, was remembered as a strong and compassionate leader. Evelyn B., who taught under her, called her a "crackerjack."

Many retired teachers remembered how easy it was to run these small country schools. Jane W., for example, described working conditions in the two-room school at Locust Grove as "wonderful": "There were two teachers, and the other teacher lived down the road a little ways. . . . She had the primary and I had the upper grades. We were just like a big family. We ate out under the trees. All we had to do, the two of us, was get together and we had a faculty meeting."

Hannah A., in contrast, remembered the job of principal as "a lot of hard work and you get the name for it."

K.W.: What kind of hard work was it?
Hannah A.: Well, records that you had to keep and you had to be responsible for materials, ordering materials, oh a lot of extra things.

Teresa D. provided a similar account:

K.W.: What do you think it meant to be principal when you're in a school with only two or three teachers?
Teresa D.: It really meant that if any problems came up, you handle them. That's what it meant, and it meant that you took a little responsibility for the planning in the school or whatever was needed . . . any problems that might come up.

K.W.: Did you think when you were principal that you had the responsibility to make sure that the other teacher or teachers in the school were doing their work right?

Teresa D.: Well, the places where I was principal, I didn't feel that. Now, if I had been in larger schools I might have, but in the places where I was, really, the teachers were good teachers, and I think that they knew that, that they did what they were supposed to do. . . . The person that's principal handles the figures for the attendance, some of the budget, turning in the budget.

In the interwar period, women also served in positions of power and authority as rural supervisors and, in some cases, as principals of graded town schools or as elected county school superintendents. Although Tulare County never elected a woman superintendent, Kings County had three women superintendents. Superintendent M. L. (Lee) Richmond, who served from 1918 to 1926, was closely associated with the ideas of progressive education championed by Helen Heffernan. Like her predecessor in office, Nannie Davidson, Richmond came from the Protestant, Anglo-American world of small farmers that defined the dominant cultural and political values of the Valley.[4] (Her father was the well-known farmer Stuart Richmond.) After moving from teaching in one-room schools to the graded schools of Lemoore and Hanford, she was appointed assistant superintendent of schools for Kings County. By the time she defeated J. E. Meadows for the county superintendency, she was well known in the county.

As an unmarried woman, Richmond seems to have moved within a cultural world of women's clubs and friendships. Consider this 1925 account of a surprise luncheon she arranged for two office workers who were retiring from her staff:

Miss M. L. Richmond, Miss Helen Heffernan, Mrs. Nella Ayers, and Mrs. Clara Coldwell, all of the office, entertained at a delightful dinner at Bernstein's on Wednesday evening. The event was a complete surprise to the honored guests, who had each been quietly invited to attend a surprise party on the other. Shasta daisies centered the pretty table which had been arranged on the mezzanine, and following the delicious chicken menu, Miss Richmond on behalf of the hostesses presented Miss Benson with a handsome luncheon cloth and napkins of Italian cut work on linen for use in her new home, and Miss Pampuel with a handsome brush and comb. Later the group chatted gaily for an hour and then left to attend various graduation exercises.[5]

This newspaper item appeared on the women's page of the *Hanford Morning Journal*; it was accompanied by reports of the Tuesday Bridge Club, the Double X Club, the E.O.S. Club, Lakeside Ladies Aid, the Wednesday Club, St. Margaret's Guild, and the E.W.O. Club, all weekly or biweekly women's groups that met in the afternoon for luncheon or cards. Thus, the social setting for these women teachers and administrators was very different from the business- and politics-oriented milieu in which male educators like J. E. Buckman or J. E. Meadows circulated. But although Lee Richmond felt most at home within the cultural world of women's clubs and organizations, she nevertheless cultivated and maintained alliances with the male-dominated public world of educational leaders and university experts. In 1920, for example, she was elected head of the Central Division of the California Teachers Association.[6]

In 1926, Lee Richmond was defeated in her bid for reelection by Elsie Felt Bozeman. She then moved to Butte County, where she took a position as rural school supervisor. She gained this position, an appointment by the county superintendent of schools, almost certainly through the influence of Helen Heffernan, who as a young woman had herself worked under Richmond as a rural supervisor. Butte County was also the home of Elizabeth Hughes, who was one of the first women elected to the state legislature, in 1918, and who was particularly interested in rural education. In 1929, Richmond was elected president of the California Rural Supervisors Association, an organization closely associated with Helen Heffernan's progressive educational ideas. A few months before her death in 1953, the Lee Richmond Elementary School in Hanford was named in her honor; Helen Heffernan spoke at the ceremony.[7]

Teachers were encouraged in progressive approaches through courses at teachers colleges and by the example and guidance of both progressive county superintendents like Lee Richmond and the rural supervisors. After rural supervision was mandated in 1921, Tulare and Kings Counties hired experienced teachers as rural supervisors, including some who specialized in music, art, and, later, physical education. Women who became rural supervisors had usually taught in rural schools themselves.

In interviews, retired rural supervisors described their own ambition and desire for better-paying and more responsible work as reasons for becoming rural supervisors. Teresa D., who had attended normal school in Kentucky and then passed the Tulare County teachers examination, decided to go on for her B.A.; she chose an external program for practicing teachers at Stanford, transferring credits from Fresno State and attending Stanford summer school for three years. She then decided to continue for her master's degree and move into supervision: "I spent three summers for my A.B. and three for my masters, and then I worked, spent one summer just doing research for my thesis. . . . I worked on the load and the cost of the Visalia school district. I could've used it for a doctor's dissertation, but I didn't have enough money saved to take a year off and spend what I'd lose [in income from teaching]." Jane W.

told a similar story of teaching for a few years, then deciding to take additional courses at Fresno State to prepare for a supervisory position.

Rural supervisors were themselves introduced to progressive approaches through meetings of the California Rural Supervisors Association and journals such as the *California Exchange Bulletin in Rural Education*. In many cases Helen Heffernan herself recruited and suggested teachers for rural supervisory positions. Mary C. was one such protégée:

I'd been teaching in Mill Valley and at first I just had regular teaching, about half the time music. And then the county schools supervisor came in to see me and I don't remember how it all began, but I made a friend out of her, and she was a lot of fun and nice. And she had a friend, and the friend was Helen Heffernan, who at that time was the rural supervisor of the state. So there were some conferences and there was this and that, we got acquainted better . . .

Mary C. later gained a position as rural music supervisor in Kings County.

K.W.: Did Helen Heffernan have anything to do with getting you that job?
Mary C.: She was a good friend of this man down here, and he had asked her how to get somebody and save himself from interviewing all of these people, because jobs were rare then.

Rural supervisors tried to support teachers in their work and to introduce them to what they considered progressive approaches to classroom teaching. By 1927, Tulare County rural supervisors were providing demonstration lessons for rural teachers at the annual teacher institutes and in one-day training sessions at local schools. Esta Aulman, the Tulare County art supervisor, claimed:

We have found as a result of these meetings that the teachers are more interested in the meetings where demonstration work occurs than in meetings without such work, as they ask for it each time. They are anxious to get the reaction of the pupils and other teachers to the work outlined in the County Manual or suggested by those in the office of the County Superintendent of Schools.

In some instances in the past, when we have found an especially weak, but hopeful, teacher we have given her a visiting day or two, so that she might spend time with one of our strongest and most resourceful teachers. We have always reserved the privilege of choosing which teacher the weak one shall visit. We have also told the strong teacher about the anticipated visit, so that she would know just what to stress. We, as well as the teachers, have found this most satisfactory.[8]

Rural supervisors were expected to work with a number of schools and teachers. In 1933 Esta Aulman created a traveling art exhibit of works created by Tulare County children that was loaned to rural schools for a week at a time. That same year, Josephine Murray, the Tulare County music supervisor, created a Joint Music Appreciation Program.

She promised that "if the pupils of any schools prepared a twenty-minute program around some theme or folk-idea," she would, in return, bring them a twenty-minute program on a subject of her choice.[9] Jane W., a rural supervisor who was frequently mentioned as an outstanding supervisor (as Evelyn B. described her, "a strong character and a very capable person"), described her work in the early 1930s:

Jane W.: When I started supervising, I had twenty-seven schools. Little ones. They were called the under–three hundred ADA schools—average daily attendance. They extended from Goshen to around Stone Corral. I had Traver, Kings River Union, Windsor, Grand View. And then the city schools could call on us for certain workshops and things, too. I used to go up to Dinuba every once in a while to do workshops.

K.W.: If you had twenty-seven schools, you couldn't possibly see them more than once a month, at the very most.

Jane W.: About twice a month.

K.W.: When you went and visited those schools, how did you see what your job was?

Jane W.: Helping a teacher improve her teaching ability, making her aware of the tremendous amount of material that existed in the county office that was available to her for the asking. Using different equipment than she had ever used, such as the motion picture machine and slide projectors. Enhancing and broadening the understanding of children. My philosophy was, and I hope it still is, that before you can teach a child to read, you need to broaden his concept of the things that are going to occur in that story so he brings something to the text and doesn't just come in cold. The child just plain needs a background to drop back on in order to really understand what he's talking about. So I wanted them to bring something to the text as well as to get something out of the text.

K.W.: When you went out to the school, how did you meet with teachers? Did you sit in on their classes, watch them teach?

Jane W.: Depended on the teacher. Some teachers yes, some teachers no.

K.W.: Would it depend on what they wanted or what you felt was good?

Jane W.: What they wanted. Because if it was anything else, you were thrusting something on them. But if it was something they felt they needed, or you could encourage them to see that they needed, then they'd take it and use it.

Some teachers were enthusiastic about the progressive ideas introduced by state leaders and county administrators. Hank G., for example, spoke of his older sister, a longtime teacher in Kings County who studied at UCLA:

Hank G.: The depression was pretty tough on us, but in 1937 we had a little family meeting, and they cashed in a little insurance policy on me and we got enough money together, and my sister went to UCLA and she graduated. One of her professors was a Dr. Seeds, who was a person for progressive education in California. I'm sure you've read some of her stuff.

K.W.: Yes, I have.

Hank G.: I've heard so much about Dr. Seeds. . . . That was the beginning, I think, to the language experience approach to reading. Because from day one my sis would always take the kids somewhere. They would come back with their little pictures of what they had seen and all, and then they would write about what they had seen.

K.W.: She got that from . . .

Hank G.: Dr. Seeds. And sis was always quoting Dr. Seeds this, and Dr. Seeds that, and Dr. Seeds everything else.

Polly O., who taught in rural elementary schools before becoming a high school English teacher, also mentioned progressive classroom practices she learned at teachers college:

Polly O.: That was a great time for grouping.

K.W.: You mentioned that everything was democratic. Where did these ideas come from?

Polly O.: From when we were doing practice teaching. We were told that it was good to have a vote on this and a vote on that, so we did. We used to always, we were always having these sharing of experiences, they would get up and tell things that happened. That was supposed to be one of the big things of that day. As far as running the class, for instance in mathematics, my girl who was in eighth grade was very poor, and she worked with the sixth graders in mathematics. In other words, we worked that way. So if they were a little faster they could work with another group.

Evelyn B. used the Deweyan discourse she had been introduced to at Fresno State to describe what it was like to teach in a one-room school: "One time, a tame crow hung over the roof, and we stopped everything, and of course, the kids just love to get out of any class, even in high school. We loved to get out of class, and you just take your lesson from the crow and make a nature study lesson out of it and you get your writing in, you get your handwriting, you get your share and tell and all of that."

Rural supervisors, progressive county superintendents, and state officials like Helen Heffernan encouraged progressive education techniques, but as we have seen, many state and local officials remained suspicious of what they considered radical ideas. Not all teachers were comfortable with the "liberal" approaches of their rural supervisors and college professors either. To some of the young rural women who attended Fresno State, the Deweyan ideas they encountered in course work and practice teaching were merely indicative of class privilege and "city ways." They described a sense of class as well as cultural difference, as in Beatrice H.'s recollection of the children who attended the Fresno State Demonstration School:

Those children were just a bunch of spoiled brats, because you know they were the professors' children or some of the leaders of the city who wanted their children out there at the Fresno State College—demonstration school, it was called. They were just, they weren't well disciplined. I didn't really enjoy that. But in '29, the year before I graduated, I went to a school on the south side of Fresno and did my practice teaching. It was a poorer end of town down in there, and they had large classes even there in Fresno back in those days. I don't remember exactly how many we had, but I remember we had large classes—there were Negro children, Japanese, Germans, it was kind of a mixture of the, I hate to use the word "lower class," but the working-class people who lived in the southern part of Fresno. So, my experience there carried over pretty well over to my experience at Earlimart, because I had so many of that type of children down there.

Ruth G., who also attended Fresno State, likewise mentioned the "children of very affluent people, professional people. We had to observe them a semester, and I thought, 'Oh, I've made the wrong choice.' Those children were horribly spoiled. Brought to school in limousines. The parents, too, I didn't enjoy too much." Ruth G. was relieved to find a place practice-teaching in a rural school rather than in the demonstration school at Fresno.

Several teachers approvingly mentioned the more practical training they received at the Miss Swopes summer schools at Long Beach and Santa Cruz, privately run schools that provided short courses on teaching methods. Hannah A., who had passed the county teachers exam, went to one such school:

Before I started teaching, that summer my sister and I went to Long Beach, and my mother went along and she kept my son. Ruth and I went to what they called the Miss Swopes school, and boy, that was right down-to-earth instruction about what to do in the school, so I had that before I started teaching. . . . Three weeks, we went three weeks. But we sure got a lot out of it.

In her use of the phrase "down-to-earth instruction," Hannah A. implicitly makes a claim for teaching as a technique or skill, not as a means of social change, in the sense in which Helen Heffernan, for example, saw it. At the same time, she asserts her own competence to teach outside the surveillance of state or county officials.

The contradictory responses of teachers to the progressive ideas they were taught at college are echoed in their memories of the rural supervisors who supported those ideas. Teresa D., who became a supervisor herself, remembered the work of the rural supervisors positively:

Teresa D.: They would come out and visit your room, and then have a conference with you. I thought it was very good.
K.W.: You didn't feel they were trying to control you? Were they helpful or . . . ?
Teresa D.: Yes, they were helpful, and they always meant to be helpful, I think. . . . As I look back, I realize that that's true, they always tried to help. So it was good. We had very good supervisors from the county office in Tulare County. We had

very good supervisors who knew what they wanted and what they were doing, and I learned along with the children, too, you know. I taught a lot of things that I learned and I hadn't really been drilled in too much. You realize it, you go through grade school and high school and years of college—a lot of things, you don't touch. So there were a lot of things that helped me when I had the good supervisors because they could give me ideas and suggestions, plans, and everything.

Other teachers, however, had a more suspicious attitude.[10] Evelyn B. described how news of a supervisor's arrival quickly spread at a graded rural school:

K.W.: How often did the supervisors come?
Evelyn B.: I think once a month. It must have been once a month that they came out.
K.W.: Did you know they were coming?
Evelyn B.: No, they came on the q.t., but we knew if they arrived in the morning. We knew that she couldn't be, you know, in every room . . . so we knew that she would be around before the day was over.

A frequently mentioned example of the tensions between classroom teachers and rural supervisors had to do with elementary reading instruction. Many teachers were committed to the earlier method of teaching reading through phonics. When rural supervisors who advocated the whole-word approach appeared, teachers would simply hide their phonics materials. Polly O. told this story of teaching in the rural graded school of Parlier:

We had county supervisors coming out. We knew who they were, of course. They would come and park in front, so we would always see when they drove up, so the word would get around. This was when they were teaching reading by the whole-word method. A lot of the teachers were not too sold on it. I was teaching eighth grade, so this didn't affect me. But a lot of teachers would do some phonetic work too. I can remember when the teacher came who was supervising that particular phase, they would often get their phonetic stuff out of sight and hide it.

Evelyn B., who believed in the phonetic method of teaching reading, would teach phonics every day before lunch. Because she didn't put it on her written schedule, however, the county supervisor never knew about it.

Race and Cultural Difference

Rural teachers in the interwar years found their work shaped by county and state officials and by changes in educational philosophy and policy. Yet teachers were also members of rural communities and shared the cultural beliefs of those communities. In Tulare and Kings Counties in this period, teachers continued to be overwhelmingly white women. In 1930, 86 percent of elementary school teachers listed in the county school directories were women; in 1940, 82 percent were women. I have been able to identify only one African-American teacher in this period, Grace Hackett, who taught in the black and Mexican school at Allensworth. The manuscript census of 1920 lists one Japanese teacher in Kings County, Masako Kitagawa, a twenty-year-old married woman who was born in Japan. Since she is not listed in the Kings County school directory, her professional status in the census probably indicates that she had been a teacher in Japan. There were Catholic teachers in both counties by 1920, particularly in Kings County, where a small number of Catholic Portuguese women taught. But the great majority of teachers in both counties continued to be native-born white Protestant women.

Schools in both Tulare and Kings Counties practiced both informal and formal racial segregation during the interwar years.[11] The school at Allensworth in essence remained a segregated school for African-American and Mexican-American children, and separate schools were held for Indian children on the Tule River reservation in Tulare County and the Ramona Rancheria in Kings County. Several teachers recalled segregation and racism in these years. Rachel B., for example, described the racial practices in Tulare in the 1920s:

When I got to Tulare all the Negroes went to school all by themselves. If it's still there today, I think it's called Lincoln. They just did it that way. I can remember when I was there for the eighth-grade ditch day, . . . I was going to have them go to the Tulare swimming school, and we couldn't because we had some Mexicans in the class. They didn't allow them in the pool.

A former superintendent described the racism of the towns of Avenal and Kettleman City in Kings County:

Avenal was a little school when they discovered oil. And then it blossomed out and they had the highest salary schedule and they attracted the best teachers and so on and so forth. They had very progressive board members—some of them were oil people, you know, and they were educated. And they really got involved and developed the program. But they did have a cute little thing going. . . . They had the school in Avenal and then the school in Kettleman City. All the Mexicans were together in Kettleman City, and all the others went over here. They had so much money they could bus them anyplace they wanted. Nobody really made any fuss about it. The word was a Negro couldn't stay overnight in Avenal. That was a Standard Oil policy. I don't know how it is now. Probably later on the Negroes had to go to Kettleman City, too. Probably you couldn't rent a place in Avenal to a Negro.

The practice of segregation was applied to Mexican-American children in a variety of ways, often justified by language differences.[12] Grace Friend, for example, described Lemoore in 1926:

There were two classes at each grade level, labeled "A" and "B," except the first grade had a class called the "High First" in addition to the other two. The students in the "A" group were presumed to be more intelligent because of their complexion or social status in the community. There was definitely a stigma in being in the "B" class. It even reflected on the teacher. "I'd love to have my child in your class, but you're teaching the 'B' group."[13]

Grace Pogue provided a similar description of her son's first-grade class in the 1920s: "In a few days, Miss Heiskell had divided the children into four groups. Son was one of twelve bluebirds. There was a slightly smaller flock of redbirds and another of yellow birds. She asked the half dozen little Spanish children what they would like to be called and they chorused, 'Blackbirds.'"[14]

The accounts of Mexican Americans of this period are similar. One respondent in the California Valley Oral History Project remembered: "Even though I was in the fifth grade, they had me in a room they called it Americanization, even though I could read and write at that age. They had all the Mexicans in one room and the rest in—all the Portuguese and Dutch—even though they couldn't speak English as well as we could, they had them mixed up."[15] In this case, children whose English was weak but who were categorized as "white"—Portuguese and Dutch children—were integrated, while bilingual Mexican-American children were segregated by means of the "Americanization" classroom.

Unlike some other areas of California, in Tulare and Kings Counties Japanese-American and Chinese-American children were integrated into the public schools.[16] Even so, they continued to face racism. Nina H., a Japanese-American woman who grew up in Tulare County, recalled her father's experiences in the 1920s:

Nina H.: My dad was here and went to school in Dinuba. It is interesting in that he was valedictorian of his graduating class, and yet he was not allowed to graduate, to take part in the graduation.
K.W.: Because he was Japanese.
Nina H.: Yeah. But four years later his brother was the president of the senior class. It just shows you how quickly they moved or tried to move. . . . My father was the captain of the baseball team, and all of this is in his annual. . . . Later he said that it was the principal—Mr. Halbalm, I believe was his name . . . my Dad said, "It was such a hard thing because he had to call me in and he was so embarrassed to give me my diploma in the office." It was really interesting. In the *Delphi* he had written the winning essay, I mean he was the valedictorian of his

class. It was with such—just a part of the times—and I think Mr. Halbalm felt very badly about that. But then four years later [when] his younger brother graduated, he helped give out the awards and spoke.

Nina H. presents this story as "interesting" and as demonstrating "how quickly they moved"; nevertheless, the racism that motivated this treatment of her father found more violent expression in 1942, when all Americans of Japanese descent in California were removed from their homes and placed in camps as potential "enemies" of white America.

In their accounts, teachers present a variety of responses to cultural and racial differences and to the racism of the period. Beth Friend, who taught in Kings County, described her first meeting with Portuguese-American children:

I was horrified to find out the little Portuguese children brought wine in their lunches instead of milk. There was a very handsome little Portuguese boy who had black curly hair. Once when he had his hair cut, he gave me a curly lock of his hair. I still have it in my Bible. Grace Awanee and I were invited to his house for dinner one night. We were greeted at the door by his mother and father and immediately were served wine. I didn't know what to do, because I had never tasted wine.[17]

Although Beth Friend approaches cultural difference here with curiosity and openness, other teachers were more suspicious of difference. The account of Ruth G., who was married to a man from an old and respected Tulare County family, reveals a strong sense of class superiority:

My next school was Thermal, which is near Delano. It was a substation for Edison employees. I had real high-class children from there and from quite wealthy wheat farmers, never any foreigners of any sort. No, it sounds like I'm bragging, but no disciplinary problems to speak of. Parents were completely behind you. A child blinked an eyelash and you told them and they really got it. So, never had any disciplinary problems at all.

For Ruth G., "foreigners" were the antithesis of the "high-class" children of the Edison employees and wheat farmers.

The belief in essential ethnic difference is striking in teachers' attitudes toward Native-American children, though here, too, views range from appreciation to suspicion. A number of women teachers seem to have been fascinated by Indian culture. Like Anna Mills Johnston, who in the late 1800s collected Indian baskets and saw herself as a defender of Indian interests, some twentieth-century teachers saw the native culture as romantic and exotic and the Indians as victims of white racism and greed. Marjorie Whited of Hanford, for example, published a book on the music of the Tache Indians at the Ramona Rancheria;[18] she also described that group's revival of the "pow wow," noting that "Mrs. Verna Brown, the teacher at the Indian school, was an interested observer. Several other teachers who had become interested in Indian culture were present and there were other neighbors and white friends of the Indians present."[19]

Other teachers, however, regarded the Indians as foreign and somewhat dangerous, as in this account about a day substitute teaching at the Tule River school:

The day I went to Tule River you could hear a pin drop in the school, just absolutely quiet. You felt like you were [about] to set off a bomb or something. I went there in my brother's car, and I hadn't used it very much. I can remember, apparently they had been told that I would be there the next day. But they all came, nobody was absent. There was a recitation bench and that sort of thing like the "good ole schools" were. There was no Indian child that spoke above a whisper all day long. All of their lessons were recited in a whisper. Like they were scared of you or something. I can remember the afternoon recess came, [we] went out to play baseball and I was the umpire, and all around the baseball diamond were these men, because they don't work. I don't know if they were in the habit of coming every day or not, but it was . . . they were just out there. I began to become goosy. "What was coming up?" We went back in after recess—I suppose it was a three o'clock recess. I can remember when the day ended I thought, "All those men are still out there." And they were, just chewing the fat. "I've got to get out of here." And I started up that car and I flooded it. Pretty soon it went over and started going, and I sure bailed out of there. There wasn't a single thing about it that was harmful, but my head worked overtime. It was a wonderful experience.

Although this teacher says there was nothing harmful in the day, her head "worked overtime" imagining possible dangers: the idle men, the children whispering as if they were afraid of something. Although she concludes by calling the day "a wonderful experience," her story is filled with a sense of strangeness and fear.

Teachers' accounts of other children, particularly African-American children, are often framed in stereotypical language. Consider this description of teaching summer school in Los Angeles: "The last summer that I taught, out on Vernon Avenue, out near the Watts district, I had thirty-five of the cutest little pickaninnies you ever saw in your life. They were third-graders, and there was one little white girl, and she stood out among the others because they were all so brown. But they were sweet and I enjoyed that summer so much." Later, this teacher recalled the first African-American children in her Tulare County school:

I remember when the first black family came in. We didn't have any; but they moved in. The cutest little pickaninnies you ever did see. I looked out, [the other teacher] had her primary grades out for recess. And here were her kids going around these little pickaninnies petting their hair. I said to her, "They can't do that." She said, "I'll talk to them." She waited until they weren't around—maybe [they] missed school, because they weren't too regular in school—and told them. But they were so fascinated by their little pigtails.

The contradictions of this account, in which the teacher presents herself as protecting African-American children, but at the same time describes them as "pickaninnies," show at best an obliviousness to racist language. This ambiguity is similar to that found in the former superintendent's account of the segregated schools at Avenal and Kettleman City, in which he uses the terms "progressive" and "educated" to describe the white school board members who created what he knew to be segregated schools.

Other teachers conveyed a more self-conscious recognition of racism. Ralph B., for example, stated:

One situation that arose was my fault, [though] I thought I was doing right at the time. There was a little girl took sick at school. So I put her in the school car and took her out to the country where she lived. And there was a car sitting in the yard and she said, "That's my mother's car." I said, "Your mother's home, all right." She said, "Yes, she's home. That's her car." So I let her out without checking. But you don't do that, you turn them over to their parents. Anyway, there wasn't anybody at home. And the little girl got scared and she ran across the field to her aunt's home about half a mile or so away. Then she told her parents that a black man came to the house and attempted to do, I don't know. . . . Our bus driver came back and said, "There was a nigger (as he called him) tried to rape this little girl out there." So I went busting out there, and by that time her folks had arrived home. They had . . . they found the little girl and everything. The little girl was sick at the time and they didn't blame me for that so much, I guess, but the little girl continued being ill for a little while. They came to me for the money to pay the doctor. I couldn't do that. So they came to the board meeting one time being a little bitter. I told the board all about it—what had happened, and it was my mistake without checking the little girl. But the board understood the problem. These parents soon moved away, but I was blamed for all that mess. They had the police out, the sheriff out looking for this nigger out there in the country. Finally it came out that the little girl just admitted that there was nobody. She hadn't seen anybody. The police were out there looking for this nigger, they could have [found a] black man out there someplace and been rough on him. Just because the guy was black, they called them niggers.

In this account, Ralph B. uses the word "nigger" self-consciously, but later calls the man in his story a "black man," shifting uneasily between terms. And he clearly frames this story (possibly because he was speaking to an urban professor from "back east") to condemn the racism it contained: "Just because the guy was black, they called them niggers."

Other teachers' narratives convey a much stronger sense of affection and respect for their students. Irma R., for example, spoke warmly of her Mexican-American and Portuguese-American students:

At Goshen quite of number of them were Mexican. One day I was walking down to the cafeteria and these Mexican girls ahead of me were just jabbering away. I didn't know what they were saying, but as I walked by I said, "Girls, be careful of some of the things you are saying." Then I went right on. One of them came up to me after school. "Do you understand Spanish?" I said, "Oh, some." I could read it—I took three years of Spanish; I can read it, but I can't speak it. She said, "Did you know what we were saying?" I said, "Well, what do you think?" She just kind of grinned at me and said, "I think we'd better be careful."

Even in this humorous story there is a hint of cultural superiority (the Mexican girls "jabbering away") that recalls the former superintendent's description of the Chinese school as separate and unknown because people "couldn't speak the language." But Irma R. was also aware of the difficulties of cultural and language differences. She told this story:

One day one of the Portuguese girls came to me and she said, "These tests are not fair to us." And I asked her to explain why, and she said, "Because at home they don't let us speak English, we have to speak Portuguese. And then we come to school and we learn to speak English and when in eighth grade we have to take these tests and we have to read it in English and we have to think it out in Portuguese and we have to write answers in English and it takes more time." She was right. But they had never taken that into consideration. Therefore these very bright children were just not scoring quite as high as they should have. That was quite an observation for a little eighth-grader.

In this passage Irma R. presents cultural difference not in terms of moral superiority or inferiority, but as an example of what the cultural anthropologist Pierre Bourdieu has called "cultural capital," that is, the linguistic and cultural knowledge the student brings from home to school.[20]

The positive impact a teacher could have on children defined as "other" is shown in this memory of a Mexican-American respondent in the California Valley Oral History Project:

Q [Interviewer]: Did you have any problem with children that maybe didn't speak English?
A [Mexican-American respondent]: [Pause.] No we didn't.
Q: You didn't have any?
A: It seems strange, but we didn't. In Cantua there were the different nationalities, we were bilingual. I mean, I can't remember when I didn't speak both languages, and I don't remember kids having problems communicating with the teacher.
Q: Did you like school?

A: I loved school. I always did like school. I particularly liked my teacher, maybe that's why I liked school.[21]

This memory is echoed in the account of another respondent in the California Valley study:

I think my education only went up to about 4th or 5th grade at the most. But like I said, when I went to that one room school house, and I, in the 3rd grade, was already reading novels and everything, because they had the library right there. We had a wonderful teacher and that's why I say it stayed with me because afterwards I didn't get any schooling. The most I ever went to school was three months of the year because we moved so much.[22]

In these two accounts, Mexican Americans remembered their experiences in country schools positively precisely because of the good feelings they had for their teachers.

One of the strongest condemnations of racism I collected is found in the narrative of Beatrice H., who presented herself as opposed to racism from an early age:

I was strong minded. Like when I, the year I was in the seventh grade and . . . we didn't have many Mexican children in our schools then, but there was one older girl in the eighth grade that year, and she was an excellent student. She was top of the class. And should have been valedictorian, but Mrs. Davis was principal of Wilson School at that time, and she wouldn't allow this girl to be valedictorian, because she was Mexican. When I heard about that I was so mad, and I went out and talked to Rosie and I asked her if it was true. She kind of looked down her nose, you know—Mexicans were in the minority at that time and they were careful about what they did say and how they acted. So she was reticent to admit it, but she finally did. I went stomping home. I went back to the house and I said to mother, "I'm not going back to that school next year. I wouldn't go to Mrs. Davis under any circumstances, I'll walk over to Lincoln School. But I will not go back"—and explained to her why. She was a little . . . she figured that I was right, but still she wanted to check on it. So Mr. Bauman's niece, Nelly Bailey, was teaching there in school, so mother went and talked to Nelly. Found out that it was all true. Mrs. Davis just didn't think . . . this girl had the grades and should have been valedictorian, but she wouldn't let her take over, just because she was a Mexican. So there was nothing more said about it.

But my folks sold their house out there and bought a lot in town and started building a house. We rented until our house was finished, and I went to school with Mr. Stadmiller in the eighth grade. They [her parents] knew that I was strong minded. If it had been something that wasn't right, you know, they wouldn't have gone along with it. But things like that, they were as much opposed to it as I was. Then the next year, the eighth grade with Mr. Stadmiller, was a wonderful experience. I felt that, actually, the Lord had his fingers in it because it was an experience that . . . I have always been glad that I went there rather than be at the other school.

The end of that year I went to high school. The day we were supposed to register, I walked up the front steps and here were several Mexican children standing here over at the side of the big front steps at Exeter High School. This same girl, Rosie, that I had known at that school, I hadn't seen her for a year because she had graduated that year and went into high school. She was there and two or three Mexican boys, and I think one more girl, because we had so few children, Mexican children, at that time. I walked over to her, glad to see them. And some of these boys had gone to school there at Lincoln School, so I did know them too. And I said, "You're all registered and finished up so early?" As usual, they kind of looked down their nose, always kind of—they didn't want to buck the system no matter how they felt, yet they were just as hurt by the way they were treated as they do now or we would feel. So finally Rosie spoke up and told me that they couldn't register until everybody else was registered. So of course I go slamming through those big front doors and down the corridor to the principal's office, and in I go. Mr. Smith was sitting down and I gave him a piece of my mind like I always do. When I got through telling him what I thought, he looked up at me and says, "You go back out and tell those young people to get in line and I'll take care of the registrar." He was already getting up out of his seat and started out of his office. Well, I went back out and told them they could get in and get in line. Of course, the boys wanted to be polite and step aside and let me go. I said, "Oh no, I'm going to be on the end and see to it that you are all registered."

This story, which documents the racist and discriminatory practices against Mexican children, also is interesting in Beatrice H.'s self-presentation as strong minded and standing up for what she believed was right. It is consistent with her earlier story of herself as a strong-willed tomboy and her later work as a champion of the rights of blind children in the 1940s and 1950s, when she was a teacher in the Tulare County schools.

Teaching in the Depression

Although schools in Tulare and Kings Counties were hard hit by the depression, the passage of the initiative of 1933 guaranteeing state support of schools through a sales tax got them through the worst, and federal programs provided additional support for schools serving migrant children. Teaching jobs, which provided a relatively good income, were desirable and difficult to obtain. The percentage of men teachers in Tulare and Kings Counties rose from 14 percent to 18 percent between 1930 and 1940, doubtless reflecting the tight job market and the relative security of teaching. Christine McCready of Kings County recalled, "It was 1934 and the depression was in full swing. Teachers went up and down the roads, stopping at towns along the way to ask about openings. I heard of one that way. The principal and a trustee were on the golf course so I had the interview there. I got the job but at a cut in salary."[23]

During the depression, the class position of teachers was not much different from that of workers. Rachel B., for example, who had to support herself and her mother on her teacher's salary, took advantage of the "school holidays" during the cotton-picking season to take on extra work:

The school closed, I don't know how many days, maybe one day a week or something like that to pick cotton. So *this* gal went into the cotton field and picked. I figured if the kids did, I'd better. But I didn't do it over there. I came home and I went to a friend of the family who had a cotton patch. And when my first sack was dumped—I guess it took me most of the day—why, he got up in the trailer to dump that cotton and before he started he said, "Hear ye, hear ye: Rachel the schoolteacher is dumping her first load of cotton!" I could have killed him. . . . I picked for at least two days, I know. And I took the money I got for it, and in Exeter I found a beautiful alarm clock with a blue front (I leaned toward blue), and I made a down payment on that clock and I said, "I'll be back to get it when I've picked enough cotton to pay for that clock."

Teaching conditions were often difficult during the depression, in part because of the influx of children of migrant workers. Beatrice H. remembered the size of her classes:

Always had forty-eight. Never had less than that. My seats were always filled. But during the height of the season, during cantaloupe season when we'd first go there in September, we'd maybe have more than forty-eight. But when the cotton started I've had as many as sixty in my room. Before they would finally hire substitute teachers, you know. They'd set up classes over there in the old school building. That would relieve of us of that. But I never had less than forty-eight.

The responses of classroom teachers to migrant children seem to have varied. Dust Bowl migrants remember harshness and prejudice vividly: teachers who referred to them as "you migrants" or the school nurse who checked them for lice, calling them "Okies."[24] In an oral history interview, Billie Pate, who came to the San Joaquin Valley in the Dust Bowl migration of the depression, remembered a fifth-grade teacher who called the migrant children "trash."

Pate: For some reason our teacher resented and made it known that she didn't like the Okies and the Arkies and the Texans. So it was a very bad relationship. . . . She was abusive towards us, calling us trash. We were really trash to her.
Interviewer: She called you trash? Why were you trash? Did you misbehave?
Pate: At first, I don't think so, because we had not been reared to misbehave, and we were good students in Texas, very good students. But somehow, we got off on the wrong foot here and that year we were not good students and we slipped into behavior that was not good at all.[25]

Jewell Egbert, who also came to the valley as a child, remembers what she felt to be the intentional cruelty of a teacher:

I had a teacher who liked to make you feel bad. In a sewing class she asked what our room was like and would we like to redecorate our room. I didn't have a room. There wasn't even any paint. I slept in the living room on a little cot. . . . I'm sure she knew that I lived like that. I don't know how much of the class, probably one-third, were migrant type people or people that didn't have the wherewithal to do things. But she went right on down the line . . . [26]

Official attitudes toward migrant children seem to have varied as well. At times, racist stereotypes of Mexican-American and African-American children were applied in turn to the white migrants from the south-central United States. R. T. Neideffer of the Kern County School Department, for example, reported in 1938 that not only were migrant children behind in grade level and suffering from health problems, but

[their parents'] home philosophies are reflected in an indifference on the part of the children toward local social standards. . . . The social habits and background of children of seasonal workers may often, if not carefully supervised, lower or break down the pupil morale of the entire school. Examples of chewing and smoking tobacco in lavatories, and sex conduct on the playground, together with social diseases in the elementary level, have become evident with the greater advent of the children of seasonal workers.[27]

Such overtly hostile views of migrant children are in fact unusual in records of public meetings and official documents. Much more common was concern with material problems of health and nutrition, which were seen as resulting from extreme poverty and deprivation. Jewell Potter, for example, a principal from Kern County, assessed the situation this way:

The shifting of these boys and girls from one school to another seems to make them difficult problems with which to work. . . . Many have poor health and are undernourished, tired from traveling, uncertain as to the future, and have insufficient clothing. With many of these their attitudes are indifferent. Is it any wonder? If these boys and girls can be given, while they are in the school, something to brighten their lives, some contact with sympathy and understanding, some advancement in knowledge and information, then all of the extra work, worry and physical strain is worthwhile.[28]

At times, however, concern over the migrants' health and nutrition is expressed in a way that presents the children as somewhat sinister and strange. Consider this description by Mildred Krohn, a nutritionist from the State Department of Public Health:

It is possible . . . for any interested layman to see the many thin, stunted, wing-shouldered children with their flabby muscles, pale cheeks and tired old-looking eyes that all contrast greatly to a robust child with his good posture and firm colorful skin. One often finds, also, the sullen, non-interested or nervous, fretful attitude of the migratory child which is a great contrast to that of a well-nourished child brimming with curiosity and good humor.[29]

While these children may have been "sullen," "nervous," and "fretful" because of poor nutrition and difficult living conditions, they are nevertheless clearly objectified as "other," positioned in opposition to the good-humored, curious, and robust children of, presumably, local residents. But at least Krohn's prescription for improvement was to provide cheap milk and oranges, nutritionally sound lunches, and instruction in the principles of good nutrition. This was surely better than obsessing about their low morals or contemplating what good cotton pickers these "inferior" children could make.

African-American and Mexican-American migrant children had to combat racism in addition to prejudice against migrant workers generally. Dust Bowl migrants themselves often brought racist attitudes toward African Americans and applied them to the Mexican children they met in California. Ruth Woodall Criswell, a white southwesterner, describes her parents' reaction when she first attended an integrated school: "My parents could hardly reconcile themselves to the fact. At first they didn't seem to mind so much about the Mexican and Chinese but the blacks bothered them."[30] Charles Newsome, another Dust Bowl migrant, remembered his first days at school in Tulare County:

The teacher assigned me and told me to go sit in this desk . . . it was right behind the only colored kid in the class. So I was a little smart ass Okie and I had never had much school with them so no way was I going to get behind no colored kid. . . . I told her, "Teacher I don't sit behind no nigger." So when recess time came naturally that's when a fight got started.[31]

Billie Pate likewise recalled: "The school at the camp [his family lived in] had many Mexican Americans, and we were not accustomed to these people. We had never been around them and so my mother wasn't comfortable with it at that time."[32] Pate's mother managed to have her children sent to the local school instead.

Christina McLanahan, an African American, described the public school she attended in Buttonwillow, which during the depression was a black settlement:

I remember a teacher who came to our class in fifth grade from Iowa. We were all in the classroom when she arrived and she walked in and said "I've never had any niggers in my class before." If she decided to pick somebody to do something she'd say, "Eeny meeny miney mo, catch a nigger," and she'd point, "nigger by his toes." . . . What are you going to do? My folks were telling us to go to school and get an education. She's already got hers. You just go on and get yours. If you don't you won't be in a position to do anything so just take the little bit that she's doing and go on and get your education.[33]

Grace Friend, a teacher in Kings County, described local reaction to African-American migrant children: "There was a great influx of people from Oklahoma and Arkansas as a result of the Dust Bowl. Quite a sprinkling of Negroes was included. This was something new and things went well except when a woman bus driver made all the black children sit in the back of the bus in regular Jim Crow fashion."[34] But white teachers showed kindness as well, as in this account by Beatrice H.:

I still have a little note stuck away some place from a Negro family, they were just destitute, had a little piece of property of their own and worked around with other people. I had gone out to visit for some reason or other—the child was sick or I had gone for something—[and] found what a destitute position they were in. I had collected up clothing, and we had an apple orchard on the old ranch, and I went over there and got apples and whatever I could find. So I went out and took it out to them and the farmer wrote me this note—sort of "i" for capital "I" . . . his education was so slight that he didn't know how to make a capital "i," things like that—but I kept that note for such a long, long time, because just the fact that he appreciated it enough to write. . . . It was really desperate for some of those people. It was really too bad.

Parents and children often felt that they received an inferior education in the migratory schools or in special classes for migratory children. Alvin Laird remembered the special class at the school at Tipton:

They had a bunch of cabins out there where they sent what they call transients and slow learners. Well, my second boy—nothing wrong with his mind—was ornery. So they stuck him out there in that cabin. So my wife went down and raised Cain and they put him back in the regular class. They put one of my nephews out there too. One of the teachers told Rosie so she went down there and jumped on the principal. "Why, Mrs. Laird, you don't know what you're talking about. They got the same teaching out there." She said, "Oh no, Mr. Stewart. One of your teachers here told me that they didn't—all they do is let them do what they want to." And that's exactly what they done. This nephew of mine—after she got him straightened out back in the regular school—said, "Aunt Rose, I'm mad at you." She said, "What for?" "Well," he said, "They make me work. At that other school I didn't do nothing."[35]

Migrant children sometimes responded to this treatment by resisting or by being disruptive. One fourteen-year-old boy recounted: "Sometimes a teacher will say to one of us, 'You ain't had good bringin' up.' . . . When they act like that we say, 'Do you know what they do with insane people in Oklahoma and Texas? They send them to California to be school-teachers.'"[36]

Migrants also remember teachers who treated them with respect and cared for them. Billie Pate, for example, whose fifth-grade teacher had called the migrant children trash, was sent to a different school the next year. There, Pate remembered, "We had a young teacher, just out of college, that appreciated us and worked with us. She's still there today. It was the best year of school. So, the fifth grade was bad but the sixth grade was super good. . . . She treated us as kids want to be treated, with dignity and respect. She showed us kindness, real kindness, which we needed."[37] After a conflict with a teacher whom Vera Criswell thought was biased against her children, she put them in another school:

I told [the new teacher] that they'd been over to another school and I said some of them haven't been doing too good because there was so much trouble in school. . . . I was hoping that they'd have a better atmosphere over here. The teacher said that she didn't allow that kind of thing in her school. That was the best school. They never had another day's harassment of any kind.[38]

Rita M., who experienced prejudice herself when she first arrived in Porterville from Texas during the depression, began teaching during the war. She described lingering bias against Dust Bowl children:

I had the children come to the seventh grade and I didn't have a record. One girl, I said, "Where did you come from?" She was new there and I didn't have her record. And she came up to my desk and whispered, "Oklahoma." I said "Oh, I guess you're my neighbor then because I'm from Texas." That seemed to help her to have the rest of them adjust to her. It was bad. I felt sorry for some of them. Some of them I just told them if I heard any more about it they could be punished.

Although former students recalled negative as well as positive experiences with teachers, not surprisingly retired teachers remembered their attitudes toward migratory children as positive. Margaret C. recalled: "We had these people from Oklahoma and they were great people. They were poor . . . they lived in tents across the road, just on some vacant land. For the floor they had cardboard. . . . They're great people. Sturdy Americans." Teresa D. put it this way:

All the cases that I had where children came from the Dust Bowl were very lovely children. They might not have been the highest in academic work that could exist, but they were good citizens because I consider citizenship a very important quality in a school anywhere. I mean, they know how to control and behave themselves and co-operate. All of them, they were all good citizens, and they were all good workers, and they all co-operated. So I had no problems. In fact, I enjoyed working with the Dust Bowl children.

Many teachers remember the poverty of the families and their need for food and clothing.[39] Local residents helped the migrants, particularly the children, most frequently by giving food. At the Liberty school in Tulare County, when migrant children came to school hungry, the teacher gave them lunch; when she no longer could meet their needs on her own, the wives of local farmers took turns "cooking a hot dish and providing the vegetables and milk."[40] In Kings County, a teacher remembers, "Children came to school from a large cotton camp nearby. Mr. Jud Bowden, who owned and operated the Superior Dairy, gave us a crate of bottled milk for the children every morning. Most of these children needed food. Since they brought no lunches, the teachers brought bread and sandwich materials so they would have something to eat at noon."[41] Wellabelle Maloney was struck by the physical signs of poverty and malnourishment of migrant children: "I remember the stick-like appearance of the arms and legs of the 'Okie' children. The Federal lunch program eventually changed that, but it took a long time and much persuasion to get the children to try foods they had never eaten such as butter, canned beef and many different vegetables."[42] Beatrice H. helped poor families in many ways, making dresses for the children and sacking staples provided in hundred-pound bags by the Red Cross:

After school the teachers took turns. We'd go over to the old school building that was still standing then—we used it for overflow and for band and things like this. We'd go over there and sack up rice and beans and flour, whatever there had been furnished to us. I remember one Mexican family that came in and got beans and rice and whatever. He had a garden, the man, the family had a garden. So whenever they had anything extra out of their garden they'd show up with that.

Teachers remember the depression in contradictory ways. Being themselves white, Protestant, and the daughters of "respectable" families, they viewed the children they taught through the lens of the cultural categories of their communities. As they looked back on this time, therefore, teachers used a racial discourse to locate themselves at the center, in a position of cultural privilege that was natural and given, with others at the margins. But their memories are not all of one piece. Like the state and local officials who oversaw their work and established school policies, they responded to the social crisis of the depression in different ways. Some viewed the migrants as dangerous and threatening; others, however, such as Irma R. and Beatrice H., saw the migrants as human beings in difficult circumstances. Many of these more sympathetic teachers provided help to their students in the form of clothing or food. In these actions, they continued to fill a traditional woman's role as social caretaker.

Although some women teachers lost their jobs because of their gender, the federal and state programs of the depression also opened up new opportunities for women educators. Rural supervisors and princi-pals such as Hazel Ledbetter (my mother's first principal), for example, took leadership positions in government programs like the Red Cross or the WPA. For such women, teaching or working in humanitarian pro-grams during the depression provided them with meaningful and re-sponsible work that seems to have been deeply satisfying.

Conclusion

The work of rural women teachers in the interwar years was shaped by state policies and by the crisis of the depression. Increasingly their work was defined and overseen by county and state officials who estab-lished policies and curriculum goals. The introduction of standardized testing and observation by rural supervisors also more closely controlled their work lives. At a structural level, too, the state educational system was strongly marked by discriminatory and racist practices, which af-fected the day-to-day lives of teachers and students. At the same time, the interwar years in California saw an institutional validation of the value and seriousness of rural teaching, thanks largely to the leadership of He-len Heffernan. Women rural supervisors and principals found an op-portunity to exercise leadership and earn higher pay; they describe their work with pride. Teachers, meanwhile, gained from their work both plea-sure and self-respect. Small one- and two-room schools still provided rel-atively autonomous settings in which teachers could control the pace and structure of the day and, in some cases at least, put into practice the pro-gressive methods they were introduced to at teachers colleges and by rural supervisors. The detail and pride with which retired teachers de-scribe their work is testimony to their sense of its importance. Rural women teachers thus led complex and ambiguous work lives, using their jobs to gain personal autonomy and accomplishing what they defined as socially useful work, but within an educational state that continued to separate and label students and to attempt greater surveillance and con-trol of teachers. With the coming of the Second World War, and particu-larly with the successful move to unify and consolidate rural schools in the immediate postwar years, the nature of rural teaching in California would be transformed.

MEN TAKE CONTROL,
1940-1950

The 1940s saw profound changes in the rural schools of Tulare and Kings Counties. Nationwide, debates over the meaning of public education in war and peace were carried on by experts, mostly men, who were seen as voices of authority. Although gender was largely absent from these discussions, in practice the lives of women teachers were deeply affected by state interventions and the ideological struggles of the 1940s.

With the onset of war, opportunities for women to work in nontraditional jobs, particularly in war-related industries, increased markedly. Between 1940 and 1945, women's participation in the work force grew from 27.6 percent to 37.0 percent of all workers. Three-quarters of these new women workers were married.[1] Nationwide, fewer than 10 percent of teachers left teaching during the war—a figure that included men who joined the service.[2] Although the war in part reaffirmed women teachers' traditional role as nurturers, it also introduced new responsibilities and new opportunities.[3] A 1945 national survey of members of Pi Lambda Theta, an honorary association of women in education, found that the majority of respondents, though still teaching, were also involved in a wide range of volunteer war work: taking first-aid courses, selling war bonds, collecting for the Red Cross, helping with civilian defense, working for the United Service Organizations (USO).[4] California women teachers, like others, felt the powerful impact of the war, both in terms of official declarations regarding patriotism in the schools and in terms of direct state intervention through conscription, the internment of Japanese Americans, and, perhaps most significantly for women, the virtual abandonment of the marriage bar because of the wartime teacher shortage.

The postwar years saw even more changes, particularly for women

achers in rural areas such as Tulare and Kings Counties. First, heightened political struggles around issues of race, patriotism, anticommunism, and progressive reform marked California education in the late
1940s, culminating in the McCarthyite attacks of the 1950s. Increasingly
aggressive conservative attacks on the tenets of progressive education
were part of this unrest. But perhaps more significant, these years saw
the triumph of school consolidation and the virtual disappearance of relatively autonomous one- and two-room schools. The simultaneous entry
of young male veterans into school administration meant that leadership
of the newly consolidated schools was assumed overwhelmingly by male
principals—often men far less experienced than the older women classroom teachers they oversaw. By 1950, then, women principals were rare
indeed, and rural consolidated and unionized schools had taken on the
familiar structure of contemporary elementary schools.

Shifts of power and authority from women to men in rural schools
were accompanied by changes in the representation of the woman
teacher. This occurred in the context of the postwar reimposition of
ideas of woman's proper role and sexual essence, which resulted in what
Betty Friedan termed the "feminine mystique." The domestic ideology
of the cold war, which emphasized woman's centrality in the suburban
nuclear family; the Freudian emphasis on normative heterosexuality; and
the disappearance of the marriage bar all contributed to the representation of the woman teacher as a sexual being living under male authority
both in the school and at home. By 1950, the idea of capable and responsible women educators in positions of power in schools had essentially disappeared from public discourse.

Tulare and Kings County Schools in 1940

The women teachers of Tulare and Kings Counties in the 1940s were
certainly affected by the political divisions that so marked California education.[5] Tulare County in particular demonstrated a continuing tension
between the progressive views of Helen Heffernan and more conservative approaches. This tension can be traced in the monthly *Tulare County
Schools Bulletin*, distributed to all teachers in the county beginning in
1935. The *Bulletin*, which was edited first by John Terry and later by Fred
Trott, both followers of Heffernan, frequently included excerpts from
the writings of progressive educators and admonitions to teachers to
build democracy and foster racial understanding. In December 1940, for
example, the *Bulletin* reprinted the "creed of democracy" put together
by 150 educators at Columbia Teachers College, and the next May it encouraged teachers to attend the UCLA summer conference for elemen-

tary teachers and supervisors organized by Helen Heffernan and Corinne Seeds around the theme "Democratic Guidance of Teachers in the Modern School." Conservatives, meanwhile, lost no opportunity to attack educators for their suspiciously "progressive" approaches. In Tulare County in 1940, for example, an attempt was made to censor school texts. Responding to growing uneasiness among conservative local business leaders about the "left wing" content of textbooks, Terry wrote in the December 1940 issue of the *Bulletin*: "Misunderstanding and poor judgment regarding school materials appear to arise from failure to give them adequate study, and articles such as 'Treason in the Textbooks' and 'Indictment of the Rugg Books' are the unfortunate results."

The Tulare County Board of Education, however, took a more conservative position. In January 1941, the board issued a declaration of its policies. After a paragraph arguing for the school's responsibility to develop "a deep and abiding loyalty to the values of Democracy—the principles of equality and brotherhood, free inquiry and discussion, the principles of honesty and stability, and the dignity of work," the declaration went on to state:

Books which attempt to debunk American heroes or cast doubt on their motives or their patriotism—books which cast aspersions upon our form of government or our Constitution, or which seek to undermine our traditional faith and ideals—such books shall have no place in the schools of Tulare County. . . . We shall see to it that the schools of Tulare County are free from all influences tending to uproot and poison and destroy our freedom, our liberty and our Democracy.[6]

Terry responded in the next month's *Bulletin*, in an article entitled "It's Not Treason," citing NEA Associate Secretary William Carr's statement that recent attacks on various school textbooks were themselves "un-American" and defending freedom of thought and civil liberties. In September, Terry reprinted a letter from Methodist bishop G. Bromley Oxnam entitled "Bearers of False Witness." In his defense of the schools, Bishop Oxnam wrote:

I have heard some men say, "The American school breeds communists. There is a little Red teacher in every red schoolhouse." Such statements are not only utterly false but are also destructive of the institutions that above all others are most effective in preserving democracy. During the most crucial years of our history, in which the nation was subjected to unprecedented economic depression, there has been no significant move of the American people toward revolutionary activities. This, I believe, is due to the fact that the American school has trained a generation who believe in democracy. . . . Any man who states that "the American schools breed communists" is stating a falsehood, and in the very statement menaces the Republic the schools seek to preserve.

Thus, by late 1941 California education was already polarized. The extent to which women teachers were affected by the conservative challenge to progressive ideas is not clear. But certainly, the declaration of war by the United States in December 1941 brought social and economic changes that directly affected the lives of women teachers.

Teachers and Japanese-American Children

The first and perhaps most dramatic impact of the war on California teachers was the removal of their Japanese-American students only a few months after the outbreak of the war—a graphic and immediate expression of racism.[7] A substantial number of Japanese-American children attended public schools in Kings County and especially Tulare County.[8] Although Japanese-American children had always been integrated into the public schools, as we have seen, they were subjected to discrimination in the prewar years, particularly in the 1920s. Editorials in the *Tulare County Schools Bulletin* often expressed concern over local anti-Japanese sentiment. In October 1937, for example, an editorial condemned the Japanese attack on Shanghai, but added: "Incidentally, let's not persecute and ostracize American-born Japanese—as we did American-born Germans twenty years ago. Remember?" In December 1941, immediately after the Japanese attack on Pearl Harbor, Tulare County Superintendent of Schools Theo Nickel wrote in the *Bulletin*:

Just because we are at war, we should not adopt the despicable creed of Adolf Hitler and other fanatical devotees of race prejudice and hatred. War has many ugly phases, but none more repulsive than the persecution mania it arouses. When World War Number One was over many people blushed at the spiteful, mean and underhand way in which they had treated some of their neighbors— and even former friends.

America, Nickels reminded teachers, was "the melting pot." Interestingly, his whole column was focused on the need to combat racism, not to encourage patriotism—perhaps in response to overt anti-Japanese feeling in the county.

In the weeks after the attack on Pearl Harbor and the U.S. declaration of war, newspaper editorials and statements by public officials moved from initial support of the Japanese-American community—as in the *Kingsburg Recorder*'s warning that "race prejudice must be guarded against"[9]—to suspicion and sometimes direct attack. In nearby Fresno County, for example, a speaker at the Selma Community Club argued that there were "300,000 persons of Japanese birth or ancestry in California and every one of them constitutes a problem socially if not from a

military standpoint."[10] In Kingsburg in Kings County, a Japanese man was
held by police because "he had been questioning employees on matters
which were none of his concern at the Kingsburg Cotton Oil Co."[11]

In February 1942 Roosevelt issued the infamous Executive Order
9066 forcing the removal of all citizens and resident aliens of Japanese
descent from the West Coast. The order for removal was put into effect
in stages, starting with the coastal areas; a number of Japanese families
came to Tulare County at that time.[12] In the San Joaquin Valley, restrictions were put into effect at different times in different counties. By the
late spring, however, all Japanese Americans, both those from the coast
and local families, had been removed to camps.

Retired teachers had powerful memories of the removal of the Japanese. Although the decision to deprive these citizens of their rights, to
force them from their homes, and to put them in camps because of race
was made at the highest level of state authority—which, by virtue of their
role as public servants, schoolteachers in a sense represented—the consequences in human terms, particularly in the lives of children, had to
be addressed by women teachers who were also expected to act as care-
takers and protectors.

This contradiction was implied but rarely directly addressed by the
teachers with whom I spoke. They described their students sympatheti-
cally but seldom questioned the government's actions. Polly O., for example, spoke of her students' reaction to the news of Pearl Harbor:

I remember the morning following Pearl Harbor. My class had the one radio in
the school. So we listened to President Roosevelt's talk. I'll never forget the look
on those faces of those kids. These Japanese youngsters were popular youngsters
and everybody just did things together. Never been any problems or anything. I
can see them, they'd been so outgoing and they sort of sat there, sort of stunned.

Karen R. described the arrival of the refugees from the coast: "It was
right after Easter, must have been in March of 1942. I went into the office and made out the absence slips and so on. And that office was lined
all the way around with Japanese from the coast and they had come over
in here because a lot of them had relatives or friends that were here. So
they had been shooed out from along the coast and came over here."

Polly O. described an incident in this same period when she was teaching in Parlier in Fresno County:

Our eighth-grade students would always come down to Mooney Grove [in Tulare
County] for a picnic just before school was out. One of the families had a big
truck and the kids would ride in the truck, and we always made a five-gallon ice
cream container. About one-third of our students were Japanese. One of the boys
was the president of the student body, very popular, [a] very smart youngster. I

would say in my class I probably had ten to twelve Japanese students out of about thirty. We had a lot of Mexican students, and some Anglo students, and quite a number of Armenian students were in Parlier at that time, too. Anyway, we had come down and the kids had a great time, it was a beautiful day. We got back to the truck a little bit early, and here was a policeman. He told us, maybe we weren't aware, but the Japanese were already interned from Tulare County. And here somebody had noticed all these Japanese running around in Mooney Grove and they had reported to the county sheriff or the Visalia police, I'm not sure just what office it was. We told him that we were just about ready to leave and we hoped they wouldn't make a big incident out of it. And they didn't. So the kids never knew. It was really very touching.

Although Polly O. described this incident as "touching," she did not question that eighth-grade children were seen as breaking the law because they went on a class picnic.

Japanese-American children often were outstanding students. Ironically, their success came in schools permeated with the rhetoric of democracy and justice. Hannah A. remembered one Japanese-American boy who assumed a show of patriotism would protect his rights:

We knew it [the deportation] was going to happen. One of these boys came to me when all that was going on. . . . We had pictures of some of the presidents, and I stored them in the storeroom when I put other pictures up. He wanted those pictures because he thought that if he had something like that in his room they wouldn't make him go. I let him have them, but it didn't help.

Polly O. described the bewilderment of children who were suddenly treated like criminals, facing a strict curfew and the knowledge that they would soon be taken from their homes:

Another thing I recall when it came to graduation. We had always had an evening graduation. They had ordered their things at the usual time, and then came the order that no Japanese were to be out after six o'clock at night. Not to be on the streets after six o'clock at night. I met with the youngsters, and they talked very freely in my presence, they knew I was their friend. [Yes,] just the Japanese students. We talked it over about what we could do. We finally thought, well, would it help if we had an afternoon graduation? But no, because most of their folks were working in the fields and they couldn't come then anyway. What we finally did was to go ahead and have the regular evening graduation without them and have a second graduation the following morning. One of the young teachers had a beautiful singing voice, and he had sung at the graduation the night before, and then he sang for them specially. He made a special little talk about it, because he had to report for army duty on Monday, and this was on a Friday. He made a special point of how much this meant to him. Then . . . instead of having a local minister give the invocation we had a speaking choir of all the girls— those who had graduated the night before and the Japanese girls. We mentioned

how much better it was now that we had all the voices. We tried to make it as special as we could. They hung around after school when we were cleaning up the
room, because they were to go Monday or Tuesday—they knew that they were to
report to be interned at Tulare at the fairgrounds. Eventually most of them were
interned in Arizona. I used to carry on correspondence with them for a number
of years, and one girl lives in Fresno now and has children who are out of college now. We hear every Christmas.

While teachers were usually sympathetic to the plight of the children,
most considered the government's action to be warranted. Polly O., for
example, who remembered her own Japanese-American children fondly,
was not sure about the adults in the community:

Many people were thinking that they were just "the Japs." One thing, too, there
was a lot of gossip. People didn't know; they thought there were a lot of under-
ground things going on in places. This boy who was the president of the student body was the son of the Buddhist minister there. I don't know if they had
many Buddhist meetings, but a lot of them did have language meetings for the
children to learn the language. And the gossip was that they were making plots
and plans in these Buddhist meetings. Whether that was true or not I don't
know.

Other teachers mentioned hearing rumors that the Japanese were not
to be trusted or that they were not completely loyal. Even after the Japanese were taken to camps, some local white educators remained hostile
to them. The petty viciousness of anti-Japanese sentiment is captured in
this letter to State Superintendent Walter Dexter from a Tulare County
principal:

We should appreciate your suggestions as to whom we may address with our com-
plaint to the effect that the educational system in the Japanese Relocation Centers is favoring the Japanese to such an extent that our regular American boys
and girls must suffer a scarcity of teachers. Since the Relocation Centers have
been seeking teachers we have lost several good prospects in the vocational field
especially. Possibly our feeling in this matter is too intense, but it seems logical
to feel that our boys and girls should have priority. The educational system in the
Relocation Centers should not be so highly developed as to increase the problem of securing teachers for the public schools. A let up in the plan of education, and also in "soft heartedness" would not start a rumor in Japan that we are
giving the interned Japs horrid treatment.[13]

This language recalls the resentment of migrant Mexican and "Okie"
children in the 1930s. Again the "regular American boys and girls" are
at the center, while Japanese-American children are framed as "others"
who must on no account be given priority.

Although most of the teachers I interviewed accepted the government's actions as justified, Karen R. was outspoken in her disapproval. She described the plight of the Japanese-American families whose children she had taught:

They were around here for a few months, and then, Kathleen, they were simply lifted up and taken over into Arizona and all these places and their ranches taken away from them. And then there were whites, I never will forgive them for it, that would rent the places and let them go down and not take care of them. Oh, the Japanese, I have a lot of sympathy for them. The feeling around was that if you had anything to do with the Japanese, you were a traitor. They were shooed over into Arizona with no shade, no nothing, and over into the Owens Valley, that camp over there. I know there were a couple over in Arizona who had to do something. [So] they got to making these paper flowers. And of course they were meticulous. I remember a couple of the students that I had wrote to me and wanted to know if I could get them some umbrellas, and some tissue paper to make flowers. Well, I got them and sent them. I guess I was a traitor. But I didn't one bit feel like a traitor to the United States, because those people had not done anything at all.

Karen R.'s angry condemnation of the governmental policy was unusual. Few voices spoke out against the removal of Japanese Americans at the time, either within or outside of education. Although the teachers I interviewed continued caring for these children (giving a boy framed pictures of the presidents; sending paper and umbrellas to the barren desert camps), they did not address the contradictions between the accepted teachers' role as caregiver and their position as agents of a state system that violated the civil rights of their own students.

Schools and the War Effort

The Japanese removal forced teachers into a morally ambiguous position, but this ambiguity was ignored in official statements by educational leaders. Instead, the dominant themes of the early years of the war were patriotism and the defense of the nation, including direct and practical support of the military.[14] By September 1942, administrators in Tulare and Kings Counties were mobilizing teachers, emphasizing civil defense and the involvement of students in war-related projects. Such measures followed the suggestions put forth by the U.S. Office of Education Wartime Commission in a bimonthly pamphlet, "Education for Victory." The commission suggested such activities as scrap collections, war stamp and bond drives, civil defense drills, and the teaching of concepts having to do with war and patriotism (including words like "bombardier" and "torpedo" in spelling lessons, for example).[15] Similar themes were raised by the National Institute on Education and the War in Washington in January 1943. In a speech at that institute reprinted in the *Sierra Educational News*, Paul McNutt argued:

Every teacher should stay at his post unless the Army or Navy or Industry should draft him for work of higher priority-rating. It is the patriotic duty of teachers to continue teaching despite the lure of service on other fronts. *Teaching is war work.* Schools must be the Company Headquarters of the Home Front. But Education "as usual" is out. Education can help materially in shortening the distance to victory. No service being rendered today is more vital to victory than education.[16]

Echoing these patriotic sentiments, the *Tulare County Schools Bulletin* suggested changing the curriculum to focus on useful military skills and love of country. The editors encouraged the showing of films supplied by the Office of War Information with titles such as *Tanks, Manpower, Salvage, Winning Your Wings, Men and the Sea, Bomber,* and *Democracy in Action.* Local radio stations advertised Write-a-Fighter Clubs to encourage schoolchildren to write to relatives and friends in the service. And teachers were referred to as soldiers in an "Army of Education."[17]

Women teachers were expected to add war-related responsibilities to their existing classroom duties. In 1943, for example, Tulare County teachers were required to register the population for ration cards. In this undertaking, school principals were given the title of Building Site Administrator and told to supervise the teachers who did the actual clerical work. Most women classroom teachers, like most other Americans, seem to have participated in war-related activities out of a sense of both obligation and patriotism. Margaret C. recalled: "You had to teach the children about airplanes. Airplane watch. Two or three times a week we used to go down and watch one of the towers, teach the kids to get under their desks, and of course they all brought money and bought liberty bonds—so many pennies a week." Not everyone was thrilled with the burden of the war effort. Erma Rambo, for example, wrote to the State Department of Education challenging a request for maps of all school bus routes:

We admit that we are not fighting on Bataan, but fighting to keep up with the questionnaires your agency and others send out is in itself a 24 hour a day job. If you and all other departments would cut out some of this unnecessary clerical detail, you certainly would release thousands for more essential jobs in our Nation.

Trusting that you will reduce forms, applications, and questionnaires, and that there will be *no maps,* we remain

Very truly yours, Mrs. Erma Rambo.[18]

One unusually enthusiastic patriotic response by a classroom teacher can be seen in the Young Americans Club organized in Visalia by Clara

Evers, which she described in an article from 1948.[19] Evers got the idea of a class club during the Miss Swopes summer school of 1940. When the war broke out, she decided to organize her classroom around a patriotic club, guided by this sentiment of another teacher at the summer school session: "Through definite development of desirable habits, any undesirable are avoided and eliminated. Thus character is molded." The focus of the club was on citizenship, with committees for Good Manners, Room, Patriotism, Character and Conduct, Health, Safety, and Thrift. A sense of the ideological motivation of the club is captured in Evers's description of one Christmas celebration:

At Christmas we put on a program featuring Christmas in other lands. . . . The decorations were made a part of the program. In front of the room was a large poster entitled The First Christmas, while along the sides were scenes of Christmas in Mexico, Switzerland, Norway and England. At the rear were posters depicting Christmas in 1944, showing GIs on a Pacific Island, and another entitled Christmas in 1945, showing a GI returning and being greeted by his wife. The last poster showed New Year's season as celebrated in China. Between the posters were Bells of Joy, with a double meaning: rejoicing in the Birth of the Savior and rejoicing in our First Peace-time Christmas.

This celebration fused cultural differences, patriotism, and an assumed Christianity in an attempt to create a common identity for children. Other activities of the club included holding mock courts and trying hunters for violations of game and forestry laws. Evers's article included somewhat ominous examples of social control, as in this description of child informers:

Shortly after the Food Drive for Relief of Europe was started two children, rushing into line for Flag Salute, had hastily discarded partially-eaten ice cream cones. Immediately a child in line whispered to me that they were wasting food. The children decided that a collection-jar should be placed on the table. They would place in the jar the money they expected to spend for ice cream and candy during the week. When the jar was opened it contained far more in my opinion than the children would have spent for themselves.[20]

In this emphasis on character improvement and social discipline, Evers's classroom demonstrated precisely the values advocated by patriotic educational leaders during the war.

Women Teachers Remember the War

The war affected teachers not only in the demand that they inject greater patriotism into classroom lessons or their acceptance of the racism and chauvinism of wartime, but also in terms of working conditions and opportunities. Probably the most important impact of the war for women teachers was the virtual elimination of the marriage bar,[21] a consequence of the severe teacher shortage created by the war, though the example of women working in nontraditional, war-related jobs likely played a role as well. By January 1943, many women were leaving teaching to take better-paying jobs in other sectors, while men were entering the service in droves.[22] School boards had little choice but to turn to married women to fill the vacated positions. By 1950, 58 percent of women elementary school teachers listed in the Tulare County school records were identified as "Mrs.," an increase of 10 percent over 1940. For women, then, in addition to the burdens of extra war work, rationing, and large classes, the war provided opportunities. As one teacher recalled: "I used to teach school, then I got married and had some babies and thought I never would do anything else but keep house. Then the war came, and presently people made me feel very guilty for not doing the thing I was originally trained to do, and so I went back to teaching and I'm not sorry."[23]

In California the war created job opportunities in the defense plants of the coastal cities. Some Tulare and Kings County teachers accompanied their husbands to the shipyards of the East Bay. Hannah A., for example, described leaving her school in the middle of the year in order to join her husband:

Hannah A.: My husband was working in the shipyards; he was a guard up there in the shipyards during the war and he was sort of batching around and he wanted me to come up there. So I left Welcome [School] in the middle of the term and went up there and stayed until he came out.
K.W.: What did you do up there?
Hannah A.: What did I do? Well, kept house. We lived in a two-room apartment and I could go out and I could drive a car and I could get around. . . . Other people were up there from down here that we knew . . . men that were working on the police force here in Porterville went up there and got work. So there were several from down here.

Hannah A. did not work during the war, because her husband could support them both with his high wartime wages. For Irma R., however, the move to the Bay Area provided another opportunity to teach, although it also led to conflicts with her husband:

Irma R.: When my second husband and I were married he was working in the shipyards at Richmond. He told me, "You're not going to teach anymore." . . . A friend of mine was teaching in Richmond, and she became quite ill and couldn't get a substitute. She asked me if I could. The rest of the year I taught. And that was a case. They put me in the sixth grade and I never had less than sixty youngsters, afternoon sessions, and they required so much book work that you were always and forever filling out all their health cards and transfer cards because more youngsters would come in and they'd have to take so many out of this room and put them in another room and shift. The morning session and my session overlapped for half an hour. They were supposed to have P.E., but they couldn't have P.E. if it was raining, so they had to be in the classroom—and my youngsters had to be in the classroom. So there were more than a hundred youngsters crammed into a room for half an hour. . . .

I drove from Walnut Creek, and my husband got a ride with other men who worked in the shipyards in order to leave me the car. Before very many months, I was picking up a load of teachers who would meet me on different corners. Here were these college graduates, who had so much more training than I, yet I was receiving the highest pay of any of them.

K.W.: Why was it your husband wanted you not to teach?

Irma R.: He just thought I'd done it enough. He wanted me to become a homebody.

Although Irma R.'s husband had told her, "You're not going to teach anymore," and wanted her "to become a homebody," she was soon teaching anyway. The teacher shortage provided her with the opportunity to assert her own desire to work, even under these difficult conditions. Other retired teachers described the teacher shortage in Tulare and Kings Counties in terms of the openings that were created for married women. Rita M., who had taught in Texas and had come to Porterville with her husband during the depression, was at home caring for her three children when the teacher shortage hit:

When my youngest one was old enough to go to school—this was World War II— they needed teachers so badly. I had known a family back in Texas who had moved out here, too, and he lived in the neighborhood of Harmony School. And the trustees were looking for a teacher. I was out in the garden barefooted and with a Texas bonnet on, and three men came by and asked my husband where I was. He said, "She's out in the garden." Before they got to me, I heard one of them say, "She's the one we're looking for." And I had no idea, I hadn't seen any of the trustees, I had no idea why they were looking for me. My mind just rushed—Why in the world could they be looking for me? Because I thought maybe they were policemen. So we came in and talked awhile. They said they wanted me: they had made up their mind even before they met me.

By February 1944 the teacher shortage was "critical" in Tulare County, and officials proposed a three-week summer course to train and certify emergency teachers.[24] George J., who was a county superintendent during the war, described the hiring process:

We had emergency teachers, that's what they were called . . . emergency teachers. I just had to hold my hand over their head, and they were emergency teachers. It was a matter of personal assessment. And evaluating. We didn't give them any tests or anything like that. If they were good with kids, they'd have a job. Most of them started out in the migrant camps because those were the most undesirable and you couldn't get all of the white people to go out there. But they were dedicated people. It is surprising how well they did. So that, then, later on, they went up a step and were called provisional teachers. There was emergency first and provisional later. You were a teacher as long as you went to school—that type of thing. And I can't recall there was much difference in salary. They must have gotten a little bit less, but I don't remember. So then our provisional people came along. They might have had two years of college or something like that. We had classes for teachers, extension through Fresno State; they had classes on Saturdays and night classes and so on. That's the way we solved the problem.

Another Kings County teacher recalled being recruited to teach, even though she had had only one year of college and had worked in an office before the war:

At the end of World War II in 1945, the county superintendent called me and wanted to know if I'd be interested in teaching a third or fourth combination [classroom] at the Cross Creek Midvalley School. And I said, "Why no, I've never taught school in my life." This was after school had started and the boys were returning from overseas and the teachers in Hanford and Cross Creek and all over the county were quitting. So he called me up on a Saturday, and he said, "Well, I'll come out and talk to you and your husband." We lived out on West Grangeville Boulevard. And he did, and my husband looked at me and I looked at him and he says, "Well, maybe she'll try it out." My daughter was in kindergarten and my son was born in 1934. He was in school, of course, and I had a wonderful baby-sitter for my daughter. And I said, "Well, okay." And my husband said, "If she doesn't like it, well, she'll quit at the end of the year." And the superintendent said, "That's fine." And I said, "Well, how do I learn how to teach school?" I'd had one year at Cal, and one year at Armstrong Business College, and I'd worked in San Francisco, commuted across the bay in a boat. Well, I stayed the one year, and my salary was $1,200 a year. And the chairman of the board came by and said, "We're very happy with you." And they offered to pay me $1,400 a year for the second year. They had been impressed with the work I had done because I had worked so hard. And I really, I loved it.

The Postwar World

Although teachers were still encouraged to hold bond drives and to plant victory gardens, by 1944 the intense focus on the war effort was beginning to abate. While the image of teachers at their posts working for victory in the schools had characterized official government pronouncements during the war, the more critical voices of progressive educators like Heffernan were never completely muted in California. Even during the war, progressive educators continued to emphasize the political and ideological nature of schooling, including the need for tolerance, though they seldom called for specific antiracist actions.[25] Instead they publicized the sufferings of the Soviet and Chinese peoples, and continued to insist that racial and ethnic differences within the United States be respected.[26]

In Tulare and Kings Counties, progressive concerns over the meaning of education in a democracy and the question of discrimination in the United States began to reappear in the schools in 1944. This change of focus was reflected in the pages of the *Tulare County Schools Bulletin*, which in 1943 came under the editorship of county administrator and Heffernan supporter Fred Trott.[27] By 1944 the *Bulletin* was again publishing excerpts from the speeches of progressive educators admonishing teachers to teach tolerance and democracy. Trott included the following anecdote, for example, in the November 1944 issue:

The children in a class were discussing suitable punishments which might be meted out to Hitler at the close of the war. The usual suggestions of hanging, shooting and torture were put forth with great vehemence when one little Negro boy spoke up and said, "If you just give him a black skin and make him wear it the rest of his life, that will be punishment enough."

As the war in Europe came to an end in the spring of 1945, teachers not only had to adjust to a new educational rhetoric for peacetime, but they also had to deal with the continuing effects of the war, including the return of Japanese-American children. Some educators reacted with hostility to their return, such as this school superintendent from Imperial County:

As an acid test of loyalty and devotion it is safe to say those Japanese who refuse to return to California for the duration are to be commended. Herein they recognize a fundamental fact; namely, that their return now, will, of a certainty, create friction, ill-will, delay in our war effort, strife, and possible bloodshed. True, it will mean loss of property, loss of home perhaps, but this too is the price every American family is also paying in tears and blood.

Although "there can be no question that they be accorded equal academic rights and privileges with all other American school children," this superintendent cautioned, "we would do well to bear in mind and jealously guard those principles of our democracy for which we are pouring our all into the present cauldron." Because, however, Japan was characterized as "a definitely merciless foe," and Japanese Americans were assumed to be loyal to "the cold reality of the Japanese religion and philosophy," just what these "equal academic rights and privileges" might consist of is questionable indeed.[28]

Anti-Japanese sentiment was high in parts of Kings County and par-

ticularly in Tulare County, which had a sizable Japanese-American minority. One Japanese-American woman I interviewed remembered returning in 1945 to a small town in Tulare County when she was six years
old:

We came back here and it was hard again because . . . there was so much distrust
and it was right during those years. But again, my parents felt that school was
safe, and if we could just get to school we'd always be safe. There were a lot of
children who had parents that had lost a brother or a father or a son in the war,
and hated our being back here. But the teachers were wonderful, really, I never
felt that I ran into a prejudiced teacher. I never had that feeling.

Some whites, however, were hostile to any kind of positive or equal treatment for the returning Japanese Americans. In Orosi, for example, when
a Japanese-American boy made the high school baseball team in the
spring of 1945, a group of local whites protested. The high school principal wrote to Sacramento for advice:

I am confronted with a problem of playing a Japanese-American boy on our baseball team. This boy recently returned to our school and has "made" our team
fairly. We have used him in one game to date. Our school and myself have been
criticized for this action by a few radical members of our community. I have explained that the boy ceased to be a Japanese as far as the school was concerned
when he entered our school and as such, we cannot make a distinction between
race, color, or creed as provided in the code. I will therefore appreciate a reply
from your office as to the law on such matters and the positions of the schools
in adopting a policy of actions on the Americans of Japanese ancestry. This matter is a most urgent one here and I will greatly appreciate a reply by return mail if
possible. I also would like your permission to publish your reply.[29]

There is, however, no reply to this letter in the Sacramento archives.

Despite these anti-Japanese feelings, many educators were supportive
of the returning Japanese-American children. Mabel Crumby, a professor of education at San Jose State College, argued in a 1945 article that

a teacher with imagination might get her class to feel what these Japanese-American children had been through—their disrupted home life, their insecurity and
fears and now their anticipation, probably mixed with dread and pleasure, of
their return home. . . . More than what the teacher says, however, is her own attitude toward the child. This she will reveal to her class as she graciously receives
each returning "citizen" and makes him feel he is welcomed home.[30]

In another article, Henry Cooke, professor of history at Claremont
Graduate School, encouraged teachers to think of the return of the
Japanese-American children as an opportunity to teach "the spirit of
world fellowship": "This is particularly so because these people have been
under a cloud. We have a chance to point out the fallacy that is inherent

in the race doctrine. We can learn to deal with individuals as human beings despite the lineage behind them. We can get in a good stroke
against the West Coast tendencies to distrust all 'Orientals.'"[31] Cooke acknowledged that "anti-Japanese feeling" and deep prejudice existed, particularly in "largely rural areas where the residents think of the Japanese
people as competitors in agriculture or regions which unfortunately lost
a good many men in the horrors of war on Corregidor and Bataan."

Similar calls for sympathy were put forward by Priscilla Beattie and Roy
Arnheim, a junior high school teacher and principal, respectively, from
Los Angeles: "We as teachers must not disappoint these young people of
Japanese ancestry, for it is to us that they will look for guidance in their
problems of assimilation once more into the American community."[32] After 1946, however, such articles disappeared from official educational
journals and the Japanese removal vanished from public discussion.

Despite the failure to address the implications of the Japanese removal, concern over prejudice in children was a common theme in California education in the immediate postwar years. In the spring of 1945
the Tulare County superintendent of schools sponsored a forum on
"Race Relations and America's Future" at Visalia Union High School; at
the 1945 fall institute in Tulare County, the keynote lecture was "Inter-
Cultural Conflicts: Problems of Race Prejudice," by Dr. Franklin Fearing,
a UCLA psychology professor.[33] In April 1946, progressive educator
Willis Sutton spoke about "the Battle for America" as a struggle "for freedom of religion, for an unshackled press, for individual liberty and for
civil and individual rights."[34]

Under Fred Trott, the *Tulare County Schools Bulletin* continued to publish stories about progressive causes, including sympathetic accounts of
the suffering of the Soviet people. In the November 1945 *Bulletin*, for example, Trott reported: "Before the war, Smolensk, a Russian city 200
miles west of Moscow, had 176,000 inhabitants, 8,000 buildings, 96 factories, 17 schools of higher education, 19 libraries. After the war it has
25,000 population, 700 buildings, no factories, no schools of higher education and no libraries. This sort of thing is one reason that the Rus-
sians feel pretty strongly about a hard peace for Germany." He also defended the schools against conservative criticism: "Attacks upon education, in recent years, usually come in the form of a 'return to
fundamentals' campaign, and are calculated to frighten school people
into their burrows like rabbits and forestall a request for more money to
build more classrooms, reduce classroom load, buy needed equipment,
or adjust teachers' salaries to meet increased costs of living."[35] Trott
reprinted progressive articles from other journals—on the founding of
UNESCO; celebrating John Dewey's eighty-eighth birthday; in defense

of the "Building America" social studies series, which was the focus of conservative attacks in California; and on Robert Hutchins's address "Atomic Bomb vs. Civilization." Teachers "having children of Mexican origin in their classrooms" were encouraged to read U.S. Office of Education pamphlets on cultural understanding.[36] Typical of Trott's approach is this comment from one of his editorials in the *Bulletin*: "To begin with, we cannot afford to have any race prejudices. . . . We need to do more toward developing an international point of view in our schools."[37]

By the late 1940s, however, the political climate in the United States as a whole was shifting. The immediate postwar years were marked by a resurgence of anticommunism and antiprogressivism.[38] In California, Helen Heffernan was the target of numerous attacks, and articles supporting American freedoms in opposition to "godless Communism" appeared with increasing frequency in educational journals and in local newspapers.[39] In 1948 two Tulare County administrators and supporters of progressive education, Fred Trott and Alan Beach, resigned. Trott then took a position as principal of the two-room Deep Creek school, a striking demotion.[40] He was replaced as director of education by Elizabeth Butler, whose interests were more narrowly focused on issues of classroom instruction. The next year, Tulare County Superintendent of Schools Theo Nickel resigned in the middle of his term to take a position in the Fresno County town of Reedley. The new superintendent was J. Post Williams, a conservative administrator who perfectly fit the profile of rural county superintendents described by Myra Strober and David Tyack in their classic article "Why Do Women Teach and Men Manage?" He was tall, Protestant, closely connected with local business groups, and a member of the Masonic Lodge, the Eastern Star Lodge, the Visalia Toastmasters Club, and the Council of Boy Scouts of America.[41] Williams's first column in the *Bulletin*, in October 1949, was a bland message entitled "Experience Is Our Best Teacher." In his September 1950 column he called for greater respect for the flag:

With our American democracy being threatened by atheistic communism it behooves us to give more attention to the ideals for which our forefathers fought. Spiritual values in public education should be emphasized in order that we may carry forward our ideals in the stress and strain of a war economy. Emphasis will be placed on this theme at the coming Tulare County Teachers' Institute.

Throughout the country in the late 1940s, the opinions of teachers were being shaped by the anticommunist crusade. Four Tulare County teachers attended the 1949 meeting of the National Education Association at which it was decided to bar Communists from employment in

American schools. Agnes Strom, a Visalia teacher, submitted an account of the meeting to the *Tulare County Schools Bulletin* that November:

Members of the Communist Party shall not be employed in the American schools. Such membership involves adherence to doctrines and discipline completely inconsistent with the principles of freedom on which American education depends. Such membership, and the accompanying surrender of intellectual integrity, render an individual unfit to discharge the duties of a teacher in this country. . . . At the same time, we condemn the careless, incorrect, and unjust use of such words as "Red" and "communist" to attack teachers and other persons who in point of fact are not communists, but who merely have views different from those of their accusers. The whole spirit of free American education will be subverted unless teachers are free to think for themselves. It is because members of the Communist Party are required to surrender this right, as a consequence of becoming part of a movement characterized by conspiracy and calculated deceit, that they shall be excluded from employment as teachers and from membership in the NEA.

Although this report reflected public concerns over education in general, such a direct discussion of politics was unusual in the *Tulare County Schools Bulletin.* By early 1950, the public statements of Tulare and Kings County school officials were conservative and cautious, reflecting the increasingly repressive political climate throughout the country. The *Bulletin* now included sections on classroom methods of art education, music education, kindergarten education, and physical education but few discussions of the goals and theories of education.

The mood of the times also affected the public stance of state officials. Although Helen Heffernan and her staff continued to argue for more democratic forms of education, their work became less openly political. In May 1950, when Heffernan spoke at public meetings on the need for long-range planning for Tulare County's education program, her statements condemning racism or defending freedom of speech were much more circumspect than they had been in the 1930s or even during the war.

Rural School Consolidation

Rural education in California in the late 1940s was marked not only by cold war political ideology but also by the closing of small rural schools and the creation of larger consolidated schools to which children were bused. Educational experts had advocated consolidation as the solution to the "rural school problem" since the turn of the century, arguing that larger schools offered more opportunities for children, that isolated teachers were unprofessional, and that larger administrative units were cheaper and more efficient. Yet community resistance to school consolidation had remained strong throughout the 1920s, and in the depression years of the 1930s few resources existed to support educational innovation of any kind.[42] Nationwide, a large percentage of one-room schools remained in use through the Second World War, despite a slow movement toward consolidation.

By the late 1940s, however, improved roads, cheap gas, the continued depopulation of rural areas, and growing suburbanization made consolidated schools not only feasible but seemingly inevitable. In 1944, a White House conference on rural education had called for a renewed emphasis on centralization and the consolidation of schools. As the war came to an end, a number of California educators began to argue for such a move.

Typical of the arguments in favor of consolidation was the 1944 proposal to the Kellogg Foundation by Paul Hanna, professor of education at Stanford, for a Rural Education Institute:

California has several hundred rural school districts controlled by lay citizens who have little vision of the possibilities of education and headed by administrators with not much greater vision. These districts maintain 1,340 one-room elementary schools many of which are so small that an adequate school program is impossible with poor buildings, poor equipment and inadequately trained teachers. Rural elementary schools are filled with teachers who have little or no training for life in rural communities and who take these positions to secure enough experience to obtain city positions later or because they cannot find positions elsewhere. The high rate of turnover in the rural schools of California is proof of this statement.[43]

In this passage Hanna recycles arguments from the turn of the century and ignores the decades of imaginative and thoughtful work by rural teachers, principals, and supervisors. His pointed reference to California schools is particularly striking, given the outstanding, nationally recognized leadership Helen Heffernan had provided in rural education in that state. Indeed, Hanna was well acquainted with Heffernan, and he himself supervised a program in which rural teachers could earn a Stanford degree through summer work. Hanna's proposal may be an example of the elitism of university professors of education or simply another example of the shallow opportunism that to this day marks so many funded educational research projects. But "inadequately trained teachers" and administrators with little "vision of the possibilities of education" refers to the very real—and professional—people who taught in and administered these schools.

In the period immediately following the Second World War, the movement to consolidate rural schools in California gained momentum, fueled in part by the arguments of experts like Hanna, but motivated even more powerfully by the demographic and social changes of the war years. In early 1945, the Strayer report on the future of California education recommended the establishment of "regional committees, made up of local persons to examine their communities for possibilities of unionizing districts, and setting up larger units of administration in order to provide better administration, more economical and logical school units, and to provide better educational opportunities for children in small rural schools."[44] Later that year, in response to this report, school district reorganization legislation was passed, with financial support pledged for the consolidation of schools in California.[45] In 1949 additional legislation was passed requiring all counties to appoint a committee on school district reorganization to study and recommend how districts should be unionized.[46] The effect of this legislation was to accelerate the pace of school consolidation and the formation of large graded schools, to which rural children were bused. Resistance to consolidation remained present in some rural areas, with objections framed in terms of local community control and solidarity, the hardship of long bus rides, and, occasionally, fear of children from other localities or of other races.[47] Such resistance, however, had little effect on the overall pace of consolidation.

By the late 1940s school officials and local leaders generally accepted consolidation as the most modern and scientific approach to rural schooling. Throughout the nonurban areas of California one- and two-room schools were abandoned and country children were bused to district graded elementary schools. The same trend occurred throughout the United States during these years, as the approximate numbers of one-room schools nationwide for the period 1930–70 graphically demonstrate:

1930	149,000
1940	114,000
1950	60,000
1960	20,000
1970	2,000[48]

Consolidation had a powerful impact on local communities, children, and particularly teachers. The new elementary schools were overwhelmingly staffed by women teachers (the same women who had taught in the country schools, along with new graduates and, in the case of California, teachers who had come west in the postwar boom) and administered by men principals, frequently young veterans who had gone to college under the GI bill.

Rural School Consolidation in Tulare and Kings Counties

Small independent school districts had reached their largest number in Tulare and Kings Counties in 1920. Following national trends, a slow movement to consolidate these districts into larger units began in the early 1920s, despite some local resistance. By 1930 a gradual but steady move toward consolidation was evident: between 1930 and 1940 the number of one-, two-, and three-teacher schools in Tulare and Kings Counties declined from 108 to 80, with one-room schools in particular declining from 41 to 24. After 1945, both counties moved to eliminate small rural schools entirely. Theo Nickel, Tulare County superintendent of schools, wrote in 1947: "Many schools are forced to consider tremendous building programs, and it appears to us that all schools should carefully study the possibilities of unionization, annexation, or unification before permanent buildings are constructed in areas which are not now logically situated for schoolroom sites."[49] Twelve graded union schools were formed between 1945 and 1956, replacing thirty small one- and two-room district schools.

Consolidation of rural schools in Tulare and Kings Counties took place through either the *unionization* of two or more small elementary school districts into one large elementary district or the *unification* of elementary districts with a high school to form a joint elementary–high school district.[50] Both of these methods led to a unified district board and central administration, in which local control of schools was given up to a larger entity. By 1960, even most unionized districts that initially retained two or more small schools had closed those schools and were busing students to larger graded schools.[51]

Numbers of rural schools differed somewhat between Kings and Tulare Counties, reflecting the different geography and size of the two counties. Tulare County had approximately twice the population of Kings County, yet it also included the small, isolated mountain communities of the Sierra Nevada. The population of Kings County, in the flat farm country of the central San Joaquin Valley, was to a large extent already centered in small towns, and where there were large, corporate-owned ranches, these were worked by migrant farm laborers. By 1950 the number of one-, two-, and three-teacher schools in the combined counties had dropped to 40, 9 of which were one-room schools. The number of teachers working in these schools also declined, particularly in Kings County, where only nine women and two men remained teaching in one-, two-, and three-room schools. In both counties, the desirability of large graded schools was accepted, at least officially, by educators and local leaders, and the process of consolidation continued throughout the 1950s.

Even in the face of school consolidation, some rural supervisors attempted to maintain a sense of community and a vision of progressive education for small schools. For example, the Visalia Rural Teachers Club was founded in late 1946 for the small country schools surrounding Visalia. The club had thirty-five members in 1946–47, both men and women, though women predominated in leadership positions. The *Tulare County Schools Bulletin* reported in February 1947:

> The Visalia Rural Teachers Club has held two meetings. Officers elected were President, Jewell Wall, Principal, East Lynne; Vice President, Mrs. Cora Harman, Principal, Goshen; Secretary, Mrs. Evelyn Worthington, Primary Teacher, Elbow; Treasurer, Mr. James Dutton, Principal, Elbow. Everyone went away from the meeting feeling refreshed and happy. The next meeting will be in February with the men in charge of the evening.

In 1947 Jewell Wall, president of the Visalia Rural Teachers Club, was made a rural supervisor for Tulare County. One of her projects in that role was to build small district schools into community centers. For example, she was instrumental in the founding of the Yettem Community Club in the Yettem school district. A report in the *Tulare County Schools Bulletin* of April 1950 described the first meeting of the club: "The mothers present enjoyed a very interesting program presented by the primary children and the principal, Mrs. Emma Russell. Miss Jewell Wall, from the County office was present as a consultant. Here we have another instance where school and community are actively working together in the solution of problems which are otherwise unconquerable."

Despite the continued work of rural supervisors like Jewell Wall to realize the democratic vision of leaders such as Helen Heffernan, such efforts paled in comparison to the powerful movement toward consolidation. In this process, teachers not only lost the autonomy of small schools, but also seemed to lose a sense of their own value. Reflecting on the continued requirement that teachers attend county institutes, one teacher commented: "I hope institute is never done away with; it helps one to keep from being a little cog in a wheel without knowing what the other cogs are doing."[52]

Consolidation was accompanied by dramatic shifts in the gender composition of school staffs. In the period 1900–1930, elementary teachers and principals in the one-, two-, and three-room schools of Tulare and Kings Counties were overwhelmingly women. In 1930, for example, there were 142 women and 5 men teaching in the small rural schools of

Tulare County (all the men were principals of two- and three-room schools), and 40 women and 2 men in Kings County (one of the men was principal of a two-room school, the other taught under a woman principal in a two-room school). By 1940, although rural school teachers were still overwhelmingly women, men increasingly held positions as principals. In Tulare County in 1940, there were 101 women and 18 men teaching in one-, two-, and three-room schools; of the 18 men, 15 were principals of two- or three-room schools. The numbers for Kings County were 31 women and 2 men, both of the men being principals of two-room schools. By 1950, 76 women and 10 men remained teaching in small rural schools in Tulare County; all 10 of the men were principals of two- or three-room schools. Kings County by this time had virtually eliminated all its small rural schools.

When schools consolidated in the late 1940s, women who had been principals of two- and three-room schools tended to return to the classroom, while younger men took positions as principals of the newly formed graded schools. Sundale Union School in Tulare County, formed by the consolidation of Nickerson School and Oakdale School in 1945, with Bliss School added in 1946, provides a typical example. All three of these schools began as one-room schools—Oakdale in 1882, Bliss in 1912, and Nickerson in 1918. The teachers and teaching principals at these schools—especially the smaller Bliss and Nickerson—were predominantly women. Bliss had sixteen women and two men teachers or teaching principals in the period 1912–46; Nickerson had eleven teachers or teaching principals, all women, in the period 1918–45; and Oakdale, the oldest and largest of the three schools, had twenty-one women and fourteen men teachers or teaching principals in the period 1882–1945. The 1946 merger of Nickerson, Oakdale, and Bliss was at the administrative level only. That is, although L. W. Ripple, teaching principal of Oakdale, was named principal of Sundale Union School District, the teaching principals at Bliss and Nickerson, Gladys Rusher and Blanche Pummill, respectively, remained in place. In 1950, however, a new union school was built, the three smaller schools were closed, and children were now bused to Sundale Union. John Holtsdorf, district principal and principal at Oakdale, was made district superintendent and principal of the nine-teacher graded school. Blanche Pummill, principal at Nickerson from 1942 to 1950, returned to the classroom.

It is important to note that the pattern of men moving into positions of administrative control over women was not unique to the consolidated rural schools of Tulare and Kings Counties. Similar changes took place in the town graded schools. In the towns, to be sure, the positions of town and district superintendent had always been held by men, although

TABLE 7
Principals of Graded Town Schools in Tulare and Kings Counties, 1930–50

	Men		Women	
	Kings	Tulare	Kings	Tulare
1930				
District Superintendents	2	5	0	0
Principals	3	10	8	17
1940				
District Superintendents	3	4	0	0
Principals	4	23	6	6
1950				
District Superintendents	3	5	0	0
Principals	14	40	7	10

SOURCE: School Directories of Tulare and Kings Counties for 1930, 1940, and 1950.

as we have seen, between 1902 and 1934 the Kings County superintendency went to women as well. In both counties, however, more women held positions as elementary graded school principals in 1930 than did men. That all changed in subsequent decades, when men came to outnumber women in principalships by quite a margin (Table 7).

One exception to this pattern of men taking over positions of administrative authority was Madeleine Cochrane of Tulare County, an outstanding rural teacher, principal of the two-room Laurel School, and a widely recognized community leader. Madeleine Cochrane recalled:

They voted to unionize in the fifties—must have been around '54. That was Linder School, Walnut Grove School, Enterprise School, and Laurel School. Those four unionized into Oak Valley. The first year I taught there I had just the regular rural kids. And then the next year I left because they wanted me to come to town anyway and I thought if I was going to make a break I should.

Cochrane was offered and accepted the principalship of a junior high school in Tulare. In this, however, she was unusual. As she remembered the 1950s, she was the only woman junior high school principal in Tulare County.

Representations of Women Teachers in the Postwar World

The conservative restoration of the later 1940s and 1950s was marked not only by anticommunism and cold war hysteria, but also by the coalescing of a rigid gender politics, what Betty Friedan later called "the feminine mystique." As has often been pointed out, the politics of the feminine mystique in many ways replicated the separate-sphere ideology of middle-class nineteenth-century society, although the twentieth-century version emphasized a normative and exaggerated female heterosexuality, expressed ideally in marriage and the nuclear family. In education, this politics played itself out in the elimination of the marriage bar and a thinly veiled homophobic attack on single women teachers and women in positions of power in administration. Thus, changes in the organization of rural schools were paralleled by shifts in the representation of the woman teacher in public discourse. Repressive social conformity, cold war anxiety, the glorification of the nuclear family, and rigid conceptions of gender were all intertwined with the resurgence of patriarchal control of the schools. The causal connections among these shifts as they relate to school reform are difficult to establish, in part because the role of women in education was rarely openly debated in the late 1940s. Nevertheless, the consequences for women of widespread school reform in the late 1940s and 1950s, particularly in rural areas, were profound.

With the elimination of the marriage bar, women teachers were redefined as heterosexual wives and mothers and encouraged to work as teachers, so long as they were under the control of male administrators. In this shift from the asexual single schoolmarm to the heterosexual married teacher, the possibility that a woman could serve in a position of power and responsibility as principal or superintendent was erased. Instead, the school once again was imagined as the patriarchal family writ large. Very little protest was heard in the public realm about this erosion of women's gains in education. One of the few exceptions was the campaign to pass an equal rights amendment in the 1940s, which was supported by articles in the *Sierra Educational News,* the official magazine of the California Teachers Association.[53] These voices, however, were isolated, and the CTA itself, which was dominated by male administrators, never addressed the changes in the gender composition of administration that were taking place.

As we have seen, the construct of the woman teacher had been contested since the late nineteenth century. In California, thanks in large part to the powerful voice of Helen Heffernan, the idea of the rural woman teacher as responsible and capable was embraced, particularly in the 1920s and 1930s. Moreover, women often held positions as principals of small rural schools and as county superintendents of schools. But despite these positive examples, the stereotype of the rural teacher as a frustrated spinster or as Ellwood Cubberley's "mere slip of a girl" did not vanish. A 1930 California report on "educational problems," for exam-

ple, advocated school consolidation in part precisely because of the dangers of rural women teachers.[54]

Negative views of the woman teacher resurfaced with force in the post-
1945 period in the context of the postwar ideology of domesticity and
the rapid growth of male administrative control. In a fascinating article
published in the *Sierra Educational News* in 1945, Ducelia Cobb, a Long
Beach teacher, argued that women in fact avoided going into teaching
because of these negative views. Cobb recognized that low pay was an issue, particularly for young men, "who cannot hope to maintain a family
approaching a standard to which a professional man might reasonably
aspire on the salary paid a teacher." Unlike critics in the earlier woman
peril panic, however, Cobb accepted that men would never enter teaching in large numbers and that teaching would therefore remain a
woman-defined job. Her interest was thus not with men teachers, but
with women (who apparently would not be concerned about low pay)
who, she argued, were reluctant to enter teaching because of "a reputation that amounts to a stigma." That reputation, she said, was one of inadequate womanliness, especially heterosexual attractiveness: "It is common practice with the majority of the public," she wrote, "to classify the
teacher as unattractive looking, as lacking in style, and as the possessor of
an overbearing, sententious personality."

In Cobb's opinion, any truth to this assumption was the fault not of
teachers, but of school boards and principals "who labor under the mis-
apprehension that it is in poor taste to wear makeup and to dress in a
manner that conforms to current style." Moreover, Cobb attacked the
still-widespread practice of regulating the teacher's private life: "Motives
should not be questioned, aspects of the applicant's life which have no
close bearing on her work should not be inspected." In essence, Cobb
argued that women teachers should be allowed, even encouraged, to
meet the same standard of female beauty and attractiveness as other
women: "It is the duty of every teacher to be as attractive as possible, not
only for her pupils but also as a gesture of public relations. As well as being physically attractive, she should strive to have a charming personality; and little by little the outmoded picture of the traditional 'school
marm' will be modified."[55] Thus, although Cobb accepted that teaching
would remain low-paid women's work, she challenged the view of women
teachers as "lacking in style" or charm. Instead she envisioned "the
woman teacher" as an individual for whom sexual attractiveness and private pleasures would be central.

In a response to Cobb's article, Alden Naud, a teacher in Calexico,
agreed that teachers should meet social ideals of attractiveness and
grooming. But she also defended the unmarried teacher:

Unmarried instructors cannot in fairness to those who have dedicated their lives to their profession be classed under the heading of "desiccated old maids" or "widows who have to be grateful for even the most meager living." It isn't a question of single-blessedness or teaching that makes a person untidy or unlovely, any more than it makes a woman in some other walk of life or in her home, messy or disagreeable or drab. A great majority of teachers are well-groomed and appropriately dressed.[56]

Both Cobb and Naud were concerned with the image of the woman teacher in terms of appearance and changing social norms of what constituted a "proper woman." Makeup, style, charm, and physical attractiveness became central to their defense of the woman teacher. And Cobb, at least, also argued for the right of women teachers to seek pleasure and to control their private lives. At the same time, Cobb and Naud ignored questions of equal pay, intellectual commitment, respect, or access to positions of authority that marked the discourse of earlier women educators. Issues of control over teachers' work and political or philosophical questions about the meaning of education in a democracy are strikingly absent from their discussion.

It is interesting to compare Cobb's and Naud's vision of the woman teacher with assumptions about teaching as work for men in this period. Typical of postwar discourse is a 1946 *Sierra Educational News* article on teaching as a career by Albert Lang, a professor at Fresno State College. Lang paid special attention to young men, arguing that "elementary school work is a man's-size job, the need for men is great, and the opportunities are permanent and far-reaching. No qualified young man needs to hesitate about entering the elementary aspect of educational work. This is actually a big field for capable men." Lang was quick to stress that this "man's-size job" involved not teaching, but administration and supervision: "There are opportunities for the capable and effective teacher to move into positions of greater responsibility and remuneration. By additional training elementary teachers, especially men, are in line for positions as principals, general supervisors and supervisors of special subjects."[57]

Two other features of teaching, according to Lang, were important in attracting young people into the profession: individual freedom and social standing. On the former point he writes: "He will not enter a vocation where his personal freedom is unduly hampered. He must keep his right to think as he wishes. He cannot allow any one else to dictate his beliefs and opinions." Again, the use of the masculine pronoun is significant here. This teacher is assumed to be a man and therefore to be concerned with autonomy and freedom of thought. As Lang describes the possibilities of education as a career, "Nothing is quite so thrilling to a capable person as the consciousness of achievement. Nothing is quite so distasteful as to follow monotonous routine and to be in work where self-expression is restricted."[58] Note that these concerns of intellectual freedom and achievement go unmentioned in Cobb's and Naud's articles, where the teacher is envisioned to be a woman.

Lang's article recalls the "woman peril" of the early years of the twentieth century, when young men were encouraged to enter teaching as crusaders and to take leadership positions as models for boys. It is striking, though, that such an article could be written *after* the achievements of women educators in California in the 1920s and 1930s. By the late 1940s, the representation of the woman teacher as capable and autonomous had essentially disappeared from public discourse, while the feminine mystique and the image of the heterosexualized woman classroom teacher in need of male control and supervision went largely unchallenged. The rapidity of school consolidation, the emergence of cold war ideology, and the construction of a feminine mystique combined to create a new world, both institutionally and discursively, while the loss of a language of feminism and of an organized movement advocating women's rights in education left women without a vocabulary to name what was happening.

Teachers Remember the Postwar Rural Schools

The dramatic changes of the postwar years in the rural schools of Tulare and Kings Counties reflected decisions at the state level, economic and social transformations, and shifts in the representation of men and women in popular culture. These changes, which led to the disappearance of rural schools presided over by women teachers and principals, paralleled the victory of ideas of centralization and efficiency in education; the almost total hegemony of heterosexuality, with its emphasis on men's and women's "essential" natures, likewise helped explain and justify the reorganization of the schools.

As is true of memories of other periods of social change, the accounts of retired teachers tend to describe these transitions in education as inevitable and, in a sense, unassailable. Even when they noted the discrimination against women teachers of these years (possibly because of assumptions they made about my own politics), they did not analyze these events as being the result of human decisions or interests, but presented them as simply a matter of fact.

Retired teachers all noted the shift from women to men principals. Martha M., for example, commented:

Martha M.: They began to encourage men to coming into teaching. They began to feel that they should be the principals.

K.W.: When was this. After the war?

Martha M.: I really don't know when it started, but it was kind of subtle. [Laughs] They began to encourage men to go into teaching. Which was fine. There were many men, some of them were quite macho and felt they should be the principal. But I really didn't run up against those.

Although Martha M. refers to the "macho" attitude of some men who "felt they should be principal," she also emphasizes that she had no personal experience with such men. Her sense of these "macho" attitudes, then, reflects a shift in gender expectations in a broader sense, part of the well-documented backlash against women in the late 1940s and 1950s. For her, the change was "subtle" and could not be attributed to a single dramatic event.

Teresa D. described the same gender shift in positions of leadership:

Teresa D.: I think that at that time there were a good many women, and then gradually it changed and then became more men. There was a time when more men came in.

K.W.: Now, I'm interested in that. Do you have any sense of why that happened?

Teresa D.: Well, it might be partly finance. You see, they paid a little better, and as they paid a little more, the men came in. I think that had something to do with it.

K.W.: It seems to have happened after the war . . .

Teresa D.: It was after the war. . . . The change was partly financial, it may have been more financial than I realize, as I look back, and also, as it became better paying financially even some amount of money would make a difference, and some of the men would use their positions as stepping stones to go to another and get a better salary from their experience.

K.W.: Well, could women do that too?

Teresa D.: Yes, they could, but for some reason, women usually stayed closer to home. You know what I mean? Now, the men, though, they were the head of the family and they could move. So there's that to think about.

In reflecting on the shift to men principals, Teresa D. first explains the change as economic, which doubtless was an important factor in making these positions attractive. But when I ask if women also might have sought these better-paying positions, Teresa D. falls back on a notion of woman's essential nature, her desire to stay "closer to home." And she describes without comment a social world in which it was accepted that men were heads of family who determined where the family would live.

Early in my research, I assumed that men had always held the positions of power in schools. Rachel B., however, made it clear that women had once been principals, and that they had lost these positions to men. She described rural schools as a woman's world in the 1920s and 1930s:

Rachel B.: . . . the early days of school teachers, women did it. And men did not. And then some people, I guess parents or maybe supervisors, got the idea they were being cheated of the male image in life. And then the first thing you knew there were male students just like the male nurses that come into the nursing profession now. And toward the end when they stopped the institute—could have been during the war, I don't know—there were as many men as there were women.

K.W.: There must have been, even when you started teaching, it must have been that most of the principals were men?

Rachel B.: No, it wasn't. There were a few men in high school and the principals in high school were men. But no, when I first started teaching, women were principals.

Rachel B. firmly corrected me in my assumption that principals were mostly men. But although there is an implied criticism here (parents feeling they were "being cheated of the male image in life"), she did not develop this critique. In a later interview she described teaching in graded schools under male principals without comment. Rachel B. also makes two statements that exaggerate the shift from women to men: first, she says that by the time the county stopped having institutes (around 1950) there were as many men as women teachers (this was never the case in Tulare County); and second, she claims that the early principals were all women. Although it is true that the great majority of teaching principals in the rural two-room schools were women in the 1930s and 1940s, in the graded town schools—where Rachel B. herself had taught—there were always a sizable number of men principals. In her memory, however, the world of the rural schools was a woman's world. It was only later that men entered the field of education in large numbers.

Let us compare Rachel B.'s account of the world of rural schools with Ralph D.'s. Ralph D. was one of three teaching brothers, all of whom rose to administrative positions in Tulare County schools.

Ralph D.: I taught in Tipton for four years; I did eighth-grade teaching. Then I was superintendent for eleven years.

K.W.: How common was it for a man to be an elementary school teacher?

Ralph D.: Most of the time the principal was a man in the larger schools. But there were a few women. I'd say looking back there were quite a few women principals.

K.W.: Did you ever teach under a woman principal?

Ralph D.: I taught at Liberty for a couple of years one time under a woman principal there. We didn't get along—my fault, I'm sure. She was like they do now, wouldn't touch a child. Well, they had some real rough characters there, and if you didn't show yourself as a man, then you were out of luck. I played football with the boys, you know. One boy took a dislike to me for some reason or other. He was in the eighth grade and I played with the seventh-graders. One day he decided he was going to carry the ball and he was going to come right after me.

He didn't know that I played football in high school, junior college, and everything. So he came up to me, I just lowered my shoulder and he hit me and bounced back. I never had any more trouble with him. That's all it took, just to show that I was a man.

When asked how common it was for men to teach in elementary schools, Ralph D. immediately mentioned that men were principals. Unlike Rachel B., Ralph D. first commented that there were "a few" women principals, but then changed that to "quite a few." For Ralph D., moreover, it was imperative to "show yourself as a man" to the boy students by means of physical strength.

Ralph D.'s account of men and women teachers and principals is both confirmed and challenged by the memories of Miriam J., who taught in the rural schools of Tulare County.

K.W.: One thing that I have talked to people about is that in the early days most of the teachers were women. Was that your experience too?

Miriam J.: The principal, if it was a large enough school, was a man.

K.W.: So that was true even back then, that the principal was a man.

Miriam J.: When I taught at Sultana I had to work with men teachers. The upper-grade teachers, they liked to have men. They had to have the boys' physical education. Although when I taught at East Orosi, I had to have the boys' physical education; they learned, had already learned from their older brothers and fathers probably, because they would tell me what to do next, what to tell them to do next. That was kind of amusing.

K.W.: In the early days they didn't seem to mind the idea that these older boys would have a woman teacher.

Miriam J.: No, they didn't seem to mind. The boys could be larger than the teacher.

Here, Miriam J. notes the relationship between male authority and graded schools, commenting that the principal would be a man if it was "a large enough school." But she also recalls that she was able to hold authority over large boys in rural schools. East Orosi School, where she mentions she had charge of boys' physical education, was a two-room school in which she was the teaching principal. Thus in Miriam J.'s memory, women controlled the small rural school and wielded authority over large boys. Unlike Ralph B., though, she did not need to demonstrate her power through physical strength.

Men's accounts of their experiences as teachers and administrators in the postwar years mirror those of women teachers. After the war, as we have seen, men were encouraged to enter teaching with the idea that they could quickly rise into administration. Hank G.'s story provides a typical example of a capable young man who came home from the war uncertain about his future and who ended up in teaching. Hank G.'s older sister, an elementary school teacher who had studied with Corinne Seeds at UCLA and was a strong advocate of progressive methods, encouraged him to go to college.

I came back here to Hanford to see my sister. And I said, "I'm going on down to Ventura to get on with the Shell Oil Company." They'd offered me a job as a roustabout. And she said, "Well I'm teaching up at Fresno State this summer. I'm a master teacher in their lab school. Why don't you come with me?" I said, "Where's Fresno State?" And she said, "Well, just get in the car, come on." I went wandering around the campus, went into the biology department, and was looking at the mammals that they have mounted, and a fellow walked up to me, the head of the department. I had on my uniform, and my ruptured duck and my wings and my medals and all that stuff, and he said, "Why don't you come in and sit down with me and we'll talk." And one hour later I was enrolled in the biology department at Fresno, and I graduated in '48 with a degree in biology.

In Hank G.'s memory, it was the influence of his wife, also a teacher, and his sister that led him into teaching:

I had passed all my fish and game examinations, and my wife was already a teacher; she taught in Sanger at the time, kindergarten. Put me through the last year of school—along with the GI bill. So I said, "We're going to have to move." She said, "Where?" And I said, "Well, I don't know, it'll have to be somewhere in the mountains, because I'm a biologist." She said, "No way." My sis called and the two of them got together, and they had two teaching openings down here at the Lakeside school. I'd taken observation-participation, but I hadn't taken practice teaching. In those days, though, you could get an emergency credential. So I came to work down here as the eighth-grade teacher and bus driver. I got $2,800 a year for teaching and $500 for driving the bus. And my wife was so mad. She had either one or two years experience, and they only offered her $2,700. And my wife is the original liberated woman to begin with. She said, "You didn't know anything about anything and they offered me a hundred dollars a year less just because you're a man." I said, "Well . . . "

Once Hank G. began teaching in the rural schools of Kings County he rose quickly into administration.

A job opening came at a five-teacher school out in the country. I went out and went around to different board members and said, "Well I'd sure like to be your teaching principal." Well, they checked around, and I'd done an adequate job, I suppose, and so they hired me. Twenty-five years old. . . . I finished the second year there, and then a principalship came open at the Lee Richmond school. Lee Richmond was one of the early-day superintendents here, and they named a school after her. It was a new school that was opening here in Hanford, and the superintendent here in town called me and said, "Don't you want to come in and be principal of the school?" Real affirmative action. I was there two years, and they had trouble with the junior high school here in town—they'd had four principals in five years—so they raised my salary to $6,000 and they said, "You go over there and take that job." So I said, "All right." So I went over there.

The ease with which Hank G. moved into the principalship (his first position, when he was twenty-five) illuminates the statistical shift from women to men principals in the postwar years. Hank G. was more outspoken than any other teacher I interviewed about gender discrimination (witness his ironic comment about "real affirmative action"). Although Hank G. was considered to be an outstanding administrator, he nonetheless benefited from social expectations in ways that equally talented women teachers in this period did not.

George J. told a similar story. George J. had attended San Jose State and began teaching in Kings County during the depression.

Well, here's the situation: I had a letter of introduction from a friend of my father's who had come from Hanford. He wrote a letter of introduction for me to the board chairman down here. Well, the thing was, I was interested in coming down here because I was going with a charming girl. She had a job in Lemoore. She had graduated college at the same time as I did and she had been a star at Lemoore High School in music, and so the elementary principal, he recruited her. She didn't even apply. So she worked there for three years as a music supervisor teacher, and I started in here. That's the way it was—it was just chance. No direction particularly. [Laughs] Just bumble along, and everything worked out fine and that's true of all my life. I just have been so fortunate in ending up doing the right thing.

George J. rose quickly to be a successful principal and administrator. Like Hank G., he was spoken of with great respect and affection by other teachers I interviewed. As George J. put it, "Everything worked out fine"; but the ease with which he rose to administrative positions also reflects the expectation that men would take positions of power in the schools.

Although men took control of school leadership in the 1940s, women, who were again relegated to the classroom, at the same time gained a measure of freedom in their private lives. As we have seen, both men and women teachers were expected to meet strict standards of behavior through the 1930s; these standards were enforced by direct orders of school boards and by the close surveillance of small-town and rural communities. By the late 1940s, however, this moral discipline began to loosen, reflecting not only changes in sexual standards and gender ideology but also the transition to larger, centralized schools. And the marriage bar, which was still in effect in many rural districts in the 1930s, disappeared with the wartime teacher shortage. Thus for some Tulare and Kings County teachers, the graded schools of the late 1940s were liberating.

Teachers in Tulare and Kings Counties remembered the late 1940s as a time of rapid social change and enhanced personal freedom. Evelyn Burke Huffman, for example, who came to teach in Kings County after the war, remembered the sense of independence from social constraints that she felt, as well as the sociability of the graded school. Huffman had been teaching at a small school in Kansas where "there were many taboos—no smoking, no sled riding in snowy fields, no slacks, etc." Conditions in Kings County, she said, were very different:

> In 1948 I was back in the classroom in Avenal, California, teaching a third grade. What a change! This year in Avenal there were 15 new teachers from around the United States.
>   That fall when I went to prepare my classroom, I found teachers wearing shorts. There was a teacher's room and they even smoked in there! There was a machine called a Ditto and study films. Salaries were $3,500 and up. Most of the teachers lived in a complex of apartments. You didn't have to spend all of your time in the community.[59]

For Huffman, being able to control one's private life (to wear shorts, to smoke) was well worth the loss of control over teaching she had enjoyed in the country school. Of course, these two forms of control are not necessarily linked. Two teachers, speaking about the graded school in Corcoran in Kings County in the late 1940s and early 1950s, specifically noted their freedom to use whatever instructional methods they wished in their classrooms. Graded schools also provided teachers with a social group and collegiality. Rachel B., for example, notes that in Orosi (the school in which teachers were given marks by the principal) "we had good times together. We had baby showers for people who were getting pregnant and birthday parties and things like that."

Despite these advantages of the centralized graded school that developed in the late 1940s and 1950s, it was nevertheless based on a rigid gender hierarchy of women classroom teachers and men administrators. Although they could now make themselves attractive in the ways demanded by Ducelia Cobb, and although they had much greater freedom in their private lives than ever before, in return for these personal pleasures they were expected to work in a world of patriarchal control.

Conclusion

The world of rural California teachers was transformed in the 1940s. The Second World War brought home the power of the state to mobilize the population through propaganda and to control the lives of individuals in direct and sometimes violent ways, as the removal of Japanese Americans so graphically demonstrated. It also led to a teacher shortage and the elimination of the married women teacher's bar. Meanwhile, the anticommunism of the postwar years and the cold war era challenged progressive ideas that had defined California education in the 1920s and 1930s. And the woman-dominated one-, two-, and three-room schools that had provided educations for country children since the 1870s were replaced by consolidated graded schools in which men principals controlled the work of women teachers. Once again decisions at the level of the state, by transforming the institutional structure of schools, transformed the lives of teachers. Underlying and accompanying these changes was the coalescing of the rigid gender ideology of the feminine mystique and the representation of the woman teacher in the mode of what Adrienne Rich has called "compulsory heterosexuality."

The accounts of this process by retired teachers and principals are complex, revealing the pride they took in their responsible and creative work in the rural schools, but also the greater freedom they enjoyed in the graded schools. Although both men and women remembered the shift to male control, their accounts lack a gender critique of this transformation, perhaps because the language of feminism was not available to them as they lived through it. In the postwar period, there was virtually no public comment as women lost administrative power and moved into male-dominated graded schools. We can only begin to explore the reasons for these shifts by means of wider social analysis, but what the shifts mean in terms of lives lived can only be learned from the narratives of the teachers themselves—narratives that document the loss of a world of country schools in which women teachers found a large measure of respect, autonomy, and satisfaction.

CONCLUSION

Subjugated knowledges are . . . those blocs of
historical knowledge which were present but
disguised within the body of functionalist and
systematizing theory and which criticism—
which obviously draws upon scholarship—has
been unable to reveal. On the other hand, I
believe that by subjugated knowledges one
should understand something else, something
which in a sense is altogether different, namely,
a whole set of knowledges that have been disqualified as inadequate to their task or insuffi-
ciently elaborated: naive knowledges, located
low down on the hierarchy, beneath the required level of cognition or scientificity.
—Michel Foucault, *Power/Knowledge*

This book was written from a personal desire to understand the lives of women teachers like my mother, women who, in my
memory, lived complex lives of value to the community and to the
schools. Knowledge of these lives has, in Foucault's terms, been subjugated, "disqualified as inadequate," considered to be "naive . . . , located
low down on the hierarchy" of significance, hidden in the shadows of the
institutional history of schools. My initial intent in writing this book was
to uncover that knowledge. Although I began this project out of a "personal trouble," however, I soon realized that my attempt to understand
the meaning of teaching for women in California was part of a collective
exploration being undertaken in a wide range of settings and from a
number of perspectives. The scholarly work of other feminist historians
and theorists has provided me with categories I have found useful. My
framing of the history of rural California teachers thus is shaped not only
by my own personal life history but also by theories circulating throughout the contemporary intellectual world.

This history became increasingly complicated as I explored social
structures—the "pre-given forms in which people shaped their lives," in
the words of Frigga Haug—and what Carolyn Steedman calls "social information."[1] As Micaela Di Leonardo points out, the use of categories

like "discourse" and "culture" leads to a focus on the immediate setting, the ways individuals make meaning out of the social and cultural world with which they are presented. But this can deflect our attention from the powerful forces shaping each individual's world, and prevent us "from perceiving the overarching effects of the global economy on our past and present lives, the variety and malleability of kin forms, the linked continuities of class division and male dominance, and the creativity and adaptability of the human construction and reconstruction of reality."[2] Di Leonardo is emphasizing here that we do not live our lives solely in terms of discursive categories. Other forces create both the representations through which we envision ourselves and the material conditions in which we move. This history of women teachers in rural California has explored the contested nature of schooling and the way women teachers have engaged in the process of making meaning and wresting pleasure from their lives, but it has also revealed the power of the state to set out policies, shape institutions, and support or restrict teachers' work, and the impact of social and economic changes over time.

In my desire to uncover knowledge of these women's lives, I have had to recognize both my own motives for reconstructing the story of this past and the contradictions that complicate what I would like to see as a heroic narrative. Beginning research from personal concern, particularly when the subject touches one's own life history, raises questions about the nature of memory and the problem of nostalgia, of romanticizing the past. So much has been lost, hidden, and denied about these lives that there is a kind of moral imperative to try to recover them. But at the same time, the past is not an artifact to be excavated; we construct it as much as we uncover it. Carolyn Steedman has commented:

We all return to memories and dreams . . . , again and again; the story we tell of our own life is reshaped around them. But the point doesn't lie back there, back in the past, back in the lost time at which they happened; the only point lies in interpretation. The past is re-used through the agency of social information, and that interpretation of it can only be made with what people know of a social world and their place within it.[3]

The tension between the story "back there" in the past and critical interpretation has not been solved in this book. I recognize my own process of interpretation at the same time that I have been drawn throughout by a desire for closure, for logic, to see an inherent meaning in these stories. But despite all of the qualifications and cautions about the "mythological" quality of history, I believe the past *does* hold lessons, if we look for them. What, then, can we learn from this history that can help us understand the present?

One powerful theme raised by this history is the highly politicized nature of schooling. Visions of teachers' capabilities and what schools ought to do are deeply contested. In conservative times, pro-business, chauvinistic, and nativist groups flourish and put forward a conception of education that emphasizes obedience, patriotism, and conformity. In opposition to these conceptions are visions of schools as institutions in which creativity and the individual value of all children should be nurtured and encouraged. These competing visions rest on opposing views of the kind of education that is necessary in a democracy. The use of the schools to encourage unquestioning loyalty to the state during the First and Second World Wars, the movement by right-wing groups to censor the books used in schools, the attempts of local communities to exclude children deemed different—the "others," in opposition to what are always called the "regular" children: all of these stories resonate with the world in which we live.

Recent conservative critics of contemporary U.S. education look back to a "golden age" in which students shared a common cultural literacy and received a solid education in facts and basic skills.[4] These critics share a nostalgic view of schools as part of a unified and coherent cultural world, a world they claim has been shattered since the 1960s, when excluded groups—among them women, African Americans, Hispanic Americans, and Asian Americans—undermined the common culture and created dissent and chaos.

The history of the schools of Tulare and Kings Counties both affirms and challenges such a romantic view of the past. According to school officials, journalists, and teachers of the time, late-nineteenth-century schools, especially rural ones, did symbolize community and affirm a common local and national culture. Yet a closer examination of education in those counties reveals the same dynamic of patriarchal and racial privilege that has characterized U.S. society since its beginnings. What needs to be examined in both nineteenth- and twentieth-century myths of schooling is how schools helped produce and reproduce a dominant culture by ignoring subordinate groups and minimizing class and racial struggles over power, work, and knowledge. These myths obscure the self-conscious ways in which schools perpetuated views of coherence and democracy that did not exist for all people. The Tulare and Kings County schools symbolized consensus for dominant groups, but this was achieved by denying the realities of a racist and unequal society; struggles over power, work, and knowledge were silenced in the classroom. As I write, members of Congress are mobilizing support for a constitutional amendment requiring school prayer, even as more cuts in federal support of education are being contemplated, cuts that will disproportionately affect children who are defined as "other," children implicitly assumed to be undeserving.

Although the lives of teachers need to be understood in a political context, teachers are more than simply agents of the state. Their role in the public schools has been and continues to be complex. One of the aspects of teaching often overlooked, for example, is the question of pleasure. For many women, teaching is not a grim moral obligation or simply a means of achieving financial security; rather, it provides the pleasure of emotionally and intellectually meaningful work. Descriptions of teaching in one-room schools are filled with stories like that of the lesson built around a tame crow hovering above the school, of the little girl learning to love reading because of its association with baking bread, of the country teacher who provided books and paints for children—the satisfactions of encouraging and seeing children's emotional and intellectual growth. These are pleasures just as certainly as the freedom of the first car purchased with a young teacher's wages or the comradeship of two women teachers sharing responsibility for an isolated country two-room school. The satisfaction of seeing children's growth or sharing the joy of a first snowfall cannot be measured by tests or controlled by the state. This pattern of teachers' lives is invisible; there is no profit in it.

While women teachers at various times have used teaching to express their creative, emotional, and intellectual talents, those talents have rarely been recognized. Instead, teachers have been expected to participate in an institutional structure that all too often has reproduced existing hierarchies and inequalities and that, particularly in the twentieth century, has envisioned children as clients to be disciplined and sorted. Teachers continue to find themselves treated variously as educators, as "social mothers," or as wage workers. In times of perceived social crisis, women teachers serve time and again as convenient scapegoats: in the panic over the "woman peril"; in the "problem of the rural school," presided over by the young and ignorant woman teacher; in homophobic attacks on the "unhealthy" spinster teacher. We see this dynamic being enacted again today in the denunciation of multiculturalism and feminism as "causing" a supposed decline in educational standards and threatening social collapse.

As workers in the public schools, teachers have been put in the morally and politically ambiguous position of caring for children while enacting what have often been racist state policies. This contradiction can be seen in discriminatory practices targeting Mexican-American, African-American, and Asian-American children and in the inadequately supported "emergency" schools for the children of migrant workers. In California, the most dramatic example was the expectation during the Second World War that teachers, who had been trusted to protect and nurture children, to maintain a sense of humanity and care, were to teach obedience to the government as Japanese-American children awaited removal to camps. In 1994, California voters passed Proposition 187, which denies all public services, including schooling, to children of "illegal immigrants." Teachers were expected to identify illegal children in their classes and report them to state authorities. Once again teachers were torn between their human responsibility to children and obedience to the state. How often have teachers been put in this position of providing the human care that might repair the damage done by the cold machinery of capital and the state?

One of the lessons I see in this history is the vital importance of discourse, of a vocabulary that allows us to name what we want and who we are. This involves the exploration of societal assumptions as they are revealed in the discursive practices—the personal narratives, scholarly studies, and policy statements—of historical actors. My reading of this history has emphasized the ways in which education has been framed by assumptions about gender that are sometimes articulated and sometimes silent. It has questioned the dominant constructs of women teachers, either as passive young women waiting for marriage or as maternal nurturers needing patriarchal guidance and control, constructs that are used to explain and justify social inequalities. Throughout I have questioned the idea of an "essential" womanly nature. Simone de Beauvoir wrote in *The Second Sex* that "one is not born a woman, but rather *becomes* one." Not only are our understandings of who we are as men and women historically and socially constructed, but even as we live within these constructed categories, these imaginative paradigms, our subject positions as "man" and as "woman" have to be constantly recreated.[5] Moreover, these identities reflect political struggles over privilege and power.

Consider the moral panic over the "woman peril" in the early twentieth century. The first wave of feminism and the suffrage movement were built on a conception of women as intelligent and capable of acting in the public world, the antithesis of the domestic "true woman" of the nineteenth century. For example, when Kate Ames, Napa County superintendent of schools, challenged the men of the California Teachers Association in 1906, she argued that "insight, industry and skill are individual rather than sex characteristics" and condemned what she called the "sex fallacy" in education. By divorcing intellectual and personal abilities from the biological fact of sex, Ames attacked the whole edifice of male privilege. The result of this public denunciation was the end of her career as an educational leader. She never again gained any position of leadership in the CTA, and she was defeated in her bid for reelection as county school superintendent. It was the challenge of feminists like Ames that led male educators to postulate the danger of the woman peril, the idea that boys taught by women never "learned to admire the masculine qualities in the Anglo-Saxon race," as Earl Barnes of Stanford put it, which in turn jeopardized the entire nation. The conflict between feminists and male educators on this issue was conducted at the level of discourse. The questions were clear: Who should have authority in the schools? What was the role of the woman teacher?

By the 1930s such direct conflicts were rare. The gendered nature of schooling and the struggles over patriarchal privilege—and, underlying these, socially reinforced assumptions about men's and women's natures—were no longer named. The discourse of educational reform in California shows a marked shift from the period before the achievement of suffrage, when women educators spoke of a common interest and experience *as women*, to the period after 1920, when gender virtually disappears as a meaningful category of discussion. This shift, of course, reflects the larger move away from a self-conscious feminism once women's suffrage was attained. Nevertheless, when women accept the idea that all people can compete equally, but fail to acknowledge the power and weight of patriarchal privilege, they render themselves vulnerable to sexist practices and ideology. In the 1920s and 1930s, as the California example shows so clearly, individual women achieved a great deal and created rich and meaningful lives. But although these women moved in the world as though they would be judged according to their abilities and accomplishments, in fact they were not universally viewed as capable human beings; rather, they were too often seen as "women," as special but subordinate beings who would find fulfillment only under male domination and control. The lack of a vocabulary to name this dynamic left women vulnerable to the patriarchal backlash. As mere "human beings," how could they defend themselves against the charge that they were "women" first?

In California, the network of women teachers and supervisors surrounding Helen Heffernan did not name themselves publicly as a group with collective interests and identity. As a result, they were vulnerable to the resurgence of male privilege in education after the Second World War. Because no vocabulary existed any longer for claiming a positive identity as a strong and competent woman, the Freudian image of the heterosexual housewife and mother as the inevitable and desirable lot for women (assumed, of course, to be white and middle class) went largely uncontested. By 1950, the "feminine mystique" was virtually unchallenged. What was lost was the naming of sexism as practice and discursive system, and with it the claim to an identity as "woman" that was complex and filled with possibilities. Again, there is a contemporary analogy in the conservative charge that feminism is itself a form of victimiza-

tion and that women need only assert their strengths in the open marketplace to succeed. While asserting strength and capability is important,
to be sure, it is equally important that patriarchy and sexism be named.
After all, there are good reasons for male anxieties: men have enormous
power and privilege under patriarchy. Feminism challenges this privilege
and calls into question both "man" and "woman" as discursive constructs
within an unequal system.

   Writing this history has been both a personal exploration and an intellectual challenge. I began from a sense of private loss, with the intent
of rescuing the lives of women teachers in one rural area of California
over a century of change. While I do not imagine I have discovered a final reality of this place and time, I do think the stories and conflicts depicted here can tell us a great deal that we need to remember: that
women and men live their lives within the confines of a language created
outside themselves, one that reflects sedimented history; that they both
confirm and contest the meanings constructed through this language in
their desires and actions. Schools, as well, are revealed in their potential
as sites for the development of both teachers and students. This is a vision not of the abstract logic of profit and loss, but of the potential of
human lives. In times like these, memories of past struggles can give us
hope in the realization that history is always in process and changing, as
the present turns into the past, and as the past reappears to us in new
light.

REFERENCE MATTER

NOTES

INTRODUCTION

1. Shulamit Reinharz, *Feminist Methods in Social Research* (New York: Oxford University Press, 1993), p. 260.

2. Carolyn Steedman, "Culture, Cultural Studies, and the Historians," in *Cultural Studies*, ed. L. Grossberg, C. Nelson, and P. Treichler (New York: Routledge, 1992), p. 621.

3. This study was published as *Women Teaching for Change* (South Hadley, Mass.: Bergin & Garvey, 1988).

4. Micaela Di Leonardo, *Varieties of Ethnic Experience* (Ithaca: Cornell University Press, 1984), p. 233.

5. See, for example, the exchange between Gordon and Scott in *Signs* 15, no. 4 (summer 1990); also the earlier discussion over women's culture and resistance among Ellen DuBois, Mary Jo Buhle, Temma Kaplan, Gerda Lerner, and Carroll Smith-Rosenberg, "Politics and Culture in Women's History," *Feminist Studies* 6 (spring 1980): 28–36.

6. Judith Newton, "History as Usual? Feminism and the New Historicism," in *The New Historicism*, ed. H. Adam Veeser (London: Routledge, 1989), p. 152.

7. See, for example, Catherine Hall, "Missionary Stories: Gender and Ethnicity in England in the 1830s and 1840s," in Grossberg, Nelson, and Treichler, eds., *Cultural Studies*, pp. 240–76; Ruth Roach Pierson, "Experience, Difference, Dominance, and Voice in the Writing of Canadian Women's History," in *Writing Women's History: International Perspectives*, ed. Karen Offen, Ruth Roach Pierson, and Jane Rendall (Bloomington: Indiana University Press, 1991), pp. 79–106; Denise Riley, *Am I That Name?* (Minneapolis: University of Minnesota Press, 1989); Joan Scott, *Gender and the Politics of History* (New York: Columbia University Press, 1989); Ann-Louise Shapiro, ed., *History and Feminist Theory* (Middletown, Conn.: Wesleyan University Press, 1992); and Steedman, "Culture, Cultural Studies, and the Historians."

8. Shapiro, ed., *History and Feminist Theory*, p. 3.

9. Joan Scott, "Experience," in *Feminists Theorize the Political,* ed. Judith Butler and Joan Scott (London: Routledge, 1992), p. 25.

10. Linda Gordon, "Response to Scott," *Signs* 15, no. 4 (summer 1990): 852–53.

11. Antonio Gramsci, *Selections from the Prison Notebooks* (New York: Monthly Review Press, 1971); Mikhail Bakhtin, *The Dialogical Imagination* (Austin: University of Texas Press, 1984).

12. Bakhtin, *Dialogical Imagination,* p. 294.

13. Alison Prentice and Marjorie Theobald, "The Historiography of Women Teachers," in *Women Who Taught,* ed. Alison Prentice and Marjorie Theobald (Toronto: University of Toronto Press, 1991), p. 15.

CHAPTER ONE

1. David Tyack and Elisabeth Hansot, "The Dream Deferred: A Golden Age for Women School Administrators?" (Stanford: Institute for Research on Educational Finance and Governance, 1981), p. 2.

2. Since teaching has not been defined as a "real" profession like medicine or law, it has not been seen as an arena for women pioneers or pathbreakers. In *Beyond Her Sphere: Women and Professions in American History* (Westport, Conn.: Greenwood Press, 1978), for example, Barbara Harris does not examine teaching; teachers, she claims, are not of the "professional class" because of their class origins and lack of formal education. Geraldine Clifford, however, points out: "In truth it is neither level, kind of completed education, nor the social class origins of participants that matters much to Harris. Like other feminist historians, her first and last test is whether most of the practitioners of a 'learned' profession are male or female" ("Eve: Redeemed by Education and Teaching School," *History of Education Quarterly* 21, no. 2 [winter 1981]: 486).

3. For a discussion of studies on women teachers in the industrialized English-speaking nations, see Prentice and Theobald, "Historiography of Women Teachers."

4. The complex development of the common school system has been the topic of much debate in the history of education, particularly in relation to class structure. See Michael Katz, *The Irony of Early School Reform* (Cambridge, Mass.: Harvard University Press, 1969); Michael Katz, "The Origins of Public Education: A Reassessment," *History of Education Quarterly* 16 (winter 1976): 381–407; Carl Kaestle, *Pillars of the Republic* (New York: Hill & Wang, 1983); Carl Kaestle and Maris Vinovskis, *Education and Social Change in Nineteenth-Century Massachusetts* (Cambridge: Cambridge University Press, 1980); David Tyack, "The Common School and American Society: A Reappraisal," *History of Education Quarterly* 26, no. 2 (summer 1986): 301–6.

5. As a number of historians have argued, by 1800 literacy was considered desirable for middle-class mothers so that they could help guide their sons to become Republican citizens. See, for example, Nancy Cott, *The Bonds of Womanhood* (New Haven: Yale University Press, 1977); Linda Kerber, *Women of the Republic*

(Chapel Hill: University of North Carolina Press, 1980); Mary Beth Norton, *Liberty's Daughters* (Boston: Little, Brown, 1980).

6. For a discussion of the shifting nature of women's wage work, see Tom Dublin, *Women at Work* (New York: Columbia University Press, 1979); and Alice Kessler-Harris, *Out to Work* (New York: Oxford University Press, 1982).

7. On the economic appeal of teaching as work for women, see John Richardson and Brenda Hatcher, "The Feminization of Public School Teaching, 1870–1920," *Work and Occupations* 10 (Feb. 1983): 81–100. The same argument is made by Susan Carter in "Incentives and Rewards to Teaching," in *America's Teachers: Histories of a Profession at Work*, ed. Donald Warren (New York: Macmillan, 1989), pp. 49–63.

8. Susan Carter, "Occupational Segregation, Teachers' Wages, and American Economic History," *Journal of Economic History* 46, no. 2 (June 1986): 379.

9. David Allmendinger, "Mount Holyoke Students Encounter the Need for Life Planning, 1837–1850," *History of Education Quarterly* 19, no. 1 (spring 1979): 27–46.

10. Carroll Smith-Rosenberg, *Disorderly Conduct* (New York: Oxford University Press, 1985), p. 18. Different approaches to the question of the meaning of women's cultural sphere can be seen in the exchange between Smith-Rosenberg and Ellen DuBois. DuBois argued that the private, "cultural" sphere of nineteenth-century women was not a site of potential resistance to the dominant sexual ideology but in fact one of acceptance and reinforcement of ideas of male dominance: "Women's culture itself did not constitute an open and radical break with dominant sexual ideology any more than slave culture openly challenged slavery. Indeed, it was part of the dominant system, sharing more of its assumptions about women and men—separate sphere, women's domesticity, male dominance" (in DuBois, Buhle, Kaplan, Lerner, and Smith-Rosenberg, "Politics and Culture in Women's History," p. 33).

11. Paula Baker, "The Domestication of Politics: Women and American Political Society, 1780–1920," *American Historical Review* 89, no. 3 (June 1984): 631.

12. For two discussions of this ideology in the period of early industrialization, see Barbara Welter, "The Cult of True Womanhood, 1820–1860," *American Quarterly* 18 (1966): 151–74; and Gerda Lerner, "The Lady and the Mill Girl," *American Studies Journal* 10 (spring 1969): 5–15.

13. Joan Kelly, *Women's History and Theory* (Chicago: University of Chicago Press, 1984), p. 59.

14. For a psychoanalytic discussion of the effects of this ideology, see Madeleine Grumet, "Pedagogy for Patriarchy: The Feminization of Teaching," *Interchange* 12, nos. 1–2 (1981): 165–84; also Geraldine Clifford, "Marry, Stitch, Die, or Do Worse," in *Work, Youth, and Schooling*, ed. Harvey Kantor and David Tyack (Stanford: Stanford University Press, 1982), pp. 223–68.

15. Quoted in Thomas Woody, *A History of Women's Education in the United States*, vol. 1 (Lancaster, Pa.: Science Press, 1929), p. 463.

16. Beecher to Mann, quoted in ibid., p. 483.

17. Deborah Fitts, "Una and the Lion: The Feminization of District School

Teaching and Its Effects on the Roles of Students and Teachers in Nineteenth-Century Massachusetts," in *Regulated Children/Liberated Children: Education in Psychohistorical Perspective*, ed. Barbara Finkelstein (New York: Psychohistory Books, 1979), p. 142.

18. Boston Board of Education, *Fourth Annual Report*, quoted in Willard Elsbree, *The American Teacher* (New York: American Book Company, 1939), p. 201.

19. Woody, *History of Women's Education*, p. 516.

20. Richard Bernard and Maris Vinovskis, "The Female School Teacher in Ante-Bellum Massachusetts," *Journal of Social History* 3 (1977): 337. Bernard and Vinovskis do argue that teaching was an important factor in shaping many women's lives; they estimated that approximately 20 percent of white women in pre–Civil War Massachusetts were at some point in their lives teachers.

21. Linda Perkins, "The History of Blacks in Teaching: Growth and Decline Within the Profession," in Warren, ed., *America's Teachers*, p. 345.

22. On the freedmen's schools, see Jacqueline Jones, *Soldiers of Light and Love* (Chapel Hill: University of North Carolina Press, 1980); Ronald Butchart, *Northern Schools, Southern Blacks, and Reconstruction* (Westport, Conn.: Greenwood Press, 1980); Nancy Hoffman, ed., *Woman's "True" Profession* (Old Westbury, N.Y.: Feminist Press, 1982); Gerda Lerner, ed., *Black Women in White America* (New York: Pantheon Books, 1972).

23. See Linda Perkins, *Fanny Jackson Coppin and the Institute for Colored Youth* (New York: Garland, 1987); Charlotte Forten, *The Journal of Charlotte Forten* (New York: W. W. Norton, 1981).

24. See, for example, the biographies of Prudence Crandell, Margaret Douglass, and Myrtilla Minor, white women who attempted to open schools for black children before the Civil War, in Philip Foner and Josephine Pacheco, *Three Who Dared* (Westport, Conn.: Greenwood Press, 1984).

25. The letters from women teachers in the 1840s cited by Polly Kaufman in *Women Teachers on the Frontier* (New Haven: Yale University Press, 1984) suggest that for these women, at least, the dominant ideology of service shaped their self-definition, but they did not envision lifelong careers as teachers.

26. Jo Anne Preston, "Female Aspiration and Male Ideology: School-Teaching in Nineteenth-Century New England," in *Current Issues in Women's History*, ed. Arina Angerman et al. (London: Routledge, 1990), pp. 179, 180.

27. Geraldine Clifford, "'Lady Teachers' and the Politics of Teaching in the United States, 1850–1930," in *Teachers: The Culture and Politics of Work*, ed. Martin Lawn and Gerald Grace (London: Falmer Press, 1987), p. 10.

28. Clifford, "Marry, Stitch, Die," p. 236. See also Sally Schwager, "Educating Women in America," *Signs* 12, no. 2 (winter 1987): 333–72.

29. For more on the developments in education in the late 1800s, see, for example, David Hogan, *Class and Reform* (Philadelphia: University of Pennsylvania Press, 1985); David Tyack, *The One Best System* (Cambridge, Mass.: Harvard University Press, 1971); Lawrence Cremin, *The Transformation of the School* (New York: Random House, 1961); and David Tyack and Elisabeth Hansot, *Managers of Virtue* (New York: Basic Books, 1982).

30. Smith-Rosenberg, *Disorderly Conduct*, p. 247.

31. The most useful source of information on the family and class origins of teachers thus far is Lotus Coffman, *The Social Composition of the Teaching Population* (New York: Teachers College, Columbia University, 1911). Coffman found the following data on the families of origin of teachers:

Children of:	Male	Female
Farmers	69.7%	44.8%
"Professional Life"	7.0%	7.5%
Businessmen	6.2%	15.3%
Artisans	8.0%	16.4%
Laborers	7.0%	11.3%
Public officials	0.8%	1.8%

According to Coffman's respondents, the parental incomes averaged $800 a year. These 1910 figures corroborate Allmendinger's study of Massachusetts in the period 1837–50.

32. John Rury, *Education and Women's Work* (Albany: State University of New York Press, 1991), p. 5.

33. Joel Perlman and Victoria Huntzinger, "How Long They Taught" (typescript, 1987).

34. Indianapolis figures cited in Grumet, "Pedagogy for Patriarchy," p. 170.

35. Coffman (*Social Composition*) provides a picture of the teaching population nationwide in 1910. Coffman analyzed questionnaires from over five thousand teachers and administrators passed out at conferences, schools, and other settings, and found the following median years of experience:

	Men	Women
Rural Schools	2	2
Town Schools	12	6
City Schools	12	7

These differences are reflected in the median ages of respondents, which ranged from 21.4 years for women in rural schools to 34.6 years for men in city schools. In urban school systems, men and women usually followed different career trajectories: virtually all elementary school teachers and a majority of high school teachers in this period were women, whereas men dominated administrative positions. Coffman comments, "The greater permanency of men in both towns and cities is no doubt due to the executive character of their work, and to the increased compensation that accompanied it" (p. 28).

36. See David Peters, *The Status of the Married Woman Teacher* (New York: Teachers College, Columbia University Bureau of Publications, 1934).

37. Clifford, "'Lady Teachers,'" p. 10.

38. On the greater control single women had over their time and finances, see Martha Vicinus's study of English single women in the nineteenth century, *Independent Women* (Chicago: University of Chicago Press, 1985).

39. Generalizations about the motivation or experiences of women teachers need to be carefully examined. Rury, for example, argues that women did not see teaching as a long-term career and accepted the dominant ideology of mar-

riage and the private sphere: "Most [women teachers] taught only as a way of supplementing their parents' income until marriage, when they left the family household and the teaching force. Others viewed teaching, whether by choice or necessity, as an interim between dependency upon their parents and their future husbands. In either case, women did not enter teaching with the perspective of pursuing a life-long career. For most women in late Victorian America, the pursuit of fulfillment through a professional career was simply not an option. The only respectable calling for a woman was a family of her own" (Rury, "Gender, Salaries, and Career: American Teachers, 1900–1910," *Issues in Education* 4, no. 3 [winter 1986]: 216).

40. Patricia Carter, "The Social Status of Women Teachers in the Early Twentieth Century," in *The Teacher's Voice*, ed. Richard Altenbaugh (London: Falmer Press, 1992), p. 135.

41. Jacqueline Jones, *Labor of Love, Labor of Sorrow* (New York: Vintage Books, 1986), p. 145.

42. Perkins, "History of Blacks in Teaching," p. 349.

43. Cited in David Tyack and Elisabeth Hansot, *Learning Together* (New Haven: Yale University Press, 1990), p. 56.

44. See Jones, *Labor of Love, Labor of Sorrow*; Linda Perkins, "The Impact of the 'Cult of True Womanhood' on the Education of Black Women," *Journal of Social Issues* 39, no. 3 (Sept. 1983): 17–28.

45. Perkins, "Impact of the 'Cult of True Womanhood,'" p. 18.

46. Phyllis McGruder Chase, "African-American Teachers in Buffalo: The First One Hundred Years," in Altenbaugh, ed., *The Teacher's Voice*, pp. 65–77; Septima Clark, *Echo in my Soul* (New York: E. P. Dutton, 1962).

47. Mamie Fields and Karen Fields, *Lemon Swamp and Other Places: A Carolina Memoir* (New York: Free Press, 1983), pp. 130–31.

48. S. Clark, *Echo in My Soul.*

49. Alison Prentice, for example, states: "The entry of large numbers of women into public school teaching was . . . accepted because their position in the schools was generally a subordinate one. Their move into public teaching facilitated—and was facilitated by—the emergence of the public school itself, and in urban centres, of large, graded school systems, in which hierarchical professional patterns were feasible. To the extent that this pattern persisted and spread, and to the extent that school children absorbed messages from the organization of the institutions in which they were educated, Canadian children were exposed to a powerful image of women's inferior position in society. One must not discount, moreover, the impact on the women themselves. The experience of public school teaching, the experience of its discipline and of its hierarchical organization, became the experience of large numbers of Canadian women by the end of the nineteenth century" ("The Feminization of Teaching in British North America and Canada, 1845–1875," *Social History/Histoire Sociale* 8 [May 1975]: 7). See also Danylewycz and Prentice, "Teachers, Gender, and Bureaucratizing School Systems."

50. Myra Strober and David Tyack, "Why Do Women Teach and Men Manage?" *Signs* 5 (1980): 494–503.

51. Myra Strober and Audry Gordon Lanford, "The Feminization of Public School Teaching: Cross-Sectional Analysis, 1850–1880," *Signs* 11, no. 2 (winter 1986): 225.

52. Danylewycz and Prentice's description of this process in nineteenth-century Quebec and Ontario applies equally well to developments in the United States: "New subjects were added to the elementary school curriculum and had to be mastered and taught. At the same time, daily classroom teaching was increasingly structured by outside authority. . . . By the end of the nineteenth century, the daily work of teachers in Quebec and Ontario was monitored not only by local school superintendents and provincial inspectors but also, in many cases, by principals and by inspectors of local boards of health" ("Teachers, Gender, and Bureaucratizing School Systems," p. 139). In a later study Danylewycz and Prentice examined the actual classroom work of Quebec and Ontario teachers in the late nineteenth and early twentieth centuries, a period of an expanding state school bureaucracy. They documented the increase in paperwork, regulation and control over space and time, over both students' and teachers' lives, through school administrators and an inspectorate which both guided and evaluated teachers' work. See "Teachers' Work: Changing Patterns and Perceptions in the Emerging School Systems of Ninteenth- and Early-Twentieth-Century Central Canada," in Prentice and Theobald, eds., *Women Who Taught*, pp. 136–59.

53. Prentice, "Feminization of Teaching," p. 7. See also Danylewycz and Prentice, "Teachers, Gender, and Bureaucratizing School Systems"; and Myra Strober and Laura Best, "The Female/Male Differential in the Public Schools: Some Lessons from San Francicso, 1879," *Economic Inquiry* 17 (April 1979): 218–36.

54. Clifford, "'Lady Teachers,'" p. 29.

55. Tyack and Hansot, "Dream Deferred," pp. 2, 16.

56. Wayne Urban, *Why Teachers Organized* (Detroit: Wayne State University Press, 1982).

57. In her study of eleven western states, "Feminization and the Woman School Administrator," in *Women and Educational Leadership*, ed. Sari Biklin and Marilyn Brannigan (Lexington, Mass.: Lexington Books, 1980), Margaret Gribskov found that in 1928 women accounted for nearly two-thirds of county superintendents (p. 84). Elsewhere, local custom accepted women in administrative positions. In Brown County, Nebraska, for example, there was only one male county superintendent between 1897 and 1975; see Andrew Gulliford, *America's Country Schools* (Washington, D.C.: Preservation Press, 1984), p. 72. Mary Cordier's study of midwestern rural women teachers, *Schoolwomen of the Prairies and Plains* (Albuquerque: University of New Mexico Press, 1992), provides more evidence of the ways women took positions of authority in rural schools.

58. Quoted in Courtney Vaughn-Roberson, "Having a Purpose in Life: Western Women in the Twentieth Century," in Altenbaugh, ed., *The Teacher's Voice*, pp. 17, 25.

59. Gribskov, "Feminization and the Woman School Administrator," p. 77.

60. Quoted in P. Carter, "Social Status of Women Teachers," p. 131.

61. Robert E. Doherty, "Tempest on the Hudson: The Struggle for 'Equal Pay

for Equal Work' in the New York City Public Schools, 1907–1911," *History of Education Quarterly* 19, no. 4 (winter 1979): 426.

62. Carter Alexander, *Some Present Aspects of the Work of Teachers' Voluntary Associations* (New York: Teachers College, Columbia University, 1910).

63. See Doherty, "Tempest on the Hudson"; Patricia Carter, "Becoming the 'New Women': The Equal Rights Campaigns of New York City Schoolteachers, 1900–1920," in Altenbaugh, ed., *The Teacher's Voice*, pp. 40–59; Tyack, *One Best System*; Dan Perlstein, "Contradictions of Governance" (typescript, 1989); Urban, *Why Teachers Organized*; Marjorie Murphy, *Blackboard Unions* (Ithaca: Cornell University Press, 1990); James Fraser, "Agents of Democracy: Urban Elementary School Teachers and the Conditions of Teaching," in Warren, ed., *American Teachers*, pp. 118–56.

64. See P. Carter, "Social Status of Women Teachers."

65. See Sari Knopp Biklen, *School Work* (New York: Teachers College Press, 1995). Biklen points out that the progressive education movement itself did not address feminist concerns, even though a number of women educators were themselves deeply affected by feminism.

66. Numerous articles decrying the woman peril in education were published in the first two decades of the twentieth century. Representative is F. E. Chadwick, "The Woman Peril in American Education," *Educational Review* 47, no. 9 (1914): 109, 115–16. See the discussion in Tyack and Hansot, *Learning Together*, pp. 146–64.

67. Cited in Redding Sugg, *Motherteacher* (Charlottesville: University of Virginia Press, 1979), p. 106. See also Edward Clark's influential *Sex in Education* (New York: Arno Press, [1873] 1972) for a response to the idea of women's participation in intellectual activities or higher education in general.

68. Frederick Burk, "The Withered Heart of the School," *Educational Review* 34 (1907): 448–56.

69. Chadwick, "Woman Peril," p. 109.

70. Robert Rogers, "Is Woman Ruining the Country?" *Literary Digest*, no. 102 (1929): 24.

71. The Male Teachers Association of New York argued in 1904 that it was contrary to nature to hire women teachers because "1.) it may diminish the extent, power and influence of the home; 2.) the continuance of such work may be too great a strain upon the physical well-being of women . . . ; 3.) differentiation by the sexes indicates a differentiation of vocation, and by employing women as teachers, and taking them away from homes, is running counter to nature" ("Report of the Male Teachers Association of New York," quoted in Woody, *History of Women's Education*, pp. 510–11).

72. David Snedden, "A Sociologist Discusses the Problem of the Married Woman Teacher," quoted in Linda McPheron, "A Historical Perspective of Career Patterns of Women in the Teaching Professions, 1900–1940" (Ph.D. diss., Illinois State University, 1981), p. 31.

73. Coffman, *Social Composition*, p. 69. Coffman was relieved to find that "among the reports sent in no teachers were found among the immigrant classes that are now pouring into the United States from Southern Europe" (p. 59).

74. David Tyack and Elisabeth Hansot, "Silence, Policy Talk, and Educational Practice: The Case of Gender" (typescript, n.d.).

75. Kessler-Harris, *Out to Work*, p. 226.

76. Women's retreat from an active involvement in feminist organizations and movements is shown strikingly in the biographies of women in *Notable American Women, 1607–1950*, ed. Edward James (Cambridge, Mass.: Harvard University Press, 1971). Among women born in the 1860s, 34 percent were involved in women's rights or feminist activity, compared to 15 percent of women born in the 1920s; see Nancy Cott, *The Grounding of Modern Feminism* (New Haven: Yale University Press, 1987), p. 239.

77. Cott, *Grounding of Modern Feminism*, p. 174.

78. Smith-Rosenberg, *Disorderly Conduct*, p. 296.

79. Stephen Ewing, "Blue Laws for Teachers," *Harper's*, Feb. 1928, p. 330.

80. Diane Manning, *Hill Country Teacher: Oral Histories from the One-Room School and Beyond* (Boston: Twayne, 1990), p. 52.

81. Howard Beale, *Are American Teachers Free?* (New York: Charles Scribner's Sons, 1936), p. 376. Lois Scharf cites a Pittsburg teacher "who only smoked in the bathroom after dinner with the skylight open" (*To Work and to Wed* [Westport, Conn.: Greenwood Press, 1980], p. 74).

82. Beale, *Are American Teachers Free?* p. 376.

83. Ibid., p. 384. Scharf (*To Work and to Wed*, p. 77) points out that by the end of the 1930s the number of urban systems barring women teachers had increased significantly. See also David Tyack, Elisabeth Hansot, and Rob Lowe, *Public Schools in Hard Times* (Cambridge, Mass.: Harvard University Press, 1984).

84. Beale, *Are American Teachers Free?* p. 504.

85. Michele Foster, "Othermothers: Exploring the Educational Philosophy of Black American Women Teachers," in *Feminism and Social Justice in Education*, ed. Madeleine Arnot and Kathleen Weiler (London: Falmer Press, 1993), pp. 101–23.

86. Fields and Fields, *Lemon Swamp*, p. 236.

87. Raymond Callahan, *Education and the Cult of Efficiency* (Chicago: University of Chicago Press, 1960).

88. Urban, *Why Teachers Organized*, p. 177.

89. For a perceptive analysis of the use of sexual stigma to control women teachers and administrators, see Jackie Blount, "Manly Men and Womanly Women: Deviance, Gender Role Polarization, and the Shift in Women's School Employment, 1900–1976," *Harvard Educational Review* 66, no. 2 (1996): 318–38.

90. Alison Oram points out in her discussion of the spinster teacher in Britain ("'Embittered, Sexless, or Homosexual': Attacks on Spinster Teachers, 1918–39," in Angerman et al., eds., *Current Issues in Women's History*) that the newly developed science of sexology and the theories of such figures as Havelock Ellis and Freud led to a new emphasis on sex as natural and healthy. This view "emphasized active heterosexuality as normal and indeed essential for women's health and happiness, while increasingly stigmatizing celibate women, spinsters, and lesbians" (p. 184). According to Oram, independent and articulate women teachers threatened male privilege; in response, men demanded both the con-

tinuance of the marriage bar *and* inferior wages for women teachers as a means of guaranteeing their own privileged place.

91. Frances Donovan, *The Schoolma'am* (New York: Frederick A. Stokes, 1938), p. 13.

92. In England, according to Oram, "abuse of spinster teachers as old maids who lacked the social and sexual qualities to find a husband was not new, but this acquired a new edge during the 1920s and 1930s. This was a period when the notion of marriage as a psychological as well as a social necessity for women was introduced. Popular sexology texts proclaimed that sexual relations with men were the only way to psychological health and fulfillment for women. They characterized women without male sexual partners as frustrated, a prey to complexes and neuroses ("'Embittered, Sexless, or Homosexual,'" p. 187).

93. Ewing, "Blue Laws," pp. 328, 329.

94. George Counts, *The American Road to Culture* (New York: Arno Press, [1930] 1971), pp. 94, 95.

95. Willard Waller, *The Sociology of Teaching* (New York: Russell & Russell, 1961), pp. 458, 454.

96. Ewing, "Blue Laws," p. 333.

97. *The Schoolma'am* was the third of Donovan's studies of women at work in the 1920s and 1930s, following her studies of salesladies and waitresses. Donovan was a popular and impressionistic writer who tended to broad and sometimes contradictory generalizations. Nonetheless, her book is valuable in presenting what we can assume to be views of women teachers that were widely held among the liberal sociologists and journalists with whom Donovan was associated.

98. Donovan, *The Schoolma'am*, pp. 115, 116.

99. Adrienne Rich, "Compulsory Heterosexuality and Lesbian Existence," in Adrienne Rich, *Blood, Bread, and Poetry* (New York: W. W. Norton, 1986), pp. 23–75.

100. Mary Ryan, *Womanhood in America: From Colonial Times to the Present* (New York: New Viewpoints, 1974), p. 282.

101. S. Carter, "Incentives and Rewards," p. 57.

CHAPTER TWO

1. See, for example, Samuel Bowles and Herbert Gintis, *Schooling in Capitalist America* (New York: Basic Books, 1976); Bruce Curtis, *Building the Educational State: Canada West, 1836–71* (Lewes, Sussex: Falmer Press, 1988); Bruce Curtis, *True Government by Choice Men?* (Toronto: University of Toronto Press, 1992); Ian Hunter, *Rethinking the School* (Sydney: Allen & Unwin, 1994); Katz, *Irony of Early School Reform*; Ira Katznelson and Margaret Weir, *Schooling for All* (Berkeley: University of California Press, 1985).

2. Curtis, in *True Government by Choice Men?*, argues persuasively that organized systems of education in the nineteenth century were part of a wider process of state formation. He defines state formation as "the centralization and concentration of relations of economic and political power and authority in society. State formation typically involves the appearance or the reorganization of

monopolies over the means of violence, taxation, administration, and over symbolic systems" (p. 5).

3. Superintendent of Public Instruction, *Biennial Report, 1930–31* (Sacramento: State Printing Office, 1931), p. 43.

4. Historical studies of California education are surprisingly weak. The best single volume is Irving Hendrick's brief *California Education* (San Francisco: Boyd & Fraser, 1980). Probably the most detailed chronology is Roy Cloud, *Education in California* (Stanford: Stanford University Press, 1952), which emphasizes the institutional history of the California Teachers Association. John Swett's early account, *History of the Public School System of California* (San Francisco: A. L. Bancroft, 1876), provides a summary of the actions of the state superintendents of public instruction in the period 1850–75. His *Public Education in California* (New York: American Book Company, 1911) is a memoir that includes useful biographical information about Swett, including his tenure as a school principal in San Francisco and his four years as state superintendent. Of less value are William Ferrier, *Ninety Years of Education in California, 1846–1936* (Berkeley: Sather Gate Bookshop, 1937), which focuses on the history of the University of California; and Charles Falk, *The Development and Organization of Education in California* (New York: Harcourt, Brace & World, 1968).

5. The initial weakness of state control of education is obvious in the reports of the state superintendents of public instruction in the 1850s. As John Swett, the most influential early superintendent, commented, these reports contained "crude and confused tabular" statements and "inaccurate statistical tables"; in 1856, the report "was a brief one, without any statistical table whatever—not even the number of census children in the state" (Superintendent of Public Instruction, *Biennial Report, 1876–77*, p. 24). With the passage of the revised school law of 1866, state and county school taxes were set "at adequate levels," teachers were required to keep registers of pupils' attendance, county institutes were called for, and county and city boards of examination were established. Swett noted: "The school year ending June 30, 1867, marks the transition period of California from rate bill common schools to an American free school system. For the first time in the history of the State, every public school was made entirely free for every child to enter" (ibid., p. 5).

In this early period the certification and examination of teachers also became more regularized. From 1850 to 1866 teaching certificates had been granted by district school trustees; in practice this meant that teachers were chosen according to need and opportunity. The 1866 revised school law attempted to impose greater control over teachers with the creation of a state board of examination, the requirement that county examiners be experienced teachers, and the establishment of a state normal school with the power to grant teaching certificates upon completion of the approved course of study. John Swett described the early system of local certification: "The old schoolmasters of San Francisco were examined every year by doctors, lawyers, dentists, contractors, and businessmen, to 'see if they were fit to teach the common school.' They had been teaching years in succession. There was no standard of qualification, except the caprice of 'accidental boards.' Throughout the state, examinations were oral and in most cases resulted in issuing to everybody who applied a certificate 'to teach school one year'" (*History of the Public School System*, p. 53).

6. The selection of teachers remained the province of local districts, but in 1872 the county boards were required to use an examination prepared by the State Board of Examination. A later state superintendent described the early scandals that surrounded the state teacher examinations: "In 1872, a law was drafted . . . compelling local boards to use exclusively the questions sent out by the State Board of Examination. Then the trouble began. The questions were sometimes difficult. It was not easy to obtain a certificate. By some means, questions were obtained from the office of the State Printer, and in various other unknown ways, until, finally, the matter culminated in an official investigation in San Francisco" (Superintendent of Public Instruction, *Biennial Report, 1880–81*, p. 18).

7. County boards of education were to be composed of the county superintendent of schools and four other members appointed by the county board of supervisors, with at least two of the four appointees teachers with first-grade teaching certificates. These boards adopted schoolbooks, prescribed and enforced rules for teacher examinations, conducted the examinations, granted teaching certificates, and could revoke certificates "for immoral or unprofessional conduct" (ibid.). The term of the elected county superintendent of schools was lengthened from two to four years.

8. Superintendent of Public Instruction, *Biennial Report, 1864–65*, p. 42.

9. Ibid., p. 43.

10. Quoted in Catherine Ann Curry, "Shaping Young San Franciscans: Public and Catholic Schools in San Francisco, 1851–1906" (Ph.D. diss., Graduate Theological Union, Berkeley, 1987), p. 85.

11. Superintendent of Public Instruction, *Biennial Report, 1868–69*, pp. 12–13.

12. Perlstein, "Contradictions of Governance."

13. Superintendent of Public Instruction, *Biennial Report, 1878–79*, p. 24.

14. Superintendent of Public Instruction, *Biennial Report, 1876–77*, p. 5.

15. Jeanne Carr, "The Industrial Education of Women: An Address Read Before the State Teachers Association, September 23, 1878," cited in Superintendent of Public Instruction, *Biennial Report, 1878–79*, pp. 242, 243.

16. Superintendent of Public Instruction, *Biennial Report, 1882–83*, p. 16.

17. The concern with women's education in California mirrored national concerns in the period 1895–1920. Educational journals such as *Education, Educational Review*, and *School Review* carried numerous articles on education for girls, some by feminists advocating suffrage and equal schooling for girls and, by the first decade of the twentieth century, others proclaiming the "woman peril." See Milicent Rutherford, "Feminism and the Secondary School Curriculum, 1890–1920" (Ph.D. diss., Stanford University, 1977), for a useful bibliography of this literature.

18. See "School Organizations in California," *Sierra Educational News* 12, no. 11 (Nov. 1916): 613–15. Schoolmasters associations continued to meet in California through the Second World War.

19. See George Kyte, "Origins of the California Schoolmasters Club" (typescript, n.d.). According to Kyte, the names and records of the early years of this

club were lost in the 1906 San Francisco earthquake and fire. Accounts of the meetings of these clubs in the early years can be found in the *Western Journal of Education* generally.

20. The by-laws of the Schoolmasters Club stated, "Any man who is now, or has heretofore, been engaged in school work, either as teacher or school officer, or who is especially interested in education, is eligible to membership in the club," but applicants also had to be sponsored by two active members of the club ("Constitution and By-Laws of the California Schoolmasters Club, 1905," Bancroft Library, University of California, Berkeley).

21. Superintendent of Public Instruction, *Biennial Report, 1895–96*, p. 83.

22. Cloud, *Education in California*, p. 104.

23. See Doherty, "Tempest on the Hudson."

24. James A. Barr, "The Reasons Why Men are Leaving School Work and Some Remedies for the Same," *California Teachers Quarterly* 1, no. 3 (June 1907): 16–18.

25. Ibid., p. 22.   26. Ibid., p. 25.

27. Quoted in ibid., p. 29.   28. Quoted in ibid., p. 31.

29. Kate Ames, "Report on State Teachers' Reading Course," *Western Journal of Education* 14, no. 6 (June 1906): 216.

30. Ellwood Cubberley, "Editorial," *Western Journal of Education* 16, no. 1 (Jan. 1908): 10.

31. Kate Ames, "Some Vital School Questions: The Woman Movement and Woman's Position in the School System," *Overland Monthly* 52 (Sept. 1908): 244–45.

32. Ellwood Cubberley, "Improving County School Supervision," *Sierra Educational News* 5, no. 2 (Feb. 1909): 29.

33. Ellwood Cubberley, *Rural Life and Education: A Study of the Rural School Problem as a Phase of the Rural Life Problem* (Boston: Houghton Mifflin, 1914), p. 283, 320.

34. Superintendent of Public Instruction, *Report* 1910, p. 13.

35. Roger Sterrett, "The Vanishing Schoolmaster," *Sierra Educational News* 9, no. 4 (April 1915): 242, 243.

36. Eleanor Smith et al., "School Women's Clubs: A Statement," *Sierra Educational News* 6, no. 3 (March 1910): 21.

37. A.H.C. "Getting Together," *Sierra Educational News* 15, no. 1 (Jan. 1919): 13.

38. Joan Jensen and Gloria Lathrop, *California Women: A History* (San Francisco: Boyd & Fraser, 1987), p. 63.

39. Oakland Schoolwomen's Club Records, 1912–25; Holt Atherton Department of Special Collections, University of the Pacific, Stockton, Calif. [hereafter cited as HADSC].

40. "School Women's Day and Luncheon," *Sierra Educational News* 9, no. 10 (Dec. 1913): 813.

41. Joyce Lobner, "A Chapter in Democracy; or, A Short History of the Oakland Schoolwomen's Club" (typescript, 1942; HADSC), pp. 6–7.

42. Ibid., p. 27, 26.

43. Ibid., p. 61.

44. Ibid., p. 64.

45. Ibid., p. 10.

46. Minutes of the Oakland Schoolwomen's Club, March 11, 1925; Oakland Schoolwomen's Club Records, 1912–25, HADSC.

47. Ibid.

48. Superintendent of Public Instruction, *Biennial Report, 1901–2*, p. 150.

49. Idem, *Biennial Report, 1915–16*, p. 98.

50. Idem, *Biennial Report, 1919–20*, p. 41.

51. Ibid., p. 40; Leighton Johnson, *Development of the Central State Agency for Public Education in California, 1849–1949* (Albuquerque: University of New Mexico Press, 1952), p. 90.

52. Although the pageant was first performed in San Francisco, it quickly became so popular that in 1913 it was moved to the Greek Theater at Berkeley; see Katherine Coddington, "King of the Radicals" (M.A. thesis, San Francisco State University, 1985), p. 138.

53. Anna M. Wiebalk, "Evergirl—A Morality Play," *Sierra Educational News* 5, no. 5 (May 1909): 35.

54. Frederick Burk, *Guild Service and Ritual of Graduation* (Sacramento: California State Printing Office, 1914).

55. Wiebalk, "Everygirl," p. 37.

56. *The Collegian*, June 1922, n.p.; Special Collections, California State University, Fresno.

57. Jensen and Lathrop, *California Women*, p. 67.

58. Tyack and Hansot, *Managers of Virtue*, pp. 180–201.

59. "Margaret Schallenberger McNaught Obituary," *San Francisco Chronicle*, June 17, 1951. In response to a request for biographical information about Moses Schallenberger, Margaret wrote: "He married an English lady, has four children, the oldest being a daughter of seventeen." That "oldest daughter," of course, was Margaret herself. See Margaret Schallenberger to Mrs. John Bidwell, Aug. 31, 1880; Annie K. Bidwell Collection, Box 80.

60. Charles Allen and Ruth Royce, *Historical Sketch of the State Normal School at San Jose, California* (Sacramento: State Printing Office, 1889), p. 128.

61. J. M. Guino, *Historical Biographical Record of Coast Counties, California* (San Jose, 1904), p. 496.

62. A key figure in this attempt to influence classroom teachers was State Superintendent Edward Hyatt, who served from 1907 to 1919. Hyatt viewed himself as a "modern" superintendent and traveled by automobile throughout the state visiting schools; he reported on what he saw and heard in his column "Little Talks by the Way" in the *Western Journal of Education*, a periodical that he hoped would be "the medium for exchange of bright ideas among the teachers of California." Hyatt took photographs of schools, teachers, and students, which he published along with his column. Unfortunately for the historian, although Hyatt was modern and forward-thinking in his love of automobiles and cameras, he distrusted statistics. In his first *Biennial Report* (1908) he wrote, "You will observe that the plan and scope . . . have been greatly changed. . . . The Idea of the

change is to condense and summarize this formal [statistical] material so as to make room for something that will be of use" (p. 5). This change entailed replacing information such as numbers of schools, teachers, and children for each county with articles on such topics as the need to celebrate Arbor Day. See Solomon Jaeckel, "Edward Hyatt, 1858–1919: California Educator," *Southern California Quarterly* 3, nos. 1–3 (March–June–Sept. 1970): 3–56, 122–54, 248–74, for a detailed discussion of his career.

63. Margaret Schallenberger McNaught, "Teach Patriotism, Hygiene, Sanitation," *California Blue Bulletin* 3, no. 4 (Dec. 1917): 26.

64. State Board of Education, *Report of the Commissioner of Elementary Schools, 1916–1918* (Sacramento: State Printing Office, 1918), p. 42. In her 1918–20 report, McNaught cited the need for investigations by "educational experts that would tend to bring facts strongly into evidence, make them known to the people and stimulate teachers toward higher professional and civic attainment" (p. 14). Between 1914 and 1920 research on "backward children" was conducted by Louis Terman, Maud Whitlock, and J. B. Sears at Stanford as well as by Cyrus Mead at Berkeley. Louis Terman at Stanford was influential in advocating and spreading ideas on testing and scientific measurement, particularly in California schools, where he did much of his early research. In 1914 a laboratory for the study of "backward and feeble-minded children" was established at Stanford under Terman's direction. "From this laboratory, which was opened in 1914," wrote one of the researchers, "trained examiners are sent out to various cities and towns of the state, and assistance is given to schools in organizing special classes for defective and backward children, and in the diagnosis and classification of pupils not adapted to the regular classes. These children are examined, and the data sent to the laboratory of the foundation for analysis and comparison" (J. Harold Williams, "The Binet-Simon Scale for Measuring the Intelligence of School Children," *Educational Digest* 1, no. 7 [1914]: 15).

65. *Report of the Commissioner of Elementary Schools, 1916–18*, p. 31.

66. Margaret Schallenberger McNaught, "The Squirrel Is a Hun," *California Blue Bulletin* 4, no. 2 (June 1918): 16.

67. Will Wood, "Radical Literature in Schools," *California Blue Bulletin* 5, no. 4 (Dec. 1919): 27.

68. Superintendent of Public Instruction, *Biennial Report, 1919–20*, p. 19. By 1920 a one-year course in American history and civics was a requirement for high school graduation, and a course on the history of the United States and the Constitution was required in every public elementary school.

69. Margaret Schallenberger McNaught, "The Enfranchised Woman Teacher: Her Opportunity," *Sierra Educational News* 13, no. 9 (Sept. 1917): 334.

70. *Report of the Commissioner of Elementary Schools, 1914–16*, p. 26.

71. "At State Convention of City and County Superintendents," *Riverside Enterprise*, Dec. 11, 1915.

72. Margaret Schallenberger [McNaught], "A Message from the Commissioner of Education," *Sierra Educational News* 10, no. 1 (Jan. 1914): 66.

73. Writing in 1915, McNaught supported a proposed bill providing for the appointment of rural school supervisors: "The county superintendent, the chief

friend and professional advisor of the country teachers, burdened with increasing office duties, can not give sufficient time and thought to the subject of supervision to do much that is constructive in this field. In most of the counties of the state the superintendent is unable to visit his rural teachers oftener than once a year. No one realizes better than he that by no stretch of the imagination can such visitation be called supervision" ("The Need of Supervision," *California Blue Bulletin* 1, no. 1 [March 1915]: 2). In the spring of 1915 this bill proposing rural supervisors was submitted but failed. McNaught had lobbied publicly and privately in support of the bill; nevertheless, as she wrote to Chester Rowell, the editor of the *Fresno Republican*, she was "not disheartened. Some day we shall surely have supervision of our rural schools" (Schallenberger to Rowell, June 17, 1915; Chester Rowell Papers, Bancroft Library, University of California, Berkeley).

74. *Report of the Commissioner of Elementary Schools, 1914*, p. 10.

75. See the extensive discussion in Callahan, *Education and the Cult of Efficiency*.

76. Margaret Schallenberger McNaught, "A Strong Personality," *California Blue Bulletin* 2, no. 2 (June 1916): 14.

77. As early as 1895 the National Education Association appointed the Committee of Twelve to study "the rural school problem as part of a larger concern with country life." The Country Life Commission, established by President Roosevelt in 1908, cited the rural school as the most important institution in rural society and the most in need of reform. See "Report of the Committee of Twelve on Rural Schools," in NEA, *Addresses and Proceedings, 1897* (Washington, D.C.: NEA, 1897), pp. 385–583; James Madison, "John D. Rockefeller's General Education Board and the Rural School Problem in the Midwest," *History of Education Quarterly* 24, no. 2 (summer 1984): 181–200; Gulliford, *America's Country Schools*; and Wayne Fuller, *The Old Country School* (Chicago: University of Chicago Press, 1982).

78. See, for example, Callahan, *Education and the Cult of Efficiency*; Tyack and Hansot, *Managers of Virtue*; Herbert Kliebard, *Struggle for the American Curriculum* (Boston: Routledge, Kegan Paul, 1986).

79. The efforts of Indiana's General Education Board to reform rural schools and the early consolidation of schools in other midwestern states are examples of attempts by educational reformers to bring rural schools under the control and guidance of scientific experts. See Madison, "Rockefeller's General Education Board"; and Fuller, *Old Country School*, for detailed discussions of the movement for school consolidation in the Midwest. Advocates of a reformed curriculum took a different approach, one grounded in nature study and the richness of rural life. Underlying their arguments was a sometimes romanticized vision of country life as the true source of American tradition. The celebration of rural life underlay both the nature study movement led by Liberty Hyde Bailey at Cornell University (see his *The Country Life Movement in the United States* [New York: Macmillan, 1911]) and the more pragmatic movement to base the curriculum of rural schools in agricultural pursuits, advocated by educators like Ellwood Cubberley, who argued for the need to prepare rural children for their life on the farm (see his *Rural Life and Education*).

80. As David Tyack has pointed out, "[Leading schoolmen] wished to enforce

in rural schools the same standards of professionalism that had been slowly developing in cities. While they justified their program as public service, educators also sought greater power and status for themselves" ("The Tribe and the Common School: Community Control in Rural Education," *American Quarterly*, no. 24 [March 1972]: 4).

81. Margaret Schallenberger McNaught, "Increasing Interest in the Union of Elementary School Districts," *California Blue Bulletin* 3, no. 2 (June 1917): 16.

82. George Schultzberg, "Consolidation of Schools," *Sierra Educational News* 14, no. 3 (March 1918): 134.

83. The need for new state laws requiring rural school supervision was debated at the 1902 CTA conference; at the 1904 meeting a resolution supporting rural school supervisors was passed. See Cloud, *Education in California*, p. 111.

84. "Report of the California Council on Education," *Sierra Educational News* 12, no. 5 (May 1916): 283.

85. "A Fair Chance for All," *California Blue Bulletin* 7, no. 1 (March 1921): 2.

86. See, for example, Evelyn Dewey, *New Schools for Old: The Regeneration of the Porter School* (New York: Dutton, 1919); and Marie Turner Harvey, "The Porter School: A New Vision of the Rural School in Country Life," in *Proceedings of the National Education Association, 1924* (Washington, D.C.: NEA, 1924), pp. 674–80.

87. Will Wood, "Rural Supervision Fund," *California Blue Bulletin* 7, no. 2 (June 1921): 5.

88. "Sympathy and Supervision," *Sierra Educational News* 11, no. 8 (Oct. 1915): 512.

89. Frederick Burk, "Excess Supervision," *Sierra Educational News* 18, no. 3 (March 1922): 120.

90. Ibid., p. 121.

91. Meta Neal Footman, "The Rural Supervisor—A Rejoinder," *Sierra Educational News* 18, no. 6 (June 1922): 339.

92. The view of rural supervision as a necessary support and guide for rural teachers was echoed frequently in the pages of the *Sierra Educational News* in the early 1920s. "A rural teacher, Shasta County," for example, described Miss Florence Hale, state rural supervisor of Maine, who gave a speech at the 1926 CTA conference, as a "plain countrywoman whose heart and soul were in the improvement of rural schools and communities" ("Rural Supervision," *Sierra Educational News* 22, no. 2 [Feb. 1926]: 99).

93. Sam Cohn, "Why Supervision of Rural Schools?" *Sierra Educational News* 20, no. 2 (Feb. 1924): 306.

94. Eugene Irwin, "Improvement of Educational Standards in Rural Schools," *Sierra Educational News* 23, no. 5 (May 1927): 280.

95. See, for example, Richard Boone, "The Choice of a Life Work—Teaching as a Career," *Sierra Educational News* 15, no. 10 (Dec. 1919): 660.

96. John Almack, "The Supervisory Program," *California Exchange Bulletin in Rural Education* 1, no. 3 (March 1927): 13.

97. Almack, "Supervisory Program," p. 15.

98. Ibid., pp. 16–17.

99. Georgiana Carden, Untitled, undated manuscript on the supervision of school attendance in California, 1921–26, p. 18; Georgiana Carden Papers, Bancroft Library, University of California, Berkeley. Unless otherwise specified, unpublished materials referred to in subsequent notes are to be found in the Georgiana Carden Papers.

100. Superintendent of Public Instruction, *Biennial Report, 1927–28*, p. 184.

101. Experts from the Bureau of Mental Hygiene suggested that mental health tests be given to children and adults showing signs of "deviance." To further this goal of prevention, in 1930 the bureau's Dr. Norman Fenton developed a "traveling clinic" that gave demonstration psychiatric examinations to "aid in the solution of individual problems of mental maladjustment" (Superintendent of Public Instruction, *Biennial Report, 1929–30*, p. 60).

102. Ruth Teiser, "Notes on Georgiana Carden and Her Father, Ralph Lynet Carden," n.d., n.p.

103. Katherine Felton to Mr. J. M. Guinn, San Francisco Superintendent of Schools, n.d.

104. Georgiana Carden Diary, Oct. 20, 1923.

105. Georgiana Carden to Ralph Merritt, Nov. 4, 1921.

106. Georgiana Carden Diary, Dec. 2, 1921.

107. Superintendent of Public Instruction, *Biennial Report, 1923–24*, p. 34.

108. Georgiana Carden, Untitled, undated manuscript on the supervision of school attendance, p. 14.

109. Georgiana Carden, Itinerary and Detailed Activities, Dec. 3, 1925.

110. Georgiana Carden, Untitled, undated manuscript on Indian education, n.p.

111. Ibid.

112. Carden continued pursuing her interest in social welfare. In 1945 she was involved in the Little House experiment, an attempt to create homelike houses where young women could congregate instead of in dance halls.

113. Stanley left her position after only eighteen months for reasons that are not clear. Like Helen Heffernan, she was a strong advocate of the advantages of rural schools. She argued in 1923: "The curse of education today is its dependence on formal tasks through the medium of strict organization. In the large cities where organization has its most deadly grip by virtue of the large masses involved, you and your personality are in danger of being lost. In the rural and village communities is the hope of salvation for you and for education" ("The New Rural School," *Sierra Educational News* 19, no. 7 [Sept. 1923]: 397).

114. In 1927 the State Department of Education had been reorganized, with Heffernan appointed head of the Division of Rural Education. (In 1931 the division was again reorganized, becoming the Division of Elementary and Rural Schools; in 1946 it became the Bureau for Elementary Education. In each case Heffernan was the head of the reorganized division.)

115. In 1925–26, for example, the administrative staff of the Kings County schools was made up entirely of women: Miss M. L. Richmond, superintendent; Mrs. G. F. Whittaker, deputy superintendent; Miss Helen Heffernan, field assistant; Mrs. Nella Ayers, superintendent of attendance; and Mrs. Leone Bradford,

music. See Superintendent of Public Instruction, *Biennial Report, 1925–26,* p. 97.

116. "Teachers of Kings County Gather at Superintendent Richmond's Call," *Hanford Sentinel,* Sept. 8, 1925, p. 1.

117. Beulah M. Hartman, "California Rural Supervisors Hold Significant Convention at Lake Tahoe, October 4th to 8th," *California Exchange Bulletin in Rural Education* 1, no. 1 (Nov. 1926): 33. Georgiana Carden, the state attendance officer, wrote in support of Heffernan's candidacy: "For the development of migratory schools, no better Commissioner of Elementary Education could have been chosen than Miss Heffernan. She was chairman of the San Joaquin Valley Association of Rural Supervisors, and as such directed a study of the seasonal school program with special reference to an adjusted course of study. She is genuinely interested in the standardizing of these schools, and has had the necessary first hand experience with them. Furthermore, she is acquainted with the work of the Supervisors of Attendance, as well as knowing the present individuals personally" (Georgiana Carden to Will Wood, Sept. 28, 1926; Georgiana Carden Papers).

118. "California Rural Supervisors Meeting, October 4–8," *Sierra Educational News* 23, no. 1 (Jan. 1927): 7.

119. Helen Heffernan, "Rural Education—A Challenge, a Responsibility," *California Exchange Bulletin in Rural Education* 1, no. 1 (Nov. 1926): 8.

120. Helen Heffernan, "Group Versus Grade Organization," *Western Journal of Education* 37, no. 6 (June 1929): 8.

121. Heffernan outlined her special concern and relationship with rural supervisors in her annual reports of the activities of the Rural Supervisors Organization, in which she glowingly described their work. A sense of her involvement can be seen in this account from the *Biennial Report* for 1931–32:

> This division has aided in increasing the effectiveness of the country programs of supervision by:
>
> Visiting teachers with the supervisor
> Discussing the work of teacher and supervisor
> Participating in teachers' meetings held by supervisors
> Arranging for supervisors to see and evaluate the work in the state demonstration rural schools
> Conducting quarterly sectional conferences of rural supervisors and annual state-wide conferences
> Conducting summer session classes in techniques of country supervision and on problems of supervision
> Preparing bulletins for the use of supervisors and teachers
> Distributing many integrated units of work suitable for use in rural schools
> Evaluating for each supervisor the supervisory accomplishment of each year and in offering constructive suggestions for the proposed program for the coming school year based upon the supervisor's annual report.
>
> It has been the purpose of the division:
>
> To maintain efficiency in supervision by encouraging a unification and co-

ordination of the efforts of every individual engaged in the work of supervision

To preserve and encourage the individuality and initiative of every
supervisor

To disseminate information concerning the excellent accomplishments of
various supervisory programs throughout the state.

Helen Heffernan, "Rural School Supervision," in Department of Education, *Biennial Report, 1931–32* (Sacramento: State Printing Office, 1932), p. 80.

122. Helen Heffernan, "Division of Rural Education," in Superintendent of Public Instruction, *Biennial Report, 1927–28,* p. 56; Richard Boone, *A History of Educational Organization in California* (San Jose: California Teachers Association, 1926), p. 99.

123. An account of the San Joaquin Valley Rural Supervisors Association meeting in Visalia in April 1928 provides a sense of the working of the organization. The morning was spent on the "usual business" and the reports of committees. In the afternoon, Helen Heffernan and several members of San Francisco State Teachers College spoke on approaches to individual instruction in rural schools. See *Western Journal of Education* 36, no. 5 (May 1928): 13.

124. Robert Treacy, "Progressivism and Corinne Seeds: UCLA and the University Elementary School" (Ph.D. diss., University of Wisconsin–Madison, 1971), p. 350.

125. "The Need of Rural School Supervision," *Department of Education Bulletin,* no. 12 (Sept. 1933): 52–53.

126. "Rural Teachers Club, Napa County," *California Exchange Bulletin in Rural Education* 1, no. 4 (May 1927): 55.

127. Helen Heffernan, "School Supervision in Three California Counties," *Western Journal of Education* 37, no. 7 (July 1929): 7.

128. Ada York, "Specific Points of Teacher Training for Rural Service," *California Exchange Bulletin in Rural Education* 2, no. 1 (Oct. 1927): 10–11.

129. Helen Heffernan, "Experimental Attempts to Improve Instruction in Rural Schools," *Western Journal of Education* 37, no. 1 (Jan. 1929): 9.

130. Heffernan, "Rural School Supervision in Three California Counties," p. 7.

131. Heffernan, "Experimental Attempts," p. 9.

132. Typical is her article "A Statement of the Philosophy and the Purposes of the Elementary School," *California Journal of Elementary Education* 1, no. 3 (Feb. 1933), which begins: "The philosophy of John Dewey is basic in the thought and practice of most advanced schools today. He maintains that education is life; education is growth; education is a social process; and education is a continuous reconstruction of experience" (p. 109).

133. Political positions continued to harden in this period. In 1935, for example, concern over "subversives" led the state legislature to consider the institution of a loyalty oath for teachers. See Irving Hendrick, "California's Response to the 'New Education' in the 1930s," *California Historical Quarterly* 53 (spring 1974): 30.

134. Gregory, *American Exodus*, p. 92.

135. Hendrick, "California's Response to the 'New Education,'" p. 26. See also Irving Hendrick, "The Impact of the Great Depression on Public School Support in California," *Southern California Quarterly* 54 (1972): 177–95.

136. Tyack, Lowe, and Hansot, *Public Schools in Hard Times*, p. 82.

137. Hendrick, *California Education*, p. 38. See also Cremin, *Transformation of the School*, for an extended discussion of this period.

138. Typical of letters complaining of Heffernan's influence and the power of local rural supervisors is one from the principal of the school at Farmersville to the state superintendent of education. The trustees in Farmersville, he wrote, "positively, do not like, nor will they tolerate being dictated to, nevertheless they are not hard to work with. . . . Two very good teachers which we had quit teaching several years ago and it is my firm belief because they thought they could not please the supervisors" (George Snowden to Walter Dexter, June 7, 1944; Walter Dexter Papers, California State Archives, Sacramento).

139. Vierling Kersey to County Superintendents of Schools, July 9, 1934; Vierling Kersey Papers, California State Archives, Sacramento.

140. Kersey to Heffernan, Aug. 24, 1934; Vierling Kersey Papers.

141. Heffernan to Kersey, Sept. 4, 1934; Vierling Kersey Papers.

142. "California School Supervisors Association," *California Journal of Elementary Education* 5, no. 1 (Aug. 1936): 4.

143. Helen Heffernan, "Report of Conference on Education of Children of Seasonal Workers—Fresno State College, December 9–10, 1938," *California Journal of Elementary Education* 7, no. 3 (Feb. 1939): 185.

144. Gladys Potter, "Specific Suggestions for the Organization of Instruction in Emergency Schools," *California Journal of Elementary Education* 7, no. 3 (Feb. 1939): 140. Like Heffernan, Potter argued for decent living conditions for farm workers and denounced the racism that was used to justify their exploitation. She tied the prejudice and fear of the Dust Bowl migrants to patterns of racism that had existed in California long before: "For many years the seasonal workers were from foreign lands. The feeling of indifference toward the education of the children of these foreigners was mainly due to the fact that they were foreigners and so not welcome in our land. Certain it is that the character of the seasonal workers has changed. There are still many foreigners in this group, but many places have been taken by American-born men and women. But the American-born workers and their children suffer from the old attitudes that were exhibited toward the Japanese and Mexicans who used to form the major portion of the agricultural workers in California" (ibid.). Potter argued that the damage done to children by prejudice and a life of exploited migrant labor was felt equally by Dust Bowl migrants and Mexican migrants: "It is inevitable that the fears, the emotional insecurity, the hunger, and the feeling of being ostracized have influenced the children of these families, and of the families of the Mexicans and other foreign groups that come into the public schools" ("Teaching the Migratory," *Sierra Educational News* 36, no. 3 [March 1940]: 35). Of course, neither Heffernan nor Potter tied this analysis to a critique of the structure of capitalist

agriculture, which gave rise to both the exploitation and the justifications (and continues to do so).

145. Potter then describes a school day in what she considers a model migratory school—a three-room building, forty children, and two teachers: "The building is an old wooden structure to which rooms have been added as the numbers have increased. The walls are not plastered. The room is heated with a stove. The old type of desks and seats have been put on skids so that they can be pushed about to make floor space available when needed. A long, low table stands at one side of the room, flanked with homemade chairs. The teacher arrived at eight (an hour before school began) with four of the older children. They heated water, got out wash basins, bars of soap, paper towels, mirrors and combs. All the children washed before starting school. A hot soup was made for lunch. During the day the children worked on 'the study of clothing,' working individually and in groups" ("Specific Suggestions," p. 146).

146. As one supervisor wrote to her in 1959, "Your inspiration to supervisors in California has no equal. I owe much of my success to you and many others do too" (Enid M. House, Supervisor of Elementary Education, Chula Vista City School District, to Heffernan, March 10, 1959; quoted in Treacy, "Progressivism and Corinne Seeds," p. 345). Helen Heffernan continued to be a controversial figure in California. She was the focus of a number of conservative and right-wing attacks in the late 1940s and 1950s, as part of a general offensive against progressive education. These attacks culminated in the election of Max Raferty to the position of state superintendent of schools in 1962. Heffernan later said, "If I'm responsible for Max Raferty, I'm sorry" (quoted in Treacy, "Progressivism and Corinne Seeds," p. 353).

147. This same pattern of male authority in conjunction with the growth of ideas of professionalism and "science" is well documented in other fields as well, such as medicine. See Barbara Melosh, *The Physician's Hand* (Philadelphia: Temple University Press, 1982).

CHAPTER THREE

1. For an excellent discussion of the area's human geography, see William Preston, *Vanishing Landscapes: Land and Life in the Tulare Lake Basin* (Berkeley: University of California Press, 1981).

2. John Muir, *The Mountains of California* (San Francisco: Sierra Club Books, 1989), pp. 1–2.

3. Fresno, Kern, and Inyo counties were created out of the original county within a few years; Kings County was established in 1893 out of the western part of Tulare County.

4. A fascinating account of life among the Yokuts can be found in Thomas Jefferson Mayfield's *Indian Summer* (Berkeley: Heyday Books/California Historical Society, 1993). Mayfield lived with the Choinumne Yokuts in the 1850s as an adopted child. His story was taken down by Frank Latta in 1928, just before his death.

5. Alice Miranda interview, January 18, 1971, p. 1, Tule River Heritage Project; Annie Mitchell History Room, Tulare County Public Library, Visalia, Calif. [hereafter cited as AMHR]. See also Robert Heizer and Alan Almquist, *The Other*

Californians (Berkeley: University of California Press, 1971), for accounts of white attitudes toward native peoples in the period 1850–80. Wars of "extermination" were common throughout the state, as was the kidnapping and selling of Indian children, forced servitude, and the taking of native lands without treaty or any other attempt at legal justification. California Indians were not allowed to vote or give testimony in court against whites until 1879.

6. The 1860 U.S. Census seems a model of science compared to the 1870 census, which counts 4 Indians out of a total Tulare County population of 4,533.

7. *Visalia Weekly Delta*, July 9, 1859, p. 1.

8. *Visalia Weekly Delta*, Oct. 24, 1861, p.1.

9. W. Preston, *Vanishing Landscapes*, p. 87.

10. Sister Mary Thomas, *Apostle of the Valley: The Life of Daniel Frances Dade—Pioneer Priest of the San Joaquin Valley* (Fresno: Academy of California Church History, 1947), p. 24.

11. Donald Pisani, *From Family Farm to Agribusiness: The Irrigation Crusade in California and the West, 1850–1931* (Berkeley: University of California Press, 1984), p. 6.

12. W. Preston, *Vanishing Landscapes*, p. 135.

13. James L. Brown, *The Mussel Slough Tragedy* (Hanford, Calif., 1980). This incident was the inspiration for Frank Norris's *The Octopus*.

14. Pisani, *From Family Farm to Agribusiness*, p. 10.

15. Ibid., p. 185.

16. The idea of a separate county was first proposed by businessmen in the towns of Lemoore and Hanford in 1886. In 1893, after several years of political pressure in favor of a new county, the Kings County Division Act was passed. See Evon Cody and Jay Clark, *Kings County: A Short History* (Hanford, Calif.: Star Stenographic Service, 1987), p. iii.

17. W. Preston, *Vanishing Landscapes*, p. 146.

18. Ibid.

19. This is now Highway 99, still a heavily traveled route between Sacramento and Bakersfield.

20. Tom Hall, "California Populism at the Grass-Roots: The Case of Tulare County, 1892," *Southern California Quarterly* 49, no. 2 (June 1967): 193.

21. Hermann Morse, *A Rural Survey of Tulare County* (New York: Presbyterian Church Board of Home Missions, 1915), p. 81. The other fourteen institutions included one Buddhist, four Catholic, five Christian Science, two United Brethren, one Gregorian Armenian, and one Latter-Day Saints.

22. "On Christmas Eve in 1892," begins:

> On Christmas Eve, in 1892
> Came a family a-traveling, who numbered not a few
> And the train from Kentucky had taken a week,
> The trip down from Fresno was made on a freight,
> And hours that had taken; were nearly eight.
> They had read in their Church paper, Dinuba was a good place
> To raise their children in God's nurture and grace.

Ione Cochran, "Samuel Davies Cochran Family" (typescript, n.d.), p. 57, AMHR.

23. Andrew Wells, *The San Joaquin Valley of California: Resources, Industries, and Advantages* (San Francisco: Southern Pacific Railroad Passenger Department, 1908), p. 68.

24. Helen Howe, "A History of Stratford," in Cody and Clark, *Kings County: A Short History*, p. 21.

25. Black people first came to California as part of the early Spanish and Mexican settlements, but they did not arrive in meaningful numbers until the gold rush of 1848. Still, in 1900 African Americans numbered only 11,045, less than 1 percent of the population of California, and remained concentrated in the cities of Oakland and San Francisco. In the decade 1900–1910, black migrants increasingly saw southern California as a place of opportunity: the 1910 U.S. Census listed 21,645 African Americans in California, nearly half of them in Los Angeles.

26. Audrey Leibold, *A History of the Chinese Taoist Temple, Hanford, California* (Hanford, Calif.: Taoist Temple Preservation Society, 1982), pp. 1–2.

27. W. Preston, *Vanishing Landscapes*, p. 133.

28. Morse, *Rural Survey*, pp. 35, 37, 36.

29. George Stewart, "Our Chinaman," *Visalia Weekly Delta*, Jan. 2, 1880.

30. "The Chinese Vegetable Man," in *Tulare County Business Directory* (Fresno: Pillsbury & Ellsworth, 1888), p. 34.

31. David Masumoto, *Country Voices* (Del Rey, Calif.: Inaka Countryside Publications, 1987), p. 14.

32. Ibid., p. 16.

33. Morse, *Rural Survey*, p. 40.

34. Quoted in Eleanor Ramsay, "Allensworth" (Ph.D. diss., University of California, Berkeley, 1972), p. 156.

35. For discussions of the movement to create black towns, see Norman Crockett, *The Black Towns* (Lawrence: University of Kansas Press, 1979); Mozell Hill, "The All-Negro Communities of Oklahoma," *Journal of Negro History* 31, no. 3 (July 1946): 254–68; August Meier, *Negro Thought in America, 1880–1915: Racial Ideologies in the Age of Booker T. Washington* (Ann Arbor: University of Michigan Press, 1963); Nell Painter, *Exodusters* (Lawrence: University of Kansas Press, 1986); and Harold Rose, "The All-Negro Town: Its Evolution and Function," *Geographical Review* 55 (July 1955): 362–81.

36. Ramsay, "Allensworth," p. 5, cites oral sources, school attendance reports, the index to the Great Register of Voters of Tulare County, and land titles as sources.

37. Henry Singleton interview, Allensworth Collection, California State Department of Parks and Recreation.

38. Early residents who were children at Allensworth in the period between 1910 and 1920 describe playing in alkali up to their knees. Henry Singleton commented, "That land was no good, to tell you the truth" (Singleton interview).

39. Singleton interview.

40. Morse, *Rural Survey*, p. 39.

41. W. Preston, *Vanishing Landscapes*, p. 169.

42. Ibid., p. 170.

43. Ibid., p. 172.

44. The size of farms in Tulare and Kings Counties increased from an average of 159 acres in 1925 to 213 acres in 1945. At the same time, the number of farms fell from 9,465 to 8,505. In the same period, large corporate interests gained power in the San Joaquin Valley. Standard Oil developed the oil fields of the Kettleman Hills, while vast cotton ranches were established on the West Side of Kings County and in the southern parts of Tulare County; in conjunction, company towns such as Avenal, where oil field workers lived, and Corcoran, a cotton-ginning center, were established. These developments created great wealth for corporate landowners, but led to an almost feudal economic and social structure that was quite different from that of the more settled eastern parts of Kings and Tulare Counties, where small family farms still predominated. See W. Preston, *Vanishing Landscapes*, p. 170.

45. Helen Heffernan commented in 1938, "The racial composition of our migrants has changed. In 1930 it was largely Mexican. Now, it is largely American stock from the drought states. These migrants have arrived and continue to arrive in cars of ancient vintage with homemade trailers attached—and, they have come to stay" ("Report of Conference on Education of Children of Seasonal Workers," p. 186).

46. Newell Bringhurst, "The Ku Klux Klan in Visalia, Tulare County, California" (typescript), pp. 7, 2.

47. Quoted in Carey McWilliams, *Factories in the Fields* (Boston: Little, Brown, 1940), p. 323.

48. Quoted in Walter Stein, *California and the Dust Bowl Migration* (Westport, Conn.: Greenwood Press, 1973), p. 61.

49. James Gregory summarizes the hostility to "Okies" thus: "The increased taxes, the changing complexion of communities, the migrants' poverty, the enlarged relief rolls, and the threat of disease—[all these] contributed to a growing sense of apprehension as residents watched more and more people, most of them poor, and most of them Southwesterners, filter into the valley" (*American Exodus* [New York: Oxford University Press, 1988], p. 88). In fact, as Stein (*California and the Dust Bowl*, pp. 279–81) points out, the 1930s migration to some extent helped rural California communities, in that it brought in state and federal assistance funds; this support, however, was not acknowledged by Central Valley residents.

50. On efforts to organize migrant farm laborers during the depression, see Gregory, *American Exodus*, pp. 154–64.

51. Ibid., p. 98.

52. See, for example, Fuller, *Old Country School*; Jonathan Sher, ed., *Education in Rural America: A Reassessment of Conventional Wisdom* (Boulder, Colo.: Westview Press, 1977); and Gulliford, *America's Country Schools*.

53. These records were apparently already lost by the early 1880s. As the writers of an 1883 history of Tulare County comment: "The first County Superintendent of Schools, or School Commissioner, was Major Gordon, who was County Clerk and ex officio School Commissioner. During his administration the records of the schools were kept in a small memorandum, which at the expiration of his

term was turned over to his successor. As to the present whereabout of this valuable record and the matter there contained, time and eternity can only reveal" (Wallace Elliott, *A History of Tulare County* [Fresno, Calif.: California History Books, (1883) 1975], p. 198).

54. "First Concern of Our Pioneers Was to Educate Their Children," *Visalia Times Delta,* May 24, 1952.

55. Waverly Dean Hall, "History of the Organization and Administration of Public Schools in Tulare County, California, 1852–1970" (Ed.D. diss., University of Southern California, 1972), p. 42.

56. "Tulare County Superintendent of Schools Report," in Superintendent of Public Instruction, *Biennial Report, 1870–71,* p. 44.

57. Superintendent of Public Instruction, *Biennial Report, 1862–63,* p. 132.

58. Joe Doctor, "A Study of the Historical and Architectural Resources of Tulare County" (typescript, n.d.), p. 4, AMHR.

59. "Recollections of Orlena Wrought," in Sigma Chapter, Delta Kappa Gamma, *Tulare County Schools 100 Years* (Visalia, Calif., 1961), p. 193. Orlena Wrought was my great-aunt.

60. Ibid. The Wilson school near Dinuba in Tulare County provides another typical example of the creation of an early school district. In the mid-1870s, when this area was first settled, children were either taught at home by their mothers or received no schooling at all. Six families with children in this district petitioned the county board of supervisors to create the Wilson School District. An early settler recalled: "When Mr. Stephen Hicks was asked to sign the petition, he not only did so but offered a building site on the northeast corner of his homestead. Later, he gave a deed to three acres, after he had made final proof of his property. The settlers donated most of the material and labor. Some hauled lumber from the mountains, while others brought rocks for the foundation from Smith Mountain. Isaac Rice, Morgan West and John and Abner Fraser were the carpenters. They constructed a 20' x 30' building with walls 12' high and made of 1" x 12" rough pine boards. The floor was of the same material and in the wintertime a constant draft of cold air came up through the cracks. The seats were home-made of redwood" ("Recollections of Maude Ledbetter," quoted in Sigma Chapter, *Tulare County Schools,* p. 29).

61. Melvin Rudholm, "A Short History and Survey of Pixley Union School District" (M.A. thesis, Fresno State College, 1953), p. 28.

62. "Tulare County Superintendent of Schools Report," in Superintendent of Public Instruction, *Biennial Report, 1874–75,* p. 227.

63. "Annual Report of the Conditions of Schools in Tulare County, 1877–1878," quoted in W. D. Hall, "History of the Organization and Administration of Public Schools," p. 107.

64. The view that a difficult examination brought higher-quality teachers was expressed in newspaper articles and pamphlets boosting the county. The *Tulare County Business Directory* of 1888, for example, claimed: "It is not presumed that gentlemen and ladies teach as a mere 'go-between' while they are preparing for some other occupation. The presumption is that teaching is their profession and

they are presumed to have made thorough preparation for their work before they appear for examination. Hence the examinations are somewhat technical. . . . This strictness of examinations serves to keep up salaries, and better than all, it keeps the schools in the hands of teachers who know what to teach and how to teach it, so that the public school fund is not frittered away by incompetents" (p. 84).

65. Tulare County Superintendent of Schools W. J. Ellis wrote in 1880: "The thorough system of irrigation introduced into many parts of the county has materially increased its wealth and importance, and changed the country from a cattle and sheep raising land to one of agriculture and permanent homes" ("Tulare County Superintendent of Schools Report," in Superintendent of Public Instruction, *Biennial Report, 1879–80*, p. 73).

66. Quoted in Katherine Small, *A History of Tulare County* (Chicago: J. Clarke, 1925), p. 338.

67. "Report of the Tulare County Superintendent of Schools, 1885–1886," quoted in W. D. Hall, "History of the Organization and Administration of Public Schools," p. 109.

68. Quoted in ibid., p. 110. In 1900 there were 107 school districts with 143 schools in Tulare County. Kings County listed 31 school districts in 1900. Local support for the schools was reflected in extremely high attendance rates. As the county superintendent wrote in 1900, "The percentage of attendance is quite remarkable when we consider the conditions surrounding the children of this county. In the early autumn and late spring months our orchardists draw heavily upon our schools for their help, thus materially reducing school attendance; yet we have been able to maintain an average attendance of a little more than 95% on the average number belonging; and this with the greatest average length of school term in the history of the county" (Superintendent of Public Instruction, *Biennial Report, 1900–1901*, p. 149).

69. In an advertisement in the *Visalia Delta* in 1860, Rev. and Mrs. Taylor promised, "Young ladies will not be permitted to receive attention or address except such as would be agreeable to their parents" (quoted in A. W. Frost, "Visalia Select Seminary" [typescript, 1941], p. 2, AMHR).

70. The first Academy of the Nativity was held in a building that had originally been used as a stable, which suggested the name to Father Dade; see Thomas, *Apostle of the Valley*, p. 80.

71. Orr, for example, claimed that "at one time" thirty-five of sixty-nine teachers in the public schools had attended the Visalia Normal School (cited in W. D. Hall, "History of the Organization and Administration of Public Schools," p. 55).

72. "The Visalia Normal School Bulletin" (Visalia, 1883), AMHR.

73. Mervyn Shippey, "The Visalia Normal School" (typescript, n.d.), p. 54, AMHR.

74. "Constitution of the Tulare County Teachers Institute, April 29, 1868," cited in Stella Bailey, "Education in Tulare County, California, 1852–1912" (M.A. thesis, Fresno State College, 1962), p. 58.

75. "Tulare County Superintendent of Schools Report 1885," in Superintendent of Public Instruction, *Biennial Report, 1886–87*, p. 22.

76. Grace Pogue, *The Swift Seasons* (Hollywood, Calif.: Cloister Press, 1957), p. 35.

77. The most detailed description of Tulare County schools in the early twentieth century is found in Morse's social survey of 1914–15. In his study, Morse differentiated the graded schools of the six largest towns—Visalia, Porterville, Tulare, Lindsay, Dinuba, and Exeter—from the one-, two-, and three-room schools of the rural back country. Almost half of the students in the county attended school in these six towns in 1914–15. Of the country schools, 72 percent were one-room schools, 21 percent were two-teacher schools, and 7 percent were three- to six-teacher schools. Morse was especially concerned with these country schools, where it was most likely that a "rural school problem" might be manifested. Echoing the concerns of progressive social scientists of the day, Morse advocated school consolidation, paid great attention to lighting, ventilation, heating, and sanitation, and encouraged the use of school buildings as community centers. While Morse was critical of the condition of the rural schools, he did acknowledge that schools built within the five years preceding his study were "highly satisfactory" (Morse, *Rural Survey*, p. 64).

78. Ibid., p. 63.

79. Ibid., p. 64.

80. In the past decade, scholars have begun to critique the consequences of the monocultural organization of schools and curriculum. Guadalupe San Miguel, for example, has argued that the treatment of Chicano and Mexican children has "aided in the reproduction and strengthening of the existing caste-like structure of dominant-subordinate relationships in the Southwest and generally limited the opportunities for social mobility among Chicano children" ("Status of the Historiography of Chicano Education: A Preliminary Analysis," *History of Education Quarterly* 26, no. 4 [winter 1986]: 526). For further discussion of racial segregation and exclusion in California, see Gilbert Gonzalez, "Segregation of Mexican Children in a Southern California City: The Legacy of Expansionism and the American Southwest," *Western Historical Quarterly* 16 (Jan. 1985): 55–76; Heizer and Almquist, *Other Californians*; Irving Hendrick, *The Education of Non-Whites in California, 1849–1970* (San Francisco: R & E Research Associates, 1979); and Charles Wollenberg, *All Deliberate Speed: Segregation and Exclusion in California Schools, 1855–1975* (Berkeley: University of California Press, 1976).

81. David Tyack has made this point in a number of works. See, in particular, "Onward Christian Soldiers: Religion in the American Common School," in *History and Education: The Educational Uses of the Past*, ed. Paul Nash (New York: Random House, 1970), pp. 212–55.

82. Wollenberg, *All Deliberate Speed*, p. 14.

83. Superintendent Andrew Moulder argued in 1858: "If this attempt to force Africans, Chinese and Diggers into our white schools is persisted in, it must result in the ruin of our schools" (Superintendent of Public Instruction, *Biennial Report, 1858–59*, p. 14).

84. See Wollenberg, *All Deliberate Speed*, for a more extensive discussion.

85. Sigma Chapter, *Tulare County Schools*, p. 164.

86. Mervyn Shippey, "A Short History of the Visalia Colored School" (typescript, n.d.), p. 1, AMHR.

87. Ibid., p. 4.

88. With this decision the court asserted the legality of the 1880 school law, which formally abolished segregation in the state of California. Various forms of segregation continued to exist in California schools, however, directed at Asian, Mexican, and Native-American children. In 1929 the school code finally repealed all earlier segregated school provisions and "specifically provided that all children, regardless of race, should be admitted to all schools" (Heizer and Almquist, *Other Californians*, p. 176). Informal practices of school segregation nonetheless continue to be widespread in California.

89. Delilah Beasley, *Negro Trailblazers of California* (Los Angeles: Times Mirror Printing and Binding House, 1919), p. 185.

90. The Allensworth schoolhouse, an outstanding example of rural school architecture, has been restored as part of the Allensworth State Park. I am indebted to Alice Royal of Visalia and Oakland for an illuminating tour of the park.

91. Mrs. Twaddle to H. E. McPherson, Feb. 3, 1915, Allensworth Vertical File, AMHR.

92. Mrs. Beatrice Rainbow Higgs, quoted in Ramsay, "Allensworth," p. 99.

93. Ramsay, "Allensworth," p. 118.

94. Helatha Smith, interview, Allensworth Collection, California State Department of Parts and Recreation.

95. "Ninth Annual Commencement of the Allensworth Public School Nineteen Hundred Nineteen," Allensworth Vertical File, AMHR.

96. Will Wood, "A Visit to Allensworth—A Colony for the Negro," *California Blue Bulletin* 3, no. 2 (June 1917): 13.

97. Irving Hendrick, "Federal Policy Affecting the Education of Indians in California, 1849–1934," *History of Education Quarterly* 16, no. 2 (summer 1976): 166.

98. Georgiana Carden, Untitled, undated manuscript on Indian education, Georgiana Carden Papers, Bancroft Library, University of California, Berkeley.

99. At the Tule River school, children's health was monitored by the Indian agent as well as the teacher. In an interview, Rachel B., who taught briefly at the school as a substitute teacher, recalled: "There were showers and places to brush your teeth out back. The children took showers and a government employee of some kind on the reservation came in and witnessed the showers. But it was the teacher's job to see that the teeth got brushed. It was just like a regular set up. You had everything under the sun that you needed that was available in those days because it was a government situation."

100. *Visalia Weekly Delta*, April 2, 1880, p. 2.

101. Thomas, *Apostle of the Valley*, p. 85.

102. Richard Wing, oral history interview, Local History Collection, Kings County Library, Hanford, Calif.

103. *Farmersville Herald*, June 24, 1981. See the description of one such school in Fresno County in Masamoto, *Country Voices*.

104. Such school records have provided invaluable information for historians where they exist. An excellent example of the historical use of school records

is Marjorie Theobald's *Knowing Women: Origins of Women's Education in Nineteenth-Century Australia* (Cambridge: Cambridge University Press, 1996). See also J. Donald Wilson, "I Am Ready to Be of Assistance When I Can: Lottie Bowron and Rural Women Teachers in British Columbia," in Prentice and Theobald, eds., *Women Who Taught*, pp. 202–31.

105. The 1880 census provides the first useful data for the lightly populated county. The 1890 manuscript census records were destroyed by fire. Information from the 1930 census will not be released until the early twenty-first century.

106. The accuracy of early census figures is questionable. The prejudices of local census takers, particularly in the period before 1900, often render data on women and nonwhites suspect.

107. The history of women in the West has been explored in a number of works during the last fifteen years. See, for example, Susan Armitage, "Women and Men in Western History: A Stereotypical Vision," *Western Historical Quarterly* 16 (Oct. 1985): 381–95; Susan Armitage and Elizabeth Jameson, eds., *The Women's West* (Norman: University of Oklahoma Press, 1987); Julie Roy Jeffrey, *Frontier Women* (New York: Hill & Wang, 1979); Joan Jensen and Darlis Miller, "The Gentle Tamers Revisited: New Approaches to the History of Women in the American West," *Pacific Historical Review* 49, no. 2 (May 1980): 173–213; Sandra Myres, *Westering Women and the Frontier Experience, 1800–1915* (Albuquerque: University of New Mexico Press, 1982); Peggy Pascoe, *Relations of Rescue* (New York: Oxford University Press, 1991); Lillian Schlissel, Vicki Ruiz, and Janice Monk, eds., *Western Women: Their Land, Their Lives* (Albuquerque: University of New Mexico Press, 1988).

108. See Peter Palquist, "Women in California Photography, 1850–1920" (paper presented at the conference "Suspect Terrain: Women in the West," Lincoln, Neb., July 1992).

109. See Kessler-Harris, *Out to Work*, for a discussion of the changing opportunities for paid work for women in this period.

110. Of the fifty-one teachers listed in the census, only thirty-seven also appear in school records. Thus over half of the teachers listed in official school records in 1880 cannot be traced through the census. The fifteen people who list their occupation in the census as "teacher" but who do not show up in the school records can probably be explained by considering the rapid population shifts in the county in this period. Settlers poured into the county seeking cheap land, and teaching positions were poorly paid and loosely supervised. Many teachers, particularly men, seem to have taught briefly as a way of making some extra money, as was the case for T. J. Vivian in 1880, whom the *Visalia Delta* of February 20, 1880, described as having "abandoned the schoolroom and turned his attention to sheep" in the middle of term. The fifteen (only three of whom were women) could very well have been teachers at some point in their lives, possibly in their home communities. Or perhaps they disappeared from the records because they moved away from Tulare County or found other work than teaching. Another problem in analyzing school records comes from the fact that teachers listed in the records sometimes taught at two schools in the same year, undoubtedly two three-month schools in different parts of the county. Some schools

list more than one teacher. In this fluid situation of rapid settlement, school-teachers must have been in demand, but for brief periods, and teaching probably provided temporary employment for literate new settlers but not necessarily a commitment to long-term careers.

111. Tulare County, Department of Education Files, California State Archives, Sacramento.

112. See Tyack and Hansot, *Managers of Virtue,* for a detailed discussion of the ideological stance of these administrators. See also Callahan, *Education and the Cult of Efficiency,* for a still-relevant discussion of the period 1890–1920.

113. "J. E. Buckman, County Superintendent, 1911–1935," in Sigma Chapter, *Tulare County Schools,* p. 9. Buckman's sympathy for ranchers was evident in the county's reluctance to provide schooling for migrant children in the 1920s. Georgiana Carden, in her diary for 1925, noted: "It appeared necessary to go personally with the County Supervisor of Attendance of Tulare County, to the school districts affected by cotton pickers because there was an unmistakable tendency on the part of the County Office to let matters drift and, above all, to ignore the provision for emergency conditions contained in Section 1543, Eighteenth" ("Itinerary and Detailed Activities Since 12/1/25, December 3," Georgiana Carden Papers).

114. Quoted in Small, *History,* p. 339.

115. A more extended discussion of Nannie Davidson's career is found in Chapter 4.

116. "Meadows the Man," *Hanford Morning Journal,* Nov. 1, 1914.

117. Lee Richmond, "Kings County Schools," *California Exchange Bulletin in Rural Education* 1, no. 1 (Nov. 1926): 32.

118. "Editorial," *Educational Digest: A Journal for Busy Teachers* 1, no. 1 (Sept. 1914): 3.

119. In 1904, for example, the superintendent of public instruction's report included an enthusiastic account by University of California professor F. B. Dressler of European (particularly German) schools with their baths, tiled floors, gymnasiums, and "filtrating of air" (*Biennial Report, 1904–5,* pp. 88–97).

120. Margaret Schallenberger McNaught, "The Best Way to Make Citizens of Aliens," *California Blue Bulletin* 6, no. 1 (March 1920): 19.

121. J. E. Buckman, "Letters from Your County Superintendents," *Educational Digest* 1, no. 1 (Sept. 1914): 26.

122. "Tulare County School Manual 1924," p. 17, AMHR.

123. These school pageants were examples of a wider cultural phenomenon. The University of California, San Francisco State Normal School, and other colleges and universities also produced elaborate pageants celebrating regional and group identity in the period immediately prior to the First World War.

124. For an example, see the 1913 graduation program of the Tipton Lindsay Grammar School, Visalia Public School Vertical File 40, AMHR.

125. "Graduation Program, Eighth Grades of the Webster and Jefferson Schools, Visalia, 1918," Visalia Public Schools Vertical File 41, AMHR.

126. Grace Pogue, *Within the Magic Circle* (Visalia, Calif.: Visalia Times Delta, n.d.), p. 80.

127. "Manual for the Public Schools of Kings County, California, 1908," Public Schools Vertical File, Kings County Public Library.

128. "School Manual of Tulare County, 1911," p. 38, AMHR.

129. Elsie Bozeman, "Kings County Notes," *Sierra Educational News* 23, no. 9 (Nov. 1927): 574.

130. *Tulare County School Bulletin* 6, no. 1 (Sept. 1940): 2.

131. W. N. Davis, "History of the Dinuba Elementary Schools, 1889–1961" (privately published, 1961), p. 25.

132. Ibid., p. 26.

133. "Visalia Schools Will Practice Rigid Economy," *Visalia Times Delta*, May 20, 1932, p. 1.

134. Writing in the *Sierra Educational News*, for example, Driggers claimed that "the public school system of Tulare County is second to none" and cited the accomplishments of Tulare County teachers. In 1936, more than two hundred of the eight hundred teachers in the county attended summer school sessions, and "approximately 350 teachers traveled extensively in this and foreign countries"—remarkable figures given the depth of the depression. See Roy Driggers, "Around the State—Tulare County," *Sierra Educational News* 33, no. 3 (March 1937): 27; also "Tulare County," *Western Journal of Education* 42, no. 8 (1938): 6.

135. "School Manual of Tulare County, 1936," p. 7, AMHR.

136. *Tulare County Schools Bulletin* 1, no. 1 (April 1936): 1.

137. *Tulare County Schools Bulletin* 1, no. 3 (Sept. 1936): 1.

138. Lillian B. Hill, "Report of the Bureau of Attendance and Migratory Schools," in Superintendent of Public Instruction, *Biennial Report, 1929–30*, p. 159. The Simon J. Lubin Society in 1938 estimated that more than 250,000 homeless migrants were working in California agriculture, including at least 30,000 children.

139. Despite its enormous productivity and abundance, California agriculture has always been characterized by large farms and ranches and a dependence on and exploitation of low-paid migrant labor. James Gregory points out, "The migrant farm labor system imposed one of the sharpest class structures found anywhere in American society. Moving from place to place, strangers in nearly every community, seasonal farm workers were a class apart, the mostly invisible underside of generally prosperous rural California" (*American Exodus*, p. 58). The composition of the migratory work force in California agriculture has shifted over time, from an early dependence on white male workers to the employment of ethnic male workers, usually under the contract system, including at various times Chinese, Japanese, Filipinos, and Mexicans. Expanding markets and the introduction of cotton to the Imperial Valley and then the San Joaquin Valley in the 1920s created an even greater need for a cheap, migratory work force. In the 1920s, growers increasingly turned to Mexican labor to fill this need. This group of workers, unlike earlier groups such as the native white "fruit tramps" of the late nineteenth and early twentieth centuries or the Asian men who had come to the United States alone, was made up of families. See Ronald Takaki, *Strangers from a Different Shore* (New York: Penguin Books, 1989), for a discussion of the forces and policies shaping the lives of Asian immigrants; for a wider discussion,

see Cletus Daniel, *Bitter Harvest: A History of California Farm Workers, 1870–1941* (Ithaca: Cornell University Press, 1981).

140. Clara Coldwell, "Teaching the Children of Seasonal Workers," *California Exchange Bulletin in Rural Education* 1, no. 2 (Jan. 1927): 59.

141. Frances Averill, "Supervision of Schools for Children of Seasonal Workers," *Western Journal of Education* 35, no. 9 (Sept. 1929): 8.

142. Mary Armour, "History of the Tagus Ranch School" (typescript), Tagus Ranch Vertical File, AMHR.

143. *Tulare County Schools Bulletin* 2, no. 2 (Oct. 1936): 1.

144. Doris Thornley, "Health Program for Tulare County," *Western Journal of Education* 36, no. 12 (Dec. 1930): 3.

145. Paul Taylor, *On the Ground in the Thirties* (Layton, Utah: Peregrine Smith Books, 1983), p. 51. The *Visalia Times Delta* of October 23, 1933, reported: "With several hundred Tulare district school children in the cotton fields at work Saturday, an informal movement to urge declaration of a school holiday for a short period was underway in Tulare" (p. 1).

146. Georgiana Carden, Untitled, undated manuscript on the supervision of school attendance, p. 14, Georgiana Carden Papers.

147. In 1936 Driggers sent this message to teachers: "Just now with the rapid influx of the seasonal workers, many of you are working under great difficulties. In some schools there is a shortage of desks, books, materials, etc. This office is doing everything possible to help in making provisions for these emergencies. It will be necessary for us all to be patient and understanding and cooperative" ("To the Principals and Teachers of Tulare County Schools," *Tulare County Bulletin* 2, no. 1 [Sept. 1936]: 1).

148. Under Nickel, the *Tulare County Schools Bulletin* took on a more cautious tone, as in this passage from his yearly message to teachers in 1940: "It shall be the duty of all teachers to endeavor to impress upon the minds of the pupils the principles of morality, truth, justice, and patriotism; to teach them to avoid idleness, profanity, and falsehood; and to instruct them in the principles of a free government, and to train them up to a true comprehension of the rights, duties, and dignity of American citizenship" (*Tulare County Schools Bulletin*, 6, no. 1 [Sept. 1940]: 1).

149. Revisionist historians have argued that schooling in industrialized and urban areas in the United States was one site of locally defined class conflict, as incipient working classes struggled with dominant bourgeois interests to define and control curriculum and teaching. In the rural West, this class conflict is less clear in terms of schooling. See Katz, *Irony of Early School Reform*; Katznelson and Weir, *Schooling for All*; Hogan, *Class and Reform*.

CHAPTER FOUR

1. See Peggy Pascoe, "The Challenge of Writing Multicultural Women's History," *Frontiers* 12, no. 1 (1991): 1–4. Pascoe argues that it is important not only to seek the history of women who have been excluded from history, but also to "mark as race and class specific the history of white middle-class women who

have so frequently been used by historians to stand in for all women." A similar argument is put forward by Elizabeth Jameson in "Toward a Multicultural History of Women in the Western United States," *Signs* 13, no. 4 (summer 1988): 761–91.

2. See Ruth Frankenberg's *White Women, Race Matters: The Social Construction of Whiteness* (Minneapolis: University of Minnesota Press, 1993).

3. Numerous published memoirs and autobiographies of teachers exist. For narratives of western women teachers, see Vaughn-Roberson, "Having a Purpose in Life." For California specifically, examples include Virginia Church, *Teachers Are People: Being the Lyrics of Virginia Church* (Hollywood, Calif.: David Graham Fischer Co., 1929); Annabel Ross Gardner, *Children and Challenges: Recollections of a Life of Teaching and Learning* (Palo Alto: Walter Hays School PTA, 1976); Eleanor Miller, *When Memory Calls* (Gardena, Calif.: Institute Press, 1936); Ferol Slotle, *School Bell Memories: Horse and Buggy to Space Age* (Los Altos, Calif.: Del Monte Press, 1986); Eleanor Tracy, *Schoolma'am, Stone Lagoon, California, 1903–1904* (Eureka, Calif.: Artcraft Print Co., 1978); and Lettie Zion, *Fairview: True Tales of a Country Schoolhouse* (Oceana, Calif.: Tower Press, 1981).

4. These include Amanda Chase, *Some California School Beginnings* (1936); and several compilations by Laura Esta Settle: *Reminiscences of Some Early California Teachers* (1937), *Yes, I'm a Pioneer Teacher* (1938), *"I Remember" Stories by Early California Teachers* (1939), and *Pages from the Past* (1940).

5. We know about Anna Mills Johnston's life from a number of sources, the most useful and interesting being her scrapbook, which has been preserved in the Annie Mitchell History Room of the Tulare County Public Library. The scrapbook is both a wonderful source and a frustrating one. It is made up of uncited newspaper clippings: although dates are sometimes provided, the name of the newspaper is rarely given. Even more frustrating is the fact that many pages of the scrapbook have been neatly cut out—whether by Anna Mills Johnston herself or by someone else at a later time we cannot know. No one remembers when the scrapbook was given to the library or by whom. The scrapbook clippings are not the only sources for Anna Mills Johnston's life, however. As the first woman to climb Mt. Whitney, she published an account of her trip in the *Mt. Whitney Club Journal*. Two letters she wrote to George Stewart, the editor of the *Visalia Delta* and a leading conservationist, have been saved in the Stewart Papers in the California State Archives. Johnston was also deeply interested in the native Yokut Indians of Tulare County and collected an outstanding collection of baskets; they can still be seen at the Tulare County Historical Museum.

6. Nannie Davidson's campaign for the office of state superintendent of public instruction, waged after twelve years as county superintendent, was not the first such attempt by a woman. In 1906 Kate Ames of Napa County had vied to become the Republican nominee for the state superintendency, but was defeated by Edward Hyatt, who subsequently defeated the Democrat Anna Williams in the November election. See Jaeckel, "Edward Hyatt," p. 144.

7. In the summer of 1883 Anna Mills traveled to Hawaii and sent a description of her trip to George Stewart, including the adventure of getting lost in a volcano for nine hours. She also described her life on the steamer: "Several of

your friends are on the steamer and I tell you we have jolly times. My appetite is good, I have a table seat at the right of the chief engineer, who is by far the handsomest man on the ship. I will not return to Visalia before the last of the month. Expect to stay at 109 Hood Street while in the City. I hope you will excuse me for sending you such a letter. Your Friend, Anna Mills" (Anna Mills to George Stewart, July 31, 1883, George Stewart Papers, Box 784, Folder 44, California State Library, Sacramento).

8. She wrote later that it was her privilege "to visit the various mountain regions in this country from the Atlantic to the Pacific and from Alaska to the Rio Grande, and to scale the volcanic mountains of Hawaii"; she "crossed the watershed of the Bavarian Alps, traversed the Austrian Tyrol, visited the German, Italian, and Swiss Alps, and gazed with admiration on the beauties of the Matterhorn and Jungfrau" (Anna Mills Johnston, "A Trip to Mt. Whitney in 1878," *Mt. Whitney Club Journal* 1, no. 1 [May 1902]: 28).

9. Johnston scrapbook.

10. Dr. Davidson was said to be the model for the doctor in Frank Norris's *The Octopus*, a novel based on the violent Mussel Slough conflict of 1880 between farmers and the Southern Pacific Railroad; see "Mrs. Davidson Candidate for State Superintendent of Schools," *Hanford Morning Journal*, April 7, 1914. On the Mussel Slough Massacre, see J. L. Brown, *Mussel Slough Tragedy*.

11. See Ned Dearborn, *The Oswego Movement in American Education* (New York: Teachers College Press, 1925).

12. Robert Brown, *History of Kings County* (Hanford, Calif.: S. H. Cawston, 1940), p. 184.

13. Johnston scrapbook.

14. Lucia Runyan, "Elbow Creek School," *Los Tulares* 33 (Dec. 1957): 1.

15. Grace Pogue, "The Golden Years," *Woodlake Echo*, May 13, 1955.

16. "Bird Day," *Visalia Times*, in Johnston scrapbook.

17. Elsie Crowley, "Carrie Barnett—An Honored Teacher," in Sigma Chapter, *Tulare County Schools*, p. 165.

18. For an analysis of white women as moral guardians, see Pascoe, *Relations of Rescue*. See also Linda Gordon, ed., *Women, the State, and Welfare* (Madison: University of Wisconsin Press, 1990), for a useful collection of essays on gender and social reform.

19. "Statement by Mrs. N. E. Davidson," *Sierra Educational News* 10, no. 5 (May 1914): 353.

20. "The Schools Are for the Children," *Hanford Morning Journal*, July 6, 1914, p. 2.

21. Carrie Barnett, "Letter to the Editor," *Visalia Times*, Feb. 6, 1914, p. 3.

22. "Women Drys Parade the Streets of City," *Visalia Times*, Feb. 12, 1914, p. 5.

23. Johnston, "Trip to Mt. Whitney," p. 18. See also Leonard Daughenbaugh, "On Top of the World: Anna Mills Johnston's Ascent of Mt. Whitney," *California History* 64, no. 1 (winter 1985): 42–51.

24. Johnston, "Trip to Mt. Whitney," p. 24. Because of her lameness, when the party finally began the final ascent Anna set out early, since it would take her longer to make the climb. In a dramatic passage she describes her experience:

"Eating a hurried breakfast, I started alone, soon after five o'clock, for Guitar Lake, where I was to rest and wait for the other members of the party. Climbing over the rocks was no easy task. . . . But I didn't mind such trifles when there was so much at stake. My heart was set on something higher, and nothing short of the highest point would satisfy me. I would reach that and die if need be" (ibid.).

25. Johnston scrapbook.

26. Ibid.

27. Ibid.

28. "Mrs. Davidson Warmly Greeted," *Hanford Morning Journal*, July 14, 1914.

29. "Friends Rally to Mrs. Davidson's Aid," *Hanford Morning Journal*, Aug. 4, 1914.

30. "Mrs. Davidson Optimistic," *Hanford Morning Journal*, Aug. 25, 1914.

31. U.S. Bureau of the Census, *Statistics of Women and Work* (Washington, D.C.: GPO, 1907), p. 111.

32. U.S. Bureau of the Census, *Thirteenth Census of the United States, 1910*, vol. 4: *Population, Occupation Statistics* (Washington, D.C.: GPO, 1914), p. 440.

33. The reporter's description—of which I have found nothing comparable for a teacher, male or female, in any of the newspapers for Tulare or Kings County—recalls the "orientalizing" of the exotic "other" described by Edward Said in *Orientalism* (New York: Vintage Books, 1979).

34. "Successful Candidates," *Visalia Weekly Delta*, Dec. 30, 1881, p. 1.

35. Ibid.

36. Ida B. Wells, *Crusade for Justice: The Autobiography of Ida B. Wells* (Chicago: University of Chicago Press, 1970), p. 24.

37. Ibid., p. 25.

38. Beasley, *Negro Trailblazers*, p. 167.

39. Will Wood ("Visit to Allensworth," p. 13) describes the first teacher at Allensworth, William Payne, who was also one of the original founders of the colony. Payne was born in West Virginia in 1879, the son of a miner; he attended normal school in that state and later graduated with a B.A. from Denison University in Ohio. He then became a teacher and principal in the segregated schools of West Virginia and Ohio. In 1906 Payne and his wife followed his parents to Pasadena; in the integrated schools of Pasadena, however, there were no openings for African-American teachers. As Margaret Prince Hubert recalled, "For him, a well-educated Black man, Pasadena only offered jobs such as taking care of offices and gardening" (quoted in Ramsay, "Allensworth," p. 147).

40. In addition, a valuable exhibit documenting life at Allensworth was held at the California Afro-American Museum in Los Angeles in 1987.

41. Quotations of Margaret Prince Hubert in the following are from Ramsay, "Allensworth," pp. 146–49.

42. On the founding of Allensworth, see Chapter 3; on Payne, see above, note 39. At the Allensworth school, the gendered pattern of instruction at white schools was duplicated: Payne was principal and taught the older children, while the primary children were taught by black women teachers. The first woman teacher was Eva Whiting, who left after two years. The second was Margaret Prince.

43. *Los Angeles New Age*, Dec. 4, 1914.

44. *Los Angeles New Age*, May 7, 1914.

45. *California Eagle*, Feb. 27, 1915.

46. See, for example, the account of the 1915 Allensworth school graduation in *The Visalia Times*, June 13, 1915.

47. "Allensworth," *Oakland Sunshine*, Oct. 27, 1913.

48. Elizabeth Payne McGee interview, Allensworth Collection, California State Department of Parks and Recreation, Sacramento.

49. *Los Angeles New Age*, April 2, 1915.

50. These segregated schools in El Centro and the Imperial Valley were criticized in the African-American press. See *California Eagle*, Oct. 17, 1914.

51. Quoted in Ramsay, "Allensworth," p. 150.

52. Information about Nevada Porch Hastings comes from a number of sources, primarily newspaper accounts of her career published after her retirement. These can be found in the Annie Mitchell History Room of the Tulare County Public Library.

53. Sigma Chapter, *Tulare County Schools*, p. 75.

54. William Hastings was eleven years older than Nevada Porch. He had been a mail rider and sheepman in his youth, and since 1885 had been farming near Terra Bella, close to Plano village. It may well be that Nevada Porch's parents died in those years between 1906 and her marriage in 1909.

55. "Nevada Porch Hastings," *Terra Bella News*, Oct. 20, 1949, p. 2.

56. Grace Pogue's association of drinking and immorality can be seen in this memory from when her son Richard was a baby: "Earl [a family friend] picked a lovely white rose bud, removed the thorns and handed it to the baby. I said, 'What a symbol of purity. If only we could keep our little son as sweet and clean as that rose.' Earl replied that one of the worst evils, intoxicating liquor, would be gone before Richard grew up. I later watched an effigy of John Barleycorn kicked into a grave, but he didn't stay there. The resistance to temptation must be developed from within" (Pogue, *Swift Seasons*, p. 52).

57. Perhaps because she saw herself in some sense as a professional writer, Grace Pogue's prose is somewhat mannered and self-conscious. For example, *The Swift Seasons* begins with this account of her own birth: "Nobody was at home except Mother and me when Doc Stork came. It was a surprise to both of us. Doc had a four-pound bundle to deliver. It was a warm June day and he was tired." This tone, in which painful or frightening events (in this case, facing a premature birth alone) are domesticated and made humorous, is characteristic of Pogue's style.

58. Pogue, *Swift Seasons*, p. 13.

59. Ibid., pp. 15, 20.

60. Ibid., p. 16.

61. See Chapter 3, p. 88.

62. Pogue, *Swift Seasons*, p. 152.

63. Ibid., p. 29.

64. Ibid., p. 38.

65. Ethel Besquette, "Pleasant Valley School," in Settle, ed., *Yes, I'm a Pioneer Teacher*, p. 99.

66. Ibid.

67. One of the most vivid accounts of teaching in California in the early twen-

tieth century can be found in Mary Ellicott Arnold and Mabel Reed's *In the Land of the Grasshopper's Song* (Lincoln: University of Nebraska Press, 1957), about teaching among the Klamath River Indians in 1908 and 1909.

68. Mrs. W. Hastings, "Remarks at Picnic," *Terra Bella News*, June 21, 1946, p. 3.

69. Besquette, "Pleasant Valley School," p. 95.

70. Hastings, "Remarks at Picnic."

71. Ibid.

72. Besquette, "Pleasant Valley School," p. 90.

73. Ibid., p. 92.   74. Ibid., pp. 92–93.

75. Ibid., p. 99.   76. Ibid., p. 97.

77. Ibid., pp. 98–99.   78. Ibid., p. 93.

79. Ibid., p. 99.

80. See, for example, Jane Roland Martin, *The Schoolhome* (Cambridge, Mass.: Harvard University Press, 1992); Madeleine Grumet, *Bitter Milk* (Albany: State University of New York Press, 1988); and Carol Gilligan, *In a Different Voice* (Cambridge, Mass.: Harvard University Press, 1982).

81. Aileen Goodin Hartwell, "Sarah Goodin—Teacher," in Sigma Chapter, *Tulare County Schools*, p. 66.

82. Pogue, *Swift Seasons*, pp. 32, 35.

83. This shifting back and forth between teaching and farm work recalls the movement between teaching and work in the textile mills in mid-nineteenth-century Massachusetts; see Dublin, *Women at Work*. My own mother, Nadine Wrought, who began teaching in 1927 when she was twenty, worked summers in fruit packing houses up until her marriage.

84. Ethel Besquette, "School Near Mt. Shasta's Grandeur," in Settle, ed., *Pages from the Past*, p. 34.

85. Pogue, *The Swift Seasons*, p. 45.

86. Ibid., p. 56.

87. Ibid., p. 59.

88. Besquette, "School Near Mt. Shasta's Grandeur," p. 31.

CHAPTER FIVE

1. Richard Quantz, in "The Complex Visions of Female Teachers and the Failure of Unionization in the 1930s: An Oral History" (in Altenbaugh, ed., *The Teacher's Voice*, pp. 139–56), argues that teachers understood their work and lives through four main metaphors: the teacher as subordinate authority figure; the school as family; teaching as the natural female avocation; and the dual self. Acceptance of these tropes, he argues, helps explain the failure of Ohio teachers to unionize in the 1930s.

2. In my discussion of these interviews, I provide actual names only when I have used passages from published sources. Otherwise I use pseudonyms. Although I want to honor the lives of these women who gave so generously of their time and memories, I also feel there are issues of confidentiality and interpretation that make the use of pseudonyms advisable. I am aware that my interpretation and analysis of these narratives might not always be accepted by the teachers

themselves, who invoke different discourses from my own academic and theoretical one. And while the accounts they have provided were given freely, I want to protect them and their families.

3. The profiles of the twenty-one retired teachers I interviewed are quite similar in several respects to those of the teachers in the 1900, 1910, and 1920 censuses. By 1900, almost half of the teachers listed in Tulare and Kings Counties in the U.S. manuscript census were born in California, a figure that remained fairly constant through 1920.

The number of teachers from farming families also remains fairly constant between 1900 and 1920, with approximately one-third of all teachers living in farming households. The following table indicates the occupations of heads of households in which Tulare and Kings County teachers resided for the period 1880–1920:

| | Women Teachers | | |
	Farmer	Teacher	Other
1880	12 (71%)	0 (0%)	5 (29%)
1900	33 (38%)	1 (1%)	54 (61%)
1910	71 (33%)	10 (5%)	131 (62%)
1920	123 (34%)	21 (6%)	220 (60%)

| | Men Teachers | | |
	Farmer	Teacher	Other
1880	9 (53%)	0 (0%)	8 (47%)
1900	4 (33%)	0 (0%)	8 (67%)
1910	6 (40%)	0 (0%)	9 (60%)
1920	4 (29%)	7 (21%)	3 (50%)

SOURCE: Bureau of the Census, Manuscript Censuses for 1880, 1900, 1910, and 1920.

NOTE: Does not include teachers who are listed as head of household.

Since both Tulare and Kings Counties are agricultural areas, this picture is hardly surprising, but it does suggest that the picture of rural childhood given in teachers' interviews and in written accounts is representative.

4. I have been influenced in my analysis by a number of approaches to personal narratives, including the work of the Popular Memory Group of the Centre for Contemporary Cultural Studies at the University of Birmingham; Luisa Passerini's studies of the Turin working class; and the ongoing feminist analysis of women's personal narratives, memory, and the construction of subjectivity in a number of fields. For specific examples, see Judith Butler, *Gender Trouble* (New York: Routledge, 1990); Teresa DeLauretis, *Alice Doesn't: Feminism, Semiotics, Cinema* (Bloomington: University of Indiana Press, 1984); Sherna Berger Gluck and Daphne Patai, *Women's Words* (New York: Routledge, 1991); Frigga Haug, *Female Sexualization: A Collective Work of Memory* (London: Verso, 1987); Luisa Passerini, *Fascism in Popular Memory: The Cultural Experience of the Turin Working Class* (Cambridge: Cambridge University Press, 1987); Luisa Passerini, "Women's Personal Narratives: Myths, Experiences, and Emotions," in Personal Narratives Group,

Interpreting Women's Lives, pp. 189-97; and Popular Memory Group, "Popular Memory: Theory, Politics, Method," in *Making Histories*, ed. Richard Johnson, Gregor McLennon, Bill Swartz, and David Sutton (Minneapolis: University of Minnesota Press, 1982), pp. 218-42.

5. Raphael Samuel, "Myth and History: A First Reading," *Oral History* 16, no. 1 (1988): 15.

6. Passerini, "Women's Personal Narratives," p. 197. Passerini's study *Fascism in Popular Memory* provides a valuable example of this approach. In that work, Passerini seeks to uncover the organizing principles that shape memory and consciousness as a collective process. She does so by reading both for structure and for culture; that is, although oral accounts can be sources for "the history of the events of everyday life," they must be analyzed in terms of the structuring processes of memory. Passerini, like the Popular Memory Group, is not primarily concerned with uncovering a fixed truth, a sense of "what really happened," from oral accounts; rather, she sees oral accounts as evidence of mental reconstructions and symbolic orderings of experience. In this, the ways in which individuals employ the structuring devices of narrative to make sense of life experience are of particular importance. Moreover, the processes of memory are not, in her view, just a matter of individual psychology, but in fact are representative and constitutive of class identity. Oral accounts, then, are narratives that reflect collective conventions and so are open to formal and structural analysis. These narratives, she argues, employ a cacophony of discourses, from authoritative hegemonic discourses to collective systems of meaning, what Gramsci would call "common sense." By emphasizing recurrent narrative forms, Passerini seeks to uncover the ways in which people reconcile contradictions, the ways they create meaning from their lives and create a coherent sense of themselves through available forms of discourse. At the same time, she is concerned with the "bad fit" or gap between "preexisting story lines" and individual constructions of the self through memory. As individuals construct their past, they leave unresolved contradictions at precisely those points where authoritative discourse conflicts with collective cultural meanings or an internal oppositional discourse of critique.

7. Bakhtin, *Dialogical Imagination*, pp. 257-366; Gramsci, *Prison Notebooks*, pp. 419-25.

8. Popular Memory Group, "Popular Memory," p. 234.

9. Ibid., p. 228.

10. See in particular the collection of essays in Personal Narratives Group, *Interpreting Women's Lives*; also Gluck and Patai, *Women's Words*.

11. Sandra Frieden, "Transformative Subjectivity in the Writings of Christa Wolf," in Personal Narratives Group, *Interpreting Women's Lives* (Bloomington: Indiana University Press, 1989), p. 172.

12. Personal Narratives Group, *Interpreting Women's Lives*, p. 7.

13. Passerini, *Fascism in Popular Memory*, p. 28.

14. These descriptions of one- and two-room rural schools echo the accounts gathered by Margaret Nelson in Vermont ("Female Schoolteachers as Community Builders," in Altenbaugh, ed., *The Teacher's Voice*, pp. 78-89). Nelson argues that rural schools often served as the focus for community activities in areas with-

out natural centers and that teachers were expected to organize activities such as dances, Christmas parties, and closing ceremonies that would bring local families together. State ratings of teachers in Vermont included the category "relation to the community," and supervisors rated teachers on their enthusiasm. See also the descriptions of local community in Manning, *Hill Country Teacher.*

15. Hazel Fowler, cited in Marie Hayden Miller, ed., "Pride in America" (pamphlet, Hanford, Calif., n.d.), p. 19.

16. Pogue, *Within the Magic Circle*, p. 79.

17. Nelson argues that in Vermont teachers were treated differently also because they were responsible for maintaining a sense of community: "As the rural school gave way to the town school built (both literally and symbolically) on a stronger foundation, the teacher herself ceased to be responsible for maintaining the community. As a young, inexperienced teacher made room for her more professional peers, a teacher no longer had to rely on a 'mantle' of difference to mark her off from other community members. And finally, when she no longer played a central role in a small, ingrown community, the teacher no longer had to be contained [because of the threat she posed to the social order]. If the teacher lost a certain kind of 'respect' in the process, she also gained the freedom to be a normal member of the community and to lead a normal life—even as a single woman" ("Female Schoolteachers as Community Builders," p. 87).

18. Quoted in M. H. Miller, "Pride in America," p. 19.

19. Ibid., p. 9.
20. Ibid., p. 5.
21. Ibid., p. 10.
22. Ibid.
23. Ibid., p. 34.
24. Ibid., p. 10.

25. In his classic study of teachers in the mid-1930s, Howard Beale commented: "Bobbed hair is pretty generally accepted, but one large teacher's agency testified in 1928 that it still advised its applicants to conceal bobbed hair while interviewing certain superintendents" (*Are American Teachers Free?* p. 390).

26. "Editorial," *Sierra Educational News* 20, no. 3 (March 1924): 156.

27. As was true throughout the United States, women made up the overwhelming majority of teachers in these two counties by 1920, when there were only 63 men teachers, as compared to 404 women teachers. Of the 63 men, 49 (78 percent) were married heads of household. This continued a trend from 1880. Twenty-six percent of women teachers listed in the 1920 census lived as boarders (versus 32 percent in 1910), while 10 percent listed themselves as heads of household and 16 percent were married. Although the number of women living independently had increased by 1920, a large number of women teachers— 47 percent of the total—still lived as dependents with parents or other relatives.

28. Quoted in M. H. Miller, "Pride in America," p. 37.

29. Ibid., p. 35.

30. Judith Butler, arguing against essentialist binary conceptions of gender, writes: "The deconstruction of identity is not the deconstruction of politics; rather, it establishes as political the very terms through which identity is articulated. This kind of critique brings into question the foundationalist frame in which feminism as an identity politics has been articulated. The internal paradox of this foundationalism is that it presumes, fixes, and constrains the very

'subjects' that it hopes to represent and liberate. The task here is not to celebrate each and every new possibility, but to redescribe those possibilities that *already* exist, but which exist within cultural domains designated as culturally unintelligible and impossible" (*Gender Trouble*, pp. 148–49).

CHAPTER SIX

1. M. H. Miller, "Pride in America," p. 8.

2. Quoted in ibid., p. 13.

3. For discussions of the role of the woman school administrator, see Tyack and Hansot, "Dream Deferred"; Urban, *Why Teachers Organized.*

4. Lee Richmond's parents settled in the Lucerne District of what was then Tulare County in 1874 when Lee was three. She first attended the one-room Lake school (the same school at which Nannie Davidson taught as a young woman) and later another one-room school, the Paddock school. For secondary schooling, she went to Stockton to the Business and Teachers Training College. She then took and passed the county teachers examination, given at Visalia. See "Mildred Lee Richmond Succumbs in Southland," *Hanford Sentinel*, May 15, 1953.

5. "Informal Dinner," *Hanford Morning Journal*, June 10, 1925.

6. "Miss M. L. Richmond Elected President of CTA Central Section," *Sierra Educational News* 16, no. 1 (1920): 24.

7. Heffernan gave the following tribute: "Miss Richmond is remembered for a tremendous vitality of interest in nature and human beings. She was always willing to give her time unselfishly and is known for a great faith and optimism. She is admired throughout the state" ("Pioneer Educator Honored at Dedication," *Hanford Sentinel*, Aug. 19, 1953).

8. Esta Aulman, "The Value of Demonstration Lessons in Rural Supervision," *California Exchange Bulletin in Rural Education* 1, no. 2 (Jan. 1927): 29–30.

9. Eleanor Russell, "Tulare County's Traveling Exhibit," *Sierra Educational News* 29, no. 6 (June 1933): 32.

10. Turn-of-the-century urban teachers likewise viewed supervision with suspicion; see, for example, Myra Kelly, "The Inquisition of the Teacher," in Hoffman, ed., *Woman's "True" Profession*, pp. 249–54.

11. For more extensive discussions of racial segregation, see, for example, Robert Alvarez, *Familia: Migration and Adaptation in Alta and Baja California, 1800–1975* (Berkeley: University of California Press, 1987); Martha Menchaca and Richard Valencia, "Anglo-Saxon Ideologies in the 1920s and 1930s: Their Impact on the Segregation of Mexican Students in California," *Anthropology and Education Quarterly* 21 (1990): 222–49; Gonzalez, "Segregation of Mexican Children"; and Wollenberg, *All Deliberate Speed.*

12. The practice of creating segregated schools for Mexican-American children was justified on the grounds of assumed differences between "Mexican" and "American" children, including the belief that the presence of Mexican or Mexican-American children would hold back what Carden termed the "regular" children. In the language of state and local officials, "Mexican" included both

Mexican nationals and Mexican Americans. For some state officials, such as William John Cooper, who was state superintendent of public instruction briefly in 1927–28, the education of migrant Mexican-American children was viewed as "only an aspect of a larger social and economic problem," namely, Mexican im-migration. "Whole families cross the border in cheap automobiles and move from district to district and county to county as various crops are ready to har-vest," Cooper wrote. "Early last fall I visited, in company with a county superin-tendent, the schools in several districts where large numbers of Mexicans were working in the fields. I recall schoolrooms provided to house the usual popula-tion overcrowded with the children of these immigrants. These newcomers re-tarded the normal progress of the class because they knew little or no English and were unaccustomed to American ways" (Superintendent of Public Instruc-tion, *Biennial Report, 1927–28*, p. 36). The language he used—"retard[ing] nor-mal progress," "unaccustomed to American ways"—recalls the earlier opposition to these children as "other," as a threat to the "regular" children.

Some local school leaders were more direct in their hostility toward Mexican and Mexican-American children. The superintendent of schools of Needles, writ-ing in the *Sierra Educational News* in 1933, argued that "the Mexican children are usually of inferior intelligence in comparison with the American children." He granted that there were "exceptions" and that some of these children "[are] clean and rate equally with the Americans in intelligence," but he was concerned with the majority of Mexican children, whom he described as "inferior" and "a waste of time" (John Branigan, "Education of Over-Age Mexican Children," *Sierra Educational News* 29, no. 10 [Oct. 1933]: 37).

Another county superintendent of schools reported in 1928, with dismay: "We find in the wealthiest districts the coldest hearts, and a very strong sentiment in opposition to any schooling for these Mexican children. We have begged and talked, and tried to sell to them the conviction that Mexican boys and girls are like any other boys and girls, and are entitled to educational opportunities. We are met with coldness, and almost an opposition to any effort to provide schools for them. The farmers flatly refuse to give a place for their schools and the trustees forbid our using the schoolhouses. Today one trustee told us, 'Here we have twenty-six of our own children in the schoolroom, and we have given up our anterooms to the Mexicans, so that our children have no place to hang their hats. We positively can not take any more, and will do nothing to help take care of them'" (quoted in Superintendent of Public Instruction, *Biennial Report, 1927–28*, p. 37). This trustee is typical in his refusal to spend money on other than "our children" and in his use of terms of inclusion and exclusion, pitting "our own children" against "the Mexicans," who are clearly defined as outside the bounds of community. Similar attitudes were expressed by a white farm manager in the Imperial Valley, who argued: "The Mexicans are a happy people, happier than we are; they don't want responsibility, they want just to float along, sing songs, smoke cigarettes. Education doesn't make them any happier; most of them continue to the same sort of work at the same wages as if they had never attended school. It only makes them dissatisfied, and teaches them to read the wrong kind of literature (IWW) and listen to the wrong kind of talk" (quoted in Taylor, *On the Ground in the Thirties,* p. 10). Here is the familiar stereotype of the "happy" Mexican, who has no need for education, as well as the fear that too much learning can be subversive, leading to their reading "the wrong kind of literature."

13. M. H. Miller, "Pride in America," p. 19.

14. Pogue, *Swift Seasons,* p. 59.

15. "California Valley Oral History Project," A 786, Subject 24, Henry A. Murray Research Center, Radcliffe College, Cambridge, Mass.

16. See the description of segregated schooling for Japanese children in the town of Walnut Grove during the interwar years in Eichiro Azuma, "Japanese Immigrant Farmers and California Alien Land Laws," *California History* 63, no. 1 (spring 1994): 14–29. In 1921, the Japanese Association of San Francisco estimated that there were forty Japanese schools, with 1,900 pupils, in California ("Schoolnotes," *Sierra Educational News* 16, no. 3 [March 1921]: 153).

17. Quoted in M. H. Miller, "Pride in America," p. 24.

18. Marjorie Whited Cummings, *The Tache-Yokuts: Indians of the San Joaquin Valley* (Fresno, Calif.: Pioneer Publishing Co., 1978).

19. Marjorie Whited, "A Tache Pow-Wow," in R. Brown, *History of Kings County,* p. 28.

20. "An educational system based on a traditional type of pedagogy can fulfill its function of inculcation only so long as it addresses itself to students equipped with the linguistic and cultural capital—and the capacity to invest it profitably—which the system presupposes and consecrates without ever expressly demanding it and without methodologically transmitting it" (Pierre Bourdieu and Jean-Claude Passeron, *Reproduction in Education, Society, and Culture* [London: Sage, 1977], p. 99).

21. "California Valley Oral History Project," A 786, Subject 18.

22. Ibid., Subject 21.

23. Quoted in M. H. Miller, "Pride in America," p. 34.

24. Gregory, *American Exodus,* p. 129.

25. Billie Pate interview, "California Odyssey Oral History Project," California State University, Bakersfield.

26. Jewell Egbert interview, "California Odyssey Oral History Project."

27. Cited in Heffernan, "Report of Conference on Education of Children of Seasonal Workers," p. 188.

28. Jewell Potter, "Teacher and Migrant: The Teacher's Problem in a Migratory Situation," *Sierra Educational News* 34, no. 8 (Aug. 1938): 26.

29. Mildred Krohn, "Migratory Home: United Efforts to Find a New Way of Living," *Sierra Educational News* 34, no. 9 (Sept. 1937): 22.

30. Quoted in Gregory, *American Exodus,* p. 166.

31. Ibid., p. 167.

32. Billie Pate interview, "California Odyssey Oral History Project."

33. Christina McLanahan interview, "California Odyssey Oral History Project."

34. Quoted in M. H. Miller, "Pride in America," p. 24.

35. Alvin Laird interview, "California Odyssey Oral History Project."

36. Quoted in Gregory, *American Exodus,* p. 134.

37. Billie Pate interview, "California Odyssey Oral History Project."

38. Vera Criswell interview, "California Odyssey Oral History Project."

39. According to Tyack, Hansot, and Lowe (*Public Schools in Hard Times*, p. 24), teachers in San Jose volunteered 5 percent of their salaries "to provide school children with clothing, blankets, medicine, and food."

40. "Liberty School," *Visalia Times Delta*, Sept. 1, 1966.

41. Helen Ritchie, quoted in M. H. Miller, "Pride in America," p. 9.

42. Quoted in ibid., p. 27.

CHAPTER SEVEN

1. Susan Hartmann, *The Home Front and Beyond* (Boston: Twayne, 1982), p. 21.

2. Doris Weatherford, *American Women and World War II* (New York: Facts on File, 1990), p. 191.

3. On the impact World War II had on women in the United States, see ibid.; Karen Anderson, *Wartime Women: Sex Roles, Family Relations, and the Status of Women During World War II* (Westport, Conn.: Greenwood Press, 1981); and Hartman, *Home Front*.

4. Eunice Hilton, "Professional Women and the War," *School and Society* 63 (Jan. 12, 1946): 35.

5. Probably the best account of the economic and social tensions in the San Joaquin Valley in the 1940s is Walter Goldschmidt's classic *As You Sow: Three Studies in the Social Consequences of Agribusiness* (Glencoe, Ill.: Free Press, 1947). Goldschmidt studied the social and economic structure of three towns, two in Kern County and one, Dinuba, in Tulare County, but did not explore contemporary political conflicts.

6. "Policies of the Tulare County Board of Education," *Tulare County Schools Bulletin* 6, no. 5 (Jan. 1941): 1.

7. Issues of the *Tulare County Schools Bulletin* for the period February–September 1942 are missing from the Tulare County History Room. I have therefore been unable to find a published official reaction to the local removal of Japanese children. For an excellent discussion of the educational experiences of Japanese-American children before and during the war, see Thomas James, *Exile Within* (Cambridge, Mass.: Harvard University Press, 1987).

8. Although the percentage of Japanese Americans in the two counties was small: 1,822 out of a total population of 107,152 (1.7 percent) in Tulare County and 249 of 23,761 (0.6 percent) in Kings County, Japanese settlement tended to be localized, so that some teachers taught large numbers of Japanese children, wheras others had no Japanese students at all.

9. Cited by Masumoto, *Country Voices*, p. 41.

10. Ibid.

11. Ibid., p. 44.

12. Although accounts of the reactions of Japanese Americans vary, the bitterness of this experience is captured in the diary of Hatsuye Egami, who was first moved to the Tulare Assembly Center in Tulare County. "Since yesterday," he

wrote, "we Japanese have ceased to be human beings. We are numbers. We are no longer Egamis, but the number 23324. A tag with that number is on every trunk, suitcase, and bag. Tags, also, on our breasts" (quoted in James, *Exile Within*, p. 25).

13. B. H. Grisener to Walter Dexter, September 2, 1943, Walter Dexter Papers, California State Archives, Sacramento.

14. In November 1942 the California State Liaison Group, whose job it was to coordinate schools and the war effort, met in Fresno. The opening address by John Sexton set out the dominant view that the schools should directly contribute to the war effort by making their facilities available for civil defense, that high schools should actively recruit students to the service, and that both elementary and high schools should encourage children in the conservation of resources, the collection of scrap metal, and the making of victory gardens. Twenty-one demands on the schools were enumerated. A sense of their overall tone can be seen in demand 3: "To utilize existing personnel and facilities for the information and guidance of those seeking their places in the nation's mobilization for victory, and to expand these facilities to expedite the recruiting of both manpower and womanpower to a point where our nation will have an armed force of some ten million armed men in the field and an industrial army of many times this number producing the goods, munitions, and arms necessary to support this army and ourselves for the duration" (John Sexton, "Education and the War," *Sierra Educational News* 38, no. 12 [Dec. 1942]: 9).

15. Ronald Cohen, "Schooling Uncle Sam's Children: Education in the USA, 1941–1945," in *Education and the Second World War: Studies in Schooling and Social Change*, ed. Roy Lowe (London: Falmer Press, 1992), p. 47.

16. Paul McNutt, "Education and War," *Sierra Educational News* 39, no. 1 (Jan. 1943): 11.

17. "Army of Education," *Tulare County Schools Bulletin* 8, no. 1 (Sept. 1942).

18. Erma Rambo to Joseph Eastman, Director, Office of Defense Transportation, February 20, 1943, Tulare County File, Subject File School Districts, Department of Education, California State Archives.

19. Clara Evers, "Young Americans Club," *Sierra Educational News* 44, no. 7 (Jan. 1948): 13–14.

20. Evers, "Young Americans Club," p. 14.

21. By 1951, only 8 percent of city school districts nationwide absolutely refused to hire married women (U.S. Women's Bureau, *Status of Women in the United States, 1953*, Women's Bureau Bulletin No. 249 [Washington, D.C.: GPO, 1953], pp. 16–17).

22. *Tulare County Schools Bulletin* 8, no. 2 (Jan. 1943).

23. Katherine Peavy, "Letter to the Editor," *Sierra Educational News* 42, no. 3 (March 1946): 37.

24. *Tulare County Schools Bulletin* 9, no. 6 (Feb. 1944).

25. In the fall of 1941, for example, the U.S. Office of Education produced a series of twenty-four thirty-minute radio programs called "Americans All . . . Immigrants All" presenting "specific information concerning the part which has been played by the various culture groups in American life and dramatiz[ing] their triumphs and achievements" (*Tulare County Schools Bulletin* 6, no. 8 (Sept.

1941). In the summer of 1942 Dean Grayson Kefauver of the Stanford School of Education led the Stanford Workshop on Education for War and Peace. In the publication *Education for War and Peace* that emerged from this conference the themes of democracy, tolerance, and inclusion were highlighted. A section on building character and the need for moral integrity, for example, advocated that teachers contribute to the achievement of worldwide democratic values by inspiring in students attitudes such as "(a) sensitivity to the interests, needs, and problems of other people; (b) a feeling that every person, regardless of race or nationality, has inherent worth; (c) respect for the worth-while achievements of all peoples and a feeling of membership in a world culture; (d) a fair, open-minded tolerance of other peoples' viewpoints and interpretations; (e) a willingness to accept the compromises and make the sacrifices which may be necessary in order to further a better world society; (f) a spirit of co-operation, responsibility, and loyalty toward individuals and organizations working for a world structure for peace; and (g) faith in education and the conference method as a means of bringing about understandings which will lead to the settling of differences and the formulation of constructive policies" (p. 31). This publication is striking in its acknowledgment of prejudice: "It would be stupid to talk about the extension of democratic ideals upon a world-wide basis and to ignore the more glaring evidences of our failures to put them into practice in this country, for the louder we talk the more conspicuous becomes our inconsistency. We have within our borders minority and race problems that have for too long been neglected, and they weaken our power as advocates of equality of opportunity" (ibid.). Ironically and significantly, this conference took place only a few months after the removal of West Coast Japanese Americans to internment camps in the spring of 1942. Despite its antiracist stance, *Education for War and Peace* made no mention of the removal of Japanese-American children from the schools.

26. Typical is Heffernan's 1943 "Greeting" to California elementary school principals: "Many school principals have seen in the war situation a new approach to the achievements of educational purposes of enduring value. In the instructional program, cultures of the various United Nations have been emphasized in order that children of elementary school age would understand why the aspirations of free men serve to unite people of different racial and cultural heritage in a stupendous global effort" (Helen Heffernan Papers, California State Archives, Sacramento).

27. In 1943 Trott had taken leave from his duties in Tulare County to help Heffernan, in fulfillment of the Lanham Act, create nursery schools for the children of mothers working in the California defense industry. When Heffernan was attacked that year in Senate hearings by conservative state senators, Trott testified on her behalf. At the same time, he distanced himself from her; in a letter to Walter Dexter, state superintendent of public instruction, Trott wrote: "The program of elementary education in the state and Miss Heffernan's program are not synonymous. To defend one is not necessarily to defend the other. Therefore, no useful purpose is served by defending Miss Heffernan in order to defend California's elementary schools. In fact, each community will make a better defense of its program if I say this to you in spite of the fact that I told the

Senate Committee, under oath, that I subscribe to Miss Heffernan's point of view about education. There is no inconsistency here." Trott concluded his letter by asking for a job with the state, noting that although he didn't have a graduate degree, he had a good deal of school experience (Fred Trott to Walter Dexter, Nov. 9, 1943, Walter Dexter Papers). Nothing seems to have come of this suggestion. In 1944 Trott defended Heffernan against Swan's continued attacks and his call for "fundamentals" in education. As Trott wrote to Dexter on January 24, 1944: "And what will the state-wide test in the 'Fundamentals' prove? In Tulare County it will prove that the youngsters have never been 'up to grade,' whatever that means, in the past ten years. The county has never been up to grade on tests that test simple literacy since the County broadened its teaching objectives to include more than simple literacy, enforced its compulsory education laws and kept youngsters in school who did not learn readily."

28. W. Wesley La Rue, "Returning Japanese," *Sierra Educational News* 41, no. 3 (March 1945): 29.

29. Lloyd Diggs to Walter Dexter, April 4, 1945, Walter Dexter Papers.

30. Mabel Crumby, "Children Are Returning," *Sierra Educational News* 41, no. 4 (April 1945): 23.

31. W. Henry Cooke, "Japanese Americans," *Sierra Educational News* 41, no. 10 (Nov. 1945): 18.

32. R. Priscilla Beattie and Roy Arnheim, "Japanese Americans: These Are America's Children," *Sierra Educational News* 41, no. 10 (Nov. 1945): 39.

33. *Tulare County Schools Bulletin* 11, no. 2 (Oct. 1945).

34. *Tulare County Schools Bulletin* 11, no. 4 (Dec. 1945).

35. *Tulare County Schools Bulletin* 11, no. 6 (Feb. 1946).

36. *Tulare County Schools Bulletin* 11, no. 4 (Dec. 1945).

37. *Tulare County Schools Bulletin* 13, no. 2 (Oct. 1947).

38. See Ellen Schrecker, *No Ivory Tower* (New York: Basic Books, 1989), for a discussion of the effects of anticommunism on higher education in this period.

39. The most vitriolic attacks were those of Aaron Sargent, head of the California Society of the Sons of the American Revolution; see the correspondence of Helen Heffernan in the Department of Education General Correspondence Files, California State Archives, Sacramento. Typical of the anticommunist tone of these years is a public service advertisement placed by the Public Policy Committee of the Advertising Council in the *Sierra Educational News* in 1949 advertising a free booklet called "The Miracle of America." The copy of the advertisement was a letter purportedly directed to Soviet teachers and setting out the advantages of capitalism over communism. Typical in this advertisement is the conflation of democracy ("free people, governing themselves and spurred by ambition . . . ") and capitalism: "Which system—yours or ours—has mass-produced for more people the daily benefits of such inventions as the automobile, telephone, radio, refrigeration, central heating, modern plumbing and better farm machinery? The world knows that it is *our* system!" ("Dear Soviet Teachers" [advertisement], *Sierra Educational News* 45, no. 5 [May 1949]: 19).

40. *Tulare County Schools Bulletin* 13, no. 9 (May 1948).

41. *Tulare County Schools Bulletin* 14, no. 6 (May 1949).

42. As Wayne Booth (*Old Country School*, p. 239) has pointed out, the pace of school consolidation decreased markedly in the Midwest in the mid-1920s, even though improvements in transportation made consolidation easier and safer.

43. Paul Hanna, "Proposal for a Rural Education Institute" (1944), Paul Hanna Papers, Hoover Institution on War, Revolution and Peace, Stanford.

44. *Tulare County Schools Bulletin* 10, no. 5 (Jan. 1945).

45. "Optional Reorganization of School Districts," *Sierra Educational News* 44, no. 2 (Feb. 1948): 6–7.

46. C. O. Fitzwater, *School District Reorganization* (Washington, D.C.: U.S. Department of Health, Education, and Welfare, 1957).

47. Robert Alford, "School District Reorganization and Community Integration," *Educational Review* 30, no. 4 (fall 1960): 350–71.

48. Jonathan Sher and Rachel Tompkins, "Economy, Efficiency, and Equality: The Myth of Rural School and District Consolidation," in *Education in Rural America*, ed. Jonathan Sher (Boulder, Colo.: Westview Press, 1977), p. 164. By the 1970s, school consolidation was being reexamined with a new sensitivity to issues of community influence. This more critical view of consolidation reflected the social critiques of the 1960s, when the bureaucratic and factorylike quality of much mass education came increasingly under attack. School consolidation was seen by some critics as part of the "urbanization" of rural schools, with the attendant evils of impersonal and regimented control of children and teachers and a lack of responsiveness to community needs. Despite these criticisms, however, the movement toward larger rural districts has continued.

49. *Tulare County Schools Bulletin* 12, no. 1 (Jan. 1947).

50. Sometimes small rural schools remained open after unification, particularly in the case of isolated mountain communities in the Sierra Nevada in Tulare County. A handful still remain.

51. The numbers of principals of rural schools in Tulare and Kings Counties for the period 1930–50, broken down by gender, are as follows:

	1-teacher schools		2-teacher schools		3-teacher schools	
	Tulare	Kings	Tulare	Kings	Tulare	Kings
1930						
Schools	32	9	38	15	13	1
Women	32	9	37	14	10	1
Men	0	0	1	1	3	0
1940						
Schools	17	7	27	11	16	2
Women	17	7	22	9	8	2
Men	0	0	5	2	8	0
1950						
Schools	6	3	14	1	14	2
Women	6	3	12	1	6	0
Men	0	0	2	0	8	2

SOURCE: School Directories of Tulare and Kings Counties for 1930, 1940, and 1950.

52. *Tulare County Schools Bulletin* 11, no. 3 (Nov. 1945).

53. Cecilia O'Neill, "Equal Rights: A Basic Principle," *Sierra Educational News* 40, no. 5 (May 1944): 33–34; Wickliffe Stack, "Full Citizenship: A Goal of Education," *Sierra Educational News* 42, no. 1 (Jan. 1946): 18–20.

54. *Report of the California Commission for the Study of Educational Problems* (Sacramento: California State Printing Office, 1931), p. 111.

55. Ducelia McLeod Cobb, "Teacher Shortage," *Sierra Educational News* 41, no. 10 (Nov. 1945): 44.

56. Alden Naud, "Teacher Shortage," *Sierra Educational News* 42, no. 2 (Feb. 1946): 21.

57. Albert R. Lang, "California Elementary School Teaching for Young Californians," *Sierra Educational News* 42, no. 9 (Sept. 1946): 25.

58. Ibid., p. 26.

59. Quoted in M. H. Miller, "Pride in America," p. 6.

CONCLUSION

1. Haug, *Female Sexualization*, p. 41.

2. Di Leonardo, *Varieties of Ethnic Experience*, p. 230.

3. Carolyn Steedman, *Landscape for a Good Woman* (New Brunswick, N.J.: Rutgers University Press, 1987), p. 5.

4. See as representative Alan Bloom, *The Closing of the American Mind* (New York: Simon & Schuster, 1987); E. D. Hirsch, *Cultural Literacy* (Boston: Houghton Mifflin, 1987); and Diane Ravitch and Chester Finn, *What Do Our 17-Year-Olds Know?* (New York: Harper & Row, 1988).

5. As Frigga Haug puts it: "The day-to-day struggle over the hearts and minds of human subjects is located not only within social structures, the pre-given forms into which individuals work themselves, but also in the *process* whereby they perceive any given situation, approve or validate it, assess its goals as proper and worthy, repugnant or reprehensible" (*Female Sexualization*, p. 41).

BIBLIOGRAPHY

GOVERNMENT DOCUMENTS AND PUBLICATIONS

California. Board of Education. *Biennial Report,* 1913/14–1925/26. Sacramento: State Printing Office.

———. *Report of the Bureau for Elementary Education,* 1946–50. Sacramento: State Printing Office.

———. *Report of the California Commission for the Study of Educational Problems.* Sacramento: California State Printing Office, 1931.

———. *Report of the Commissioner of Elementary Schools,* 1913/14–1925/26. Sacramento: State Printing Office.

———. *Report of the Commissioner of Rural Education,* 1927–31. Sacramento: State Printing Office.

———. *Report of the Division of Elementary and Rural Schools,* 1931–45. Sacramento: State Printing Office.

California. Department of Education. *California Blue Bulletin.* Vols. 1–7: 1915–21. Sacramento: State Printing Office.

———. *California Exchange Bulletin in Rural Education.* Vols. 1–2: 1926–27. Sacramento: State Printing Office.

California. Superintendent of Public Instruction. *Biennial Report,* 1858/59–1930/31. Sacramento: State Printing Office.

United States. Bureau of the Census. *Ninth Census of the United Sates, 1870.* Washington, D.C.: U.S. Government Printing Office, 1873.

———. *Tenth Census of the United States, 1880.* Washington, D.C.: U.S. Government Printing Office, 1883.

———. *Eleventh Census of the United States, 1890.* Washington, D.C.: U.S. Government Printing Office, 1893.

———. *Twelfth Census of the United States, 1900.* Washington, D.C.: U.S. Government Printing Office, 1903.

———. *Thirteenth Census of the United States, 1910.* Vols. 1–3. Washington, D.C.: U.S. Government Printing Office, 1913.

————. *Thirteenth Census of the United States, 1910.* Vol 4: *Population, Occupation Statistics.* Washington, D.C.: Government Printing Office, 1914.

————. *Fourteenth Census of the United States, 1920.* Washington, D.C.: U.S. Government Printing Office, 1923.

————. *Statistics of Women and Work.* Washington, D.C.: Government Printing Office, 1907.

United States. Women's Bureau. *Status of Women in the United States, 1953.* Women's Bureau Bulletin No. 249. Washington D.C.: Government Printing Office, 1953.

TULARE AND KINGS COUNTY SCHOOL
REPORTS AND MANUALS

Kings County School Manual, 1894–1908.
Kings County Schools Directory, 1910–50.
Tulare County School Manual, 1911–42.
Tulare County Schools Bulletin, 1935–50.
Tulare County Schools Directory, 1910–50.

MANUSCRIPT COLLECTIONS

Many of the materials used in this study are in small and sometimes uncatalogued collections. I relied most heavily on the materials in the Annie Mitchell History Room [AMHR] at the Tulare County Public Library in Visalia and the Local History Collection at the Kings County Public Library in Hanford. I have cited unpublished manuscripts in these collections by author.

Allensworth Collection, California State Department of Parks and Recreation, Sacramento

Annie K. Bidwell Papers, Bancroft Library, University of California, Berkeley

California Odyssey Oral History Project, California State University, Bakersfield

California Valley Oral History Project, Henry A. Murray Research Center, Radcliffe College, Cambridge, Mass.

Georgiana Carden Papers, Bancroft Library, University of California, Berkeley

The Collegian, Special Collections, California State University, Fresno

Department of Education General Correspondence Files, California State Archives, Sacramento

Walter Dexter Papers, California State Archives, Sacramento

Paul Hanna Papers, Hoover Institution on War, Revolution, and Peace, Stanford University, Stanford

Helen Heffernan Papers, California State Archives, Sacramento

Helen Heffernan Papers, Special Collections, Tomas Rivera Libary, University of California at Riverside

Vierling Kersey Papers, California State Archives, Sacramento

Oakland Schoolwomen's Club Records, 1912–25, Holt Atherton Department of Special Collections, University of the Pacific, Stockton, Calif.

The Prospect, Special Collections, California State University, Fresno
Chester Rowell Papers, Bancroft Library, University of California, Berkeley
George Stewart Papers, California State Library, Sacramento
Tulare County, Department of Education Files, California State Archives, Sacramento

BOOKS AND ARTICLES

A.H.C. "Getting Together." *Sierra Educational News* 15, no. 1 (Jan. 1919): 13–14.

Alexander, Carter. *Some Present Aspects of the Work of Teachers' Voluntary Associations*. New York: Teachers College, Columbia University, 1910.

Alford, Robert. "School District Reorganization and Community Integration." *Educational Review* 30, no. 4 (fall 1960): 350–71.

Allen, Charles, and Ruth Royce. *Historical Sketch of the State Normal School at San Jose, California*. Sacramento: State Printing Office, 1889.

Allmendinger, David. "Mount Holyoke Students Encounter the Need for Life Planning, 1837–1850." *History of Education Quarterly* 19, no. 1 (spring 1979): 27–46.

Almack, John. "The Supervisory Program." *California Exchange Bulletin in Rural Education* 1, no. 3 (March 1927): 12–25.

Alvarez, Robert. *Familia: Migration and Adaptation in Alta and Baja California, 1800–1975*. Berkeley: University of California Press, 1987.

Ames, Kate. "Report on State Teachers' Reading Course." *Western Journal of Education* 4, no. 5 (June 1906): 214–17.

———. "Some Vital School Questions: The Woman Movement and Woman's Position in the School System." *Overland Monthly* 52 (Sept. 1908): 243–46.

Anderson, Karen. *Wartime Women: Sex Roles, Family Relations, and the Status of Women During World War II*. Westport, Conn.: Greenwood Press, 1981.

Armitage, Susan. "Women and Men in Western History: A Stereotypical Vision." *Western Historical Quarterly* 16 (Oct. 1985): 381–95.

Armitage, Susan, and Elizabeth Jameson, eds. *The Women's West*. Norman: University of Oklahoma Press, 1987.

Armour, Mary. "History of the Tagus Ranch School." Typescript, n.d.; Annie Mitchell History Room, Tulare County Public Library, Visalia, Calif.

Arnold, Mary Ellicott, and Mabel Reed. *In the Land of the Grasshopper's Song*. Lincoln: University of Nebraska Press, 1957.

Aulman, Esta. "The Value of Demonstration Lessons in Rural Supervision." *California Exchange Bulletin in Rural Education* 1, no. 2 (Jan. 1927): 29–30.

Averill, Frances. "Supervision of Schools for Children of Seasonal Workers." *Western Journal of Education* 35, no. 9 (Sept. 1929): 8–10.

Azuma, Eichiro. "Japanese Immigrant Farmers and California Alien Land Laws." *California History* 63, no. 1 (spring 1994): 14–29.

Bailey, Liberty Hyde. *The Country Life Movement in the United States*. New York: Macmillan, 1911.

Bailey, Stella. "Education in Tulare County, California, 1852–1910." M.A. thesis, Fresno State College, 1962.

Baker, Paula. "The Domestication of Politics: Women and American Political Society, 1780–1920." *American Historical Review* 89, no. 3 (June 1984): 620–47.

Bakhtin, Mikhail. *The Dialogical Imagination.* Austin: University of Texas Press, 1984.

Barr, James A. "The Reasons Why Men Are Leaving School Work and Some Remedies for the Same." *California Teachers Quarterly* 1, no. 3 (June 1907): 16–31.

Beale, Howard. *Are American Teachers Free?* New York: Charles Scribner's Sons, 1936.

Beasley, Delilah. *Negro Trailblazers of California.* Los Angeles: Times Mirror Printing and Binding House, 1919.

Beattie, R. Priscilla, and Roy Arnheim. "Japanese Americans: These Are America's Children." *Sierra Educational News* 41, no. 10 (Nov. 1945): 39–41.

Bernard, Richard, and Maris Vinovskis. "The Female School Teacher in Ante-Bellum Massachusetts." *Journal of Social History* 3 (1977): 332–45.

Besquette, Ethel. "Pleasant Valley School." In *Yes, I'm a Pioneer Teacher,* edited by Laura Esta Settle, pp. 89–100. Sacramento: California Retired Teachers Association, 1938.

———. "School Near Mt. Shasta's Grandeur." In *Pages from the Past,* edited by Laura Esta Settle, pp. 28–35. Sacramento: California Retired Teachers Association, 1940.

Biklen, Sari Knopp. *School Work.* New York: Teachers College Press, 1995.

Bloom, Alan. *The Closing of the American Mind.* New York: Simon & Schuster, 1987.

Blount, Jackie. "Manly Men and Womanly Women: Deviance, Gender Role Polarization, and the Shift in Women's School Employment, 1900–1976." *Harvard Educational Review* 66, no. 2 (1996): 318–38.

Boone, Richard. "The Choice of a Life Work—Teaching as a Career." *Sierra Educational News* 15, no. 10 (Dec. 1919): 660–61.

———. *A History of Educational Organization in California.* San Jose: California Teachers Association, 1926.

Bourdieu, Pierre, and Jean-Claude Passeron. *Reproduction in Education, Society, and Culture.* London: Sage, 1977.

Bowles, Samuel, and Herbert Gintis. *Schooling in Capitalist America.* New York: Basic Books, 1976.

Branigan, John. "Education of Over-Age Mexican Children." *Sierra Educational News* 29, no. 10 (Oct. 1933): 37–39.

Bringhurst, Newell. "The Ku Klux Klan in Visalia, Tulare County, California." Typescript, n.d.; Annie Mitchell History Room, Tulare County Public Library, Visalia, Calif.

Brown, James L. *The Mussel Slough Tragedy.* Hanford, Calif., 1980.

Brown, Robert. *History of Kings County.* Hanford, Calif.: S. H. Cawston, 1940.

Buckman, J. E. "Letters from Your County Superintendents." *Educational Digest* 1, no. 1 (Sept. 1914): 26.

Burk, Frederick. "Excess Supervision." *Sierra Educational News* 18, no. 3 (March 1922): 120–21.

———. *Guild Service and Ritual of Graduation.* Sacramento: California State Printing Office, 1914.

———. "The Withered Heart of the School." *Educational Review* 34 (1907): 448–56.

Butchart, Ronald. *Northern Schools, Southern Blacks, and Reconstruction.* Westport, Conn.: Greenwood Press, 1980.

Butler, Judith. *Gender Trouble.* New York: Routledge, 1990.

Callahan, Raymond. *Education and the Cult of Efficiency.* Chicago: University of Chicago Press, 1960.

Carter, Patricia. "Becoming the 'New Women': The Equal Rights Campaigns of New York City Schoolteachers, 1900–1920." In *The Teacher's Voice,* edited by Richard Altenbaugh, pp. 40–59. London: Falmer Press, 1992.

———. "The Social Status of Women Teachers in the Early Twentieth Century." In *The Teacher's Voice,* edited by Richard Altenbaugh, pp. 127–38. London: Falmer Press, 1992.

Carter, Susan. "Incentives and Rewards to Teaching." In *America's Teachers: Histories of a Profession at Work,* edited by Donald Warren, pp. 49–63. New York: Macmillan, 1989.

———. "Occupational Segregation, Teachers' Wages, and American Economic History." *Journal of Economic History* 46, no. 2 (June 1986): 373–83.

Chadwick, F. E. "The Woman Peril in American Education." *Educational Review* 47, no. 9 (1914): 109, 115–16.

Chase, Amanda. *Some California School Beginnings.* Sacramento: California Retired Teachers Association, 1936.

Chase, Phyllis McGruder. "African-American Teachers in Buffalo: The First One Hundred Years." In *The Teacher's Voice,* edited by Richard Altenbaugh, pp. 65–77. London: Falmer Press, 1992.

Church, Virginia. *Teachers Are People: Being the Lyrics of Virginia Church.* Hollywood, Calif.: David Graham Fischer Co., 1929.

Clark, Edward. *Sex in Education.* New York: Arno Press, [1873] 1972.

Clark, Septima. *Echo in My Soul.* New York: E. P. Dutton, 1962.

Clifford, Geraldine. "Eve: Redeemed by Education and Teaching School." *History of Education Quarterly* 21, no. 4 (winter 1981): 479–92.

———. "'Lady Teachers' and the Politics of Teaching in the United States, 1850–1930." In *Teachers: The Culture and Politics of Work,* edited by Martin Lawn and Gerald Grace, pp. 3–30. London: Falmer Press, 1987.

———. "Marry, Stitch, Die, or Do Worse." In *Work, Youth, and Schooling,* edited by Harvey Kantor and David Tyack, pp. 223–68. Stanford: Stanford University Press, 1982.

Cloud, Roy. *Education in California.* Stanford: Stanford University Press, 1952.

Cobb, Ducelia McLeod. "Teacher Shortage." *Sierra Educational News* 41, no. 10 (Nov. 1945): 44–45.

Cochrane, Ione. "Samuel Davies Cochrane Family." Typescript, n.d.; Annie Mitchell History Room, Tulare County Public Library, Visalia, Calif.

Coddington, Katherine. "King of the Radicals." M.A. thesis, San Francisco State University, 1985.

Cody, Evon, and Jay Clark. *Kings County: A Short History.* Hanford, Calif.: Star Stenographic Service, 1987.

Coffman, Lotus. *The Social Composition of the Teaching Population.* New York: Teachers College, Columbia University, 1911.

Cohen, Ronald. "Schooling Uncle Sam's Children: Education in the USA, 1941–1945." In *Education and the Second World War: Studies in Schooling and Social Change,* edited by Roy Lowe, pp. 47–58. London: Falmer Press, 1992.

Cohn, Sam. "Why Supervision of Rural Schools?" *Sierra Educational News* 20, no. 2 (Feb. 1924): 305–7.

Coldwell, Clara. "Teaching the Children of Seasonal Workers." *California Exchange Bulletin in Rural Education* 1, no. 2 (Jan. 1927): 59–60.

Cooke, W. Henry. "Japanese Americans." *Sierra Educational News* 41, no. 10 (Nov. 1945): 18.

Cordier, Mary. *Schoolwomen of the Prairies and Plains.* Albuquerque: University of New Mexico Press, 1992.

Cott, Nancy. *The Bonds of Womanhood.* New Haven: Yale University Press, 1977.

———. *The Grounding of Modern Feminism.* New Haven: Yale University Press, 1987.

Counts, George. *The American Road to Culture.* New York: Arno Press, [1930] 1971.

———. *Dare the Schools Build a New Social Order?* New York: Arno Press, [1934] 1969.

Cremin, Lawrence. *The Transformation of the School.* New York: Random House, 1961.

Crockett, Norman. *The Black Towns.* Lawrence: University of Kansas Press, 1979.

Crumby, Mabel. "Children Are Returning." *Sierra Educational News* 41, no. 4 (April 1945): 23.

Cubberley, Ellwood. "Editorial." *Western Journal of Education* 16, no. 1 (Jan. 1908): 10.

———. "Improving County School Supervision." *Sierra Educational News* 5, no. 2 (Feb. 1909): 29–30.

———. *Rural Life and Education: A Study of the Rural School Problem as a Phase of the Rural Life Problem.* Boston: Houghton Mifflin, 1914.

Cummings, Marjorie Whited. *The Tache-Yokuts: Indians of the San Joaquin Valley.* Fresno, Calif.: Pioneer Publishing Co., 1978.

Curry, Catherine Ann. "Shaping Young San Franciscans: Public and Catholic Schools in San Francisco, 1851–1906." Ph.D. diss., Graduate Theological Union, Berkeley, 1987.

Curtis, Bruce. *Building the Educational State: Canada West, 1836–71.* Lewes, Sussex: Falmer Press, 1988.

———. *True Government by Choice Men?* Toronto: University of Toronto Press, 1992.

Daniel, Cletus. *Bitter Harvest: A History of California Farm Workers, 1870–1941.* Ithaca: Cornell University Press, 1981.

Danylewycz, Marta, and Alison Prentice. "Teachers, Gender, and Bureaucratizing School Systems in Nineteenth-Century Montreal and Toronto." *History of Education Quarterly* 24, no. 1 (spring 1984): 75–99.

———. "Teachers' Work: Changing Patterns and Perceptions in the Emerging

School Systems of Nineteenth- and Early-Twentieth-Century Central Canada." In *Women Who Taught*, edited by Alison Prentice and Marjorie Theobald, pp. 136–59. Toronto: University of Toronto Press, 1990.

Daughenbaugh, Leonard. "On Top of the World: Anna Mills Johnston's Ascent of Mt. Whitney." *California History* 64, no. 1 (winter 1985): 42–51.

Davis, W. N. "History of the Dinuba Elementary Schools, 1889–1961." Privately published, 1961.

Dearborn, Ned. *The Oswego Movement in American Education*. New York: Teachers College Press, 1925.

DeLauretis, Teresa. *Alice Doesn't: Feminism, Semiotics, Cinema*. Bloomington: University of Indiana Press, 1984.

Dewey, Evelyn. *New Schools for Old: The Regeneration of the Porter School*. New York: Dutton, 1919.

Di Leonardo, Micaela. *Varieties of Ethnic Experience*. Ithaca: Cornell University Press, 1984.

Doctor, Joe. "A Study of the Historical and Architectural Resources of Tulare County." Typescript, n.d.; Annie Mitchell History Room, Tulare County Public Library, Visalia, Calif.

Doherty, Robert E. "Tempest on the Hudson: The Struggle for 'Equal Pay for Equal Work' in the New York City Public Schools, 1907–1911." *History of Education Quarterly* 19, no. 4 (winter 1979): 413–34.

Donovan, Frances. *The Schoolma'am*. New York: Frederick A. Stokes, 1938.

Driggers, Roy. "Around the State—Tulare County." *Sierra Educational News* 33, no. 3 (March 1937): 27.

Dublin, Tom. *Women at Work*. New York: Columbia University Press, 1979.

DuBois, Ellen, Mary Jo Buhle, Temma Kaplan, Gerda Lerner, and Carroll Smith-Rosenberg. "Politics and Culture in Women's History." *Feminist Studies* 6 (spring 1980): 28–36.

Dunn, Fannie, and Marcia Everett. *Four Years in a Country School*. New York: Teachers College, Columbia University, 1926.

Elliott, Wallace. *A History of Tulare County*. Fresno, Calif.: California History Books, [1883] 1975.

Elsbree, Willard. *The American Teacher*. New York: American Book Company, 1939.

Evers, Clara. "Young Americans Club." *Sierra Educational News* 44, no. 7 (Jan. 1948): 13–14.

Ewing, Stephen. "Blue Laws for Teachers." *Harper's*, Feb. 1928, pp. 328–31.

Falk, Charles. *The Development and Organization of Education in California*. New York: Harcourt, Brace & World, 1968.

Ferrier, William. *Ninety Years of Education in California, 1846–1936*. Berkeley: Sather Gate Bookshop, 1937.

Fields, Mamie, and Karen Fields. *Lemon Swamp and Other Places: A Carolina Memoir*. New York: Free Press, 1983.

Fitts, Deborah. "Una and the Lion: The Feminization of District School Teaching and Its Effects on the Roles of Students and Teachers in Nineteenth-Century Massachusetts." In *Regulated Children/Liberated Children: Education in*

Psychohistorical Perspective, edited by Barbara Finkelstein, pp. 140–57. New York: Psychohistory Books, 1979.

Fitzwater, C. O. *School District Reorganization.* Washington, D.C.: U.S. Department of Health, Education, and Welfare, 1957.

Foner, Philip, and Josephine Pacheco. *Three Who Dared.* Westport, Conn.: Greenwood Press, 1984.

Footman, Meta Neal. "The Rural Supervisor—A Rejoinder." *Sierra Educational News* 18, no. 6 (June 1922): 339–40.

Forten, Charlotte. *The Journal of Charlotte Forten.* New York: W. W. Norton, 1981.

Foster, Michele. "Othermothers: Exploring the Educational Philosophy of Black American Women Teachers." In *Feminism and Social Justice in Education,* edited by Madeleine Arnot and Kathleen Weiler, pp. 101–23. London: Falmer Press, 1993.

Frankenberg, Ruth. *White Women, Race Matters: The Social Construction of Whiteness.* Minneapolis: University of Minnesota Press, 1993.

Fraser, James. "Agents of Democracy: Urban Elementary School Teachers and the Conditions of Teaching." In *American Teachers: Histories of a Profession at Work,* edited by Donald Warren, pp. 118–56. New York: Macmillan, 1989.

Freedman, Estelle. "Separatism as Strategy: Female Institution Building and American Feminism, 1870–1930." *Feminist Studies* 5 (fall 1979): 512–29.

Frieden, Sandra. "Transformative Subjectivity in the Writings of Christa Wolf." In Personal Narratives Group, *Interpreting Women's Lives,* pp. 172–88. Bloomington: Indiana University Press, 1989.

Frost, A. W. "Visalia Select Seminary." Typescript, 1941; Annie Mitchell History Room, Tulare County Public Library, Visalia, Calif.

Fuller, Wayne. *The Old Country School.* Chicago: University of Chicago Press, 1982.

Gardner, Annabel Ross. *Children and Challenges: Recollections of a Life of Teaching and Learning.* Palo Alto: Walter Hays School PTA, 1976.

Geertz, Clifford. *Works and Lives: The Anthropologist as Author.* Stanford: Stanford University Press, 1988.

Gilligan, Carol. *In a Different Voice.* Cambridge, Mass.: Harvard University Press, 1982.

Gluck, Sherna Berger, and Daphne Patai. *Women's Words.* New York: Routledge, 1991.

Goldschmidt, Walter. *As You Sow: Three Studies in the Social Consequences of Agribusiness.* Glencoe, Ill.: Free Press, 1947.

Gonzalez, Gilbert. "Segregation of Mexican Children in a Southern California City: The Legacy of Expansionism and the American Southwest." *Western Historical Quarterly* 16 (Jan. 1985): 55–76.

Gordon, Linda. "Response to Scott." *Signs* 15, no. 4 (summer 1990): 852–53.

———, ed. *Women, the State, and Welfare.* Madison: University of Wisconsin Press, 1990.

Gramsci, Antonio. *Selections from the Prison Notebooks.* New York: Monthly Review Press, 1971.

Gregory, James. *American Exodus.* New York: Oxford University Press, 1988.

Gribskov, Margaret. "Feminization and the Woman School Administrator." In

Women and Educational Leadership, edited by Sari Biklen and Marilyn Brannigan, pp. 77–92. Lexington, Mass.: Lexington Books, 1980.

Grumet, Madeleine. *Bitter Milk*. Albany: State University of New York Press, 1988.

———. "Pedagogy for Patriarchy: The Feminization of Teaching." *Interchange* 12, nos. 1–2 (1981): 165–84.

Guino, J. M. *Historical Biographical Record of Coast Counties, California*. San Jose, 1904.

Gulliford, Andrew. *America's Country Schools*. Washington, D.C.: Preservation Press, 1984.

Hall, Catherine. "Missionary Stories: Gender and Ethnicity in England in the 1830s and 1840s." In *Cultural Studies*, edited by L. Grossberg, C. Nelson, and P. Treichler, pp. 240–76. New York: Routledge, 1992.

Hall, Tom. "California Populism at the Grass-Roots: The Case of Tulare County, 1892." *Southern California Quarterly* 49, no. 2 (June 1967): 193–204.

Hall, Waverly Dean. "History of the Organization and Administration of Public Schools in Tulare County, California, 1852–1970." Ed.D. diss., University of Southern California, 1972.

Harding, Sandra. *The Science Question in Feminism*. Ithaca: Cornell University Press, 1986.

Harris, Barbara. *Beyond Her Sphere: Women and Professions in American History*. Westport, Conn.: Greenwood Press, 1978.

Hartman, Beulah M. "California Rural Supervisors Hold Significant Convention at Lake Tahoe, October 4th to 8th." *California Exchange Bulletin in Rural Education* 1, no. 1 (Nov. 1926): 33.

Hartmann, Susan. *The Home Front and Beyond*. Boston: Twayne, 1982.

Harvey, Marie Turner. "The Porter School: A New Vision of the Rural School in Country Life." In *Proceedings of the National Education Association, 1924*, pp. 674–80. Washington, D.C.: NEA, 1924.

Haug, Frigga. *Female Sexualization: A Collective Work of Memory*. London: Verso, 1987.

Heffernan, Helen. "Experimental Attempts to Improve Instruction in Rural Schools." *Western Journal of Education* 37, no. 1 (Jan. 1929): 9–10.

———. "Group Versus Grade Organization." *Western Journal of Education* 37, no. 6 (June 1929): 7–8.

———. "Introduction." In *Organization of Learning Experiences in Small Rural Schools*, pp. ii–iv. Sacramento: California School Supervisors Association, Northern Section, 1938.

———. "Report of Conference on Education of Children of Seasonal Workers—Fresno State College, December 9–10, 1938." *California Journal of Elementary Education* 7, no. 3 (Feb. 1939): 181–92.

———. "Rural Education—A Challenge, a Responsibility." *California Exchange Bulletin in Rural Education* 1, no. 1 (Nov. 1926): 8.

———. "Rural School Supervision." In Department of Education, *Biennial Report, 1931–32*, pp. 76–88. Sacramento: State Printing Office, 1932.

———. "Rural School Supervision in Three California Counties." *Western Journal of Education* 37, no. 7 (July 1929): 4–8.

————. "A Statement of the Philosophy and the Purposes of the Elementary School." *California Journal of Elementary Education* 1, no. 3 (Feb. 1933): 109–13.

————. "To Our Visitors: Information to Visitors Concerning California's State Rural Demonstration School." Woods School, San Joaquin County, Woodbridge, California, n.d.

Heizer, Robert, and Alan Almquist. *The Other Californians.* Berkeley: University of California Press, 1971.

Hendrick, Irving. *California Education.* San Francisco: Boyd & Fraser, 1980.

————. "California's Response to the 'New Education' in the 1930s." *California Historical Quarterly* 53 (spring 1974): 25–40.

————. *The Education of Non-Whites in California, 1849–1970.* San Francisco: R & E Research Associates, 1979.

————. "Federal Policy Affecting the Education of Indians in California, 1849–1934." *History of Education Quarterly* 16, no. 2 (summer 1976): 163–86.

————. "The Impact of the Great Depression on Public School Support in California." *Southern California Quarterly* 54 (1972): 177–95.

Hill, Mozell. "The All-Negro Communities of Oklahoma." *Journal of Negro History* 31, no. 3 (July 1946): 254–68.

Hilton, Eunice. "Professional Women and the War." *School and Society* 63 (Jan. 12, 1946): 35–37.

Hirsch, E. D. *Cultural Literacy.* Boston: Houghton Mifflin, 1987.

Hoffman, Nancy, ed. *Woman's "True" Profession.* Old Westbury, N.Y.: Feminist Press, 1981.

Hogan, David. *Class and Reform.* Philadelphia: University of Pennsylvania Press, 1985.

Hunter, Ian. *Rethinking the School.* Sydney: Allen & Unwin, 1994.

Irwin, Eugene. "Improvement of Educational Standards in Rural Schools." *Sierra Educational News* 23, no. 5 (May 1927): 280–82.

Jaeckel, Solomon. "Edward Hyatt, 1858–1919: California Educator." *Southern California Quarterly* 3, nos. 1–3 (March–June–Sept. 1970): 3–56, 122–54, 248–74.

James, Thomas. *Exile Within.* Cambridge, Mass.: Harvard University Press, 1987.

Jameson, Elizabeth. "Toward a Multicultural History of Women in the Western United States." *Signs* 13, no. 4 (summer 1988): 761–91.

Jeffrey, Julie Roy. *Frontier Women.* New York: Hill & Wang, 1979.

Jensen, Joan, and Gloria Lathrop. *California Women: A History.* San Francisco: Boyd & Fraser, 1987.

Jensen, Joan, and Darlis Miller. "The Gentle Tamers Revisited: New Approaches to the History of Women in the American West." *Pacific Historical Review* 49, no. 2 (May 1980): 173–213.

Johnson, Leighton. *Development of the Central State Agency for Public Education in California, 1849–1949.* Albuquerque: University of New Mexico Press, 1952.

Johnston, Anna Mills. "A Trip to Mt. Whitney in 1878." *Mt. Whitney Club Journal* 1, no. 1 (May 1902): 18–28.

Jones, Jacqueline. *Labor of Love, Labor of Sorrow.* New York: Vintage Books, 1986.

————. *Soldiers of Light and Love*. Chapel Hill: University of North Carolina Press, 1980.

Kaestle, Carl. *Pillars of the Republic*. New York: Hill & Wang, 1983.

Kaestle, Carl, and Maris Vinovskis. *Education and Social Change in Nineteenth-Century Massachusetts*. Cambridge: Cambridge University Press, 1980.

Katz, Michael. *The Irony of Early School Reform*. Cambridge, Mass.: Harvard University Press, 1969.

————. "The Origins of Public Education: A Reassessment." *History of Education Quarterly* 16 (winter 1976): 381–407.

Katznelson, Ira, and Margaret Weir. *Schooling for All*. Berkeley: University of California Press, 1985.

Kaufman, Polly. *Women Teachers on the Frontier*. New Haven: Yale University Press, 1984.

Kelly, Joan. *Women's History and Theory*. Chicago: University of Chicago Press, 1984.

Kelly, Myra. "The Inquisition of the Teacher." In *Woman's "True" Profession*, edited by Nancy Hoffman, pp. 249–54. Old Westbury, N.Y.: Feminist Press, 1981.

Kerber, Linda. *Women of the Republic*. Chapel Hill: University of North Carolina Press, 1980.

Kessler-Harris, Alice. *Out to Work*. New York: Oxford University Press, 1982.

Kliebard, Herbert. *Struggle for the American Curriculum*. Boston: Routledge, Kegan Paul, 1986.

Krohn, Mildred. "Migratory Home: United Efforts to Find a New Way of Living." *Sierra Educational News* 34, no. 9 (Sept. 1937): 22–24.

Kyte, George. "Origins of the California Schoolmasters Club." Typescript, n.d.; Bancroft Library, University of California, Berkeley.

Lang, Albert R. "California Elementary School Teaching for Young Californians." *Sierra Educational News* 42, no. 9 (Sept. 1946): 24–26.

La Rue, W. Wesley. "Returning Japanese." *Sierra Educational News* 41, no. 3 (March 1945): 28–29.

Leibold, Audrey. *A History of the Chinese Taoist Temple, Hanford, California*. Hanford, Calif.: Taoist Temple Preservation Society, 1982.

Lerner, Gerda. "The Lady and the Mill Girl." *American Studies Journal* 10 (spring 1969): 5–15.

————, ed. *Black Women in White America*. New York: Pantheon Books, 1972.

Lobner, Joyce. "A Chapter in Democracy; or, A Short History of the Oakland Schoolwomen's Club." Typescript, 1942; Holt Atherton Department of Special Collections, University of the Pacific, Stockton, Calif.

Lundberg, Ferdinand, and Marynia Farnham. *Modern Woman: The Lost Sex*. New York: Harper, 1947.

Madison, James. "John D. Rockefeller's General Education Board and the Rural School Problem in the Midwest." *History of Education Quarterly* 24, no. 2 (summer 1984): 181–200.

Manning, Diane. *Hill Country Teacher: Oral Histories from the One-Room School and Beyond*. Boston: Twayne, 1990.

Martin, Jane Roland. *The Schoolhome.* Cambridge, Mass.: Harvard University Press, 1992.

Masumoto, David. *Country Voices.* Del Rey, Calif.: Inaka Countryside Publications, 1987.

Mayfield, Thomas Jefferson. *Indian Summer.* Berkeley: Heyday Books/California Historical Society, 1993.

McNaught, Margaret Schallenberger. "The Best Way to Make Citizens of Aliens." *California Blue Bulletin* 6, no. 1 (March 1920): 19–21.

———. "The Enfranchised Woman Teacher: Her Opportunity." *Sierra Educational News* 13, no. 9 (Sept. 1917): 334.

———. "Increasing Interest in the Union of Elementary School Districts." *California Blue Bulletin* 3, no. 2 (June 1917): 16–17.

———. "A Message from the Commissioner of Education." *Sierra Educational News* 10, no. 1 (Jan. 1914): 66.

———. "The Need of Supervision." *California Blue Bulletin* 1, no. 1 (March 1915): 2–3.

———. "The Squirrel Is a Hun." *California Blue Bulletin* 4, no. 2 (June 1918): 15–16.

———. "A Strong Personality." *California Blue Bulletin* 2, no. 2 (June 1916): 14.

———. "Teach Patriotism, Hygiene, Sanitation." *California Blue Bulletin* 3, no. 4 (Dec. 1917): 24–26.

McNutt, Paul. "Education and War." *Sierra Educational News* 39, no. 1 (Jan. 1943): 11–12.

McPheron, Linda. "A Historical Perspective of Career Patterns of Women in the Teaching Professions, 1900–1940." Ph.D. diss., Illinois State University, 1981.

McWilliams, Carey. *Factories in the Fields.* Boston: Little, Brown, 1940.

Meier, August. *Negro Thought in America, 1880–1915: Racial Ideologies in the Age of Booker T. Washington.* Ann Arbor: University of Michigan Press, 1963.

Melosh, Barbara. *The Physician's Hand.* Philadelphia: Temple University Press, 1982.

Menchaca, Martha, and Richard Valencia. "Anglo-Saxon Ideologies in the 1920s and 1930s: Their Impact on the Segregation of Mexican Students in California." *Anthropology and Education Quarterly* 21 (1990): 222–49.

Miller, Eleanor. *When Memory Calls.* Gardena, Calif.: Institute Press, 1936.

Miller, Marie Hayden, ed. "Pride in America." Pamphlet, Hanford, Calif., n.d.

Morse, Hermann. *A Rural Survey of Tulare County.* New York: Presbyterian Church Board of Home Missions, 1915.

Muir, John. *The Mountains of California.* San Francisco: Sierra Club Books, 1989.

Murphy, Marjorie. *Blackboard Unions.* Ithaca: Cornell University Press, 1990.

Myres, Sandra. *Westering Women and the Frontier Experience, 1800–1915.* Albuquerque: University of New Mexico Press, 1982.

National Education Association. "Report of the Committee of Twelve on Rural Schools." In *Addresses and Proceedings, 1897*, pp. 385–583. Washington, D.C.: NEA, 1897.

Naud, Alden. "Teacher Shortage." *Sierra Educational News* 42, no. 2 (Feb. 1946): 20–21.

Nelson, Margaret K. "Female Schoolteachers as Community Builders." In *The Teacher's Voice*, edited by Richard Altenbaugh, pp. 78–89. London: Falmer Press, 1992.

Newton, Judith. "History as Usual? Feminism and the New Historicism." In *The New Historicism*, edited by H. Adam Veeser, pp. 152–67. London: Routledge, 1989.

Norton, Mary Beth. *Liberty's Daughters*. Boston: Little, Brown, 1980.

O'Neill, Cecilia. "Equal Rights: A Basic Principle." *Sierra Educational News* 40, no. 5 (May 1944): 33–34.

Oram, Alison. "'Embittered, Sexless, or Homosexual': Attacks on Spinster Teachers, 1918–39." In *Current Issues in Women's History*, edited by Arina Angerman, Geerte Binnema, Annemieke Keunen, Vefie Poels, and Jacqueline Zirksee, pp. 183–202. London: Routledge, 1989.

Painter, Nell. *Exodusters*. Lawrence: University of Kansas Press, 1986.

Palquist, Peter. "Women in California Photography, 1850–1920." Paper presented at the conference "Suspect Terrain: Women in the West," Lincoln, Neb., July 1992.

Pascoe, Peggy. "The Challenge of Writing Multicultural Women's History." *Frontiers* 12, no. 1 (1991): 1–4.

———. *Relations of Rescue*. New York: Oxford University Press, 1991.

Passerini, Luisa. *Fascism in Popular Memory: The Cultural Experience of the Turin Working Class*. Cambridge: Cambridge University Press, 1987.

———. "Women's Personal Narratives: Myths, Experiences, and Emotions." In Personal Narratives Group, *Interpreting Women's Lives*, pp. 189–97. Bloomington: Indiana University Press, 1989.

Perkins, Linda. *Fanny Jackson Coppin and the Institute for Colored Youth*. New York: Garland, 1987.

———. "The History of Blacks in Teaching: Growth and Decline Within the Profession." In *America's Teachers: Histories of a Profession at Work*, edited by Donald Warren, pp. 344–69. New York: Macmillan, 1989.

———. "The Impact of the 'Cult of True Womanhood' on the Education of Black Women." *Journal of Social Issues* 39, no. 3 (Sept. 1983): 17–28.

Perlman, Joel, and Victoria Huntzinger. "How Long They Taught." Typescript, 1987.

Perlstein, Dan. "Contradictions of Governance." Typescript, 1989.

Peters, David. *The Status of the Married Woman Teacher*. New York: Teachers College, Columbia University Bureau of Publications, 1934.

Pierson, Ruth Roach. "Experience, Difference, Dominance, and Voice in the Writing of Canadian Women's History." In *Writing Women's History International Perspectives*, edited by Karen Offen, Ruth Roach Pierson, and Jane Rendall, pp. 79–106. Bloomington: Indiana University Press, 1991.

Pisani, Donald. *From Family Farm to Agribusiness: The Irrigation Crusade in California and the West, 1850–1931*. Berkeley: University of California Press, 1984.

Pogue, Grace. *The Swift Seasons*. Hollywood, Calif.: Cloister Press, 1957.

———. *Within the Magic Circle*. Visalia, Calif.: Visalia Times Delta, n.d.

Popular Memory Group. "Popular Memory: Theory, Politics, Method." In *Mak-*

ing Histories, edited by Richard Johnson, Gregor McLennon, Bill Swartz, and David Sutton, pp. 218–42. Minneapolis: University of Minnesota Press, 1982.

Potter, Gladys L. "Specific Suggestions for the Organization of Instruction in Emergency Schools." *California Journal of Elementary Education* 7, no. 3 (Feb. 1939): 138–48.

———. "Teaching the Migratory." *Sierra Educational News* 36, no. 3 (March 1940): 34–36.

Potter, Jewell. "Teacher and Migrant: The Teacher's Problem in a Migratory Situation." *Sierra Educational News* 34, no. 8 (Aug. 1938): 25–27.

Prentice, Alison. "The Feminization of Teaching in British North America and Canada, 1845–1875." *Social History/Histoire Sociale* 8 (May 1975): 5–20.

Prentice, Alison, and Marjorie Theobald. "The Historiography of Women Teachers: A Retrospect." In *Women Who Taught*, edited by Alison Prentice and Marjorie Theobald, pp. 3–36. Toronto: University of Toronto Press, 1991.

Preston, Jo Anne. "Female Aspiration and Male Ideology: School-Teaching in Nineteenth Century New England." In *Current Issues in Women's History*, edited by Arina Angerman, Geerte Binnema, Annemieke Keunen, Vefie Poels, and Jacqueline Zirksee, pp. 171–82. London: Routledge, 1989.

Preston, William. *Vanishing Landscapes: Land and Life in the Tulare Lake Basin.* Berkeley: University of California Press, 1981.

Quantz, Richard. "The Complex Visions of Female Teachers and the Failure of Unionization in the 1930s: An Oral History." In *The Teacher's Voice*, edited by Richard Altenbaugh, pp. 139–56. London: Falmer Press, 1992.

Ramsay, Eleanor. "Allensworth." Ph.D. diss., University of California, Berkeley, 1972.

Ravitch, Diane, and Chester Finn. *What Do Our 17-Year-Olds Know?* New York: Harper & Row, 1988.

Reinharz, Shulamit. *Feminist Methods in Social Research.* New York: Oxford University Press, 1993.

Rich, Adrienne. "Compulsory Heterosexuality and Lesbian Existence." In *Blood, Bread, and Poetry*, pp. 23–75. New York: W. W. Norton, 1986.

Richardson, John, and Brenda Hatcher. "The Feminization of Public School Teaching, 1870–1920." *Work and Occupations* 10 (Feb. 1983): 81–100.

Riley, Denise. *Am I That Name?* Minneapolis: University of Minnesota Press, 1989.

Rogers, Robert. "Is Woman Ruining the Country?" *Literary Digest* 102 (1929): 23–26.

Rose, Harold. "The All-Negro Town: Its Evolution and Function." *Geographical Review* 55 (July 1955): 362–81.

Rudholm, Melvin. "A Short History and Survey of Pixley Union School District." M.A. thesis, Fresno State College, 1953.

Runyan, Lucia. "Elbow Creek School." *Los Tulares* 33 (Dec. 1957): 1.

Rury, John. "Gender, Salaries, and Career: American Teachers, 1900–1910." *Issues in Education* 4, no. 3 (winter 1986): 215–35.

Russell, Eleanor. "Tulare County's Traveling Exhibit." *Sierra Educational News* 29, no. 6 (June 1933): 32–33.

Rutherford, Milicent. "Feminism and the Secondary School Curriculum, 1890–1920." Ph.D. diss., Stanford University, 1977.

Ryan, Mary. *Womanhood in America: From Colonial Times to the Present.* New York: New Viewpoints, 1974.

Said, Edward. *Orientalism.* New York: Vintage Books, 1979.

Samuel, Raphael. "Myth and History: A First Reading." *Oral History* 16, no. 1 (1988): 10–17.

San Miguel, Guadalupe. "Status of the Historiography of Chicano Education: A Preliminary Analysis." *History of Education Quarterly* 26, no. 4 (winter 1986): 467–80.

Schallenberger, Margaret. *See* McNaught, Margaret Schallenberger.

Scharf, Lois. *To Work and to Wed.* Westport, Conn.: Greenwood Press, 1980.

Schlissel, Lillian, Vicki Ruiz, and Janice Monk, eds. *Western Women: Their Land, Their Lives.* Albuquerque: University of New Mexico Press, 1988.

Schrecker, Ellen. *No Ivory Tower.* New York: Basic Books, 1989.

Schwager, Sally. "Educating Women in America." *Signs* 12, no. 2 (winter 1987): 333–72.

Scott, Joan. "Experience." In *Feminists Theorize the Political,* edited by Judith Butler and Joan Scott, pp. 22–41. London: Routledge, 1992.

———. *Gender and the Politics of History.* New York: Columbia University Press, 1989.

———. "Response to Gordon." *Signs* 15, no. 4 (summer 1990): 859.

Sexton, John. "Education and the War." *Sierra Educational News* 38, no. 12 (Dec. 1942): 8–9.

Shapiro, Ann-Louise, ed. *History and Feminist Theory.* Middletown, Conn.: Wesleyan University Press, 1992.

Schultzberg, George. "Consolidation of Schools." *Sierra Educational News* 14, no. 3 (March 1918): 134–36.

Settle, Laura Esta. *"I Remember" Stories by Early California Teachers.* Sacramento: California Retired Teachers Association, 1939.

———. *Pages from the Past.* Sacramento: California Retired Teachers Association, 1940.

———. *Reminiscences of Some Early California Teachers.* Sacramento: California Retired Teachers Association, 1937.

———. *Yes, I'm a Pioneer Teacher.* Sacramento: California Retired Teachers Association, 1938.

Sher, Jonathan, ed. *Education in Rural America: A Reassessment of Conventional Wisdom.* Boulder, Colo.: Westview Press, 1977.

Sher, Jonathan, and Rachel Tompkins. "Economy, Efficiency, and Equality: The Myth of Rural School and District Consolidation." In *Education in Rural America,* edited by Jonathan Sher, pp. 152–68. Boulder, Colo.: Westview Press, 1977.

Shippey, Mervyn. "A Short History of the Visalia Colored School." Typescript, n.d.; Annie Mitchell History Room, Tulare County Public Library, Visalia, Calif.

———. "The Visalia Normal School." Typescript, n.d.; Annie Mitchell History Room, Tulare County Public Library, Visalia, Calif.

Sigma Chapter, Delta Kappa Gamma. *Tulare County Schools 100 Years.* Visalia, Calif.: Privately printed, 1961.

Slotle, Ferol. *School Bell Memories: Horse and Buggy to Space Age.* Los Altos, Calif.: Del Monte Press, 1986.

Small, Katherine. *A History of Tulare County.* Chicago: J. Clarke, 1925.

Smith, Dorothy. *The Everyday World as Problematic.* Boston: Northeastern University Press, 1987.

Smith, Eleanor, Emily Dodge, Mary Post, Anna Wiebalk, and Flora Conover. "School Women's Clubs: A Statement." *Sierra Educational News* 6, no. 3 (March 1910): 21.

Smith-Rosenberg, Carroll. *Disorderly Conduct.* New York: Oxford University Press, 1985.

Stack, Wickliffe. "Full Citizenship: A Goal of Education." *Sierra Educational News* 42, no. 1 (Jan. 1946): 18–20.

Stanford Workshop on Education for War and Peace. *Education for War and Peace.* Stanford: Stanford University Press, 1942.

Stanley, Grace. "The New Rural School." *Sierra Educational News* 19, no. 7 (Sept. 1923): 396–97.

Steedman, Carolyn. "Culture, Cultural Studies, and the Historians." In *Cultural Studies,* edited by L. Grossberg, C. Nelson, and P. Treichler, pp. 613–22. New York: Routledge, 1992.

———. *Landscape for a Good Woman.* New Brunswick, N.J.: Rutgers University Press, 1987.

Stein, Walter. *California and the Dust Bowl Migration.* Westport, Conn.: Greenwood Press, 1973.

Sterrett, Roger. "The Vanishing Schoolmaster." *Sierra Educational News* 9, no. 4 (April 1915): 242–45.

Strober, Myra, and Laura Best. "The Female/Male Differential in the Public Schools: Some Lessons from San Francicso, 1879." *Economic Inquiry* 17 (April 1979): 218–36.

Strober, Myra, and Audry Gordon Lanford. "The Feminization of Public School Teaching: Cross-Sectional Analysis, 1850–1880." *Signs* 11, no. 2 (winter 1986): 212–35.

Strober, Myra, and David Tyack. "Why Do Women Teach and Men Manage?" *Signs* 5 (1980): 494–503.

Sugg, Redding. *Motherteacher.* Charlottesville: University of Virginia Press, 1979.

Swett, John. *History of the Public School System of California.* San Francisco: A. L. Bancroft, 1876.

———. *Public Education in California.* New York: American Book Company, 1911.

Takaki, Ronald. *Strangers from a Different Shore.* New York: Penguin Books, 1989.

Taylor, Paul. *On the Ground in the Thirties.* Layton, Utah: Peregrine Smith Books, 1983.

Theobald, Marjorie. *Knowing Women: Origins of Women's Education in Nineteenth-Century Australia.* Cambridge: Cambridge University Press, 1996.

Thomas, Sister Mary. *Apostle of the Valley: The Life of Daniel Frances Dade—Pioneer*

Priest of the San Joaquin Valley. Fresno: Academy of California Church History, 1947.

Thornley, Doris. "Health Program for Tulare County." *Western Journal of Education* 36, no. 12 (Dec. 1930): 3–4.

Tracy, Eleanor. *Schoolma'am, Stone Lagoon California, 1903–1904.* Eureka, Calif.: Artcraft Print Co., 1978.

Treacy, Robert. "Progressivism and Corinne Seeds: UCLA and the University Elementary School." Ph.D. diss., University of Wisconsin–Madison, 1971.

Tulare County Business Directory. Fresno, Calif.: Pillsbury & Ellsworth, 1888.

Tyack, David. "The Common School and American Society: A Reappraisal." *History of Education Quarterly* 26, no. 2 (summer 1986): 301–6.

———. *The One Best System.* Cambridge, Mass.: Harvard University Press, 1971.

———. "Onward Christian Soldiers: Religion in the American Common School." In *History and Education: The Educational Uses of the Past,* edited by Paul Nash, pp. 212–55. New York: Random House, 1970.

———. "The Tribe and the Common School: Community Control in Rural Education." *American Quarterly,* no. 24 (March 1972): 3–19.

Tyack, David, and Elisabeth Hansot. "The Dream Deferred: A Golden Age for Women School Administrators?" Stanford: Institute for Research on Educational Finance and Governance, 1981.

———. *Learning Together.* New Haven: Yale University Press, 1990.

———. *Managers of Virtue.* New York: Basic Books, 1982.

———. "Silence, Policy Talk, and Educational Practice: The Case of Gender." Typescript, n.d.

Tyack, David, Elisabeth Hansot, and Rob Lowe. *Public Schools in Hard Times.* Cambridge, Mass.: Harvard University Press, 1984.

Urban, Wayne. *Why Teachers Organized.* Detroit: Wayne State University Press, 1982.

Vaughn-Roberson, Courtney. "Having a Purpose in Life: Western Women in the Twentieth Century." In *The Teacher's Voice,* edited by Richard Altenbaugh, pp. 13–25. London: Falmer Press, 1992.

Vicinus, Martha. *Independent Women.* Chicago: University of Chicago Press, 1985.

Waller, Willard. *The Sociology of Teaching.* New York: Russell & Russell, 1961.

Weatherford, Doris. *American Women and World War II.* New York: Facts on File, 1990.

Weiler, Kathleen. *Women Teaching for Change.* South Hadley, Mass.: Bergin & Garvey, 1988.

Wells, Andrew. *The San Joaquin Valley of California: Resources, Industries, and Advantages.* San Francisco: Southern Pacific Railroad Passenger Department, 1908.

Wells, Ida B. *Crusade for Justice: The Autobiography of Ida B. Wells.* Chicago: University of Chicago Press, 1970.

Welter, Barbara. "The Cult of True Womanhood, 1820–1860." *American Quarterly* 18 (1966): 151–74.

Wiebalk, Anna M. "Everygirl—A Morality Play." *Sierra Educational News* 5, no. 5 (May 1909): 30–37.

Williams, J. Harold. "The Binet-Simon Scale for Measuring the Intelligence of School Children." *Educational Digest* 1, no. 7 (1914): 13–15.

Wilson, J. Donald. "I Am Ready to Be of Assistance When I Can: Lottie Bowron and Rural Women Teachers in British Columbia." In *Women Who Taught*, edited by Marjorie Theobald and Alison Prentice, pp. 202–31. Toronto: University of Toronto Press, 1991.

Wollenberg, Charles. *All Deliberate Speed: Segregation and Exclusion in California Schools, 1855–1975.* Berkeley: University of California Press, 1976.

Wood, Will. "Radical Literature in Schools." *California Blue Bulletin* 5, no. 4 (Dec. 1919): 26–27.

———. "Rural Supervision Fund." *California Blue Bulletin* 7, no. 2 (June 1921): 5–6.

———. "A Visit to Allensworth—A Colony for the Negro." *California Blue Bulletin* 3, no. 2 (June 1917): 13.

Woody, Thomas. *A History of Women's Education in the United States.* Vol. 1. Lancaster, Pa.: Science Press, 1929.

Wylie, Philip. *A Generation of Vipers.* New York: Rinehart, 1942.

York, Ada. "Specific Points of Teacher Training for Rural Service." *California Exchange Bulletin in Rural Education* 2, no. 1 (Oct. 1927): 10–11.

Zion, Lettie. *Fairview: True Tales of a Country Schoolhouse.* Oceana, Calif.: Tower Press, 1981.

INDEX

Library of Congress Cataloging-in-Publication Data

Weiler, Kathleen.
    Country schoolwomen : teaching in rural California,
1850–1950 / Kathleen Weiler.
        p.   cm.
    Includes bibliographical references (p.) and index.
    ISBN 0-8047-3004-0
        1. Women teachers—California—History—19th century.
        2. Women teachers—California—History—20th century.
        3. Education, Rural—California—History—19th century.
        4. Education, Rural—California—History—20th century.
        5. Women teachers—California—Social conditions—
    History—19th century.   6. Women teachers—California—
    Social conditions—History—20th century.   I. Title.
    LB2837.W445   1998
    371.1'0082—dc21   97-42647
                                                   CIP

  ⊗ This book is printed on acid-free, recycled paper.

Original printing 1998
Last figure below indicates year of this printing:
07   06   05   04   03   02   01   00   99   98